PowerShell 7 for IT Pros

PowerShell 7 for IT Pros

A Guide to Using PowerShell 7 to Manage
Windows® Systems

Thomas Lee

WILEY

To my wife, Susan, who has been my loving companion and a constant source of strength, affection, and humour, especially during the COVID-19 crisis.

To my daughter, Rebecca. Your smiles keep me going.

To my grandmother, Louise Runk Robinson, who worked in the US Library of Congress and lit a spark in me that would ultimately lead me to write books.

To my friend, Jeffrey Snover, who has been an inspiring role model.

Thank you all for your support. You mean the world to me.

About the Author

Thomas Lee is a technical trainer, consultant, and author who specializes in the Microsoft Windows platform. Thomas began in the IT industry in 1968 as a computer operator operating an IBM 360/67 running IBM's Time-Sharing System. His career spans five decades and has included the mainframe, mini-computers, time sharing (aka very early cloud computing), AI, and other emerging technologies.

Thomas has worked in the consulting field, first with Arthur Andersen (today known as Accenture), where he witnessed the birth of the PC as a tool for clients across the board. He continues to provide consulting services to many long-standing clients.

He has also written extensively, both for the technical trade in the United Kingdom and for the worldwide publishing industry. This book marks his fourth on PowerShell. He has written hundreds of articles about Microsoft and other technologies and maintains a technical blog at tfl09.blogspot.com.

Thomas was a Microsoft-certified trainer for more than 25 years and was awarded the Microsoft MVP award 17 times. He was a fellow in the British Computer Society and a chartered engineer. He serves as a global board member for the MVP Reconnect program.

He lives today in an old cottage in the English countryside. He enjoys his garden, a well-stocked wine cellar, an extensive collection of Grateful Dead live recordings, and the love of his family. He loves working with PowerShell too!

About the Technical Editor

Jim Topp is a Windows Server systems administrator with more than 16 years of experience. He has been scripting and automating with PowerShell for more than 12 years. He is a community member of PowerShell.org and has edited several books written by Don Jones. Jim lives in Bloomington, Indiana.

Acknowledgments

Every book requires a great team of talented people to ensure a great product. While an author can write text and code, the developmental and technical editors focus the writing and ensure that the scripts are accurate and work as shown. Publishing a book is an honour as well as an incredible learning experience for me. I have always believed that you truly have to know your subject to write a book, and I certainly have learned a lot in the process.

First, my deepest gratitude to Wiley, and the fantastic team at Wiley, for bringing this book to life: Kenyon Brown, Pete Gaughan, and others. Thank you for recognizing that I had a story to tell.

A huge thank-you to my developmental editor, Jim Compton, for your wisdom, kindness, and patience during through my writing "process." You have been a great inspiration to me, and I am indebted for your contributions.

Writing hundreds of lines of PowerShell 7 code and transcribing it accurately into both the book's text and the screenshots is an amazingly difficult job. Jim Topp did an outstanding job of checking every line of code and every screenshot as well as making great suggestions to improve what we have here.

In writing this book, I have been impressed on a daily basis with the entire PowerShell development team. You folks have delivered high-quality code consistently, been able to listen to and accept the views of the community, and deliver a world-class product. Joey Aiello, Steve Lee, and Jim Truher, among others, have been an inspiration.

Another significant inspiration is Jeffrey Snover. From that day in L.A. when he first introduced Monad, he has been an awesome role model. He is smart, focused, and one of the best presenters I have ever had the good fortune to watch. When I noted, on Twitter, that PowerShell Core 6.1 was kind of like Windows PowerShell 2.0 all over again, Jeffrey noted in his understated way that, while it was true, PowerShell had better velocity. An understatement at the very least.

The PowerShell 7 code in this book was developed and tested on a variety of Hyper-V virtual machines running Windows Server 2019. Because I am a member of the MVP Reconnect program, the Visual Studio team at Microsoft generously provided me with a subscription to Visual Studio Online, from which I obtained the necessary ISO images with which you (and I) can build the VMs. I could not have written this book without their generous assistance.

Thanks too to the PowerShell community. The community has created a massive number of PowerShell resources, code, and documentation. Deep dives, new modules, tips, and tricks—so much awesome content. Thanks to Jeff Hick, Don Jones, Richard Siddaway, and many more.

Lastly, a shout-out to the PowerShell community at Spiceworks—a friendly bunch of helpful PowerShell addicts (`community.spiceworks.com/programming/powershell`). If you are keen on PowerShell, consider visiting and joining in.

Foreword

Ten years after the release of Windows PowerShell 1.0, the PowerShell team announced PowerShell Core 6. The work toward PowerShell Core 6 started a few years earlier, and that was when I became the engineering manager for PowerShell. It was not easy early on, particularly in terms of compatibility with Windows PowerShell, but with the PowerShell 7 release we are officially starting a new chapter for PowerShell in which PowerShell 7 can be used as a replacement for (or side by side with) Windows PowerShell 5.1.

PowerShell 7 represents the future of PowerShell based on three big changes:

- **A single automation language for Windows, Linux, and macOS:** Windows PowerShell has been heavily adopted by the Windows community. With IT moving toward the cloud, this presented an opportunity for PowerShell to be the glue language for the cloud. Improvements to the web cmdlets make it simple to call REST APIs. Early partnerships with Azure, Amazon Web Services, Google Compute Cloud, and VMware ensured PowerShell cmdlet coverage for any cloud you would want to use on any platform. Along the way, we also made PowerShell a great shell to use whether you are using Windows, Linux, or macOS.

- **Moving to open source:** This was a huge change in how we write software and also how we engage with the community. We could now be much more transparent with our plans and also accept contributions from the community to address issues or add features that would not have necessarily been a priority for the team. With about 50 percent of the pull requests coming from the community, PowerShell's future really is a community-driven project!

- **Early adopter of .NET Core:** It was not without challenges that we moved from .NET Framework to .NET Core (and now just .NET). Compatibility with Windows PowerShell modules was the biggest issue initially. .NET has come a long way in addressing the compatibility gap, adding back many APIs to enable PowerShell to be compatible with existing modules. In addition, .NET Core has substantial performance improvements that make existing PowerShell scripts and modules simply work faster without any modifications!

The mission statement of PowerShell is to make it easier for users to use compute resources. With PowerShell 7, this includes different platforms such as Windows, Linux, and macOS, but also new architectures such as ARM32 and ARM64. With PowerShell modules available for the major public and private clouds, you can leverage PowerShell to be more productive in cross-cloud or hybrid scenarios. We still maintain PowerShell's "sacred vow"— that learning a new language is hard, but with time invested learning PowerShell, we will continue to enable PowerShell users to expand their impact and productivity, such as serverless functions as a service and Jupyter Notebooks. I'm excited about the next phase of PowerShell that we started with PowerShell 7, but for me, this is really just a beginning, with many more great things to come! This book from Thomas is a great way to get started on PowerShell 7, leveraging existing experience from Windows PowerShell.

Thomas Lee has been part of the PowerShell community far longer than I have been the engineering manager for PowerShell. Some of the things I've learned about PowerShell have come from reading his articles and blog posts. As the PowerShell team was making progress toward our substantial PowerShell 7 release, Thomas was there the whole way, promoting, teaching, and informing the community of all the great things to come with PowerShell 7. The most important aspect of what makes PowerShell successful has been the community, and Thomas has been a significant part of that.

Steve Lee
Principal Software Engineering Manager
PowerShell Team

Contents at a Glance

Contents

Introduction

Hello, and thank you for buying this book. I sat in the audience at the Professional Developers Conference in Los Angeles in 2003, where Jeffrey Snover introduced Monad, which was later to become Windows PowerShell. I was excited about what I saw and heard; it was a seminal moment in my career.

Today we have a new version of PowerShell, PowerShell 7, to get excited about all over again. The PowerShell development team, combined with a fantastic community, has taken PowerShell to a new level. I continue to be excited, and I hope you are.

Before you dive into the body of this book, I hope you might take a few moments to read this short introduction where I explain my motivation for writing the book, its structure, and how you can use the PowerShell scripts in this book using Hyper-V VMs.

This book contains 10 chapters. The first chapter looks at setting up PowerShell 7 in your environment. Chapter 2 examines the issue of Windows PowerShell compatibility and shows how PowerShell 7 addresses this challenge. The remaining eight chapters cover various Windows Server features and how you manage them with PowerShell 7. Here's a short overview of what is in this book:

Chapter 1: Setting Up a PowerShell 7 Environment: In this chapter, you look at how to install PowerShell 7 and VS Code. VS Code is your replacement for the older Windows PowerShell ISE. The screenshots in this book show PowerShell code running in VS Code. In production, you could consider not using VS Code, or any GUI tool for that matter, on your server and instead rely on the PowerShell 7 console and remote text editing.

Chapter 2: PowerShell 7 Compatibility with Windows PowerShell: Compatibility with Windows PowerShell is both an important objective and a significant engineering task. This chapter describes the compatibility issue as well as providing some additional background on modules. The chapter then looks at how backward compatibility works and discusses the small number of Windows PowerShell that you cannot use in PowerShell 7.

Chapter 3: Managing Active Directory: AD is at the heart of almost every organization's network. This chapter shows how you can deploy and manage AD, including creating forests and domains as well as linking forests with cross-forest trusts. The chapter also looks at how you manage AD users, computers, groups, and more.

Chapter 4: Managing Networking: In this chapter, you look at managing your network with PowerShell 7. You examine NIC configuration, as well as installing and managing both DNS and DHCP.

Chapter 5: Managing Storage: Storage is a crucial aspect of any computer system. You need somewhere to store your files and other data. This chapter looks at managing disks and volumes/partitions as well as using a third-party module to manage NTFS permissions. The chapter also examines Storage Replica to replicate storage, possibly for disaster recovery. Finally, the chapter looks at using File Server Resource Manager to manage file quotas and file screening.

Chapter 6: Managing Shared Data: Once you have disks configured as volumes and partitions and you have set up permissions appropriately, you need to share that data across the network. This chapter looks at how you set up and configure an SMB file server and how to create and secure SMB file shares. The chapter also looks at setting up an iSCSI target and then using that target to deploy a highly resilient clustered scale-out file server.

Chapter 7: Managing Printing: Printing has been a core feature of Windows since the beginning of Windows itself. This chapter shows how to set up and manage a print server. The chapter shows how to add a printer, how to add print drivers, how to print a test page, and how to set up a printer pool.

Chapter 8: Managing Hyper-V: Hyper-V is Microsoft's core virtualization product. This chapter shows you how to set up and manage Hyper V and how to create and manage Hyper-V VMs. The chapter also looks at VM and VM storage movement and replication, vital topics for today's VM-focused world.

Chapter 9: Using WMI with CIM Cmdlets: Windows Management Instrumentation has been a feature within Windows since NT 4. WMI provides you with access to information about your system and allows you to manage aspects of the system. WMI is useful to provide you with access to Windows functionality you cannot get via PowerShell cmdlets. This chapter explores the WMI components and shows you how to discover more. The chapter also looks at managing WMI events and shows how you can set up a permanent event handler to manage critical security events.

Chapter 10: Reporting: Knowing the status of your IT infrastructure is vital to being able to manage your computing estate. This chapter demonstrates how you can use PowerShell 7 to learn more about your infrastructure. The chapter looks at reporting on AD users and computers, the filesystem via FSRM, printer usage, and Hyper-V host and VM usage. This chapter also looks at using performance logging and alerting to capture detailed performance information and create rich performance reports and graphs that show the performance of your infrastructure.

I wrote this book to show you, the IT pro, that moving to PowerShell 7 is easy and worth your while. Just like when moving your home, things are a bit different in PowerShell 7. But once you get settled in, you are unlikely to look back. Along with VS Code, PowerShell 7 is just better. And I hope that each chapter of this book demonstrates that.

This book assumes you are an IT professional wanting to learn how to make the most of PowerShell 7. You might be an active administrator, a consultant, or a manager. You should have a background in both Windows Server features and broadly what they do, along with an understanding of Windows PowerShell itself.

The book looks at a variety of core Windows features including Active Directory, File Services Resource Manager, WMI, printing, and more. Each chapter describes a feature area and the components with which you interact. Then the chapter shows you how you can use PowerShell 7 to deploy, manage, and leverage that feature.

In this book (and indeed any book on PowerShell), it's not possible to cover every aspect of every feature set of Windows. As Jeffrey Snover says, "To ship is to choose," and I hope I have chosen wisely. I have also provided pointers to where you can find more information. You are welcome to email me and give me feedback (`DoctorDNS@Gmail.Com`).

This book contains a variety of scripts that you can use to manage some aspects of Windows using PowerShell 7. You can download these scripts either from the Wiley site or from my GitHub repository at `github.com/doctordns/Wiley20`. In the unlikely event you discover an issue with any of the scripts or find issues with the documentation, please file an issue report on the GitHub repository (`github.com/doctordns/Wiley20/issues`).

A key goal in developing this book is to demonstrate how easily you can use PowerShell 7 to manage a Windows Server infrastructure. There is a difference in how you install it, and you have to get used to VS Code as a replacement to the ISE. Along the way, I discovered a few issues around compatibility with

Windows PowerShell, and I discuss these in Chapter 2. It is time to move forward to PowerShell 7.

I built the scripts and the book content based on a set of Windows Server 2019 Datacenter edition Hyper-V VMs. To get the most value from this book and the scripts it contains, you should build the VMs yourself and use them to test the scripts. Of course, you can use physical hosts as an alternative to virtual machines, but VMs are simpler to use. For readers who may not have the necessary hardware at hand, I include screenshots showing the output of each step of each script. To assist in creating the VMs, I have created a set of scripts. You can find these on GitHub; see Chapter 1 for more information on these scripts and how to obtain them.

One impressive aspect of PowerShell, from the beginning, is the rich and vibrant PowerShell community. There are hundreds of people around the world who love PowerShell and have delivered all kinds of goodness: tweets, forum posts, blog articles, scripts, modules, web sites, and more. A fair number of features in PowerShell 7 come from the community.

Should you have any problem with any aspect of any component of this book—or any aspect of Windows—there is no shortage of help and guidance you can find on the Internet.

Pretty much any social media site where techies can congregate is going to have PowerShell content, help, and assistance. Feel free to visit the PowerShell forum on Spiceworks where I am a moderator (`community.spiceworks.com/programming/powershell`).

With that said, enjoy the book and enjoy PowerShell 7.

Fare thee well now,
Let your life proceed by its own design.
Nothing to tell now,
Let the words be yours; I'm done with mine.
"Cassidy," John Barlow/Robert Weir

Thomas Lee
June 2020
Cookham, England

Setting Up a PowerShell 7 Environment

The first versions of Windows PowerShell were provided via a user-installed download, initially for Windows XP and Windows Server 2008. Today, both Windows Server and Windows 10 come with Windows PowerShell version 5.1—which in this book I'll call simply Windows PowerShell to distinguish it from PowerShell 7 (and the Windows PowerShell Integrated Scripting Environment) installed and available by default. Windows PowerShell comes with a range of commands available for basic administration of Windows.

PowerShell 7 itself does not ship as part of Windows at the time of writing. At some point, the PowerShell team may ship PowerShell 7 as a Windows component, but until that time, you need to download and install it yourself.

The Windows PowerShell Integrated Scripting Environment (ISE) does not support PowerShell 7. IT pros who want a good interactive development environment for PowerShell can use Visual Studio Code (VS Code), a free tool you can also easily download and install. VS Code comes with an array of extensions that provide a much-improved development experience for IT pros (and others).

With earlier versions of PowerShell, the vast majority of commands came bundled into Windows or were added as part of installing an application (such as Exchange Server) or adding a Windows feature to your system. With PowerShell 7, the PowerShell Gallery has become a core source of modules/commands that you can use to perform various administrative tasks. To ensure that you can take advantage of the PowerShell Gallery, you need to be sure that the PowerShellGet module is up to date.

What Is New in PowerShell 7

PowerShell 7 is the latest version of PowerShell. The PowerShell development team released PowerShell 7.0 in March 2020. By the time you read this, the development team is certain to have released newer minor updates. PowerShell 7 has a number of key new features that IT pros can leverage.

If you are familiar with and can use Windows PowerShell to manage your Windows systems, almost all your knowledge is directly transferable to the new environment. Need to get help on a command? Just type `Get-Help` at the PowerShell command line. The basic architecture of PowerShell remains the same, with many internal changes, significant improvements, and a few breaking issues.

From the perspective of an IT professional with a working knowledge of managing Windows using Windows PowerShell, here are the key changes you can find:

- **Redeveloped cmdlets, based on .NET Core and open sourced via GitHub:** You can now read and even help to extend any cmdlet in PowerShell 7. This also means that the cmdlets were written to use .NET Core—which has created a few small compatibility issues.

- **A robust compatibility layer:** You use this to access Windows PowerShell modules that do not directly work on PowerShell 7. This means that all but a small number of Windows PowerShell 5.1 modules are available with and work under PowerShell 7. Chapter 2, "PowerShell 7 Compatibility with Windows PowerShell," describes this compatibility layer in more detail and notes how it works and its limitations as well as providing work-around solutions.

- **Significant performance enhancements:** In porting the Windows PowerShell modules to PowerShell 7, the development team was able to review the code and deliver performance enhancements. Processing large collections, for example using `Foreach`, is now a lot faster. The `Foreach-Object` cmdlet now has a `-Parallel` switch that allows you to run script blocks in parallel, which can provide substantially shorter run times, especially on larger multiprocessor and multicore servers.

- **New PowerShell language operators:** There are three new operator sets in PowerShell: the Ternary operator (a ? b : c), the Pipeline chain operators (|| and &&), and the Null coalescing operators (?? and ??=). These operators were implemented in other shells such as Bash or Zsh, and you can now use them in PowerShell 7.

- **Simplified error views:** Windows PowerShell error messages were excellent and contained a lot of information. But in most cases the rich output was more than you normally need. Error messages in PowerShell 7 are now much more succinct. And when you *do* need that additional information, you can use `Get-Error` to retrieve the full details of any error. You can set the `$ErrorView` variable to `NormalView` to view the older Windows PowerShell–style error messages or `CategoryView` to see just the error category.

▪ **Experimental features:** The PowerShell team has implemented a raft of new features that are at an experimental stage. You can opt in (or not) to these features. This gives you the opportunity to try new things and provide feedback.

▪ **Automatic new version notification:** At the time of writing, there is no support for PowerShell 7 within the Windows Store or via Windows Update. That means you need to manage the updates yourself, and these messages provide timely notification that a newer version of PowerShell exists for you to download.

▪ **`Set-Location` now supports a path of - and +:** When you use `Set-Location` to reset your current working directory, you can use `-Path "-"` to instruct `Set-Location` to move to the last folder. Having moved back, you can set location using + to move forward.

▪ **Ability to invoke a DSC resource directly:** PowerShell 7 does not support desired state configuration, so no pull/report servers, local configuration manager, and so on. You can, however, manually invoke DSC resources on a given host, which provides a partial solution.

The PowerShell 7 snippets in this book use and demonstrate most of these new features. For more information on any of these features, including use cases and examples, use your favorite search engine as the PowerShell community has produced a significant amount of content that describes the features. You can find numerous higher-level posts, such as the article at `https://www.thomasmaurer.ch/2020/03/whats-new-in-powershell-7-check-it-out`. There are also more detailed articles that cover specific new features such as `tfl09.blogspot.com/2020/03/introduction-and-background-welcome-to.html`, for example, which provides details on the new Pipeline Chain and Ternary operators.

Systems Used in This Book and Chapter

This book examines how you can use PowerShell 7 to carry out a wide range of tasks, including setting permissions on a file share, collecting and reporting on performance data, and installing and configuring Active Directory. To demonstrate these and many other tasks, this book uses a set of hosts and two domains: Reskit.Org and Kapoho.Com. You have options as to how you provision these systems.

Server VM Build Scripts

The scripts in this book assume you have a set of servers ready to configure. You could, if you choose, build each computer used in this book based on physical hardware. A simpler alternative is to build the necessary server VMs using Hyper-V using the build scripts you can find at github.com/doctordns/ ReskitBuildScripts. This GitHub repository contains a README.MD file (github .com/doctordns/ReskitBuildScripts/blob/master/README.md) that explains how you can use these scripts to build your VM farm.

By way of background, these scripts are used to create VMs for a variety of training courses and other books. You do not need to create *all* the VMs. In the introduction to each chapter, you discover the specific VMs that the chapter uses.

These build scripts build VMs, but you need to take some care in terms of the order in which you build the VMs, where you store VMs and virtual hard disks, and so on.

The build scripts build VMs with basic networking (one NIC) although you can always add more should you wish. The scripts build the VMs you need for this book using a specific set of network addresses. The document github. com/doctordns/ReskitBuildScripts/blob/master/ReskitNetwork.md shows the details of the network hosts and IP addresses.

VM Internet Access

The VMs (or hosts if you choose to use physical computers) require Internet access. The VMs are all on the 10.10.10.0/24 IPv4 network implemented as an internal Hyper-V network, using an internal Hyper-V virtual switch. There are two broad mechanisms you can use to provide this.

First, you can configure each VM to have a second virtual NIC. You configure this NIC to use an external switch that you bind to your VM host's external NIC. This is a simple solution and can be set up quickly.

Another alternative is to set up a Windows Server VM running Routing and Remote Access. You configure the VM with two NICs (one internal, the other external) and configure routing between the 10.10.10.0/24 subnet used by the VMs in this book and the internet.

Systems in Use for This Chapter

In this chapter, you use PowerShell 7 to manage various networking aspects. The scripts in this chapter make use of one.

DC1: For the purposes of this chapter, DC1 is just a Windows Server 2019 host. Figure 1.1 shows the systems in use in this chapter.

Figure 1.1: Systems used in this chapter

For the purposes of this chapter, DC1 is a VM running Windows Server 2019 Data-center. You can create this server using the build scripts noted earlier. In Chapter 3, "Managing Active Directory," you promote this server to be a domain controller.

Installing PowerShell 7

By default, Microsoft does not include PowerShell 7 within any version of Windows, including Window 10, Windows Server 2019, or any earlier supported versions of Windows client and server. To install and use PowerShell 7, you need to install it for your operating system.

The PowerShell team supports PowerShell 7, at the time of writing, on the following operating systems:

- Windows 7, 8.1, and 10
- Windows Server 2008 R2, 2012, 2012 R2, 2016, and 2019
- macOS 10.13+
- Red Hat Enterprise Linux (RHEL) / CentOS 7+
- Fedora 29+
- Debian 9+
- Ubuntu 16.04+
- openSUSE 15+
- Alpine Linux 3.8+

This list is constantly being reviewed and updated. The PowerShell product team will add distributions of Linux to the list and provide support for later versions of all platforms.

This book describes installing and using PowerShell 7 on the Windows platform. The chapters in this book leverage Windows Server features such as Active Directory, which have no counterpart on other platforms. Nevertheless, you can use PowerShell 7 on a non-Windows platform to manage Windows servers and clients.

In this book, you need to install PowerShell 7 on each host you use, since all the scripts shown in this book require PowerShell 7.

Before You Start

You run the code in this section on a Windows 2-++++-+--+-019 Server, DC1. You can also use the snippets on other hosts that you use to install VS Code on those hosts.

You begin by running the code snippets using the Windows PowerShell 5.1 (or the ISE), run in an elevated console. You can download the relevant script files, open them locally, and run them inside each VM in the ISE (initially). Once you have installed PowerShell 7, you use the PowerShell 7 console. (You use VS Code later in this chapter.)

Enabling the Execution Policy

By default, PowerShell does not allow you to run scripts. To do so, you must first set the execution policy.

```
# 1. Enable scripts to be run
Set-ExecutionPolicy -ExecutionPolicy Unrestricted -Force
```

Here you set the execution policy to Unrestricted. On production systems you may want to set a more restrictive execution policy.

Installing the Latest Version of NuGet and PowerShellGet

PowerShell 7 comes with a large number of modules containing a useful set of commands, but it does not provide commands and modules to cover every situation. The PowerShell community has stepped up and created some outstanding added modules you can download and use, some of which are discussed in this book.

You use the PowerShell Gallery to download the PowerShell modules used in this book. For example, you use the NTFS Security module in later chapters to manage NTFS file and folder security.

You download and install a module from the PowerShell Gallery, or other module repositories, using `Import-Module`. To work with the PowerShell Gallery, you need to ensure you have the latest versions of the underlying tools that `Install-Module` uses to work against the PowerShell Gallery.

To ensure that you download the most up-to-date versions of the key modules from the PowerShell Gallery, use the following commands:

```
# 2. Install latest versions of Nuget and PowerShellGet
Install-PackageProvider Nuget -MinimumVersion 2.8.5.201 -Force |
```

```
  Out-Null
Install-Module -Name PowerShellGet -Force -AllowClobber
```

You use the commands in the PowerShellGet module to download content from the PowerShell Gallery. That, in turn, requires at least version 2.8.5.201 of NuGet.

For more details on the PowerShell Gallery, see `docs.microsoft.com/power-shell/scripting/gallery/overview`. To view the commands in the PowerShellGet module, see `docs.microsoft.com/powershell/module/powershellget/`.

Creating the Foo Folder

Throughout this book, sample code snippets use the `C:\Foo` folder to hold various files that you use in the code snippets. You create it using the `New-Item` command.

```
# 3. Create local folder C:\Foo
$LFHT = @{
  ItemType    = 'Directory'
  ErrorAction = 'SilentlyContinue' # should it already exist
}
New-Item -Path C:\Foo @LFHT | Out-Null
```

These commands use a PowerShell technique known as *splatting*. First, you create a hash table containing parameter names and values. Then, you pass the hash table to a cmdlet, in this case `New-Item`. You pass the hash table instead of the parameters and their values. This book makes extensive use of this feature for a few reasons. First, it enables all the commands to fit within the width of the page, avoiding a single command that spans multiple lines. But for production code, this approach also makes it a bit easier to see and, as needed, to update scripts that contain commands with a larger number of parameters. For more information, you can type **Get-Help about _ splatting** inside PowerShell or view the help file online at `docs.microsoft.com/powershell/module/microsoft.powershell.core/about/about _ splatting`. Note that you need to run `Update-Help` within PowerShell 7 before you can view the splatting help file.

Downloading the PowerShell 7 Installation Script

There are a variety of ways you can install PowerShell 7. One simple way is to download and use an installation script created by the PowerShell team. The script is available via the Internet (from GitHub), and you download it as follows:

```
# 4. Download PowerShell 7 installation script
Set-Location C:\Foo
$URI = "https://aka.ms/install-powershell.ps1"
Invoke-RestMethod -Uri $URI |
  Out-File -FilePath C:\Foo\Install-PowerShell.ps1
```

These commands download the installation script from GitHub and store it in C:\Foo.

Viewing Installation File Help Information

It is always a good idea to examine any script you download to see how the developer intended it to be used. To that end, the installation script contains some basic help information, which you can view with Get-Help.

```
# 5. View Installation Script Help
Get-Help -Name C:\Foo\Install-PowerShell.ps1
```

You can see the output from this command in Figure 1.2.

```
PS C:\Foo> # 5. View Installation Script Help
Get-Help -Name C:\Foo\Install-PowerShell.ps1
Install-PowerShell.ps1 [-Destination <string>] [-Daily] [-DoNotOverwrite] [-AddToPath] [-Preview] [<CommonParameters>]
Install-PowerShell.ps1 [-UseMSI] [-Quiet] [-AddExplorerContextMenu] [-EnablePSRemoting] [-Preview] [<CommonParameters>]
```

Figure 1.2: Viewing help information

The installation script allows you to install PowerShell 7 by using an MSI file or by installing it by downloading a ZIP file and expanding it into a folder of your choice. You can install the current version of PowerShell 7, the latest Preview of the next version of PowerShell 7, or you can install PowerShell's daily build. You can install each version alongside the latest fully released version of PowerShell 7.

For most IT pros, using the MSI and installing silently is quick and easy. Evaluating future versions and bug fixes rolled into the daily build is for the brave. Obviously, you should proceed with all necessary caution when using an unsupported version of any product. With that being said, the advanced versions have been very stable and allow you early access to new functionality and bug fixes.

Installing PowerShell 7

To install PowerShell 7 on DC1, you run the installation script with this code snippet:

```
# 6. Install PowerShell 7
$EXTHT = @{
  UseMSI                 = $true
  Quiet                  = $true
  AddExplorerContextMenu = $true
  EnablePSRemoting       = $true
}
C:\Foo\Install-PowerShell.ps1 @EXTHT
```

The installation script that downloads the PowerShell 7 MSI Installation package then runs this code silently. You should see no meaningful output. Because you are using the MSI, it installed PowerShell into a well-known location and updated the registry to indicate which versions of PowerShell are installed on this system.

Without using the MSI, for example when installing the build of the day, the installation script downloads the appropriate version as a ZIP file and expands it into a folder you specify.

When the `Install-PowerShell` script completes, you have installed PowerShell 7 on your system.

Examining the Installation Folder

Now that you have installed PowerShell 7, you can take a look at the installation folder with the following syntax:

```
# 7. Examine the installation folder
Get-Childitem -Path $env:ProgramFiles\PowerShell\7 -Recurse |
  Measure-Object -Property Length -Sum
```

You can see the output from these commands in Figure 1.3.

```
PS C:\Foo> # 7. Examine the installation folder
PS C:\Foo> Get-Childitem -Path $env:ProgramFiles\PowerShell\7 -Recurse |
           Measure-Object -Property Length -Sum

Count    : 986
Average  :
Sum      : 234332610
Maximum  :
Minimum  :
Property : Length
```

Figure 1.3: Examining the installation folder

As you can see in the figure, PowerShell 7's installation folder is different from that of Windows PowerShell (where, as a component of Windows, it is within the `C:\Windows\System32\WindowsPowerShell` folder).

If you examine the files in that folder carefully, you can see some differences in PowerShell 7. With PowerShell 7, there are significantly more files in the `$PSHome` folder (which can be confusing), and the name of the executable program you run to bring up the PowerShell 7 console is `pwsh.exe`. Another noticeable difference is that with PowerShell 7, there are no `.PS1XML` files. In Windows PowerShell, these XML files defined the default formatting for a wide range of objects and provided for IT pro–focused extensions to .NET Framework objects. PowerShell 7 brings the formatting XML inside PowerShell itself for improved performance.

The type extensions files were highly useful for ensuring consistency of property names across .NET classes, and PowerShell now has this functionality as well. You can still create your own type or format XML and extend PowerShell with updated types or default formatting that better meets your needs.

Viewing Module Folder Locations

In Windows PowerShell, commands you use are contained in modules. You can implicitly import a module before use to ensure it's available. Or you can make use of Windows PowerShell's module autoload feature. With module autoload, if you use a command that is not contained in modules already loaded, PowerShell searches all available modules to see if that command exists in some other module. If so, PowerShell loads the module and executes the command. PowerShell uses a built-in Windows environment variable to hold a semicolon-delimited list of paths. PowerShell searches each path in turn to discover any needed module. You can view the set of module folders in Windows PowerShell with this code:

```
# 8. View Module folders
#  View module folders for autoload
$I = 0
$env:PSModulePath -split ';' |
  Foreach-Object {
     "[{0:N0}]    {1}" -f $I++, $_}
```

You can see the output from these commands in Figure 1.4.

```
PS C:\Foo> # 8. View Module folders
PS C:\Foo> #  View module folders for autoload
PS C:\Foo> $I = 0
PS C:\Foo> $env:PSModulePath -split ';' |
             Foreach-Object {
                "[{0:N0}]    {1}" -f $I++, $_}

[0]    C:\Users\tfl\Documents\WindowsPowerShell\Modules
[1]    C:\Program Files\WindowsPowerShell\Modules
[2]    C:\Windows\system32\WindowsPowerShell\v1.0\Modules
```

Figure 1.4: Viewing module paths

As you can see, with Windows PowerShell there are just three module paths by default. If you add features or other applications/tools to your system(s), you may find installation programs add additional paths to the module file path variable.

To optimize performance, each time Windows PowerShell starts up, it spawns a low-priority thread that looks at the modules available and stores the details in a local cache. The module autoload makes use of this cache to discover the modules that need to be imported before a command can be used. One side effect is that if different modules implement a given command name, the module in the higher-placed path is imported. This means you can create your own versions of `Get-Command`.

Viewing Profile File Locations

PowerShell defines four profile files.

- AllUsersAllHosts
- AllUsersCurrentHost
- CurrentUserAllHosts
- CurrentUserCurrentHost

Each profile file is associated with a well-known profile filename. PowerShell has a built-in variable, `$Profile`. At startup, PowerShell adds four properties to this variable that hold the well-known paths to each of the profile files. To see these properties, you need to use the `-Force` parameter explicitly.

These profile files allow you considerable flexibility with respect to startup profiles. Each profile file (which PowerShell runs as part of its startup) can create objects/variables, set environment options, send email, create a transcript, create PowerShell drives, and so on. In effect, profile files are a way of persisting a customized environment. You add commands to the profile that you want to have executed before you begin to work in a PowerShell session.

You can use PowerShell profile files for all users, perhaps to define some corporate or departmental aliases, create some "well-known" file locations for all users, or do more customized actions for just the current user. You have profiles for all PowerShell hosts (programs that host and use the PowerShell runtime) or separate profile files for different hosts. The ISE, for example, has the `$PSISE` variable, which allows you to control the ISE environment. This variable does not exist in either the PowerShell console or VS Code. Having different profiles for different PowerShell hosts allows you to customize each host using different techniques.

You can address a variety of deployment scenarios using different combinations of these four profile files as needed. Most IT pros just use the Current User Current Host profile, which is the value of `$Profile`.

You view the four profiles and their associated well-known filenames as follows:

```
# 9. View Profile File locations
# Inside the ISE
$PROFILE |
  Format-List -Property *Host* -Force
# from Windows PowerShell Console
powershell -Command '$Profile|  Format-List -Property *Host*' -Force
```

The output, which you can see in Figure 1.5, shows the profile file locations for both the ISE and the Windows PowerShell console.

```
PS C:\Foo> # 9. View Profile File locations
PS C:\Foo> # Inside the ISE
PS C:\Foo> $PROFILE |
              Format-List -Property *Host* -Force

AllUsersAllHosts        : C:\Windows\System32\WindowsPowerShell\v1.0\profile.ps1
AllUsersCurrentHost     : C:\Windows\System32\WindowsPowerShell\v1.0\Microsoft.PowerShellISE_profile.ps1
CurrentUserAllHosts     : C:\Users\tfl\Documents\WindowsPowerShell\profile.ps1
CurrentUserCurrentHost  : C:\Users\tfl\Documents\WindowsPowerShell\Microsoft.PowerShellISE_profile.ps1

PS C:\Foo> powershell -Command '$PROFILE |
              Format-List -Property *Host*' -Force

AllUsersAllHosts        : C:\Windows\System32\WindowsPowerShell\v1.0\profile.ps1
AllUsersCurrentHost     : C:\Windows\System32\WindowsPowerShell\v1.0\Microsoft.PowerShell_profile.ps1
CurrentUserAllHosts     : C:\Users\tfl\Documents\WindowsPowerShell\profile.ps1
CurrentUserCurrentHost  : C:\Users\tfl\Documents\WindowsPowerShell\Microsoft.PowerShell_profile.ps1
```

Figure 1.5: Viewing profile file locations

Starting PowerShell 7

Now that you have installed PowerShell 7, you can click the Windows Start button, enter **pwsh**, and hit Enter to open a PowerShell 7 console. After you open the PowerShell 7 console, verify the version by viewing the $PSVersionTable variable.

```
# 10. Run PowerShell 7 console and then...
$PSVersionTable
```

As you can see in Figure 1.6, I was running PowerShell 7 when I captured the output. There are almost certainly going to be newer versions released by the time you read this (such as 7.0.1 or 7.0.2), so you may well see a slightly later version for PowerShell 7.

```
PS C:\Users\tfl> # 10. Run PowerShell 7 console and then...
PS C:\Users\tfl> $PSVersionTable

Name                           Value
----                           -----
PSVersion                      7.0.0
PSEdition                      Core
GitCommitId                    7.0.0
OS                             Microsoft Windows 10.0.18363
Platform                       Win32NT
PSCompatibleVersions           {1.0, 2.0, 3.0, 4.0}
PSRemotingProtocolVersion      2.3
SerializationVersion           1.1.0.1
WSManStackVersion              3.0
```

Figure 1.6: Viewing help information

Viewing New Locations for Module Folders

In the previous section "Viewing Module Folder Locations" you viewed the folders where Windows PowerShell looked to find modules. With PowerShell 7, you repeat this as follows:

```
# 11. View Modules folders
$ModFolders = $Env:PSModulePath -split ';'
$I = 0
$ModFolders |
  ForEach-Object {"[{0:N0}]   {1}" -f $I++, $_}
```

You can see the output from these commands in Figure 1.7.

```
PS C:\Foo> # 11. View Modules folders
PS C:\Foo> $ModFolders = $Env:PSModulePath -split ';'
PS C:\Foo> $I = 0
PS C:\Foo> $ModFolders |
              ForEach-Object {"[{0:N0}]   {1}" -f $I++, $_}

[0]    C:\Users\tfl\Documents\PowerShell\Modules
[1]    C:\Program Files\PowerShell\Modules
[2]    c:\program files\powershell\7\Modules
[3]    C:\Program Files\WindowsPowerShell\Modules
[4]    C:\Windows\system32\WindowsPowerShell\v1.0\Modules
```

Figure 1.7: Viewing PowerShell 7 module paths

In the output, notice that you now have five module file paths.

Viewing New Locations for Profile Files

As in Windows PowerShell, you have multiple profile files with PowerShell 7, although these are now in a slightly different place on the disk. You can view the locations for the four PowerShell 7 profile files like this:

```
# 12. View Profile Locations
$PROFILE | Format-List -Property *Host* -Force
```

As you can see in Figure 1.8, there are four profiles files, each at a location separate from Windows PowerShell.

```
PS C:\Foo> # 12. View Profile Locations
PS C:\Foo> $PROFILE | Format-List -Property *Host* -Force

AllUsersAllHosts       : C:\Program Files\PowerShell\7\profile.ps1
AllUsersCurrentHost    : C:\Program Files\PowerShell\7\Microsoft.PowerShell_profile.ps1
CurrentUserAllHosts    : C:\Users\tfl\Documents\PowerShell\profile.ps1
CurrentUserCurrentHost : C:\Users\tfl\Documents\PowerShell\Microsoft.PowerShell_profile.ps1
```

Figure 1.8: Viewing PowerShell profile file locations

Creating a Current User/Current Host Profile

To demonstrate how PowerShell profile files work with PowerShell 7, you can download a sample profile from the Internet and create the Current User Current Host Profile using the following commands:

```
# 13. Create Current user/Current host profile
$URI = 'https://raw.githubusercontent.com/doctordns/Wiley20/master/' +
       'Goodies/Microsoft.PowerShell_Profile.ps1'
$ProfileFile = $Profile.CurrentUserCurrentHost
New-Item $ProfileFile -Force -WarningAction SilentlyContinue |
   Out-Null
(Invoke-WebRequest -Uri $uri -UseBasicParsing).Content |
   Out-File -FilePath  $ProfileFile
```

You can obtain the scripts for this book both from Wiley and from the author's GitHub repository. The author's repository contains a Goodies folder that has a sample profile file to illustrate the use of profiles with the PowerShell 7 console.

This sample sets some useful defaults and aliases, creates some variables, configures the console heading, and sets the current working folder to the eponymous C:\Foo folder. Feel free to adjust this profile to suit your working style. Once you run these commands, you need to restart PowerShell to have the new profiles take effect.

Installing and Configuring VS Code

The PowerShell ISE is an interactive development environment for Windows PowerShell. The ISE allows you to edit, manage, and run scripts within a single program. While there have been other IDEs available for PowerShell, the ISE is free and built in and has good functionality for the IT pro. The screenshots taken for this book that show PowerShell 7 code are shown running in VS Code.

Microsoft has indicated it has no plans to update the ISE to support PowerShell 7. A recommended alternative is VS Code. VS Code is a free, Microsoft-created, open source, cross-platform source code editor. VS Code runs as a desktop application on Windows, macOS, and Linux and provides great support for PowerShell. VS Code is an excellent tool for managing not only PowerShell source code but also documents containing Perl, Python, Markdown, and a host of other formats.

Although VS Code is cross-platform, this chapter deals with VS Code on Windows. For more information on VS Code, see code.visualstudio.com/.

VS Code supports a rich set of extensions that further enhance the development experience. You can install a spell checker, for example. If you work with Markdown (en.wikipedia.org/wiki/Markdown), the community has built VS Code extensions to help you. You can use VS Code itself to add new extensions to your environment, and you can install specific extensions when you install VS Code.

To install VS Code on your computer, you download and run an installation script from Microsoft's Visual Studio site that enables you to install VS Code and any required extensions in a single operation.

If you work with more than just PowerShell, visit the Visual Studio marketplace at `marketplace.visualstudio.com`, where you can find a large selection of extensions. Some extensions are free, while others are commercial (usually with a free trial).

Once you have installed VS Code, you can easily alter the font it uses. VS Code can use any of the fonts installed on your system, and you can change the font via the VS Code GUI or via a JSON user settings file.

Microsoft recently published a new font, Cascadia Code. This font looks good when you are using VS Code. All the screenshots in this book containing PowerShell code use this font.

Finally, if you plan to use VS Code and PowerShell 7, you might like to add shortcuts to your taskbar.

> **NOTE**   The screenshots in this book were taken using VS. You can use VS Code in all your VMs to test the scripts contained in this book, although in some environments this may not be allowed or may not be considered best practice.

Before You Start

The code in this section runs on a VM running Windows Server 2019 Datacenter, DC1. You can also use the snippets on other hosts that you use to install VS Code and test the scripts in this book.

You run the scripts in this section using PowerShell 7, which you installed in the previous section "Installing PowerShell 7."

Downloading the VS Code Installation Script

The VS Code team has created an installation script to enable you to install VS Code and uploaded this script to the PowerShell Gallery. You download the script as follows:

```
# 1. Download the VS Code Installation Script
$VSCPATH = 'C:\Foo'
Save-Script -Name Install-VSCode -Path $VSCPATH
Set-Location -Path $VSCPATH
```

This snippet retrieves the `Install-VSCode` script and saves it to the `C:\Foo` folder.

Installing VS Code and Extensions

You install VS Code using the `Install-VSCode.ps1` file you just downloaded. You can specify certain VS Code extensions that the installer should install along with VS Code itself, as follows:

```
# 2. Now run it and add in some popular VSCode Extensions
$Extensions =  "Streetsidesoftware.code-spell-checker",
               "yzhang.markdown-all-in-one"
$InstallHT = @{
  BuildEdition          = 'Stable-System'
  AdditionalExtensions  = $Extensions
  LaunchWhenDone        = $true
}
.\Install-VSCode.ps1 @InstallHT
```

You can see the output generated by the VS Code installation script in Figure 1.9.

```
PS C:\Foo> # 2. Now run it and add in some popular VSCode Extensions
PS C:\Foo> $Extensions =  "Streetsidesoftware.code-spell-checker",
                          "yzhang.markdown-all-in-one"
PS C:\Foo> $InstallHT = @{
              BuildEdition          = 'Stable-System'
              AdditionalExtensions = $Extensions
              LaunchWhenDone        = $true
              }
PS C:\Foo> .\Install-VSCode.ps1 @InstallHT

Installing extension ms-vscode.PowerShell...
Installing extensions...
Installing extension 'ms-vscode.powershell' v2020.4.0...
Extension 'ms-vscode.powershell' v2020.4.0 was successfully installed.

Installing extension Streetsidesoftware.code-spell-checker...
Installing extensions...
Installing extension 'streetsidesoftware.code-spell-checker' v1.8.0...
Extension 'streetsidesoftware.code-spell-checker' v1.8.0 was successfully installed.

Installing extension yzhang.markdown-all-in-one...
Installing extensions...
Installing extension 'yzhang.markdown-all-in-one' v2.8.0...
Extension 'yzhang.markdown-all-in-one' v2.8.0 was successfully installed.

Installation complete, starting Visual Studio Code (64-bit)...
```

Figure 1.9: Installing VS Code on *DC1*

This snippet retrieves and installs the latest stable version of VS Code from the Internet. As part of the installation two extensions are added. The first is a good spellchecker, and the second is helpful if you are editing Markdown files.

Depending on what your workload consists of, there are other extensions you might find useful. The community is active in developing, extending, and maintaining a wide variety of extensions.

These commands also start VS Code, so as additional output you see a VS Code window. You can use this window to run code snippets in the rest of this chapter.

Creating a Sample Personal Profile File

PowerShell profile files are quite powerful as a way of persisting customizations to PowerShell sessions. You can create new PowerShell drives, create and populate custom variables, define useful functions, and much more. By default, PowerShell 7 ships without profile files. As with Windows PowerShell, you create an (empty) profile file by running the following commands in the VS Code window:

```
# 3. Create a Sample Profile File
$SAMPLE = 'https://raw.githubusercontent.com/doctordns/Wiley20/master/' +
          'Goodies/Microsoft.VSCode_profile.ps1'
(Invoke-WebRequest -Uri $Sample).Content |
  Out-File $Profile
```

This snippet downloads a sample VS Code profile and saves it as the Current Host/Current User profile. Depending on your organization, this sample may be all you need. If you use both the PowerShell 7 console and VS Code, you need to maintain two separate versions of that profile—one for each host. You should review the two sample profiles and amend them as needed.

Downloading the Cascadia Code Font

Along with VS Code, Microsoft has also developed a new fixed-width font, named Cascadia Code, for use with VS Code (and any other Windows applications that use fixed-width fonts, including the PowerShell and Windows PowerShell console, Microsoft Office Word, and more). The Cascadia Code font's developers ship released versions of this font via GitHub (as well as via the Microsoft Store). There are several versions of the font, including the basic font (Cascadia.ttf). You can also download a variant that supports Powerline symbols (CascadiaPL.ttf). To download the latest version of the basic font, use the following code:

```
# 4. Download Cascadia Code font from GitHub
# Get File Locations
$CascadiaFont   = 'Cascadia.ttf'   # font file name
```

Continues

continued

```
$CascadiaRelURL   = 'https://github.com/microsoft/cascadia-code/releases'
$CascadiaRelease = Invoke-WebRequest -Uri $CascadiaRelURL # Get&all of them
$CascadiaPath     = "https://github.com" + ($CascadiaRelease.Links.href |
                    Where-Object { $_ -match "($CascadiaFont)" } |
                    Select-Object -First 1)
$CascadiaFile     = "C:\Foo\$CascadiaFont"
# Download Cascadia Code font file
Invoke-WebRequest -Uri $CascadiaPath -OutFile $CascadiaFile
```

Installing the Cascadia Code Font in Windows

There is no direct support in PowerShell to install fonts. To install the font you have just downloaded, you make use of the `Shell.Application` COM object, as shown here:

```
# 5. Install Cascadia Code font
$FontShellApp = New-Object -Com Shell.Application
$FontShellNamespace = $FontShellApp.Namespace(0x14)
$FontShellNamespace.CopyHere($CascadiaFile, 0x10)
```

Although you downloaded the font file previously, you only now install it. As long as you have not previously loaded this font, these commands produce no output.

Updating VS Code User Settings

VS Code is highly configurable. Many of the individual configuration preferences are stored in a JSON file that you can modify as you choose. Here is how you can update your user settings for VS Code:

```
# 6. Update Local User Settings for VS Code
#    This step in particular needs to be run in PowerShell 7!
$JSON = @'
{
  "workbench.colorTheme": "PowerShell ISE",
  "powershell.codeFormatting.useCorrectCasing": true,
  "files.autoSave": "onWindowChange",
  "files.defaultLanguage": "powershell",
  "editor.fontFamily": "'Cascadia Code',Consolas,'Courier New'",
  "workbench.editor.highlightModifiedTabs": true,
  "window.zoomLevel": 1
}
'@
$JHT = ConvertFrom-Json -InputObject $JSON -AsHashtable
$PWSH = "C:\\Program Files\\PowerShell\\7\\pwsh.exe"
```

```
$JHT += @{
  "terminal.integrated.shell.windows" = "$PWSH"
}
$Path = $Env:APPDATA
$CP   = '\Code\User\Settings.json'
$Settings = Join-Path  $Path -ChildPath $CP
$JHT |
  ConvertTo-Json  |
    Out-File -FilePath $Settings
```

This code snippet sets several VS Code settings for the current user, including using the newly added Cascadia Code font, setting the VS Code color theme to the PowerShell ISE, and more. Note that this snippet overwrites any user settings you may have. As you continue using VS Code and updating settings, the contents of the JSON file are likely to change.

The snippet also shows how you can manage JSON documents by using a new feature in PowerShell 7 that converts a JSON document to a PowerShell hash table. In the snippet, you import the JSON document and convert it to a PowerShell hash table. You can add a new value—in this case the name of the PowerShell 7 executable file. Once you have finished adding the user settings, you convert the hash table back to JSON and write it away.

Note that if you run this snippet in VS Code, you see the color theme and font change once these commands complete execution.

Creating a Shortcut to VS Code

You next create a shortcut to VS Code (which you use later in this section), as follows:

```
# 7. Create a short cut to VS Code
$SourceFileLocation  = "$env:ProgramFiles\Microsoft VS Code\Code.exe"
$ShortcutLocation    = "C:\foo\vscode.lnk"
# Create a  new wscript.shell object
$WScriptShell        = New-Object -ComObject WScript.Shell
$Shortcut            = $WScriptShell.CreateShortcut($ShortcutLocation)
$Shortcut.TargetPath = $SourceFileLocation
#Save the Shortcut to the TargetPath
$Shortcut.Save()
```

These steps create a shortcut in the C:\Foo folder to VS Code.

Creating a Shortcut to the PowerShell 7 Console

You can also create a shortcut to the PowerShell 7 console in a similar manner.

```
# 8. Create a shortcut to PowerShell 7
$SourceFileLocation  = "$env:ProgramFiles\PowerShell\7\pwsh.exe"
```

Continues

continued

```
$ShortcutLocation    = 'C:\Foo\pwsh.lnk'
# Create a new wscript.shell object
$WScriptShell        = New-Object -ComObject WScript.Shell
$Shortcut            = $WScriptShell.CreateShortcut($ShortcutLocation)
$Shortcut.TargetPath = $SourceFileLocation
#Save the Shortcut to the TargetPath
$Shortcut.Save()
```

These steps create a shortcut in the C:\Foo folder to the PowerShell 7 console.

Building Layout.XML

If you are going to use VS Code and PowerShell a lot, it's useful to add a shortcut to these two tools in the Windows taskbar. To do that, you first create an XML file that tells Windows to add the two recently created shortcuts to the taskbar, as follows:

```
# 9. Build Updated Layout XML
$XML = @'
<?xml version="1.0" encoding="utf-8"?>
<LayoutModificationTemplate
  xmlns="http://schemas.microsoft.com/Start/2014/LayoutModification"
  xmlns:defaultlayout=
    "http://schemas.microsoft.com/Start/2014/FullDefaultLayout"
  xmlns:start="http://schemas.microsoft.com/Start/2014/StartLayout"
  xmlns:taskbar="http://schemas.microsoft.com/Start/2014/TaskbarLayout"
  Version="1">
<CustomTaskbarLayoutCollection>
<defaultlayout:TaskbarLayout>
<taskbar:TaskbarPinList>
 <taskbar:DesktopApp DesktopApplicationLinkPath="C:\Foo\vscode.lnk"/>
 <taskbar:DesktopApp DesktopApplicationLinkPath="C:\Foo\pwsh.lnk"/>
</taskbar:TaskbarPinList>
</defaultlayout:TaskbarLayout>
</CustomTaskbarLayoutCollection>
</LayoutModificationTemplate>
'@
$XML | Out-File -FilePath C:\Foo\Layout.Xml
```

This snippet creates a new Layout.XML file and stores it in the C:\Foo folder.

Importing the New Layout.XML File

To add these shortcuts to the taskbar, you need to import the start layout XML file you just created, as follows:

```
# 10. Import the start layout XML file
#     You get an error if this is not run in an elevated session
Import-StartLayout -LayoutPath C:\Foo\Layout.Xml -MountPath C:\
```

As noted in the snippet, you must run this final command in an elevated console or run VS Code elevated. Elevated mode allows you to run commands with administrative privileges. You do this by clicking Start, typing **Code**, right-clicking the VS Code icon, and then clicking Run As Administrator.

To see the two new shortcuts on the taskbar, you sign out of Windows and then sign back in. After you sign in again, your desktop should resemble Figure 1.10.

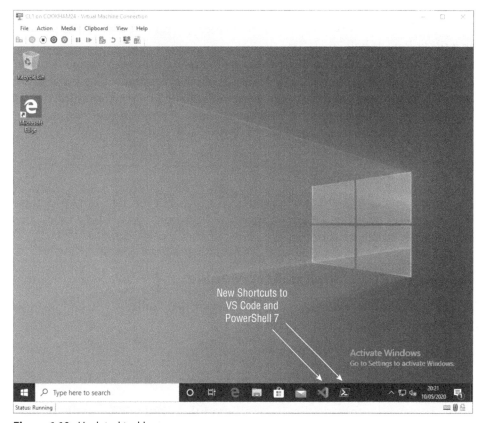

Figure 1.10: Updated taskbar

You may see a slightly different desktop depending on the media you used to install Windows 10 (for example, evaluation or fully licensed versions).

For the more adventurous, you might install both the daily build and the latest Preview build with taskbar shortcuts to all of the versions of PowerShell (and Windows PowerShell) on your computer.

Using the PowerShell Gallery

Almost since the beginning of the PC, IT pros have had to find and deploy additional software and tools. For PowerShell users, Microsoft's PowerShell

Gallery (www.powershellgallery.com/) is a repository of PowerShell add-ins including additional modules, scripts, and more. You used the PowerShell Gallery in "Installing and Configuring VS Code" to download the script to install VS Code, for example.

To discover, download, install, and update these add-ins, you use the commands in the PowerShellGet module. This module is installed by default. Given the pace of change in the PowerShell world and the importance of security, you need to ensure that you have the latest versions of this module (which is true of any module you download from the Gallery). You did that in the section "Installing PowerShell 7."

The PowerShell Gallery is run by Microsoft, and a number of the items in the PowerShell Gallery were created by Microsoft employees and Microsoft product teams. There are also a variety of excellent tools created by the community. This book shows how to use a number of these modules. The snippets in this section show how you can leverage and use the PowerShell Gallery.

Before You Start

You run the snippets in this section on a Windows Server host, DC1. You must have installed PowerShell 7, and optionally VS Code, on this host using the scripts earlier in this chapter.

Discovering PowerShell Gallery Modules

To discover modules available from the PowerShell Gallery, you can use the Find-Module command.

```
# 1. Get Details of all PS Gallery Modules
$PGSM = Find-Module -Name *
"There are {0:N0} Modules in the PS Gallery" -f $PGSM.count
```

This snippet downloads details of all modules available from the PowerShell Gallery and displays a count of how many are available, as you can see in Figure 1.11.

```
PS C:\Foo> # 1. Get Details of all PS Gallery Modules
PS C:\Foo> $PGSM = Find-Module -Name *
PS C:\Foo> "There are {0:N0} modules in the PS Gallery" -f $PGSM.Count
There are 5,526 modules in the PS Gallery
```

Figure 1.11: Count of modules available in the PowerShell Gallery

The number of available modules changes constantly but was more than 5,000 at the time of writing. While many of these modules are useful, some may be less than helpful, incomplete, or not working. Care is needed when using third-party modules.

Determining the Modules That Support .NET Core

Some, but not all, of the modules support .NET Core and thus should work natively within PowerShell 7. To report on how many modules support .NET Core, you can run these commands:

```
# 2. Get Details of packages tagged with 'PSEdition_Core'
$PGSMC = Find-Module -Name * -Tag 'PSEdition_Core'
"There are {0:N0} modules supporting PowerShell Core" -f $PGSMC.Count
```

As you can see in Figure 1.12, there are about 800 modules that support .NET core, although this number, too, is increasing.

```
PS C:\Foo> # 2. Get Details of packages tagged with 'PSEdition_Core'
PS C:\Foo> $PGSMC = Find-Module -Name * -Tag 'PSEdition_Core'
PS C:\Foo> "There are {0:N0} modules supporting PowerSell Core" -f $PGSMC.Count
There are 798 modules supporting PowerShell Core
```

Figure 1.12: Count of available modules that support .NET core

Finding NTFS Modules

As an example of how to search for modules in the PowerShell Gallery, you might want to search for a module that works with the Windows NTFS filesystem. You can search for possible modules with this code:

```
# 3. Find NTFS Modules
$PGSM | Where-Object Name -match 'NTFS'
```

This command searches the set of modules you previously obtained and displays those that have "NTFS" in the module name. Figure 1.13 shows the output.

```
PS C:\Foo> # 3. Find NTFS Modules
PS C:\Foo> $PGSM | Where-Object Name -match 'NTFS'

Version   Name                 Repository   Description
-------   ----                 ----------   -----------
4.2.6     NTFSSecurity         PSGallery    Windows PowerShell Module for managing file and folder security …
1.4.1     cNtfsAccessControl   PSGallery    The cNtfsAccessControl module contains DSC resources for NTFS ac…
1.0       NTFSPermissionMigration PSGallery This module is used as a wrapper to the popular icacls utility t…
```

Figure 1.13: NTFS-related modules

As you can see in the figure, three modules are available. One of those is the NTFSSecurity module, which you can use to manage NTFS access control lists

(ACLs) and inheritance (you use this module in several chapters in this book to adjust file ACLs).

Installing the NTFSSecurity Module

You install the NTFSSecurity module by using the `Install-Module` command.

```
# 4. Install the NTFSSecurity module
Install-Module -Name NTFSSecurity
```

Viewing Available Commands

Now that you have downloaded the module, you can use `Get-Command` to view the commands available within the NTFSSecurity module.

```
# 5. View Commands in the NTFSSecurity module
Get-Command -Module NTFSSecurity
```

You can see the output of this command in Figure 1.14.

Creating a Local PowerShellGet Repository

Public repositories such as the PowerShell Gallery are great resources for IT professionals. They provide you with a wide range of useful modules, scripts, and other resources. Modules such as NTFSSecurity make it easier to administer NTFS permissions and inheritance, for example. This book makes use of a number of modules you download from the PowerShell Gallery.

At the same time as you can leverage external modules, you can also develop modules for your own use and create your own internal module repository. You can create a module to manage users in your Active Directory, for example, that takes into account your specific business requirements. Once it is created, you can store this module on an internal repository for use by other IT professionals, or even end users, within your organization.

You have several alternative methods of creating an internal PowerShell repository. A simple implementation of a PowerShell repository would be an SMB share within your organization where you publish packages for others to use.

Before You Start

You run the code in this section on a Windows Server 2019 host, DC1. This is a Windows Server 2019 host on which you have installed PowerShell 7 and, optionally, VS Code.

```
PS C:\Foo> # 5. View Commands in the NTFS Security module
PS C:\Foo> Get-Command -Module NTFSSecurity

CommandType    Name                              Version   Source
-----------    ----                              -------   ------
Cmdlet         Add-NTFSAccess                    4.2.6     NTFSSecurity
Cmdlet         Add-NTFSAudit                     4.2.6     NTFSSecurity
Cmdlet         Clear-NTFSAccess                  4.2.6     NTFSSecurity
Cmdlet         Clear-NTFSAudit                   4.2.6     NTFSSecurity
Cmdlet         Copy-Item2                        4.2.6     NTFSSecurity
Cmdlet         Disable-NTFSAccessInheritance     4.2.6     NTFSSecurity
Cmdlet         Disable-NTFSAuditInheritance      4.2.6     NTFSSecurity
Cmdlet         Disable-Privileges                4.2.6     NTFSSecurity
Cmdlet         Enable-NTFSAccessInheritance      4.2.6     NTFSSecurity
Cmdlet         Enable-NTFSAuditInheritance       4.2.6     NTFSSecurity
Cmdlet         Enable-Privileges                 4.2.6     NTFSSecurity
Cmdlet         Get-ChildItem2                    4.2.6     NTFSSecurity
Cmdlet         Get-DiskSpace                     4.2.6     NTFSSecurity
Cmdlet         Get-FileHash2                     4.2.6     NTFSSecurity
Cmdlet         Get-Item2                         4.2.6     NTFSSecurity
Cmdlet         Get-NTFSAccess                    4.2.6     NTFSSecurity
Cmdlet         Get-NTFSAudit                     4.2.6     NTFSSecurity
Cmdlet         Get-NTFSEffectiveAccess           4.2.6     NTFSSecurity
Cmdlet         Get-NTFSHardLink                  4.2.6     NTFSSecurity
Cmdlet         Get-NTFSInheritance               4.2.6     NTFSSecurity
Cmdlet         Get-NTFSOrphanedAccess            4.2.6     NTFSSecurity
Cmdlet         Get-NTFSOrphanedAudit             4.2.6     NTFSSecurity
Cmdlet         Get-NTFSOwner                     4.2.6     NTFSSecurity
Cmdlet         Get-NTFSSecurityDescriptor        4.2.6     NTFSSecurity
Cmdlet         Get-NTFSSimpleAccess              4.2.6     NTFSSecurity
Cmdlet         Get-Privileges                    4.2.6     NTFSSecurity
Cmdlet         Move-Item2                        4.2.6     NTFSSecurity
Cmdlet         New-NTFSHardLink                  4.2.6     NTFSSecurity
Cmdlet         New-NTFSSymbolicLink              4.2.6     NTFSSecurity
Cmdlet         Remove-Item2                      4.2.6     NTFSSecurity
Cmdlet         Remove-NTFSAccess                 4.2.6     NTFSSecurity
Cmdlet         Remove-NTFSAudit                  4.2.6     NTFSSecurity
Cmdlet         Set-NTFSInheritance               4.2.6     NTFSSecurity
Cmdlet         Set-NTFSOwner                     4.2.6     NTFSSecurity
Cmdlet         Set-NTFSSecurityDescriptor        4.2.6     NTFSSecurity
Cmdlet         Test-Path2                        4.2.6     NTFSSecurity
```

Figure 1.14: Commands in the NTFSSecurity module

In Chapter 3, you convert the DC1 host to be a domain controller. However, for the purposes of this section, DC1 is just a Windows Server 2019 host.

Creating the Repository Folder

The repository you create in this section is based on a simple SMB file share. You start by creating the underlying folder.

```
# 1. Create Repository Folder
$LPATH = 'C:\RKRepo'
New-Item -Path $LPATH -ItemType Directory | Out-Null
```

In production, you would most likely protect this folder from being updated with ACLs. You can use the techniques covered in Chapter 4 , "Managing Networking," for this.

Sharing the Repository Folder

You create the repository share by using the New-SMBShare command.

```
# 2. Share the Repository Folder
$SMBHT = @{
  Name        = 'RKRepo'
  Path        = $LPATH
  Description = 'Reskit Repository'
  FullAccess  = 'Everyone'
}
New-SmbShare @SMBHT
```

These commands create a new SMB share named RKREPO on the DC1 host. This share is the basis for the repository.

Creating a Module Working Folder

While you're developing any module, prior to publishing it and using it in production, you can store it in any folder. In this case, you create a new folder, C:\ HW, that is to hold the module as you develop it.

```
# 3. Create a Working Folder for a Module
New-Item C:\HW -ItemType Directory | Out-Null
```

In production, you might want to create the working module in a separate volume. You would also want to put your module under source code control, for example using Git for this purpose.

Creating a Simple Module

The simplest module is a .PSM1 file with just a function definition (and in this case an alias).

```
# 4. Create a simple module
$HS = @'
Function Get-HelloWorld {'Hello World'}
Set-Alias GHW Get-HelloWorld
'@
$HS | Out-File C:\HW\HW.psm1
```

These commands create a PowerShell module with one function and an alias. You save this "module" in your module working folder (C:\HW).

Loading and Testing the Module

Before you upload the module to a repository, you should test it. A simple way to do this is to load the module from the module's working folder and then use the GHW alias you added to the .PSM1 file.

```
# 5. Load and Test the Module
Import-Module -Name C:\HW -Verbose
GHW
```

You can see the output from these two commands in Figure 1.15.

```
PS C:\Foo> # 5. Load and Test the Module
PS C:\Foo> Import-Module -Name C:\HW -Verbose
VERBOSE: Loading module from path 'C:\HW\HW.psm1'.
VERBOSE: Exporting function 'Get-HelloWorld'.
VERBOSE: Exporting alias 'GHW'.
VERBOSE: Importing function 'Get-HelloWorld'.
VERBOSE: Importing alias 'GHW'.
PS C:\Foo> GHW
Hello World
```

Figure 1.15: Testing the Hello World module

In the figure, you first see the verbose output from Import-Module. You can see in that output that PowerShell loads the module, adds a function to your PowerShell session, and then adds an alias to the function. Once imported, you can use the module's GHW alias.

Creating a Module Manifest

PowerShell repository and commands such as Install-Module are based on NuGet. Each item in your repository is a NuGet package. For more information on NuGet, see docs.microsoft.com/en-us/nuget/what-is-nuget.

NuGet requires all packages to have a module manifest (a .PSD1 file that you add to the folder holding the module). You can create one using New-ModuleManifest.

```
# 6. Create a Module Manifest for this module
$NMHT = @{
  Path              = 'C:\HW\HW.psd1'
  RootModule        = 'HW.psm1'
  Description       = 'Hello World module'
  Author            = 'DoctorDNS@Gmail.com'
  FunctionsToExport = 'Get-HelloWorld'
  ModuleVersion     = '1.0.0'
}
New-ModuleManifest @NMHT
```

These commands create a module manifest, HW.psd1, in the module folder. You could re-import the module, using the -Verbose switch parameter, to see that PowerShell now loads the module via the manifest.

Trusting the Repository

If you use a repository that is not trusted, attempting to use commands such as Install-Module results in a prompt asking whether to use an untrusted repository. You can trust a repository to avoid this warning. Note that a trusted repository is just a NuGet repository that a given system trusts. To trust any repository, you use the Register-PSRepository command.

```
# 7. Create the repository as trusted
#    Repeat on every host that uses this repository
$Path = '\\DC1 \RKRepo'
$REPOHT = @{
  Name              = 'RKRepo'
  SourceLocation    = $Path
  PublishLocation   = $Path
  InstallationPolicy = 'Trusted'
}
Register-PSRepository @REPOHT
```

These commands make the new RKRepo repository trusted from DC1. Note that if you want other hosts to trust this repository, you need to run this command on those hosts.

Viewing Configured Repositories

You use the Get-PSRepository command to view the currently configured repositories.

```
# 8. View configured repositories
Get-PSRepository
```

You can see the output from this command in Figure 1.16.

```
PS C:\Foo> # 8. View configured repositories
PS C:\Foo> Get-PSRepository


Name       InstallationPolicy  SourceLocation
----       ------------------  --------------
PSGallery  Untrusted           https://www.powershellgallery.com/api/v2
RKRepo     Trusted             \\DC1\RKRepo
```

Figure 1.16: Viewing configured repositories

As shown in the figure, DC1 currently has two repositories you can use. The PowerShell 7 installation process created the first, the PowerShell Gallery, although the installation process creates it as untrusted. You can configure PowerShell to trust the PowerShell Gallery should you wish.

Publishing a Module

To publish a module to your repository, you use the `Publish-Module` command.

```
# 9. Publish the module to the repository
Publish-Module -Path C:\HW -Repository RKRepo -Force
```

`Publish-Module` requires an up-to-date version of the NuGet provider. You added this explicitly to DC1 in the section "Installing PowerShell 7." By using the parameter `-Force`, you instruct PowerShell to download an appropriate version or the NuGet provider, if needed, before completing the publishing process.

If you plan to make use of repositories, whether public or private, as part of your deployment of PowerShell 7, you should install the latest versions of all modules (and have a process in place to ensure that you keep the downloaded modules up to date on each host in your infrastructure).

Viewing the Repository Folder

You can view the NuGet packages in your RKRepo repository using `Get-ChildItem`.

```
# 10. View the repository folder
Get-ChildItem -Path C:\RKRepo
```

Figure 1.17 shows the output from this command. You can see that there is just one package in the repository.

```
PS C:\Foo> # 10. View the repository folder
PS C:\Foo> Get-ChildItem -Path C:\RKRepo


    Directory: C:\RKRepo


Mode          LastWriteTime    Length Name
----          -------------    ------ ----
-a--- 11/05/2020     09:20      3463 HW.1.0.0.nupkg
```

Figure 1.17: Viewing the repository folder

Finding a Module

With the module published to your private repository, you can use `Find-Module` to view the module.

```
# 11. Find the module in the RKRepo repository
Find-Module -Repository RKRepo
```

You can see basic module detail in Figure 1.18.

```
PS C:\Foo> # 11. Find the module in the RKRepo repository
PS C:\Foo> Find-Module -Repository RKRepo

Version  Name   Repository   Description
-------  ----   ----------   -----------
1.0.0    HW     RKRepo       Hello World module
```

Figure 1.18: Viewing the RKRepo modules

In this section, you created, trusted, and used a PowerShell repository. In production, you would need policies and procedures to govern who can upload packages to the repository and how to set them up.

Creating a Code-Signing Environment

PowerShell has the ability to control the execution of digitally signed scripts, via settings of the PowerShell execution policy. If you set the execution policy to All Signed, for example, PowerShell does not run any script that is not signed or whose signature is untrusted. If you are developing PowerShell code for customers, you may find it useful to sign your code to ensure that the code you ship is the code the customer has received and to flag any unauthorized changes.

For script signing, PowerShell requires two X.509 digital certificates. The first, the signing certificate, is the certificate you use to sign a script using `Set-AuthenticodeSignature`. The second, the CA certificate, tells Windows and PowerShell to trust the actual signing certificate.

In most organizations that use digitally signed PowerShell scripts, there would be at least one certificate authority (CA) deployed along with the necessary procedures to issue signing keys and to ensure that other systems trust those keys. The instructions for setting up a CA and issuing certificates are outside the scope of this book.

As an alternative to a full-blown CA, you can use self-signed certificates to test a code-signing environment. A self-signed certificate is one that is signed by itself. You can create one with `New-SelfSignedCertifcate`. You can copy this certificate to the trusted root certificate store on the computer to enable Windows to trust the signing certificate.

The script fragments in this section show you how to create and use a self-signed certificate. Although using self-signed certificates works, in production you should use certificates issued by your organization or from public CAs.

Before You Start

This section uses the Windows Server 2019 host, DC1, that you used previously in this chapter. For this section, DC1 is a Windows 2019 Server (prior to being promoted to be a domain controller in Chapter 3).

Creating a Self-Signed Certificate

You use the `New-SelfSignedCertificate` cmdlet to create a new self-signed code-signing certificate.

```
# 1. Create a self-signed certificate
Import-Module PKI -WarningAction SilentlyContinue
$CERTHT = @{
  Subject           = 'Sign.Reskit.Org'
  Type              = "CodeSigningCert"
  CertStoreLocation = "Cert:\CurrentUser\my"
}
$SignCert = New-SelfSignedCertificate @CERTHT
```

The `New-SelfSignedCertificate` cmdlet adds a new code-signing certificate in the current user's personal certificate store.

Viewing the Certificate

You can view the new certificate.

```
# 2. View Certificate
$SignCert
```

You see the output of this command in Figure 1.19.

```
PS C:\Foo> # 2. View Certificate
PS C:\Foo> $SignCert

   PSParentPath: Microsoft.PowerShell.Security\Certificate::CurrentUser\my

Thumbprint                               Subject           EnhancedKeyUsageList
----------                               -------           --------------------
017D2305332E66C1E109EED14DDC2A9E1379E491 CN=Sign.Reskit.Org Code Signing
```

Figure 1.19: Viewing the certificate

Each certificate has a unique thumbprint. When you create a new certificate, the cmdlet creates a new thumbprint for you.

Creating a Simple Script

To demonstrate signing PowerShell scripts, create a simple script and store it in the C:\Foo folder.

```
# 3. Create a simple .PS1 File
$File = @"
# A script to be signed
"Hello World"
"@
$SignedFile = "C:\Foo\HelloWorld.ps1"
$File |
  Out-File -FilePath $SignedFile -Force
```

Setting Execution Policy

To test the requirement to use a signed script, you set the execution policy to All Signed as follows:

```
# 4. Set Execution Policy to ALL Signed
Set-ExecutionPolicy -ExecutionPolicy AllSigned
```

Attempting to Run the Script

You can try to run the script as follows:

```
# 5. Attempt to Run the script (pre-signing)
& $SignedFile
```

You can see the output from this command in Figure 1.20.

```
PS C:\Foo> # 5. Attempt to Run the File (pre-signing)
PS C:\Foo> & $SignedFile
&: File C:\Foo\HelloWorld.ps1 cannot be loaded. The file C:\Foo\HelloWorld.ps1
is not digitally signed. You cannot run this script on the current system.
For more information about running scripts and setting execution policy, see
about_Execution_Policies at https://go.microsoft.com/fwlink/?LinkID=135170.
```

Figure 1.20: Attempting to run the script

As expected, PowerShell does not run the script file, since it is unsigned and you previously set the execution policy to All Signed.

Signing the Script

You next attempt to sign the script using Set-AuthenticodeSignature, as follows:

```
# 6. Sign the script with the $SignCert certificate
Set-AuthenticodeSignature -FilePath $SignedFile -Certificate $SignCert
```

You can see the output from this command in Figure 1.21.

```
PS C:\Foo> # 6. Sign the script with the $SignCert certificate
PS C:\Foo> Set-AuthenticodeSignature –FilePath $SignedFile –Certificate $SignCert
Set-AuthenticodeSignature:
Line |
   2 |   Set-AuthenticodeSignature –FilePath $SignedFile –Certificate $SignCer …
     |   ~~~~~~~~~~~~~~~~~~~~~~~~~~~~~~~~~~~~~~~~~~~~~~~~~~~~~~~~~~~~~~~~~~~~~~~~~~~
     |   Cannot sign code. The specified certificate is not suitable for code signing.
```

Figure 1.21: Signing a PowerShell script

As you can see, PowerShell declined to sign the script. This is because the signing certificate is not trusted.

Copying a Certificate to the Trusted Publisher Certificate and Trusted Root Stores

One way to trust the self-signed certificate is to copy the certificate into the local machine's Trusted Root certificate store. You also need to ensure that PowerShell trusts code that you sign with a code-signing certificate, which you do by also copying the certificate into the local machine's Trusted Publisher certificate store, as follows:

```
# 7. Copy the cert to the Trusted Root Cert store of Local Machine
#    And to the Trusted Publisher cert store
# local Machine Trusted Root store
$CertStore = 'System.Security.Cryptography.X509Certificates.X509Store'
$CertArgs  = 'Root','LocalMachine'
$Store     = New-Object -TypeName $CertStore -ArgumentList $CertArgs
$Store.Open('ReadWrite')
$Store.Add($SignCert)
$Store.Close()
# Local Machine Trusted Publisher store
$CertStore = 'System.Security.Cryptography.X509Certificates.X509Store'
$CertArgs  = 'TrustedPublisher','LocalMachine'
$Store     = New-Object -TypeName $CertStore -ArgumentList $CertArgs
$Store.Open('ReadWrite')
$Store.Add($SignCert)
$Store.Close()
```

The PKI module you use to create a self-signed certificate has no commands to copy a certificate into either the Local Machine Trusted Publisher store or the Local Machine Trusted Root certificate store. You use the .NET Framework directly to perform the copy.

Signing the Script Again

Now that your signing certificate is trusted, you can attempt to sign the script again, like this:

```
# 8. Re-Sign the script
$SignCert = Get-ChildItem -Path Cert:\CurrentUser\my -CodeSigningCert
Set-AuthenticodeSignature -FilePath $SignedFile -Certificate $SignCert |
    Format-Table -AutoSize -Wrap
```

These commands first retrieve the signing certificate from the current user's personal certificate store. You retrieve a signing cert by using `Get-ChildItem` with the `-CodeSigningCert` parameter. If you had more than one code signing certificate, you would need to amend the snippet to select the correct one.

You can see the output from these commands in Figure 1.22.

```
PS C:\Foo> # 8. Re-Sign the script
PS C:\Foo> $SignCert = Get-ChildItem -Path Cert:\CurrentUser\my -CodeSigningCert
PS C:\Foo> Set-AuthenticodeSignature -FilePath $SignedFile -Certificate $SignCert |
            Format-Table -AutoSize -Wrap

    Directory: C:\Foo

SignerCertificate                          Status StatusMessage        Path
-----------------                          ------ -------------        ----
017D2305332E66C1E109EED14DDC2A9E1379E491 Valid  Signature verified. HelloWorld.ps1
```

Figure 1.22: Signing a PowerShell script with a trusted certificate

Running the Script

Now that the script is signed, you can run it.

```
# 9. Run the script
& $SignedFile
```

You can see the output from running the signed script in Figure 1.23. As you can see in the output, this script runs successfully.

```
PS C:\Foo> # 9. Run the script
PS C:\Foo> & $SignedFile
Hello World
```

Figure 1.23: Running a signed PowerShell script

Testing the Script's Digital Signature

After you sign a script, you can test the digital signature by using the `Get-AuthenticodeSignature` cmdlet, like this:

```
# 10. Test the script's digital signature
Get-AuthenticodeSignature -FilePath $SignedFile |
  Format-Table -AutoSize&
```

You can see the output from this command in Figure 1.24, which shows that the signature is trusted.

```
PS C:\Foo> # 10. Test the script's digital signature
Get-AuthenticodeSignature -FilePath $SignedFile |
  Format-Table -AutoSize

    Directory: C:\Foo

SignerCertificate                          Status StatusMessage        Path
-----------------                          ------ -------------        ----
017D2305332E66C1E109EED14DDC2A9E1379E491 Valid  Signature verified. HelloWorld.ps1
```

Figure 1.24: Testing a script's digital signature

In a production environment using signed scripts, certificates may be revoked or expire over time. If you rely on signed PowerShell scripts, a best practice would be to test all script signatures regularly or after any changes to the signing certificates. Of course, if you are using signed scripts, ensure that you have a certificate authority set up within your organization or use third-party certificates from firms such as Digicert.

Now that you have tested script signing, you should use `Set-ExecutionPolicy` to reset the execution policy on DC1 back to Unrestricted. If you want to retain an All Signed execution policy, you must also digitally sign your profile files.

Summary

In this chapter, you learned how you can set up a PowerShell 7 environment. You installed PowerShell 7 and VS, and then you configured PowerShell (and

VS Code) with a profile file. You then used the PowerShell gallery and saw how you can create your own trusted code repository. You finished by looking at signing PowerShell scripts by using self-signed certificates.

With the introduction of PowerShell 7, you should consider how best to deploy PowerShell and associated tools such as VS Code and the new Cascadia Code font. You also need to consider whether you need to use digitally signed scripts, and if so, you need to plan to deploy a code-signing environment.

PowerShell 7 Compatibility with Windows PowerShell

PowerShell 7, like Windows PowerShell, is a .NET application—an application built on top of and leveraging the .NET Framework, particularly the base class libraries.

Microsoft built Windows PowerShell using the full .NET Framework employing a design in which cmdlets are a thin and intelligent layer above the .NET Framework. Cmdlets rely on the .NET Framework to do all the heavy lifting. Windows PowerShell 5.1 leverages the Microsoft .NET Framework version 4.5.2.

PowerShell 7 is a complete and open source reimplementation of Windows PowerShell based on the open source .NET Core Framework using .NET Core 3.1. This has been a huge reengineering job and one that has thrown up a few challenges.

In PowerShell, commands are contained within modules. To run any command, PowerShell must first load a module that contains that command. PowerShell can only load modules that contain cmdlets and other binary artifacts if their developer has enabled this.

The PowerShell team reimplemented most of the commands contained in the core PowerShell convert to modules and ensured that the Active Directory module works with PowerShell 7.

Some Microsoft product teams and other external teams have not yet ported their modules for you to use natively in PowerShell 7. To get around this issue, the PowerShell team developed a compatibility solution that enables most commands previously developed for Windows PowerShell to work in PowerShell 7.

The compatibility solution enables you to use PowerShell 7 to manage a wide range of features in Windows Server, as demonstrated throughout this book. That does leave, however, a small set of features, modules, and commands that you are not able to use with PowerShell 7. For those, there are work-arounds.

This chapter looks at the following topics:

- In "Examining PowerShell Modules," you'll learn what the various modules contain and how they work.

- In "Introducing the Compatibility Solution," you'll see what the solution is and how you use it.

- In "Things That Do Not Work with PowerShell 7," you'll examine the Windows PowerShell features that do not work within PowerShell 7, with or without the compatibility solution. You'll also discover work-arounds to issues caused by incompatibility.

System Used in This Chapter

In this chapter, you use one host, DC1. This is a Windows Server 2019 Datacenter Edition host.

Figure 2.1 shows the system you use in this chapter.

DC1
(Windows Server 2019)

Figure 2.1: System used in this chapter

Examining PowerShell Modules

Before looking at compatibility with Windows PowerShell, you should understand PowerShell *modules*. Modules are fundamental to PowerShell, and understanding how they work is important when dealing with compatibility.

A PowerShell module is a package of commands. A module contains *members*, which can include cmdlets, providers, functions, variables, and aliases. Modules are the means that developers use to package and distribute PowerShell commands. You import a module into PowerShell to use the members of the module.

Understanding Module Types

There are four main module types in PowerShell. Each one is used differently and solves different problems.

Script modules: These modules are contained in a file with a .PSM1 extension and contain function definitions. When you import a script module, the functions defined in the .PSM1 files are imported into the current Power-Shell session.

Manifest modules: These are modules that have a module *manifest*. A module manifest is a file with a .PSD1 extension that contains details about a module. This information includes metadata (author, copyright) and instructions on what the module contains and how PowerShell should load it.

Binary modules: At its simplest, a binary module is a .NET assembly containing commands stored in a DLL file. A cmdlet developer writes the cmdlet code in C# and compiles it into a DLL; at this point, you can load the assembly by using Import-Module and specifying the DLL. To simplify loading of a binary module, you use a module manifest to help PowerShell load the needed members such as related help files.

Dynamic modules: These are dynamically created modules that PowerShell creates in memory from a script block you supply. Dynamic modules enable you to use a script to create a module on demand that does not need to be loaded or saved to persistent storage.

Any module can have additional members, although PowerShell needs to have a manifest to enable it to load those members. For example, you could include some XML for formatting or include a help file for the module.

Script modules were an easy way to distribute functions and replaced the practice of dot sourcing of .PS1 files, which was a common approach many users took with PowerShell version 1.

A *manifest* module is one that has a PowerShell module manifest file. This is a text file that contains the module details in the form of a hash table. With a module manifest, a developer can repackage a snap-in into a binary module. You can create a module manifest using New-ModuleManifest, as described at docs.microsoft.com/powershell/module/microsoft.powershell.core/new-modulemanifest.

You use dynamic modules to create a module on the fly based on the script block. As such, these are intended to be short-lived, and you cannot look at them using Get-Module. Dynamic modules do not require manifests.

To demonstrate the use of modules, you can create a simple module on DC1, as follows:

```
# 1. Create a simple script module—MyModule1
```

```
$MyModulePath = "C:\Users\$env:USERNAME\Documents\PowerShell\Modules\
MyModule1"
$MyModule = @"
# MyModule1.PSM1
Function Get-HelloWorld {
  "Hello World from My Module"
}
"@
New-Item  -Path $MyModulePath -ItemType Directory -Force | Out-Null
$MyModule | Out-File -FilePath $MyModulePath\MyModule1.PSM1
Get-Module—Name MyModule1 -ListAvailable
```

You can see the output from these commands in Figure 2.2.

```
PS C:\Foo> # 1. Create a simple script module - MyModule1
PS C:\Foo> $MyModulePath = "C:\Users\$env:USERNAME\Documents\PowerShell\Modules\MyModule1"
PS C:\Foo> $MyModule = @"
          # MyModule1.PSM1
          Function Get-HelloWorld {
          "Hello World from My Module"
          }
          "@
PS C:\Foo> New-Item  -Path $MyModulePath -ItemType Directory —Force | Out-Null
PS C:\Foo> $MyModule | Out-File —FilePath $MyModulePath\MyModule1.PSM1
PS C:\Foo> Get—Module —Name MyModule1 —ListAvailable

    Directory: C:\Users\tfl\Documents\PowerShell\Modules

ModuleType Version  PreRelease Name        PSEdition ExportedCommands
---------- -------  ---------- ----        --------- ----------------
Script     0.0                 MyModule1   Desk      Get—HelloWorld
```

Figure 2.2: Creating a new module

These commands create a new module, MyModule1, which is a simple script module created as a .PSM1 file. You can see in the output that this module exports a single command, the Get-HelloWorld function.

Importing PowerShell Modules

There are three ways PowerShell imports a module into the current PowerShell session. First, you can use the Import-Module cmdlet to import a module explicitly. Second, you can use the module autoload feature, introduced with PowerShell version 2. Finally, if you use Get-Command to discover the commands within a module, PowerShell ensures the module is imported and then returns the requested commands.

Using Import-Module allows you to load any module from any location. You can load just a single .PSM1 file, a single .NET assembly, or a rich multimember module with the help of a module manifest.

With module autoload, when you use any command that is in a module you have not yet imported, PowerShell loads the module and then runs the command. This also loads any members of the module, such as a help file. You can turn this off by setting the PowerShell environment variable $PSModuleAutoloadingPreference to none.

You can use Import-Module to import the MyModule1 module you just created.

```
# 2. Import the MyModule1 module

Import-Module -Name MyModule1 -Verbose
```

You can see the output from these commands in Figure 2.3.

```
PS C:\Foo> # 2. Import the MyModule1 module
PS C:\Foo> Import-Module -Name MyModule1 -Verbose
VERBOSE: Loading module from path 'C:\Users\tfl\Documents\PowerShell\Modules\MyModule1\MyModule1.psm1'.
VERBOSE: Exporting function 'Get-HelloWorld'.
VERBOSE: Importing function 'Get-HelloWorld'.
```

Figure 2.3: Importing the *MyModule1* module

You could also use module autoload by just specifying the Get-HelloWorld function.

Using PowerShell Module Manifests

A module manifest in PowerShell is a file with a .PSD1 extension that contains a hash table of values. These values, which are held in a PowerShell hash table, include module metadata, such as the author, plus other information to enable PowerShell to load the module.

The article at docs.microsoft.com/powershell/scripting/developer/module/how-to-write-a-powershell-module-manifest provides more information about manifests and describes how to write one.

You can add a manifest to the MyModule1 module as follows:

```
# 3. Create and Test a new module manifest
$NMMFHT = @{
  Path        = "$MyModulePath\MyModule1.PSD1"
  Author      = "Thomas Lee"
  CompanyName = 'PS Partnership'
  Rootmodule  = 'MyModule1.psm1'
}
New-ModuleManifest @NMMFHT
Get-Module -Name MyModule1 -List
# remove and re-import
Get-Module -Name MyModule1 | Remove-Module
Import-Module -Name MyModule1 -Verbose
Get-HelloWorld
```

These commands first create a new module manifest and review the module after you create the manifest. Then you import the module explicitly and finally run the `Get-HelloWorld` function, as you can see in Figure 2.4.

```
PS C:\Foo> # 3. Create and Test a new module manifest
PS C:\Foo> $NMMFHT = @{
            Path        = "$MyModulePath\MyModule1.PSD1"
            Author      = "Thomas Lee"
            CompanyName = 'PS Partnership'
            Rootmodule  = 'MyModule1.psm1'
           }
PS C:\Foo> New-ModuleManifest @NMMFHT
PS C:\Foo> Get-Module -Name MyModule1 -List

    Directory: C:\Users\tfl\Documents\PowerShell\Modules

ModuleType Version  PreRelease Name          PSEdition ExportedCommands
---------- -------  ---------- ----          --------- ----------------
Script     0.0.1               MyModule1 Desk           Get-HelloWorld

PS C:\Foo> Get-Module -Name MyModule1 | Remove-Module
PS C:\Foo> Import-Module -Name MyModule1 -Verbose
VERBOSE: Loading module from path 'C:\Users\tfl\Documents\PowerShell\Modules\MyModule1\MyModule1.psd1'.
VERBOSE: Loading module from path 'C:\Users\tfl\Documents\PowerShell\Modules\MyModule1\MyModule1.psm1'.
VERBOSE: Exporting function 'Get-HelloWorld'.
VERBOSE: Importing function 'Get-HelloWorld'.

PS C:\Foo> Get-HelloWorld
Hello World from My Module
```

Figure 2.4: Creating and using a manifest

You can view the hash table by viewing `MyModule1.PSD1`, or you can use your favorite code editor to update it as necessary.

Module Naming

In general, a module is a folder that contains one or more members. The simplest module is a `.PSM1` file with function definitions. In this case, you have a folder, perhaps called `MyModule`. Below this folder you have a file, `MyModule.PSM1`. PowerShell requires the folder name and the `.PSM1` filename to be the same; otherwise, `Import-Module` does not import the module.

You can convert a script module into a manifest module by adding a `.PSD1` file to the module folder. In this case, the `.PSD1` file must have the same name as the module folder. In such a case, the manifest contains the filename of the `.PSM1` file. The filenames can be different but should be the same to avoid confusion.

After you have created `MyModule1`, you can view the files contained in the module using Windows Explorer. In Figure 2.5, you can see the module, with both the `.PSM1` and `.PSD1` files.

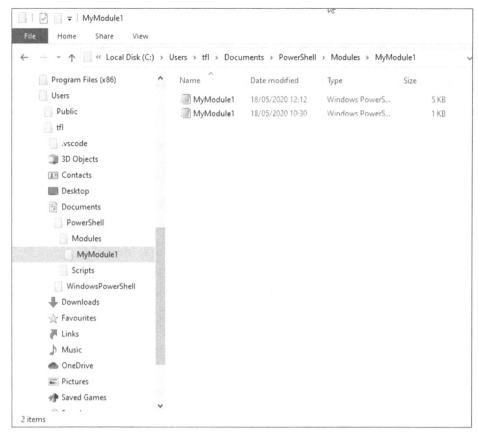

Figure 2.5: Viewing files in *MyModule1*

PowerShell supports *module versioning*, which allows you to have multiple versions of a module on a host. You use `Import-Module` to load a specific version or let it take the default of loading the latest version. For example, you could have both versions 1.0.0 and 1.1.0 of `MyModule`. By default, `Import-Module` (and module autoload) would load the latest version, which is 1.1.0. You can specify the earlier module as needed.

Creating a Module with Multiple Versions

You can create and use a module with multiple versions with the following code:

```
# 4. Create MyModule2 with 2 versions
# Create Module folders
$MyModule2Path   =
  "$env:USERPROFILE\Documents\PowerShell\Modules\MyModule2"
```

```
$MyModule2V1Path = "$MyModule2Path\1.0.0"
$MyModule2V2Path = "$MyModule2Path\2.0.0"
New-Item -Path $MyModule2Path -ItemType Directory -Force | Out-Null
New-Item -Path $MyModule2Path -Name '1.0.0' -ItemType Directory -Force |
  Out-Null
New-Item -Path $MyModule2Path -Name '2.0.0' -ItemType Directory -Force |
  Out-Null
# Create MyModule2V1.PSM1
$MyModule2V1 = @"
Function Get-HelloWorld2 {
  "Hello World from MyModule2 (V1)"
}
"@
$MyModule2V1 | Out-File -Path "$MyModule2V1Path\MyModule2.PSM1"
# Create MyModule2V2.PSM1
$MyModule2V2 = @"
Function Get-HelloWorld2 {
  "Hello World from MyModule2 (V2)"
}
"@
$MyModule2V2 | Out-File -Path "$MyModule2V2Path\MyModule2.PSM1"
# Create manifests for both versions of this module
$NMMFHV1HT = @{
  Path        = "$MyModule2V1Path\MyModule2.PSD1"
  Author      = "Thomas Lee"
  CompanyName = 'PS Partnership'
  Rootmodule  = 'MyModule2.psm1'
}
New-ModuleManifest @NMMFHV1HT -ModuleVersion '1.0.0'
$NMMFHV2HT = @{
  Path        = "$MyModule2V2Path\MyModule2.PSD1"
  Author      = "Thomas Lee"
  CompanyName = 'PS Partnership'
  Rootmodule  = 'MyModule2.psm1'
}
New-ModuleManifest @NMMFHV2HT -ModuleVersion '2.0.0'
```

These commands create the module folders and create the module itself.

Using Module Versions

In the previous section, you created a new module (MyModule2) with two versions. You can use the functions within the different versions of a module as follows:

```
# 5. Use MyModule2
# Discover, import and use MyModule2
Get-Module MyModule2 -ListAvailable
Import-Module -Name MyModule2 -Verbose -RequiredVersion '1.0.0'
```

```
Get-HelloWorld2
# Re-import MyModule2—by default the highest version
Import-Module -Name MyModule2 -Force -Verbose
# Use V2 Function
Get-HelloWorld2
```

You can see the results of these commands in Figure 2.6.

```
PS C:\Foo> # 5. Use MyModule2
# Discover, import and use MyModule2
Get-Module MyModule2 -ListAvailable

    Directory: C:\Users\tfl.COOKHAM\Documents\PowerShell\Modules

ModuleType Version  PreRelease Name         PSEdition ExportedCommands
---------- -------  ---------- ----         --------- ----------------
Script     2.0.0               MyModule2    Desk      Get-HelloWorld2
Script     1.0.0               MyModule2    Desk      Get-HelloWorld2

PS C:\Foo> Import-Module -Name MyModule2 -Verbose -RequiredVersion '1.0.0'
VERBOSE: Loading module from path 'C:\Users\tfl.COOKHAM\Documents\PowerShell\Modules\MyModule2\1.0.0\MyModule2.psd1'.
VERBOSE: Loading module from path 'C:\Users\tfl.COOKHAM\Documents\PowerShell\Modules\MyModule2\1.0.0\MyModule2.psm1'.
VERBOSE: Exporting function 'Get-HelloWorld2'.
VERBOSE: Importing function 'Get-HelloWorld2'.
PS C:\Foo> Get-HelloWorld2
Hello World from MyModule2 (V1)
PS C:\Foo> # Re-import MyModule2 - by default the highest version
PS C:\Foo> Get-Module -Name MyModule2 | Remove-Module
PS C:\Foo> Import-Module -Name MyModule2 -Verbose
VERBOSE: Loading module from path 'C:\Users\tfl.COOKHAM\Documents\PowerShell\Modules\MyModule2\2.0.0\MyModule2.psd1'.
VERBOSE: Loading module from path 'C:\Users\tfl.COOKHAM\Documents\PowerShell\Modules\MyModule2\2.0.0\MyModule2.psm1'.
VERBOSE: Exporting function 'Get-HelloWorld2'.
VERBOSE: Importing function 'Get-HelloWorld2'.
PS C:\Foo> # Use V2 Function
PS C:\Foo> Get-HelloWorld2
Hello World from MyModule2 (V2)
```

Figure 2.6: Using *MyModule2*

In this code snippet, you use `Get-Module` to discover `MyModule2`. You then load version 1.0.0 of `MyModule2`. If you use the `-Verbose` switch, PowerShell displays the process of importing your module. Verbose output like this can be useful in debugging more complex modules. With version 1 of `MyModule2` loaded, you run the first version of the `Get-HelloWorld2` function, showing the expected version 1 output. You then remove the old module explicitly and reimport the `MyModule2` module and use the function. You can see that because you did not specify a version, PowerShell loads the highest version of the function, which then returns the expected version 2 output.

You can have a simple module with just a `.PSM1` file. However, you must use a module manifest if you want to support multiple versions of the same module. In that case, the folder containing a given version must match the corresponding version number contained in the manifest. You can see the structure of `MyModule2` in the filestore in Figure 2.7.

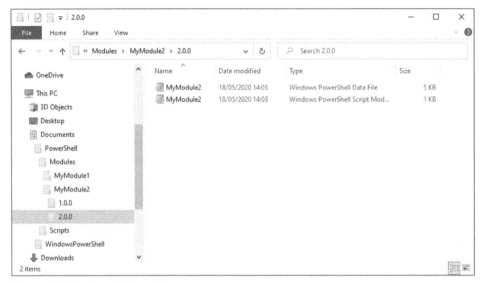

Figure 2.7: Viewing *MyModule2*

Using Module Autoload

With module autoload, PowerShell loads the module that contains the command you are using before running the command. PowerShell uses the environment variable PSModulePath to hold a comma-separated value list of paths in the Windows filesystem. PowerShell can discover the commands in any module. You can view this variable by typing **$Env:PSModulePath**.

In "Module Naming," you created MyModule2, with two versions of the module. To demonstrate autoload, you can do the following:

```
# 6. Demonstrate autoload of MyModule2
Get-Module MyModule* | Remove-Module -Verbose
Get-HelloWorld2
```

In these commands you first remove all the MyModule modules and then, with no modules loaded, use a command in the module MyModule2, namely, Get-HelloWorld2, provided for test purposes like this. You can see the output in Figure 2.8.

You can modify the module path environment variable(s) externally to PowerShell by using the sysdm.cpl applet. If you do so, the next time you enter PowerShell, you should see the updated environment variable value.

Windows supports two environment variables (of the same name)—one for the user and one for the system. PowerShell adds the values contained in the user and system Windows environment variables into the value $Env:PSModulePath. You can define both the system- and user-level PSModulePath variables using sysdm.cpl. In most cases, the module autoload path is sufficient.

```
PS C:\Foo> # 6. Demonstrate autoload of MyModule2
Get-Module Mymodule* | Remove-Module -Verbose
VERBOSE: Performing the operation "Remove-Module" on target "MyModule2
(Path: 'C:\Users\tfl.COOKHAM\Documents\PowerShell\Modules\MyModule2\2.0.0\MyModule2.psm1')".
VERBOSE: Removing the imported "Get-HelloWorld2" function.
PS C:\Foo> Get-HelloWorld2
Hello World from MyModule2 (V2)
```

Figure 2.8: Using module autoload

Third-party publishers ship installers that install their module(s) into a module-specific location by extending the PSModulePath variable.

PowerShell does not persist any changes you make to the value of $Env:PSModulePath inside a PowerShell session. You can make any changes to your profile scripts if necessary.

Viewing the Module Analysis Cache

When PowerShell uses autoloading, it has a large number of modules to search to discover which module has the requested command. To improve performance, PowerShell maintains an internal module analysis cache of all the modules on your system and the commands they contain. By default, PowerShell stores this cache at $Env:LOCALAPPDATA\Microsoft\Windows\PowerShell\ModuleAnalysisCache. You can view the cache file using Get-ChildItem.

```
# 7. View Module Analysis Cache
$CF = "$Env:LOCALAPPDATA\Microsoft\Windows\PowerShell\"+
      'ModuleAnalysisCache'
Get-ChildItem -Path $CF
```

Figure 2.9 shows the output and the file containing the cache.

```
PS C:\Foo> # 7. View Module Analysis Cache
PS C:\Foo> $CF = "$Env:LOCALAPPDATA\Microsoft\Windows\PowerShell\"+
                 'ModuleAnalysisCache'
PS C:\Foo> Get-ChildItem -Path $CF


    Directory: C:\Users\tfl\AppData\Local\Microsoft\Windows\PowerShell

Mode            LastWriteTime    Length Name
----            -------------    ------ ----
-a---     18/05/2020    14:58     63053 ModuleAnalysisCache
```

Figure 2.9: Viewing the module analysis cache

At the start of each session, PowerShell spawns a low-priority background thread that discovers the modules and the commands and updates the cache file accordingly. To learn more about the module analysis cache, see:

docs.microsoft.com/powershell/module/microsoft.powershell.core/about/
about_windows_powershell_5.1?view=powershell-5.1#module-analysis-cache.

In most cases, your module analysis cache remains constant, since in most cases, you rarely change the modules on your system. Should you want, you can change the location of the cache file. There is really little reason to do so, however, and it could just introduce more troubleshooting challenges.

Introducing the Compatibility Solution

Windows PowerShell was first launched in 2006 and has been a built-in component in Windows for more than a decade. The first two releases of what is now PowerShell 7 were known as PowerShell Core, with the emphasis on Core as in .NET Core. The development team released two versions (6.0 and 6.1). As part of the planning for the third major version of PowerShell, Microsoft decided to rename the product PowerShell 7, dropping the Core moniker. This book focuses on PowerShell 7.

With the first version PowerShell Core, it became clear that some Windows PowerShell modules did not work in the version of PowerShell based on .NET Core. An early solution to this issue was to use explicit remoting. You could create a PowerShell remoting session to your host using a PowerShell 5.1 remoting endpoint and then run your commands in that remoting session. That method works, but it means you have to manage the process and so is not ideal.

Implicit remoting is a feature of PowerShell that lets you use commands that are not available in locally installed modules. Exchange Server uses implicit remoting, and this is a handy solution cross-platform. It could be used, for example, if you want to run AD commands from a Mac or Linux computer.

In PowerShell 7, whenever `Import-Module` attempts to import any module, it looks to see whether that module is compatible with PowerShell 7. If the module is compatible, then `Import-Module` loads it into PowerShell 7, but if not, then PowerShell loads the module in compatibility mode.

When `Import-Module` imports a module in compatibility mode, it creates a PowerShell remoting session to the local host using a Windows PowerShell remoting endpoint, named `WinPSCompatSession`. PowerShell then imports the module into the remote session running Windows PowerShell and finally uses `Import-PSSession` to import the commands into the current PowerShell 7 session. This creates functions that duplicate the names of the commands imported from the remote session. Those functions use implicit remoting to run the actual cmdlet logic in the remote session.

You can view the use of the compatibility solution as follows:

```
# 8. Import Server Manager Module on DC1 and use it
Get-Module ServerManager -ListAvailable
Import-Module ServerManager
Get-Module ServerManager | Format-Table -AutoSize -Wrap
Get-WindowsFeature -Name Hyper-V | Format-Table -AutoSize
```

```
$CS = Get-PSSession -Name WinPSCompatSession
Invoke-Command -Session $CS -ScriptBlock {
  Get-WindowsFeature -Name Hyper-V | Format-Table -AutoSize
}
```

You can see the output from these commands in Figure 2.10.

```
PS C:\Foo> # 8. Import Server Manager Module on DC1 and use it
PS C:\Foo> Get-Module ServerManager -ListAvailable
PS C:\Foo> Import-Module ServerManager
WARNING: Module ServerManager is loaded in Windows PowerShell using
WinPSCompatSession remoting session; please note that all input and
output of commands from this module will be deserialized objects. If
you want to load this module into PowerShell Core please use
'Import-Module -SkipEditionCheck' syntax.


PS C:\Foo> Get-Module ServerManager | Format-Table -AutoSize

ModuleType Version PreRelease Name        ExportedCommands
---------- ------- ---------- ----        ----------------
Script     1.0                ServerManager {Disable-ServerManagerStandardUserRemoting,
                                            Enable-ServerManagerStandardUserRemoting,
                                            Get-WindowsFeature, Install-WindowsFeature,
                                            Uninstall-WindowsFeature, Add-WindowsFeature,
                                            Remove-WindowsFeature}

PS C:\Foo> Get-WindowsFeature -Name Hyper-V | Format-Table -AutoSize

Display Name Name    Install State
------------ ----    -------------
             Hyper-V Available

PS C:\Foo> $CS = Get-PSSession -Name WinPSCompatSession
PS C:\Foo> Invoke-Command -Session $CS -ScriptBlock {
             Get-WindowsFeature -Name Hyper-V | Format-Table -AutoSize
           }

Display Name Name    Install State
------------ ----    -------------
[ ] Hyper-V  Hyper-V Available
```

Figure 2.10: Loading the ServerManager module

In the output, you can see that when you first use Get-Module to find the ServerManager module, you see no output, which is expected because you have not yet loaded the module. You can then manually import the ServerManager module and review it. As you can see, this is a script module. Finally, you use a command to view a windows feature. The first time you attempt to view the Hyper-V feature, you can see that the normal DisplayName field is missing from the output. This is because Import-Module has not also imported the module's display XML into the PowerShell 7 session. As you can see, you can get the output by using the compatibility remoting session and having PowerShell do the formatting in that remote session.

If your script uses `Import-Module` to enable you to access commands from multiple modules, `Import-Module` checks to see whether `WinPSCompatSession` exists. If so, PowerShell uses the existing session to autoload additional modules. This means you only ever have one compatibility remoting session. You can read more about implicit remoting and `Import-PSSession` at docs.microsoft .com/powershell/module/microsoft.powershell.utility/import-pssession.

Using the Module Load Deny List

During the development of PowerShell 7, it became clear that a small number of modules would never work either natively or via the compatibility solution. If you did attempt to use them in the compatibility session, commands in the modules failed. The failure usually resulted in error messages that were unclear and not actionable. This was not a good user experience, particularly to new users.

To avoid that bad experience, PowerShell 7 has a list of modules that `Import-Module` does not load (natively or via the compatibility solution), by default. You can override this logic by using `Import-Module` with the `-SkipEditionCheck` parameter, although that is unlikely to be successful.

In the PowerShell installation folder, you can find PowerShell's configuration file `$PSHOME\PowerShell.config.json`. You can view the contents of this file, as follows:

```
# 8. View JSON Configuration File on DC1
Get-Content -Path $PSHOME\powershell.config.json
```

You can see the output of this command in Figure 2.11.

```
PS C:\Foo> # 9. View JSON Configuration File on DC1
PS C:\Foo> Get-Content -Path $PSHOME\powershell.config.json
{
    "WindowsPowerShellCompatibilityModuleDenyList":  [
                                                "PSScheduledJob",
                                                "BestPractices",
                                                "UpdateServices"
                                            ],
    "Microsoft.PowerShell:ExecutionPolicy":  "Unrestricted"
}
```

Figure 2.11: Viewing the module deny list

This configuration file, which you can change as needed, contains a list of modules that `Import-Module` does not load. These are based on module names, so if the product team updates these modules so that they become usable, you can change the file. Also, if and when those denied modules do change and you can use them in PowerShell 7, PowerShell may update the configuration file at the next PowerShell update.

Things That Do Not Work with PowerShell 7

Thanks to the great work by a combination of the PowerShell 7 product team and the PowerShell community, the majority of Windows PowerShell commands function properly in PowerShell 7. This means your Windows PowerShell scripts should run just fine in PowerShell 7, as this book amply demonstrates.

The compatibility solution does impose minor limitations caused by the serialization of data between the PowerShell 7 session and the compatibility remoting session. When you transfer data via remoting, PowerShell serializes the data into XML, transports the data, and then deserializes it at the other end. When a command receives commands from the remote session, that data is deserialized. This means that there are no object methods (aside from a few default ones that *all* objects have) returned. This is why, for example, the UpdateServices module does not work—it relies on object methods instead of cmdlets. Also, PowerShell changes the object type name to reflect the serialization.

Despite those limitations, almost all the modules supported by the compatibility solution work. (That is, the commands function and do their jobs.) That means you should be able to run Windows PowerShell scripts in PowerShell 7 successfully—as this book more than adequately demonstrates. But there are some features, modules, and commands PowerShell 7 does not support either natively or via the compatibility solution.

Windows PowerShell Incompatibilities

Despite a lot of hard work by the PowerShell team and others, there remains a small set of PowerShell 5.1 and earlier features, modules, and cmdlets that simply do not work with PowerShell 7, with or without the compatibility solution. These include the following:

- PowerShell workflows
- PowerShell snap-ins
- WMI cmdlets
- The -ComputerName parameter on some cmdlets
- Desired State Configuration (DSC)
- Windows Server Update Services (WSUS)
- The Best Practices module
- The WebAdministration module IIS provider
- The Add-Computer, Checkpoint-Computer, Remove-Computer, and Restore-Computer commands from the Microsoft.PowerShell.Management module

PowerShell workflows were based on the Windows Workflow Framework component of the full NET Framework. The .NET Core team did not choose to implement the necessary components to support workflows in .NET Core. The workflow feature was not heavily used, and the PowerShell team decided not to carry it forward. If you are using workflows, you can either continue to use them by using Windows PowerShell or look into alternatives.

One use of workflows was to improve performance using the Workflow component's built-in parallelism. With the implementation of `Foreach-Object-Parallel`, you can get the needed parallelism (and improve script run times) without using Windows PowerShell workflows.

It is not likely that workflows are going to be implemented with PowerShell 7. See the release notes at `docs.microsoft.com/en-us/powershell/scripting/whats-new/breaking-changes-ps6?view=powershell-6`.

PowerShell 7 does not support Windows PowerShell snap-ins. In Windows PowerShell V1, you used snap-ins to hold commands, but this approach lacked flexibility. With snap-ins, you had to use a compiled language such as C# to write your command—you could not write your commands using PowerShell. The developer also needed to create an installer program (although there is a default installation program included with .NET). Also, the installer stored details of the module in a protected area of the registry, meaning you needed administrative permissions to install a module.

The module feature, which was added in Windows PowerShell 2, in effect replaced the snap-in. Snap-ins continue to be supported in Windows PowerShell. In some cases, you may be able to convert a snap-in into a module by using a manifest. For other snap-ins, you may need to ask your internal developer or external vendor to update their product (or seek alternative solutions that support PowerShell 7).

The WMI cmdlets are not supported in PowerShell 7. You can, and should, use the CIM cmdlets. The CIM cmdlets are lighter weight and provide improved usability and reduced network bandwidth. Although the article is old, you can read more about the CIM cmdlets at `devblogs.microsoft.com/powershell/introduction-to-cim-cmdlets/`.

Some Windows PowerShell commands contain the `-ComputerName` parameter. For example, you can specify a value of that parameter to `Get-Service` to have the cmdlet get services on the specified machine. In PowerShell 7, the following commands do not support the `-ComputerName` parameter:

```
Clear-EventLog

Get-Process

Get-Service

Limit-EventLog
```

```
New-EventLog

Remove-Computer

Remove-EventLog

Set-Service

Test-EventLog

Show-EventLog
```

The -ComputerName parameter is still used in PowerShell 7, just not to indicate that the cmdlet does remote processing internally, and it does not leverage PowerShell remoting.

PowerShell 7 does not implement the full Windows DSC feature. PowerShell 7 does implement Invoke-DSCResource to invoke a DSC resource, but there is no local configuration manager, no push servers, or any of the other great features you used with DSC in Windows PowerShell.

The WSUS feature includes a module that is not compatible natively with PowerShell 7 and does not function acceptably in a compatibility session. The design of the UpdateServices module makes use of object methods, instead of the more usual approach of using cmdlets. Since methods are removed via serialization, you cannot use this module within the compatibility solution. If you want to manage WSUS, you must use Windows PowerShell.

Also, it is unlikely that there is an easy fix for the overall architecture of this module, since it relies on Simple Object Access Protocol (SOAP) for communications with the WSUS server. The .NET Core team has not implemented SOAP and appears to have no plans to do so. The long-term solution is for the WSUS team to redesign their client-server implementations to use Representational State Transfer (REST) or other supported protocols. At the time of writing, no plans have been announced.

The Best Practices module also does not work either natively or via the compatibility solution. The Best Practices team needs to redevelop the module, and feature, to make use of .NET Core.

The WebAdministration module, part of the IIS Management tools, includes a PowerShell provider. When you load this module in Windows PowerShell, Windows PowerShell loads the provider and creates an IIS: drive you use when you administer IIS. While the commands in both the IISAdministration and WebAdministration modules more or less work, any command that uses the provider would fail.

The Microsoft.PowerShell.Management module in PowerShell does not contain the Add-Computer, Checkpoint-Computer, Remove-Computer, or Restore-Computer cmdlets. You can use these commands by creating a Windows PowerShell remote session and invoking the commands in that remoting session.

Compatibility Issue Work-Arounds

The default work-around for any Windows PowerShell compatibility issue is simply to not use PowerShell 7 until there is a solution to your specific issues. Microsoft offers full support for Windows PowerShell 5.1 for the foreseeable future, so there is little risk in continuing to use Windows PowerShell.

What might be more effective is a hybrid strategy that combines running PowerShell 7 natively where you can or via the compatibility solution. Then use Windows PowerShell as needed until you can migrate fully to PowerShell 7.

For the few Windows PowerShell features not in PowerShell 7, there is no easy work-around aside from continuing to use Windows PowerShell.

That is made more complex by the cross-platform nature of PowerShell. It is harder to add features to PowerShell where .NET and the OS itself do not provide the necessary supporting features.

The modules and providers that do not work natively in PowerShell or via the compatibility list also have no easy solution. The code that would need to be updated to support PowerShell 7 natively is proprietary. The Microsoft product teams currently would need to make those changes, and for some teams, particularly the WSUS team, that could be a lot of otherwise unplanned work.

Some Microsoft product teams, for example the Active Directory team, were able to ensure the Active Directory module works with PowerShell 7, although you do need the latest version of that module. As Chapter 3, "Managing Active Directory," demonstrates, this means you can manage your AD database within PowerShell 7. But at the same time, the AD Deployment module, which you need to deploy AD in your environment, works only via the compatibility mechanism. So, you can install new forests, new domains, and new domain controllers via the compatibility solution.

For commands that formerly used the `-ComputerName` parameter, you can use `Invoke-Command` to run the command remotely and return the results. This book makes extensive use of this feature to run commands on different computers.

Summary

In summary, PowerShell 7 has done a good job implementing backward compatibility with Windows PowerShell. Almost all of the features of Windows PowerShell are available to you in PowerShell.7. The compatibility solution, which uses implicit remoting, extends the set of commands available to you, although there are some minor issues in some cases. Finally, there are a few things that do not work in PowerShell 7, and for those you have other options.

Managing Active Directory

Active Directory (AD) is at the heart of just about all modern organizations, both small and large. Microsoft first introduced AD with Windows 2000, where it replaced the domain structures previously implemented with Windows NT.

This chapter looks at how you can use PowerShell 7 to install, configure, and manage AD, as follows:

- In "Establishing a Forest Root Domain," you create the first domain in a new forest.

- In "Installing a Replica DC," you create a second domain controller in a domain.

- In "Installing a Child Domain," you create a child domain in the forest.

- In "Creating a Cross-Forest Trust," you create another forest and implement and use a cross-forest trust.

- In "Managing AD Users, Computers, and OUs," you add, remove, and manage AD users and AD computers and organize objects using organizational units.

- In "Adding Users to AD via a CSV File," you add users to the AD via a CSV file.

- In "Configuring Just Enough Administration (JEA)," you set up delegated administration.

Since introducing Active Directory, Microsoft has expanded it to include a number of separate features you can install, as follows:

Active Directory Domain Service (AD DS): Provides a central network directory that is the basis for user and computer authentication as well as environment management via Group Policy. AD DS is used in almost every organization, where it's usually just referred to as AD. You can find more information about AD DS at `docs.microsoft` `.com/en-us/windows-server/identity/ad-ds/get-started/virtual-dc/` `active-directory-domain-services-overview`.

Active Directory Certificate Services (AD CS): Enables you to create an X.509 certificate authority that you can use to issue and manage digital certificates for your organization. AD CS is used by many organizations to provide certificates for internal web sites and for smart cards. You can find more information about AD CS at `docs.microsoft.com/en-us/` `previous-versions/windows/it-pro/windows-server-2012-r2-and-2012/` `hh831740(v%3Dws.11`. This URL links to older content but should be accurate for Windows Server 2019.

Active Directory Federation Services (AD FS): Provides a simple and secure mechanism for Single Sign-On (SSO) and federated identity. AD FS is in use in larger organizations but less so in smaller firms. You can find more information on AD FS at `docs.microsoft.com/en-us/windows-server/` `identity/ad-fs/ad-fs-overview`.

Active Directory Lightweight Directory Services (AD LDS): Enables you to create directory-based applications that have their own directory database unrelated to AD DS. This is used in a few larger enterprises. See the following for an introduction to AD LDS: `docs.microsoft.com/en-us/` `previous-versions/windows/it-pro/windows-server-2012-r2-and-2012/` `hh831593(v%3Dws.11)`. Like Microsoft's online material about AD CS, this introduction was written for an earlier version of Windows Server, but it should be accurate for Server 2019.

Active Directory Rights Management Services (AD RMS): Enables you to protect documents from unauthorized use. RMS is complex to set up and is not widely used. You can find an introduction to an earlier version of AD RMS at `docs.microsoft.com/en-us/previous-versions/windows/` `desktop/adrms_sdk/ad-rms-overview`.

A full study of all these aspects could take up an entire book. This chapter covers the AD DS component and refers to it simply as "AD."

Active Directory consists of a logical structure of forests and domains (which contain users and computers and other objects). AD also has a physical structure including AD sites, subnets, and replication partners. The physical architecture is transparent to end users; AD clients "just work," via the magic of DNS name resolution and AD replication.

To enable administrators to deploy and manage AD, the Microsoft AD team has created two modules. You use commands in the AD Deployment module to build your forests and domains. You use the commands in the Active Directory module to manage the contents of the AD database (that is, managing users, computers, and so on).

In AD, a *forest* contains one or more *domains* in a hierarchy with a contiguous namespace (each child domain has a unique name plus the name of its parent). This contiguous namespace is known as a *tree*. A forest usually consists of a single tree but can contain multiple trees. The forest is a fundamental component of AD and is a key security boundary.

A domain is effectively a collection of objects including users, computers, groups, and so on. Domains enable you to support different sized organizations from small to large and globally distributed organizations. Best practice calls for a simple hierarchy with one or at most two levels of domains. This chapter demonstrates how to create and configure parent and child domains.

Each forest has a single *forest root domain*. That domain can have one or more subdomains, which in turn can contain subdomains. This allows you to have a forest with a forest root name; for example, `Reskit.Org` with a child domain such as `UK.Reskit.Org`.

Note that best AD naming practice suggests you name your AD forest root as a delegation of your registered Internet name. For example, if your organization has a registered name of `Reskit.Org`, then the AD should be named something like `AD.Reskit.Org` or `Corp.Reskit.Org`. That being said, the example code in this book uses shorter AD names, to produce shorter and simpler code. And although longer forest/domain names make scripts a bit easier to read and code, they also impose a small performance hit: every DNS/LDAP query is that little bit longer and the Distinguished Name of every object in the AD database is that little bit larger.

Best practice calls for each forest to be a single tree. But AD does allow you to add domain trees to a forest. This feature, first introduced with Windows Server 2000, was intended to assist large decentralized organizations. For example, you *could* add a separate domain tree, say `Kapoho.Com`, to the `Reskit.Org` forest. This would mean having two domain trees in a single AD Forest. You might consider this to support a subsidiary that needs a brand and email identity separate from the parent organization.

Placing noncontiguous namespace trees in a single forest is not a best-practice solution, however, because AD has no prune-and-graft feature to enable you to prune a domain or domain tree from one forest and graft it into another, unrelated forest. Best practice, and a far simpler method, is to just deploy two independent forests and then connect them with a cross-forest trust. These trusts are easy to remove as part of a company sale and allow the buyer to establish and utilize a new cross-forest trust. This chapter also demonstrates how to create a cross-forest trust.

Every domain in your forest has at least one domain controller (DC) and preferably more. A domain controller is a Windows Server system with the AD DS feature installed and configured that authenticates computers and users. DCs also provide user and computer Group Policy to domain client computers. DCs in each domain replicate with others so that any DC in a domain can authenticate a user or a computer. This chapter shows how to install a replica DC in a domain.

Within each domain you can define *users* and *computers* to represent individual computer users and the systems they access. AD enables an AD user to log on securely to any AD computer within the AD domain, subject to permissions. You can create AD *groups*, which can contain computers, users, and other groups. AD groups are invaluable for assigning permissions to resources in your domain as well as for delegating permissions in larger organizations. You can use organizational units to group users, computers, and group objects. This chapter shows how you can manage the user, group, and organizational unit objects.

AD is a complex subject. There are important aspects to AD that this book does not have space to cover, such as sites and subnets, AD replication, Global Catalog, and more. A great book on the wider subject is Brian Desmond's *Active Directory: Designing, Deploying, and Running Active Directory* (O'Reilly, 5th ed., 2013). Also, take a look at docs.microsoft.com/en-us/windows-server/identity/ ad-ds/active-directory-domain-services for more information on AD.

Group Policy is an AD feature that enables you to define and deploy rich policies to configure a user or computer automatically. This book does not really cover Group Policy. An excellent book on the subject is Jeremy Moskowitz's *Group Policy: Fundamentals, Security, and the Managed Desktop* (Sybex, 3rd ed., 2015).

In this chapter, you use PowerShell 7 to build a forest with two domains (one of which has two DCs) and a second forest with one domain. You then create a cross-forest trust between these two forests. Finally, you manage user, computer, and group objects and see how to add AD users to the domain with a comma-separated value (CSV) file.

Systems Used in This Chapter

In this chapter, you use PowerShell 7 to install and manage Active Directory. This chapter makes use of the following host systems and forests/domains:

DC1.Reskit.Org and DC2.Reskit.Org: These are, initially, stand-alone Windows Server 2019 hosts without any added features. You then install Active Directory on these two servers in a parent domain, Reskit.Org.

UKDC1.Reskit.Org: This is a single domain–joined host on which you install a child domain, `UK.Reskit.Org`. Once you complete the promotion of this server, the host name becomes `UKDC1.UK.Reskit.Org`.

KAPDC1.Kapoho.Com: This is a server you use to create the `Kapoho.Com` forest/domain to demonstrate establishing a cross-forest trust.

Figure 3.1 shows the systems you use in this chapter and the two forests and their respective domains.

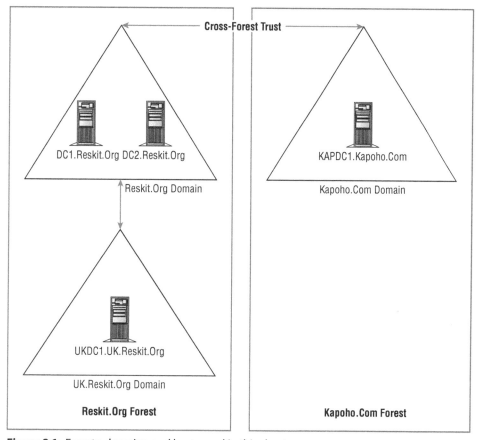

Figure 3.1: Forests, domains, and hosts used in this chapter

If you are using the Reskit build scripts (from `github.com/doctordns/ReskitBuildScripts`) to deploy your VMs, ensure you wait until `DC1` is fully deployed as a DC before building `DC2`. The build scripts use setup XML for deploying `DC2`, `UKDC1`, and `KAPDC1` that require the existence of the `Reskit.Org` forest.

Note that each host should have PowerShell 7, VS Code, and the Cascadia Code font installed. You can do that manually, using the scripts from Chapter 1, "Setting Up a PowerShell 7 Environment."

Establishing a Forest Root Domain

To establish your first AD forest, you need to create a first domain controller in the forest. This DC is known as the *forest root domain controller*. Upon creation, this DC holds all the forest and domain *Flexible Single Master Operation* (FSMO) roles.

FSMO roles designate one specific domain controller to be the master for certain forest-wide or domain-wide operations. For example, the Schema Master FSMO role holder, initially the forest root DC, is where any AD Schema changes are first made. If you update your AD Schema, the tools you use make the updates on this DC. If a given FSMO role holder is offline, certain operations cannot take place until you either bring the role holder back online or move the FSMO role to another online DC. For more details on FSMO roles, see `techgenix.com/fsmo-roles-in-active-directory/`.

To promote `DC1` to a domain controller in a new domain, you log on to the `DC1` server as a local administrator. Then you run the PowerShell code shown in this section. Once you have installed AD, you need to reboot the server and log back in using the username `RESKIT\Administrator` along with the password you used when you installed `DC1` (such as `Pa$$w0rd` or whatever password you chose to use for `DC1`'s local administrator).

Before You Start

In this section you create the forest root domain controller in a new domain/forest. You perform this on `DC1.Reskit.Org`, a Windows Server 2019 Data Center workgroup host with the Desktop Experience option installed and a working Internet connection.

You also need to have installed PowerShell 7 on this host (and possibly more tools) using the scripts in Chapter 1.

Importing the Server Manager Module

The Server Manager module does not work natively in PowerShell 7, but you can use it using the Windows PowerShell compatibility solution discussed in Chapter 2, "PowerShell 7 Compatibility with Windows PowerShell." To access the commands in the module, you first import it manually using the `Import-Module` command.

```
# 1. Explicitly Load the Server Manager Module
Import-Module ServerManager -WarningAction SilentlyContinue
```

With this command, you import the Server Manager module and avoid generating the warning message that `Import-Module` generates. Once imported, the commands in the module are available for use.

Installing the AD Domain Services Feature

With the Server Manager module imported, you can now add the AD Domain Services feature to DC1. Note that doing so does *not* configure DC1 as a domain controller. Rather, it installs the components that enable you to install a DC in whatever role is appropriate (as the first DC in a forest, the first DC in a child domain, or a DC in an existing domain).

Use the `Install-WindowsFeature` command to add the necessary components to the server.

```
# 2. Install the AD Domain Services feature and management tools
$FEATUREHT = @{
  Name                  = 'AD-Domain-Services'
  IncludeManagementTools = $True
  WarningAction         = 'SilentlyContinue'
}
Install-WindowsFeature @FEATUREHT
```

This code produces the output shown in Figure 3.2.

```
# 2  Install the AD Domain Services feature and management tools
PS C:\Foo> $FEATUREHT = @{
          Name                  = 'AD-Domain-Services'
          IncludeManagementTools = $True
          WarningAction         = 'SilentlyContinue'
          }
PS C:\Foo> Install-WindowsFeature @FEATUREHT

Success Restart Needed Exit Code     Feature Result
------- -------------- ---------     --------------
True    No             Success       {Active Directory Domain Services, Group Pol...
```

Figure 3.2: Installing AD DS Domain Services

As you can see in the figure, you do not need to reboot the server before continuing.

Loading the AD DS Deployment Module Explicitly

In the previous step, you installed the ADDSDeployment module as part of installing the AD-Domain-Services feature. This module is not supported by PowerShell 7 natively but does work using the compatibility mechanism described in Chapter 2. You load the module with the Import-Module command.

```
# 3. Import the AD DS Deployment Module
Import-Module -Name ADDSDeployment -WarningAction SilentlyContinue
```

Because this module is supported only via the Windows PowerShell compatibility mechanism, importing the module generates by default a warning message explaining that the module has been loaded using the compatibility mechanism. But this is a message you can safely ignore. To avoid this message, you set the value of `WarningAction` to `SilentlyContinue`.

Creating a Forest Root Domain Controller

With the AD DS feature installed, you create a new AD forest by promoting your server, `DC1`, to be a DC in a new forest/domain, `Reskit.Org`. Since this is the first DC in the domain, the DC becomes the forest root DC. You initiate the promotion process by performing the following:

```
# 4. Install Forest Root Domain and DC
$ADINSTALLHT = @{
   String      = 'Pa$$w0rd'
   AsPlainText = $True
   Force       = $True
}
$SECUREPW = ConvertTo-SecureString @ADINSTALLHT
$ADHT = @{
   DomainName                     = 'Reskit.Org' # Forest Root
   SafeModeAdministratorPassword  = $SECUREPW
   InstallDNS                     = $True
   DomainMode                     = 'WinThreshold' # latest
   ForestMode                     = 'WinThreshold' # Latest
   Force                          = $True
   NoRebootOnCompletion           = $True
   WarningAction                  = 'SilentlyContinue'
}
Install-ADDSForest @ADHT
```

By setting the `WarningAction` parameter to `SilentlyContinue`, the `Install-ADDSForest` command generates no warning messages. The command normally generates a number of warning messages, but they are benign. If you are using this snippet in production, you may want to view the error messages if only to satisfy yourself that they are indeed benign in your environment.

You can see the output from this code in Figure 3.3. These commands promote `DC1` to be a DC, but you need to reboot to complete the installation. This would enable you to carry out any other necessary configuration on the DC before the required reboot. Depending on your environment, you could instead not set the `NoRebootOnCompletion` parameter and the reboot would occur automatically.

This example shows a great use of hash tables with PowerShell commands. A hash table is a set of key/value pairs that PowerShell treats as a single object. You add parameter names (keys) and their values to the hash table and then call the cmdlet passing only the hash table object. This makes the source code a lot easier to read (and is a common feature this book uses for code snippets). For more details on hash tables, see docs.microsoft.com/en-us/powershell/module/microsoft.powershell.core/about/about_hash_tables?view=powershell-7.

```
PS C:\Foo> # 4. Install Forest Root Domain and DC
PS C:\Foo> $ADINSTALLHT = @{
             StringI       = 'Pa$$w0rd'
             AsPlainText = $True
             Force       = $True
           }
PS C:\Foo> $SECUREPW = ConvertTo-SecureString @ADINSTALLHT
PS C:\Foo> $ADHT = @{
             DomainName                    = 'Reskit.Org' # Forest Root
             SafeModeAdministratorPassword = $SECUREPW
             InstallDNS                    = $True
             DomainMode                    = 'WinThreshold' # Latest
             ForestMode                    = 'WinThreshold' # Latest
             Force                         = $True
             NoRebootOnCompletion          = $True
             WarningAction                 = 'SilentlyContinue'
           }
PS C:\Foo> Install-ADDSForest @ADHT

RunspaceId    : f0e468bc-35eb-4ac8-a531-5842ac888d74
Message       : You must restart this computer to complete the operation.

Context       : DCPromo.General.4
RebootRequired : True
Status        : Success
```

Figure 3.3: Promoting DC1

Restarting the Computer

To complete the installation of the new forest, you need to reboot the server. You do this using Restart-Computer as follows:

```
# 5. Restart computer
Restart-Computer -Force
```

Viewing the Directory Server Entry (DSE)

After the server, DC1.Reskit.Org, has rebooted, log in to the server (as the domain administrator Reskit\Administrator) and examine details of the forest by viewing the Root Directory Services Entry, or Root DSE. The Root DSE is the root of your directory tree, and Get-ADRootDSE provides information about a directory server.

```
# 6. After reboot, log back into DC1 as Reskit\Administrator
Get-ADRootDSE |
  Format-Table -Property DNS*, *Functionality
```

You can get the Root DSE for any standards-based LDAP server, including Windows Active Directory. You can think of the DSE as a road map of what's inside this DC and the features it supports.

An important security point is that the Root DSE is provided without requiring any authentication. If you have DCs exposed to the Internet, they provide their information anonymously. This could enable an attacker to learn more about your domain structure, and for that reason exposing DCs on the Internet is to be avoided.

As you can see in Figure 3.4, our host now has a fully qualified host name of `DC1.Reskit.Org`, is a DC in a Windows domain and forest, and has both domain and forest functionality set at the Windows 2016 level. There were no additional AD features in Windows Server 2019, so this setting means that all existing features are available.

```
PS C:\Foo> # 6. After reboot, log back into DC1 as Reskit\Administrator
PS C:\Foo> Get-ADRootDSE |
                Format-Table -Property DNS*, *Functionality

dnsHostName        domainControllerFunctionality domainFunctionality forestFunctionality
-----------        ----------------------------- ------------------- -------------------
DC1.Reskit.Org                     Windows2016   Windows2016Domain   Windows2016Forest
```

Figure 3.4: Viewing the DSE

Viewing Details of the New AD DS Forest

You can use the `Get-ADForest` command to view details of the new `Reskit.Org` forest, including forest-level FSMOs, the servers presently acting as a Global Catalog (GC), and the set of domains in the forest by using the following:

```
# 7. Examine ADDS forest
Get-ADForest |
    Format-Table -Property *master*, global*, Domains
```

Figure 3.5 shows the output of this code.

```
PS C:\Foo> # 7. Examine ADDS forest
PS C:\Foo> Get-AdForest |
                Format-Table -Property *master*, global*, Domains

DomainNamingMaster SchemaMaster    GlobalCatalogs      Domains
------------------ ------------    --------------      -------
DC1.Reskit.Org     DC1.Reskit.Org  {DC1.Reskit.Org}  {Reskit.Org}
```

Figure 3.5: Viewing the Reskit.Org forest

A GC provides access to a partial replica of *all* objects in a given forest and is used for lookups. Exchange Server, for example, makes heavy use of GC servers.

This page provides some additional detail on the role of a GC: `docs.microsoft` `.com/en-us/windows/win32/ad/global-catalog`.

In this figure, you can see that all forest-level FSMO roles are held by `DC1` `.Reskit.Org`. As you deploy more DCs, you can move the forest-level FSMOs as needed. In general, forest-level FSMOs should be held by DCs at your network core.

Getting Details of the Domain

You can view details of the `Reskit.Org` domain using the `Get-ADDomain` command. You may find that some of the default output provided by `Get-ADDomain` is not very useful, so you can refine the information displayed as follows:

```
# 8. View details of the domain
Get-ADDomain |
   Format-Table -Property DNS*, PDC*, *master, Replica*
```

You can view the output from this step in Figure 3.6. This shows that, so far, there is only one domain in the forest and one DC in that domain.

```
PS C:\Foo> # 8. View details of the domain
Get-ADDomain |
  Format-Table -Property DNS*, PDC*, *master, Replica*

DNSRoot     PDCEmulator    InfrastructureMaster RIDMaster     ReplicaDirectoryServers
-------     -----------    -------------------- ---------     -----------------------
Reskit.Org DC1.Reskit.Org DC1.Reskit.Org        DC1.Reskit.Org {DC1.Reskit.Org}
```

Figure 3.6: Viewing the Reskit.Org domain

In this figure, you can see that all domain-level FSMO roles are held by `DC1` `.Reskit.Org`. As you deploy more DCs, you can move FSMO roles as needed. As with forest-level FSMOs, you probably want the domain FSMOs to be held centrally. If you have multiple levels of domains, you may want to move domain-level FSMOs "nearer" to the center of each domain. Ultimately, you need to ensure that DCs can locate and connect to all FSMO role holders.

Viewing DNS Settings

When you promoted `DC1.Reskit.Org` as a DC, in "Creating a Forest Root Domain Controller," the promotion process added a DNS server on `DC1`, created a zone for your domain, and populated a number of DNS resource records (RRs). You can view the DNS details by using the following steps:

```
# 9. View DNS Settings
Get-Service -Name DNS
Get-DnsServerZone
Get-DnsServerResourceRecord -ZoneName 'Reskit.Org'
```

As you can see in Figure 3.7, the DNS Server service is up and running on
DC1. You can see the zones created in this DNS server, including the Reskit
.Org DNS domain. Finally, you can see the various DNS RRs that the AD service
creates and uses. If you are using multiple virtual NICs in your VM, you will
see more resource records.

```
PS C:\Foo> # 9. View DNS Settings
Get-Service -Name DNS

Status    Name          DisplayName
------    ----          -----------
Running   DNS           DNS Server

PS C:\Foo> Get-DnsServerZone

ZoneName                ZoneType    IsAutoCreated   IsDsIntegrated  IsReverseLookupZone  IsSigned
--------                --------    -------------   --------------  -------------------  --------
_msdcs.Reskit.Org       Primary     False           True            False                False
0.in-addr.arpa          Primary     True            False           True                 False
127.in-addr.arpa        Primary     True            False           True                 False
255.in-addr.arpa        Primary     True            False           True                 False
Reskit.Org              Primary     False           True            False                False

PS C:\Foo> Get-DnsServerResourceRecord -ZoneName 'Reskit.Org'

HostName             RecordType Type   Timestamp            TimeToLive  RecordData
--------             ---------- ----   ---------            ----------  ----------
@                    A          1      28/12/2019 14:00:00  00:10:00    10.10.10.10
@                    NS         2      0                    01:00:00    dc1.reskit.org.
@                    SOA        6      0                    01:00:00    [52][dc1.reskit.org.][hostmaster.reskit.org.]
@                    AAAA       28     28/12/2019 14:00:00  00:10:00    fd00::88b6:682b:e79b:511
_msdcs               NS         2      0                    01:00:00    dc1.reskit.org.
_gc._tcp.Default-First-S…  SRV  33    28/12/2019 15:00:00  00:10:00    [0][100][3268][DC1.Reskit.Org.]
_kerberos._tcp.Default-F… SRV   33    28/12/2019 15:00:00  00:10:00    [0][100][88][DC1.Reskit.Org.]
_ldap._tcp.Default-First… SRV   33    28/12/2019 15:00:00  00:10:00    [0][100][389][DC1.Reskit.Org.]
_gc._tcp             SRV        33     28/12/2019 15:00:00  00:10:00    [0][100][3268][DC1.Reskit.Org.]
_kerberos._tcp       SRV        33     28/12/2019 15:00:00  00:10:00    [0][100][88][DC1.Reskit.Org.]
_kpasswd._tcp        SRV        33     28/12/2019 15:00:00  00:10:00    [0][100][464][DC1.Reskit.Org.]
_ldap._tcp           SRV        33     28/12/2019 15:00:00  00:10:00    [0][100][389][DC1.Reskit.Org.]
_kerberos._udp       SRV        33     28/12/2019 15:00:00  00:10:00    [0][100][88][DC1.Reskit.Org.]
_kpasswd._udp        SRV        33     28/12/2019 15:00:00  00:10:00    [0][100][464][DC1.Reskit.Org.]
dc1                  A          1      0                    01:00:00    10.10.10.10
dc1                  AAAA       28     0                    01:00:00    fd00::88b6:682b:e79b:511
DomainDnsZones       A          1      28/12/2019 14:00:00  00:10:00    10.10.10.10
DomainDnsZones       AAAA       28     28/12/2019 14:00:00  00:10:00    fd00::88b6:682b:e79b:511
_ldap._tcp.Default-First… SRV   33    28/12/2019 15:00:00  00:10:00    [0][100][389][DC1.Reskit.Org.]
_ldap._tcp.DomainDnsZones SRV   33    28/12/2019 15:00:00  00:10:00    [0][100][389][DC1.Reskit.Org.]
ForestDnsZones       A          1      28/12/2019 14:00:00  00:10:00    10.10.10.10
ForestDnsZones       AAAA       28     28/12/2019 14:00:00  00:10:00    fd00::88b6:682b:e79b:511
_ldap._tcp.Default-First… SRV   33    28/12/2019 15:00:00  00:10:00    [0][100][389][DC1.Reskit.Org.]
_ldap._tcp.ForestDnsZones SRV   33    28/12/2019 15:00:00  00:10:00    [0][100][389][DC1.Reskit.Org.]
```

Figure 3.7: Viewing DNS settings and configuration

In AD, the Netlogon service writes the AD-related DNS RRs to DNS each time
the service starts and every 24 hours thereafter. You can test this self-healing feature by stopping the Netlogon service, removing the AD-related RRs, and then
restarting the service. You should see that the necessary RRs are now restored.
Of course, be careful when testing this on a production domain controller.

Installing a Replica DC

In "Establishing a Forest Root Domain," you created an AD domain with a single
DC. In test environments, this might be more than adequate. For production,

best practice suggests having more than one DC. If you are using virtualization to host domain controller VMs, you should ensure that AD VMs are hosted on independent virtualization hosts (irrespective of the virtualization platform). This avoids a single point of failure.

Before You Start

In this section you add a domain-joined server, DC2.Reskit.Org (built using Windows Server 2019), to the Reskit.Org domain. If you are using the Reskit build scripts to deploy this DC, make sure you do not build the DC2 VM until after you have finished promoting DC1 to be a domain controller.

As with other servers you use in this chapter, you should have installed PowerShell 7 on DC2. To install PowerShell 7 and optionally VS Code, you can use the scripts in Chapter 1.

Importing the Server Manager Module

You start the process of promoting DC2 by loading the Server Manager module. This module is not supported natively by PowerShell 7. The command, however, works using the Windows PowerShell compatibility mechanism mentioned in Chapter 2.

You install it using the Import-Module command.

```
# 1. Import the Server Manager module
Import-Module -Name ServerManager -WarningAction SilentlyContinue
```

By specifying the -WarningAction parameter, you avoid seeing the warning message that would be generated to warn you that this module is being used in a compatibility session.

Checking Network Connectivity

Before promoting the server DC2.Reskit.Org to be a DC, you need to ensure that another DC is online and can be reached. If this fails, it means that promotion is not going to succeed. Tests you can run prior to promoting the server include these:

```
# 2. Check DC1 can be resolved and can be reached from DC2
Resolve-DnsName -Name DC1.Reskit.Org -Type A
Test-NetConnection -ComputerName DC1.Reskit.Org -Port 445
Test-NetConnection -ComputerName DC1.Reskit.Org -Port 389
```

You can see the output of these commands in Figure 3.8.

```
PS C:\Foo> # 2. Check DC1 can be resolved and can be reached from DC2
PS C:\Foo> Resolve-DnsName -Name DC1.Reskit.Org -Type A

Name                                      Type  TTL   Section   IPAddress
----                                      ----  ---   -------   ---------
DC1.Reskit.Org                            A     3600  Answer    10.10.10.10

PS C:\Foo> Test-NetConnection -ComputerName DC1.Reskit.Org -Port 445

ComputerName     : DC1.Reskit.Org
RemoteAddress    : 10.10.10.10
RemotePort       : 445
InterfaceAlias   : Ethernet
SourceAddress    : 10.10.10.11
TcpTestSucceeded : True


PS C:\Foo> Test-NetConnection -ComputerName DC1.Reskit.Org -Port 389

ComputerName     : DC1.Reskit.Org
RemoteAddress    : 10.10.10.10
RemotePort       : 389
InterfaceAlias   : Ethernet
SourceAddress    : 10.10.10.11
TcpTestSucceeded : True
```

Figure 3.8: Testing connectivity with DC1

In the figure, you can see that DC2 is able to connect to resolve DC1's IP address and then connect over ports 445 and 389. Typical issues are related to IP addressing/configuration and DNS. And if you are using virtualization, the virtualization network configuration can also be an issue.

Adding the AD DS Features on DC2

Another prerequisite step is getting the relevant features onto your host, using `Install-WindowsFeature` as follows:

```
# 4. Add the AD DS features on DC2
Install-WindowsFeature -Name AD-Domain-Services
-IncludeManagementTools
```

Running the `Install-WindowsFeature` cmdlet generates the output you see in Figure 3.9.

```
PS C:\Foo> # 3. Add the AD DS features on DC2
PS C:\Foo> Install-WindowsFeature -Name AD-Domain-Services -IncludeManagementTools

Success Restart Needed Exit Code     Feature Result
------- -------------- ---------     --------------
True    No             Success       {Active Directory Domain Services, Group Pol...
```

Figure 3.9: Installing Windows features

Promoting DC2

To promote DC2, you run the following commands:

```
4. Promote DC2
Import-Module -Name ADDSDeployment -WarningAction SilentlyContinue
$URK    = "Administrator@Reskit.Org"
$PW     = 'Pa$$w0rd'
$PSS    = ConvertTo-SecureString -String $PW -AsPlainText -Force
$CredRK = [PSCredential]::New($URK,$PSS)
$INSTALLHT = @{
  DomainName                      = 'Reskit.Org'
  SafeModeAdministratorPassword   = $PSS
  SiteName                        = 'Default-First-Site-Name'
  NoRebootOnCompletion            = $true
  InstallDNS                      = $false
  Credential                      = $CredRK
  Force                           = $true
  }
Install-ADDSDomainController @INSTALLHT | Out-Null
```

These commands promote DC2 to be a domain controller. Once the command has completed its work, you must reboot the system to complete the promotion process. The installation command you use to promote DC2 can generate warning messages that refer to Knowledge Base article 942564. In general, these are benign errors, and you can ignore them.

Rebooting DC2

To finalize the promotion process, restart DC2, like this:

```
# 5. Reboot manually
Restart-Computer -Force
```

This command restarts the system. If you had unsaved work, possibly in another window, you may have lost it.

Reviewing DCs in Reskit.Org Domain

After the reboot process has completed, you can log in to DC2 as the domain administrator. One of the first things you can do is to check to see which computers are now in the Domain Controllers organizational unit, with these commands:

```
# 6. Check DCs in Reskit.Org
$SB = 'OU=Domain Controllers,DC=Reskit,DC=Org'
Get-ADComputer -Filter * -SearchBase $SB |
  Format-Table -Property DNSHostname, Enabled
```

The output, which you can see in Figure 3.10, shows that you now have two DCs in the Domain Controllers OU and by implication in the domain.

```
PS C:\Foo> # 6. Check DCs in Reskit.Org
PS C:\Foo> $SB = 'OU=Domain Controllers,DC=Reskit,DC=Org'
PS C:\Foo> Get-ADComputer -Filter * -SearchBase $SB |
             Format-Table -Property DNSHostname, Enabled


DNSHostname     Enabled
-----------     -------
DC2.Reskit.Org    True
DC1.Reskit.Org    True
```

Figure 3.10: Viewing DCs in the `Reskit.Org` domain

Viewing the Reskit.Org Domain

In addition to verifying that you have a second DC, another useful test is to view the AD's domain details using `Get-ADDomain`, like this:

```
# 7. View Reskit.Org Forest
Get-ADDomain |
   Format-Table -Property Forest, Name, Replica*
```

These commands return the name of the forest, the name of the domain, and the DCs in the domain, as shown in Figure 3.11.

```
PS C:\Foo> # 7. View Reskit.Org Domain
PS C:\Foo> Get-ADDomain |
             Format-Table -Property Forest, Name, Replica*


Forest      Name    ReplicaDirectoryServers
------      ----    -----------------------
Reskit.Org Reskit {DC1.Reskit.Org, DC2.Reskit.Org}
```

Figure 3.11: Viewing DNS settings and configuration

As you can see in the figure, you now have a second working domain controller in the `Reskit.Org` domain. There are a variety of other tests you might want to do before proceeding, including checking the various network ports on DC2, validating DNS entries, and ensuring that replication is happening between the two DCs.

Installing a Child Domain

For many organizations, a single domain forest with multiple DCs is adequate and has the benefit of being simple to manage. But in some cases, having one or more child domains can be advantageous. For example, you might have two parts of your organization that are geographically distant. An advantage of using a child domain is that some parts of AD are not replicated between domains, which can reduce WAN usage. For geographically dispersed organizations, you also have the option of using a single domain and placing DCs in separate AD sites.

In this section, you create a new child domain, UK.Reskit.Org, as a child of the Reskit.Org domain you set up earlier in this chapter.

Before You Start

In this section you extend the Reskit.Org forest (set up in "Establishing a Forest Root Domain") by adding a child domain named UK.Reskit.Org with a single DC, named UKDC1.UK.Reskit.Org. This host is built using Windows Server 2019. You also need to install and configure PowerShell 7 on the host and optionally install VS Code using the scripts in Chapter 1.

Importing the Server Manager Module

To add the AD DS tools onto the host, you need to use the Server Manager module. This module is one that Import-Module detects as not supported natively in PowerShell 7 and makes use of the compatibility solution described in Chapter 2. You load the module as follows:

```
# 1. Import the ServerManager module
Import-Module ServerManager -WarningAction SilentlyContinue
```

This command loads the Server Manager module using the Windows PowerShell compatibility mechanism discussed in Chapter 2. It creates a PowerShell remoting session, loads the module in that remote session, and creates local proxy functions for the commands in the Server Manager module. You can view the remoting session details using the Get-PSSession command.

Verifying That DC1 Can Be Resolved

To create the new subdomain, your server (UKDC1) needs to have connectivity to the parent domain. In particular, this host needs access to the Domain Naming Master FSMO forest role holder in the parent domain. If you are following the steps so far in this chapter, that server would be DC1.Reskit.Org. Before promoting the server, it is useful to test that you can connect to that server, using Test-NetConnection as follows:

```
# 2. Check DC1 can be resolved and can be reached over 445 and 389
from UKDC1
Resolve-DnsName -Name DC1.Reskit.Org -Type A
Test-NetConnection -ComputerName DC1.Reskit.Org -Port 445
Test-NetConnection -ComputerName DC1.Reskit.Org -Port 389
```

You can see the output from these commands in Figure 3.12. It shows that you can resolve the parent DC and can connect to it via both port 445 and port 389.

```
PS C:\Foo> # 2. Check DC1 can be resolved and can be reached over 445 and 389 from UKDC1
PS C:\Foo> Resolve-DnsName -Name DC1.Reskit.Org -Type A

Name              Type   TTL   Section   IPAddress
----              ----   ---   -------   ---------
DC1.Reskit.Org    A      3600  Answer    10.10.10.10

PS C:\Foo> Test-NetConnection -ComputerName DC1.Reskit.Org -Port 445

ComputerName      : DC1.Reskit.Org
RemoteAddress     : 10.10.10.10
RemotePort        : 445
InterfaceAlias    : Ethernet
SourceAddress     : 10.10.10.12
TcpTestSucceeded  : True


PS C:\Foo> Test-NetConnection -ComputerName DC1.Reskit.Org -Port 389

ComputerName      : DC1.Reskit.Org
RemoteAddress     : 10.10.10.10
RemotePort        : 389
InterfaceAlias    : Ethernet
SourceAddress     : 10.10.10.12
TcpTestSucceeded  : True
```

Figure 3.12: Verifying connectivity to DC1

If for any reason you cannot connect to the parent domain, you need to troubleshoot and resolve that issue. Without connectivity to the parent, the new domain cannot be created. Typical issues with connection failure include network configuration and DNS. And in production, ensure that you have and use the correct credentials.

Adding the AD DS Features to UKDC1

Before you can make UKDC1 a domain controller, you must add the AD Domain Services features to the server, as follows:

```
# 3. Add the AD DS features on UKDC1
$Features = 'AD-Domain-Services'
Install-WindowsFeature -Name AD-Domain-Services
 -IncludeManagementTools
```

You can view the output from installing this feature in Figure 3.13.

In production, the output from the Install-WindowsFeature command is probably not very helpful. If anything, it's more useful when it fails. When it succeeds, you can largely ignore the output and proceed to the next step. If it fails, you need to discover why and resolve the issue. Once the issue is resolved, you can retry this step.

```
PS C:\Foo> # 3. Add the AD DS features on UKDC1
PS C:\Foo> $Features = 'AD-Domain-Services'
PS C:\Foo> Install-WindowsFeature -Name $Features -IncludeManagementTools


Success Restart Needed Exit Code   Feature Result
------- -------------- ---------   --------------
True    No             Success     {Active Directory Domain Services, Group Pol…
```

Figure 3.13: Adding features to UKDC1

Creating the Child Domain

You create the new domain as follows using the `Install-ADDSDomain` command, like this:

```
# 4. Create New Domain
Import-Module -Name ADDSDeployment -WarningAction SilentlyContinue
$URK    = "Administrator@Reskit.Org"
$PW     = 'Pa$$w0rd'
$PSS    = ConvertTo-SecureString -String $PW -AsPlainText -Force
$CredRK = [PSCredential]::New($URK,$PSS)
$INSTALLHT    = @{
  NewDomainName                   = 'UK'
  ParentDomainName                = 'Reskit.Org'
  DomainType                      = 'ChildDomain'
  SafeModeAdministratorPassword   = $PSS
  ReplicationSourceDC             = 'DC1.Reskit.Org'
  Credential                      = $CredRK
  SiteName                        = 'Default-First-Site-Name'
  InstallDNS                      = $false
  Force                           = $true
}
Install-ADDSDomain @INSTALLHT
```

These commands promote UKDC1 to be a new DC in a child domain. Once the installation is complete, the machine reboots to complete the configuration of UKDC1.

Viewing the Updated AD Forest

After the server reboots, you can log in. You have the option of logging in as either Reskit\Administrator or UK\Administrator. That demonstrates the ability to log into a child domain with credentials from another domain in the forest.

If you log in as UK\Administrator, you can view the details of the UK.Reskit.Org domain as follows:

```
# 5. Look at AD forest
Get-ADForest -Server UKDC1.UK.Reskit.Org
```

It's worth taking a moment to study the output from this step, which you can see in Figure 3.14.

```
PS C:\Foo> # 5. Look at AD forest
PS C:\Foo> Get-ADForest -Server UKDC1.UK.Reskit.Org

ApplicationPartitions : {DC=DomainDnsZones,DC=Reskit,DC=Org, DC=ForestDnsZones,DC=Reskit,DC=Org}
CrossForestReferences : {}
DomainNamingMaster    : DC1.Reskit.Org
Domains               : {Reskit.Org, UK.Reskit.Org}
ForestMode            : Windows2016Forest
GlobalCatalogs        : {DC1.Reskit.Org, DC2.Reskit.Org, UKDC1.UK.Reskit.Org}
Name                  : Reskit.Org
PartitionsContainer   : CN=Partitions,CN=Configuration,DC=Reskit,DC=Org
RootDomain            : Reskit.Org
SchemaMaster          : DC1.Reskit.Org
Sites                 : {Default-First-Site-Name}
SPNSuffixes           : {}
UPNSuffixes           : {}
```

Figure 3.14: Viewing the `Reskit` forest

In this figure, you see that the forest now has two domains (`Reskit.Org` and `UK.Reskit.Org`). Additionally, both forest-wide FSMO roles are held by `DC1.Reskit.Org` (in the parent domain).

Viewing the Child Domain

You can also view the details of the newly created `UK.Reskit.Org` domain using the `Get-ADDomain` command, as follows:

```
# 6. Look at the UK domain
Get-ADDomain -Server UKDC1.UK.Reskit.Org
```

Figure 3.15 shows the details for the `UK.Reskit.Org` domain.

This output provides more details about the newly created child domain. You can see that the domain-wide FSMO role holders all point to this newly created DC. In production you would want a second DC (or more as appropriate) and may need to move the FSMO roles. This output also shows further domain-wide configuration information.

Once you have completed these steps, you have a working child domain (`UK.Reskit.Org`) in addition to the parent domain (`Reskit.Org`).

```
PS C:\Foo> # 6. Look at the UK domain
PS C:\Foo> Get-ADDomain -Server UKDC1.UK.Reskit.Org

AllowedDNSSuffixes                    : {}
ChildDomains                          : {}
ComputersContainer                    : CN=Computers,DC=UK,DC=Reskit,DC=Org
DeletedObjectsContainer               : CN=Deleted Objects,DC=UK,DC=Reskit,DC=Org
DistinguishedName                     : DC=UK,DC=Reskit,DC=Org
DNSRoot                               : UK.Reskit.Org
DomainControllersContainer            : OU=Domain Controllers,DC=UK,DC=Reskit,DC=Org
DomainMode                            : Windows2016Domain
DomainSID                             : S-1-5-21-2299411520-220244118-2741742863
ForeignSecurityPrincipalsContainer    : CN=ForeignSecurityPrincipals,DC=UK,DC=Reskit,DC=Org
Forest                                : Reskit.Org
InfrastructureMaster                  : UKDC1.UK.Reskit.Org
LastLogonReplicationInterval          :
LinkedGroupPolicyObjects              : {CN={31B2F340-016D-11D2-945F-00C04FB984F9},CN=Policies,CN=System,DC=UK,DC=Reskit,DC=Org}
LostAndFoundContainer                 : CN=LostAndFound,DC=UK,DC=Reskit,DC=Org
ManagedBy                             :
Name                                  : UK
NetBIOSName                           : UK
ObjectClass                           : domainDNS
ObjectGUID                            : 31e58b46-4f42-4799-b4ce-77bae4ee2083
ParentDomain                          : Reskit.Org
PDCEmulator                           : UKDC1.UK.Reskit.Org
PublicKeyRequiredPasswordRolling      : True
QuotasContainer                       : CN=NTDS Quotas,DC=UK,DC=Reskit,DC=Org
ReadOnlyReplicaDirectoryServers       : {}
ReplicaDirectoryServers               : {UKDC1.UK.Reskit.Org}
RIDMaster                             : UKDC1.UK.Reskit.Org
SubordinateReferences                 : {}
SystemsContainer                      : CN=System,DC=UK,DC=Reskit,DC=Org
UsersContainer                        : CN=Users,DC=UK,DC=Reskit,DC=Org
```

Figure 3.15: Viewing the child domain information

Configuring a Cross-Forest Trust

In this chapter thus far, you have installed a forest with two domains, namely, Reskit.Org and the child domain UK.Reskit.Org. In most organizations a one- or two-level domain structure is best practice. That means either a single-domain forest or a forest with a single root domain and one or more child domains.

Having a two-level domain structure with multiple child domains has some advantages for large distributed organizations. In particular, separate child domains can help to avoid replication between domains (which typically means additional WAN traffic).

While you can have multiple domain trees within a single forest, that is usually not a good idea. In most cases, the desire for multiple noncontiguous domain trees arises from the need of different parts of the organization to have their own domains (and therefore email and FQDN server names). For example, if a large conglomerate bought a company with a strong brand identity, it might make commercial sense to keep that separate with a separate domain tree.

However, because you cannot prune and graft parts of your AD forest between other external forests, when you buy or sell that strongly named subsidiary, a buyer might face challenges integrating the old attached domain/forest into the new environment. A much better approach is to create two separate and independent forests and then implement a *cross-forest trust*. A cross-forest trust means that you can use accounts in one domain in the access control list (ACL) of a resource in a different domain to support resource access between different forests.

In this section, you create a new forest (Kapoho.Com) on a newly installed server (KAPDC1). You create this server initially as a workgroup server and then promote it to be a DC in a new forest. Once this new forest is created, you can create and leverage the cross-forest trust.

Before You Start

In this section, you create a cross-forest trust between the Kapoho.Com and Reskit.Org forests and then use this trust to update ACLs to facilitate cross-forest resource access. To achieve this, you need to have created the domain controllers in the two forests (DC1.Reskit.Org and KAPDC1.Kapoho.Org). You run the steps in this section on KAPDC1. As with other servers, you need to install PowerShell 7 and optionally VS Code on this server. You can use the scripts in Chapter 1 to do so.

Importing the Server Manager Module

To add the AD DS tools onto the host, you need to use the Server Manager module. This module is one that Import-Module detects as not supported natively in PowerShell 7 and makes use of the compatibility solution described in Chapter 2. You load the module using Import-Module as follows:

```
# 1. Import the ServerManager module on KAPDC1
Import-Module ServerManager -WarningAction SilentlyContinue
```

This command loads the module using the Windows PowerShell compatibility mechanism described in Chapter 2. In doing so, it creates a PowerShell remoting session to the local host, loads the module in that remote session, and creates local proxy functions for the commands in the Server Manager module. You can view the remoting session details by using the Get-PSSession command.

Installing the AD Domain Services Feature and Management Tools

You can now install the AD Domain Services feature, including the necessary management tools, as follows:

```
# 2. Install the AD Domain Services feature and Management Tools
$Features = 'AD-Domain-Services'
Install-WindowsFeature -Name $Features -IncludeManagementTools
```

This step produces the output you can see in Figure 3.16.

```
PS C:\Foo> # 2. Install the AD Domain Services feature and Management Tools
PS C:\Foo> $Features = 'AD-Domain-Services'
PS C:\Foo> Install-WindowsFeature -Name $Features -IncludeManagementTools

Success Restart Needed Exit Code  Feature Result
------- -------------- ---------  --------------
True    No             Success    {Active Directory Domain Services, Group Pol…
```

Figure 3.16: Installing the AD DS feature

This command adds the AD Domain Services to the host but does not promote the host to be a DC. You promote KAPDC1 to be a new DC in a separate step ("Promoting KAPDC1").

Testing Network Connectivity with DC1

To create the cross-forest trust, KAPDC1.Kapoho.Com needs to be able to connect with DC1.Reskit.Org. So, before trying to create the trust, you test this connectivity between the two DCs, as follows:

```
# 3. Test Network Connectivity with DC1
Test-NetConnection -ComputerName DC1
```

Assuming DC1 and KAPDC1 are both online and working, the output you see should look like Figure 3.17.

```
PS C:\Foo> # 3. Test Network Connectivity with DC1
PS C:\Foo> Test-NetConnection -ComputerName DC1

ComputerName            : DC1
RemoteAddress           : fe80::651f:f0cb:cd4d:41f3%6
InterfaceAlias          : Ethernet
SourceAddress           : fe80::545c:b2eb:a778:cdcb%6
PingSucceeded           : True
PingReplyDetails (RTT)  : 0 ms
```

Figure 3.17: Testing network connectivity

You can extend these tests to verify full network connectivity using relevant ports such as 389 and 445.

Importing the AD DS Deployment Module

To promote KAPDC1 to be a DC in the Kapoho.Com domain, you need to import the AD DS Deployment module as follows:

```
# 4. Import the AD DS Deployment Module
Import-Module -Name ADDSDeployment -WarningAction SilentlyContinue
```

This command imports the module using the Windows Compatibility mechanism described in Chapter 2. Once you load the module, you can use Get-Command to view the proxy commands created.

Promoting KAPDC1

Next, you promote KAPDC1 to be a forest root DC in the Kapoho.Com forest/domain, as follows:

```
# 5. Promote KAPDC1 to be DC in its own forest
$ADINSTALLHT = @{
  String      = 'Pa$$w0rd'
  AsPlainText = $True
  Force       = $True
}
$SECUREPW = ConvertTo-SecureString @ADINSTALLHT
$ADINSTALLHT = @{
  DomainName                   = 'Kapoho.Com' # Forest Root
  SafeModeAdministratorPassword = $SecurePW
  InstallDNS                   = $True
  DomainMode                   = 'WinThreshold' # latest
  ForestMode                   = 'WinThreshold' # Latest
  Force                        = $True
  WarningAction                = 'SilentlyContinue'
}
Install-ADDSForest @ADINSTALLHT | Out-Null
```

This step produces no output. Because you did not use the -NoRebootOn-Completion parameter, once the promotion process has completed, the cmdlet reboots to finalize the server to be a DC. Specifying this parameter means that no reboot happens automatically; thus, you can control when the reboot happens. In production, you might be doing other operations in parallel with promoting the server, such as copying some files or configuring applications on the server. This parameter allows you to reboot when appropriate. Note that until you reboot, the new domain is not available.

View Kapoho.Com Forest Details

After rebooting, you can log in as the administrator in the new domain using either Administrator@Kapoho.Com or Kapoho\Administrator. Once logged in, it is useful to review and verify details of the new forest. You can view the forest details as follows:

```
# 6. View Kapoho.Com Forest Details
Get-ADForest
```

The output from this command, which you see in Figure 3.18, shows key details about the new forest. It is useful to validate that the DC has been created and promoted as you expect and that the relevant FSMO roles are set.

```
PS C:\Foo> # 6. View Kapoho.Com forest details
PS C:\Foo> Get-ADForest

ApplicationPartitions : {DC=ForestDnsZones,DC=Kapoho,DC=Com, DC=DomainDnsZones,DC=Kapoho,DC=Com}
CrossForestReferences : {}
DomainNamingMaster    : KAPDC1.Kapoho.Com
Domains               : {Kapoho.Com}
ForestMode            : Windows2016Forest
GlobalCatalogs        : {KAPDC1.Kapoho.Com}
Name                  : Kapoho.Com
PartitionsContainer   : CN=Partitions,CN=Configuration,DC=Kapoho,DC=Com
RootDomain            : Kapoho.Com
SchemaMaster          : KAPDC1.Kapoho.Com
Sites                 : {Default-First-Site-Name}
SPNSuffixes           : {}
UPNSuffixes           : {}
```

Figure 3.18: Viewing details of the Kapoho.Com forest

With the steps so far in this section, you have created another forest and domain. At present, there is no relationship between the two forests; thus, there is no cross-forest resource access yet. There are a number of further steps you need to take to implement a cross-forest trust.

Adjusting the DNS to Resolve Reskit.Org from KAPDC1

With two independent forests, you need to ensure that DNS clients in both forests are able to resolve hosts in the other forest. A simple way to do that is to create a *conditional DNS forwarder* on each forest's DNS server(s). That way, a DHCP client in Reskit.Org can resolve details of hosts in the Kapoho.Com zone by way of the forwarder. To do this locally on KAPDC1, you run the following:

```
# 7. Adjust DNS on KAPDC1 to resolve Reskit.Org from DC1
$CFHT = @{
   Name          = 'Reskit.Org'
   MasterServers = '10.10.10.10'
   Passthru      = $True
}
Add-DnsServerConditionalForwarderZone @CFHT
```

You can see the output of this command in Figure 3.19.

By performing this step, you configure the DNS server on KAPDC1 to resolve Reskit.Org-related addresses by forwarding requests to the DNS server at 10.10.10.10, which is DC1.Reskit.Org.

```
PS C:\Foo> # 7. Adjust DNS on KAPDC1 to resolve Reskit.Org from DC1
PS C:\Foo> $CFHT = @{
           Name          = 'Reskit.Org'
           MasterServers = '10.10.10.10'
           Passthru      = $True
        }
Add-DnsServerConditionalForwarderZone @CFHT


ZoneName     ZoneType    IsAutoCreated   IsDsIntegrated  IsReverseLookupZone  IsSigned
--------     --------    -------------   --------------  -------------------  --------
Reskit.Org   Forwarder   False           False           False
```

Figure 3.19: Adding a DNS conditional forwarder

This step demonstrates one of two methods you can deploy to implement cross-forest DNS lookups. The other method is to use stub zones. Each method has some advantages and disadvantages; for more information, see this article: win-admin.org/questions-answers/2-windows/2-windows/5-what-is-the-difference-between-stub-zone-and-conditional-forwarders-when-are-they-used-2.

Testing Conditional DNS Forwarding

With conditional DNS forwarding set up on KAPDC1, you test it using Resolve-DNSName. To attempt to resolve the IP address of the DC1.Reskit.Org server, enter the following:

```
# 8. Test Conditional Forwarding
Resolve-DNSName -Name DC1.Reskit.Org -Type A
```

As you can see in the output in Figure 3.20, DC1 has an A resource record for the IPv4 address of DC1.

```
# 8. Test Conditional Forwarding
Resolve-DNSName -Name DC1.Reskit.Org -Type A

Name              Type   TTL   Section   IPAddress
----              ----   ---   -------   ---------
DC1.Reskit.Org    A      3297  Answer    10.10.10.10
```

Figure 3.20: Testing conditional DNS forwarding

Setting Up a Conditional Forwarder on Reskit.Org

With the conditional forwarder set up on KAPDC1.Kapoho.Com, you can now set up and validate a forwarder on DC1.Reskit.Org to forward queries for Kapoho.Com to KAPDC1.Kapoho.Com, as follows:

```
# 9. Create a Script Block to Add Conditional Forwarder on DC1
$SB = {
```

```
    # Add CF zone
    $CFHT = @{
      Name          = 'Kapoho.Com'
      MasterServers = '10.10.10.131'
      }
    Add-DnsServerConditionalForwarderZone @CFHT
    # Test it
    Resolve-DNSName -Name KAPDC1.Kapoho.Com | Format-Table
}
```

These instructions create a script block that you use to add a conditional forwarder on DC1 to the DNS service on KAPDC1.

Create Credentials to Run a Command on DC1

Because DC1 is in a separate AD forest, you have to create a credentials object you can use to run the script block on DC1, as follows:

```
# 10. Create Credentials to Run A Command on DC1
$URK    = 'Reskit\Administrator'
$PRK    = ConvertTo-SecureString 'Pa$$w0rd' -AsPlainText -Force
$CREDRK =   [PSCredential]::New($URK,$PRK)
```

Setting WinRM

To run the script block remotely, on a system in another Kerberos realm, you need to adjust the WinRM service. To enable WinRM to run the script block, you need to update the Trusted Hosts list. This list defines which hosts you can connect to (without using Kerberos). You do this as follows:

```
# 11. Set WinRM
$PATH = 'WSMan:\localhost\Client\TrustedHosts'
Set-Item -Path $PATH -Value '*.Reskit.Org' -Force
```

After running this snippet, your system trusts any server in the Reskit.Org domain as being who it says it is. This is a potential security risk, and you should consider whether wildcard values like this are acceptable. Once you've demonstrated the capability for yourself, you may want to disable it on your system.

Invoking the Script Block on DC1

Now that you have created a script block and configured the environment, you can run the script block on the remote server as follows:

```
# 12. Run the Script Block on DC1
$NZHT = @{
```

Continues

continued

```
    Computername = 'DC1.Reskit.Org'
    Script       = $SB
    Credential   = $CREDRK
}
Invoke-Command @NZHT
```

In the output, shown in Figure 3.21, you can see that after setting up conditional forwarding, a DNS client on DC1 is able to resolve a RR for a host in the Kapoho .Com domain. Depending on how you have configured Internet access and whether you have IPv6 enabled, you may see additional RRs resolved.

```
PS C:\Foo> # 12. Run the Script Block On DC1
PS C:\Foo> $NZHT = @{
           Computername = 'DC1.Reskit.Org'
           Script       = $SB
           Credential   = $CREDRK
           }
PS C:\Foo> Invoke-Comand @NZHT

Name                  Type   TTL   Section    IPAddress
----                  ----   ---   -------    ---------
KAPDC1.Kapoho.Com     A      3599  Answer     10.10.10.131
```

Figure 3.21: Setting up a conditional forwarder on DC1

Getting the Domain Detail Objects

The AD modules do not support creating a cross-forest trust. To set up a cross-forest trust, you must make use of .NET objects and their methods.

To set up the cross-forest trust, first get the NET objects representing each of the two forests, as follows:

```
# 13. Get Reskit.Org and Kapoho.Com details
$Reskit        = 'Reskit.Org'
$User          = 'Administrator'
$UserPW        = 'Pa$$w0rd'
$Type          = 'System.DirectoryServices.' +
                 'ActiveDirectory.DirectoryContext'
$RKFHT = @{
  TypeName     = $Type
  ArgumentList = 'Forest',$Reskit,$User,$UserPW
}
$RKF           = New-Object @RKFHT
$ReskitForest =
  [System.DirectoryServices.ActiveDirectory.Forest]::GetForest($RKF)
$KapohoForest =
  [System.DirectoryServices.ActiveDirectory.
Forest]::GetCurrentForest()
```

This snippet creates variables that contain details of the two forests you are working with. These forest objects also have useful methods that are not available via PowerShell commands.

Since you store the output from these last two method calls in variables, you see no output.

The .NET namespace System.DirectoryServices.ActiveDirectory contains objects that represent the key AD components, including forest, domain, site, subnet, partition, and schemas. These classes have properties and methods that perform a variety of AD tasks. In many cases, these classes and methods overlap with commands in the Active Directory module. The classes do, however, provide properties and methods not available in the AD modules.

Viewing the Reskit Forest Details

Now that you have obtained the forest details for the Reskit.Org forest, you can display the information as follows:

```
# 14. View Reskit.Org Forest Details
$ReskitForest
```

This produces the output shown in Figure 3.22.

```
PS C:\Foo> # 14. View Reskit Forest Details
PS C:\Foo> $ReskitForest

Name                   : Reskit.Org
Sites                  : {Default-First-Site-Name}
Domains                : {Reskit.Org, UK.Reskit.Org}
GlobalCatalogs         : {DC1.Reskit.Org, DC2.Reskit.Org, UKDC1.UK.Reskit.Org}
ApplicationPartitions  : {DC=DomainDnsZones,DC=Reskit,DC=Org, DC=ForestDnsZones,DC=Reskit,DC=Org}
ForestModeLevel        : 7
ForestMode             : Unknown
RootDomain             : Reskit.Org
Schema                 : CN=Schema,CN=Configuration,DC=Reskit,DC=Org
SchemaRoleOwner        : DC1.Reskit.Org
NamingRoleOwner        : DC1.Reskit.Org
```

Figure 3.22: Viewing the Reskit.Org forest

Viewing the Kapoho Forest Details

You can also view the details of the Kapoho.Com forest, using similar syntax:

```
# 15. View Kapoho Forest Details$KapohoForest
```

The output, which you can see in Figure 3.23, is similar to that of the Reskit forest.

```
PS C:\Foo> # 15. View Kapoho Forest Details
PS C:\Foo> $KapohoForest

Name                 : Kapoho.Com
Sites                : {Default-First-Site-Name}
Domains              : {Kapoho.Com}
GlobalCatalogs       : {KAPDC1.Kapoho.Com}
ApplicationPartitions : {DC=ForestDnsZones,DC=Kapoho,DC=Com, DC=DomainDnsZones,DC=Kapoho,DC=Com}
ForestModeLevel      : 7
ForestMode           : Unknown
RootDomain           : Kapoho.Com
Schema               : CN=Schema,CN=Configuration,DC=Kapoho,DC=Com
SchemaRoleOwner      : KAPDC1.Kapoho.Com
NamingRoleOwner      : KAPDC1.Kapoho.Com
```

Figure 3.23: Viewing the Kahopo.Com forest

Establishing a Cross-Forest Trust

Now that you have the objects representing the two forests, you can establish a trust between the forests, using the `CreateTrustRelationship()` method as follows:

```
# 16. Establish a trust
$KapohoForest.CreateTrustRelationship($ReskitForest,"Bidirectional")
```

In this case, you are establishing a bidirectional trust, meaning that both domains now trust each other; you can now specify that security principals in either domain can access resources in the other domain.

Creating a Script Block to Adjust the ACL of a File on DC1

With the cross-forest trust set up, you can now make use of the trust. In particular, the trust means you can create a file (on DC1) and adjust the ACL to allow access both from members of the Reskit.Org forest and from users in the Kapoho.Com forest.

The simplest way to set ACLs on NFTS files and folders is to use the external NTFSSecurity module. You download this module from the PowerShell Gallery using the Install-Module command. After installing the module, you can create a file (on DC1) and configure the ACL to enable cross-forest access.

You do this by first creating a script block, as follows:

```
# 17. Create SB to Adjust ACL on DC1
$SB2 = {
   # Ensure NTFSSecurity module is loaded on DC1
   Install-Module -Name NTFSSecurity -Force -ErrorAction
SilentlyContinue
   # Create a file in C:\Foo
   'XFT Test' | Out-File -FilePath 'C:\Foo\XFTTEST.Txt'
   # Test ACL
   Get-NTFSaccess -Path C:\Foo\XFTTEST.Txt | Format-Table
```

```
# Add Kapoho\Administrators into ACL for this file
$NTHT = @{
  Path         = 'C:\Foo\XFTTEST.TXT'
  Account      = 'Administrator@Kapoho.Com'
  AccessRights = 'FullControl'
}
Add-NTFSAccess @NTHT
# Retest ACL
Get-NTFSaccess -Path C:\Foo\XFTTEST.Txt | Format-Table
}
```

This code snippet creates a script block (on KAPDC1), which creates a new file (on the remote system) and then looks at the initial ACL. After adding the Kapoho\Administrator to the ACL of this file, the script block retrieves and displays the updated ACL.

Running the Script Block on DC1 to Demonstrate the Cross-Forest Trust

To view the cross-forest trust in action, you can run the script block as follows:

```
# 18. Run the ScriptBlock on DC1 To Demonstrate X-Forest Trust
$PHT = @{
  ComputerName = 'DC1.Reskit.Org'
  Credential   = $CREDRK
  ScriptBlock  = $SB2
}
Invoke-Command  @PHT
```

Note that you need to ensure that connectivity between KAPDC1 and DC1. Figure 3.24 shows the output of this step. The NTFS Security cmdlets produce an extra white space in the output. You can avoid that by piping the output of, for example, Get-NTFSAccess to Format-Table and specifying -AutoSize.

In practice, you should be using the AGDLP (account, global, domain, local permissions) approach to setting permissions (see en.wikipedia.org/wiki/AGDLP for more information on this approach). The mechanism shown in this section works well but may not be as scalable. For larger enterprises, the AGDLP approach is easier to deploy and manage.

With AGDLP, you place user and group accounts that need to access resources into global groups in each forest/domain. Then you add those global groups into Domain Local groups on each domain. Once these Domain Local groups are created, you can assign permissions to a resource in either forest based on the Domain Global groups in each forest. In this book's scenario, you create a Domain Local group in the Reskit domain and then add a global group from the Kapoho domain to it.

```
PS C:\Foo> # 18. Run the Script Block on DC1 To Demonstrate X-Forest Trust
PS C:\Foo> $PH
T = @{
            ComputerName = 'DC1.Reskit.Org'
            Credential   = $CREDRK
            ScriptBlock  = $SB2
        }
PS C:\Foo> Invoke-Command  @PHT

   Path: C:\Foo\XFTTEST.Txt (Inheritance enabled)

Account                 Access Rights              Applies to        Type    IsInherited  InheritedFrom
-------                 -------------              ----------        ----    -----------  -------------
NT AUTHORITY\SYSTEM     FullControl                ThisFolderOnly    Allow   True         C:
BUILTIN\Administrators  FullControl                ThisFolderOnly    Allow   True         C:
BUILTIN\Users           ReadAndExecute, Synchron_  ThisFolderOnly    Allow   True         C:


   Path: C:\Foo\XFTTEST.Txt (Inheritance enabled)

Account                 Access Rights              Applies to        Type    IsInherited  InheritedFrom
-------                 -------------              ----------        ----    -----------  -------------
KAPOHO\Administrator    FullControl                ThisFolderOnly    Allow   False
NT AUTHORITY\SYSTEM     FullControl                ThisFolderOnly    Allow   True         C:
BUILTIN\Administrators  FullControl                ThisFolderOnly    Allow   True         C:
BUILTIN\Users           ReadAndExecute, Synchron_  ThisFolderOnly    Allow   True         C:
```

Figure 3.24: Updating the ACL and viewing its details

Managing AD Users, Computers, and OUs

Once you have your Active Directory infrastructure built, the next step in deployment is to add objects to the directory and subsequently manage them.
There are four sets of AD objects you are most likely to use.

- Users
- Computers
- Groups
- Organizational units

An AD *user* object represents a user account that can be used to log on and can be used in resource ACLs. An AD *computer* object represents a computer that can log in to the domain and onto which a user can log. AD computers can also be used in ACLs. An AD *group* is an account that contains other user, computer, or group objects. To simplify ACL management, you use a group in an ACL instead of individual users/computers. An *organizational unit* (OU) is an AD object that contains other AD objects, including other OUs. You also use OUs for two main purposes: to delegate administration and to support group policies.

You use the commands in the Active Directory module to manage the objects in your AD. This module is supported natively in PowerShell 7.

Before You Start

You run the code snippets in this section on the Windows Server domain controller, DC1.Reskit.Org. You created this server in "Establishing a Forest Root Domain" and have used it throughout this chapter.

Creating a Hash Table for General User Attributes

Creating a user object requires specifying a number of parameters, which can lead to long lines of code (that can be harder to troubleshoot). To simplify the creation of AD user (and other) objects, you can use a hash table to hold the properties you want to set when creating the object.

You create this hash table by assigning values to the $NewUserHT variable as follows:

```
# 1. Create a hash table for general user attributes
$PW  = 'Pa$$w0rd'
$PSS = ConvertTo-SecureString -String $PW -AsPlainText -Force
$NewUserHT = @{
  AccountPassword       = $PSS
  Enabled               = $true
  PasswordNeverExpires  = $true
  ChangePasswordAtLogon = $false
}
```

This hash table contains values for all the users to be added to AD in this section.

Creating Two Users

Now that you have the basic user properties hash table set up, you extend it to include user-specific details and then add the user to the AD as follows:

```
# 2. Create two users - adding to basic hash table
# First user
$NewUserHT.SamAccountName   = 'ThomasL'
$NewUserHT.UserPrincipalName = 'ThomasL@reskit.Org'
$NewUserHT.Name             = 'ThomasL'
$NewUserHT.DisplayName      = 'Thomas Lee (IT)'
New-ADUser @NewUserHT  # add first user
# Second user
$NewUserHT.SamAccountName   = 'RLT'
$NewUserHT.UserPrincipalName = 'RLT@Reskit.org'
$NewUserHT.Name             = 'Rebecca Lee-Tanner'
$NewUserHT.DisplayName      = 'Rebecca Lee-Tanner (IT)'
New-ADUser @NewUserHT  # Add second user
```

This snippet creates two new users in the AD. By default, these users are added to the Users container in AD. This container is not an OU.

This snippet shows some basic user settings. As noted earlier, you may want to extend the hash table to set additional properties on the user object being created.

Creating an OU for IT

An OU is a container object inside AD. When you added the two users to AD, it added them into the Users container. This is not helpful, as you can only apply group policies to an OU. Most organizations therefore use OUs to hold user, computer, and group objects.

It is important to note that both an OU and the Users container are container-type objects (AD objects that can contain other objects). The difference is that you can only apply group policies to an OU. It is best practice to have your AD computers, groups, and users in OUs.

To create an OU, in this case for the Reskit IT team, you can do the following:

```
# 3. Create an Organizational Unit for IT
$OUHT = @{
    Name        = 'IT'
    DisplayName = 'Reskit IT Team'
    Path        = 'DC=Reskit,DC=Org'
}
New-ADOrganizationalUnit @OUHT
```

This code creates a new OU at the top level of the `Reskit.Org` domain. Initially, it contains no objects.

Moving Users into an OU

With the IT OU created, you can now move each of the two users created earlier in this section into this OU, as follows:

```
# 4. Move the two users into the OU
$MHT1 = @{
    Identity   = 'CN=ThomasL,CN=Users,DC=Reskit,DC=ORG'
    TargetPath = 'OU=IT,DC=Reskit,DC=Org'
}
Move-ADObject @MHT1
$MHT2 = @{
    Identity = 'CN=Rebecca Lee-Tanner,CN=Users,DC=Reskit,DC=ORG'
    TargetPath = 'OU=IT,DC=Reskit,DC=Org'
}
Move-ADObject @MHT2
```

This snippet illustrates how to move an AD object. In this case, you move two specific users contained in the Users container into the IT OU. Once you have moved these user objects, the next time either user logs in, any OU-specific GPOs are applied.

Creating a User in an OU

As an alternative to creating an AD user in the Users container (and then moving the user to an appropriate OU), you can specify an OU path to the OU in which to create the new user, like this:

```
# 5. Create a third user directly in the IT OU
$NewUserHT.SamAccountName    = 'JerryG'
$NewUserHT.UserPrincipalName = 'jerryg@reskit.org'
$NewUserHT.Description        = 'Virtualization Team'
$NewUserHT.Name              = 'Jerry Garcia'
$NewUserHT.DisplayName        = 'Jerry Garcia (IT)'
$NewUserHT.Path               = 'OU=IT,DC=Reskit,DC=Org'
$NewUserHT.PasswordNeverExpires  = $true
$NewUserHT.ChangePasswordAtLogon = $false
New-ADUser @NewUserHT
```

You use this user in "Configuring Just Enough Administration (JEA)." In this example, you explicitly set the account password to never expire and to enable the user to log in a first time without changing passwords. That might be a security risk in a larger organization but is useful for this book.

Adding Two Additional Users

To demonstrate removing AD objects, begin by creating two users that you will later delete, as follows:

```
# 6. Add two users who are then removed
# First user to be removed
$NewUserHT.SamAccountName    = 'TBR1'
$NewUserHT.UserPrincipalName = 'tbr1@reskit.org'
$NewUserHT.Name              = 'TBR1'
$NewUserHT.DisplayName        = 'User to be removed'
$NewUserHT.Path               = 'OU=IT,DC=Reskit,DC=Org'
New-ADUser @NewUserHT
# Second user to be removed
$NewUserHT.SamAccountName    = 'TBR2'
$NewUserHT.UserPrincipalName = 'tbr2@reskit.org'
$NewUserHT.Name              = 'TBR2'
New-ADUser @NewUserHT
```

This snippet creates two new users (TBR1 and TBR2) in the IT OU.

Viewing Existing Users

With an OU and several users created, you can use `Get-ADUser` to view the existing AD users, as follows:

```
# 7. See the users that exist so far
Get-ADUser -Filter * -Properties DisplayName |
    Format-Table -Property Name, DisplayName, SamAccountName
```

You can see the output of this command in Figure 3.25. Depending on your needs, you may want to add more parameters to this display.

```
PS C:\Foo> # 7. See the users that exist so far
PS C:\Foo> Get-ADUser -Filter * -Properties DisplayName |
              Format-Table -Property Name, DisplayName, SamAccountName


Name                   Displayname                 SamAccountName
----                   -----------                 --------------
Administrator                                      Administrator
Guest                                             Guest
krbtgt                                            krbtgt
UK$                                               UK$
KAPOHO$                                           KAPOHO$
ThomasL                Thomas Lee (IT)            ThomasL
Rebecca Lee-Tanner    Rebecca Lee-Tanner (IT)    RLT
Jerry Garcia          Jerry Garcia (IT)          JerryG
TBR1                   User to be removed         TBR1
TBR2                   User to be removed         TBR2
```

Figure 3.25: Viewing users in Reskit.Org

As you can see in the figure, there are not many users in this domain. Also, note that the users added by default lack a `DisplayName` property, whereas the users you added did have a value set for that property.

Removing a User with a Get | Remove Pattern

There are at least two ways you can remove AD objects, including AD users. The first uses a `Get | Remove` pattern. In this pattern you first get objects (using, for example, `Get-ADUser`) and then pipe them to a command (for example, `Remove-ADUser`) to remove the objects (in this case, users). This pattern is particularly useful interactively. You use the `Get` portion to get the specific objects you need, verify that you are getting the right objects, and only then remove them. You can do this as follows:

```
# 8. Remove via a Get | Remove Pattern
Get-ADUser -Identity 'CN=TBR1,OU=IT,DC=Reskit,DC=Org' |
    Remove-ADUser -Confirm:$false
```

Removing a User Directly

A second way to remove a user is to use `Remove-ADUser` and specify the identity for the user to be removed. There are several ways to specify the identity of the object; in this case, you use the full distinguished name, as follows:

```
# 9. Remove user directly
$RUHT = @{
  Identity = 'CN=TBR2,OU=IT,DC=Reskit,DC=Org'
  Confirm  = $false}
Remove-ADUser @RUHT
```

This demonstrates how you can remove a specific user directly. This approach is possibly quicker than using the `Get | Remove` pattern, but arguably less safe in the case of typos.

Updating and Displaying a User Object

Once you create an object, whether a user, a group, or whatever, you may need to update it. You may need to update a user object with a revised phone number or office name. You can update and view a user object with the `Set-ADUser` and `Get-ADUser` commands, as follows:

```
# 10. Update and display a user
$TLHT =@{
  Identity     = 'ThomasL'
  OfficePhone  = '4416835420'
  Office       = 'Marin Office'
  EmailAddress = 'ThomasL@Reskit.Org'
  GivenName    = 'Thomas'
  Surname      = 'Lee'
  HomePage     = 'Https://tfl09.blogspot.com'
}
Set-ADUser @TLHT
Get-ADUser -Identity ThomasL -Properties  DisplayName, Office,
                                    OfficePhone, EmailAddress |
  Format-Table -Property DisplayName, Name, Office,
                     OfficePhone, EmailAddress
```

You can see the output of this step in Figure 3.26.

As in any script that outputs user details, you are likely to want to manage, retrieve, and view many different object properties; thus, you may want to extend the properties displayed by `Format-Table`. Also, remember that if you want to display a property, you may need to extend the value of the `-Properties` parameter in `Get-ADUser` as well so as to ensure you retrieve the property in the first place before displaying it. Note that retrieving additional properties adds performance overhead. Retrieving all properties can take two to three times as long as retrieving only the default set. Best practice is to retrieve only the properties you need.

```
PS C:\Foo> # 10. Update and display a user
PS C:\Foo> $TLHT =@{
            Identity    = 'ThomasL'
            OfficePhone = '4416835420'
            Office      = 'Marin Office'
            EmailAddress = 'ThomasL@Reskit.Org'
            GivenName   = 'Thomas'
            Surname     = 'Lee'
            HomePage    = 'Https://tfl09.blogspot.com'
          }
PS C:\Foo> Set-ADUser @TLHT
PS C:\Foo> Get-ADUser -Identity ThomasL -Properties  DisplayName, Office,
                             OfficePhone, EmailAddress  |
           Format-Table -Property DisplayName, Name, Office,
                     OfficePhone, EmailAddress


DisplayName      Name    Office      OfficePhone EmailAddress
-----------      ----    ------      ----------- ------------
Thomas Lee (IT) ThomasL Marin Office 4416835420  ThomasL@Reskit.Org
```

Figure 3.26: Viewing updated user details

Creating an AD Group

You create an AD group similarly to creating an AD user, with the `New-ADGroup` command as follows:

```
# 11. Create a new group for RK DNS Admins
$NGHT1 = @{
  Name        = 'RKDnsAdmins'
  Path        = 'OU=IT,DC=Reskit,DC=org'
  Description = 'Reskit DNS Universal admins'
  GroupScope  = 'Universal'
}
New-ADGroup @NGHT1
```

This creates a new group, `RKDnsAdmins`, which is stored in the IT OU. An AD group object is similar to an AD user object in that you can move it, remove it, or update it.

AD supports two types of groups: distribution groups and security groups. A security group can be used when adjusting ACLs. A distribution group, on the other hand, cannot be used for that. Even though the distribution group object actually contains a value for the SID attribute (a little-known fact), the AD UI prevents you from using distribution groups in ACLs.

For more details on how security groups are used in access control, see this document: docs.microsoft.com/en-us/windows/win32/ad/how-security-groups-are-used-in-access-control.

Creating and Viewing Group Membership

Once you create the group, you need to populate it (and view the results). To do that, you use the Add-ADGroupMember and Get-ADGroupMember commands, as follows:

```
# 12. Add a user to the DNS Admins group and view group members
Add-ADGroupMember -Identity 'RKDnsAdmins' -Members 'JerryG' | Out-Null
Get-ADGroupMember -Identity 'RKDnsAdmins'
```

The output, shown in Figure 3.27, shows the new user, JerryG, is the only member of the RKDnsAdmins group.

```
PS C:\Foo> # 12. Add a user to the DNS Admins group and view group members
PS C:\Foo> Add-ADGroupMember -Identity 'RKDnsAdmins' -Members 'JerryG' | Out-Null
PS C:\Foo> Get-ADGroupMember -Identity 'RKDnsAdmins'

distinguishedName : CN=Jerry Garcia,OU=IT,DC=Reskit,DC=Org
name              : Jerry Garcia
objectClass       : user
objectGUID        : 90d7922e-f4c8-4c2c-99ec-83667bda6c2c
SamAccountName    : JerryG
SID               : S-1-5-21-629383343-2974153759-1939089791-1107
```

Figure 3.27: Viewing updated user details

Note that you use this group (and the JerryG user) in "Configuring Just Enough Administration (JEA)."

Make a New Group for the IT Team

You next make a further Universal group that is to contain all members of the IT team.

```
# 13. Make a group for the IT Team
$NGHT2 = @{
  Name        = 'IT Team'
  Path        = 'OU=IT,DC=Reskit,DC=org'
  Description = 'All members of the IT Team'
  GroupScope  = 'Universal'
}
New-ADGroup @NGHT2
```

Make All Users in IT Members of the IT Team Group

Having created the group, you now add all members of the IT OU into this new group, with this code:

```
# 14. Make all Users in IT a Member Of This Group
$SB = 'OU=IT,DC=Reskit,DC=Org'
$ItUsers = Get-ADUser -Filter * -SearchBase $SB
Add-ADGroupMember -Identity 'IT Team' -Members $ItUsers
```

Displaying Group Membership

It is often useful to view the membership of a group after you update the members. The output of the following code, using Get-ADGroupMember, could be useful in documenting membership of key groups:

```
# 15. Display Group Members of the IT Team Group
Get-ADGroupMember -Identity 'IT Team' |
   Format-Table -Property SamAccountName, DistinguishedName
```

The output, which you can see in Figure 3.28, shows the SamAccountName and the DistinguishedName of the members of the IT Team group.

```
PS C:\Foo> # 15. Display Group Members of the IT Team Group
PS C:\Foo> Get-ADGroupMember -Identity 'IT Team' |
             Format-Table -Property SamAccountName, DistinguishedName


SamAccountName DistinguishedName
-------------- -----------------
JerryG         CN=Jerry Garcia,OU=IT,DC=Reskit,DC=Org
RLT            CN=Rebecca Lee-Tanner,OU=IT,DC=Reskit,DC=Org
ThomasL        CN=ThomasL,OU=IT,DC=Reskit,DC=Org
```

Figure 3.28: Viewing group membership

As you run the scripts in this section, it can also be handy to have the Active Directory Users and Computers MMC console open and available. This makes it easy to view the results of your scripts. It also allows you to quickly undo anything done incorrectly due, for example, to a typo in your code. As an alternative, you could also use the Active Directory Administrative Center (ADAC) for this purpose. See docs.microsoft.com/en-us/windows-server/identity/ad-ds/ad-ds-getting-started for details on the ADAC.

Adding a Computer to the AD

Adding a computer to an AD is simple and similar to adding a new user or group, as follows:

```
# 16. Add a computer to the AD
$NCHT = @{
  Name                    = 'Wolf'
  DNSHostName             = 'Wolf.Reskit.Org'
  Description             = 'One for Jerry'
  Path                    = 'OU=IT,DC=Reskit,DC=Org'
  OperatingSystemVersion  = 'Windows Server 2019 Data Center'
}
New-ADComputer @NCHT
```

This code adds a single computer, called `Wolf.Reskit.Org`, into the IT OU.

For the computer to utilize the AD domain, you also need to update the computer to be a member of the domain. Adding the computer first, known as *pre-staging*, requires administrative privilege, but once a computer has been added to AD, you can then join that computer to the AD without needing elevated credentials. You can find more details in this article: `websistent.com/how-to-prestage-a-computer-in-active-directory/`. The article is several years old, but the principles it covers remain valid.

Displaying Computers in an AD Domain

The final step in this demonstration of managing AD users, computers, and OUs is to get and output the names of the computers in your AD domain and the last time they were logged on, as follows:

```
# 17. See the computer accounts
Get-ADComputer -Filter * -Properties DNSHostName,LastLogonDate |
  Format-Table -Property Name, DNSHostName,LastLogonDate
```

The output from this step, in Figure 3.29, shows the computers currently contained in the `Reskit.Org` domain. Depending on your needs, you may want to adjust the properties you display.

```
PS C:\Foo> # 17. See the computer accounts
PS C:\Foo> Get-ADComputer -Filter * -Properties DNSHostName,LastLogonDate |
            Format-Table -Property Name, DNSHostName,LastLogonDate

Name  DNSHostName       LastLogonDate
----  -----------       -------------
DC1   DC1.Reskit.Org    06/01/2020 12:37:22
DC2   DC2.Reskit.Org    06/01/2020 12:44:30
Wolf  Wolf.Reskit.Org
```

Figure 3.29: Viewing computers in the AD

Note that the Wolf computer you added in the previous step shows no last logon date, since no one has yet logged on to this host. Also remember that the value for the `LastLogonDate` property can be off by up to 14 days. For more information, see blogs.technet.microsoft.com/askds/2009/04/15/the-lastlogontimestamp-attribute-what-it-was-designed-for-and-how-it-works/.

The code snippets in this section have demonstrated how you can use the PowerShell cmdlets to add/remove/update objects in the AD including computers, OUs, and users.

Adding Users to AD via a CSV

In "Managing AD Users, Computers, and OUs," you saw how you can use PowerShell 7 to add/remove/update objects in the AD. In production, you may need to automate the regular changes to AD. In almost all organizations, users and computers come, change, and go. Most organizations try to automate those regular changes.

How to automate the regular changes is a popular question in many support forums, such as the PowerShell forum on Spiceworks (`community.spiceworks .com/programming/powershell`). A common question is how to add users to AD using a CSV file.

In many organizations, an enterprise resource planning (ERP) tool, such as SAP, might hold the master copy of user details. Any changes to that information are made within the ERP system, which can then create a CSV file containing the information to be updated in other systems (such as AD). In a smaller organization, those details might be contained in a CSV file originating from the HR department using an Excel spreadsheet.

The basic concept is that the CSV file contains a collection of users to be added (or changed/removed). When you import the CSV file into PowerShell, you create objects that represent user properties, including name, password, and so on.

There are some user properties that are always required to add a user into the AD; the password, for example. Others, such as office name or phone number, are optional. Some organizations make use of a large number of AD User attributes; others use only the bare minimum. You can easily tailor your CSV files and the scripts that process them to meet the needs of your organization.

Before You Start

In this example you build a simple CSV file and then use it to create users in the Reskit.Org domain. You run the script on the DC1.Reskit.Org host. This host is a domain controller you created in "Establishing a Forest Root Domain" and have used throughout this chapter.

Creating a CSV File

The first step in this process is to create a CSV file. This file contains the basic information about each user to be added to the AD. It looks like this:

```
# 1 Create CSV
$CSVDATA = @'
Firstname, Initials, Lastname, UserPrincipalName, Alias, Description,
Password
S,K,Masterly, SKM, Sylvester, Data Team, Christmas42
C,B, Smith, CBS, Claire, Receptionist, Christmas42
Billy, Bob, JoeBob, BBJB, BillyBob, A Bob, Christmas42
Malcolm, Dudley, Duelittle, Malcolm, Malcolm, Mr Danger, Christmas42
'@
$CSVDATA | Out-File -FilePath C:\Foo\Users.Csv
```

This CSV file contains seven properties, including a plain-text password to be assigned to the user. If you want to include more information about each user in the AD, such as office phone number, you can add additional columns to the CSV file.

Importing and Viewing the CSV

With the CSV file created, the next step is to import it and, optionally, display the input data, as follows:

```
# 2. Import a CSV file containing the details of the users you
#    want to add to AD:
$Users = Import-CSV -Path C:\Foo\Users.Csv |
  Sort-Object -Property Alias
$Users | Format-Table
```

This creates the $Users array that contains the values for properties of the users to be added. You can see the output generated by this step in Figure 3.30.

```
PS C:\Foo> # 2. Import a CSV file containing the details of the users you
PS C:\Foo> #    want to add to AD:
PS C:\Foo> $Users = Import-CSV -Path C:\Foo\Users.Csv |
            Sort-Object  -Property Alias
PS C:\Foo> $Users | Format-Table


Firstname Initials Lastname  UserPrincipalName Alias     Description  Password
--------- -------- --------  ----------------- -----     -----------  --------
Billy     Bob      JoeBob    BBJB              BillyBob  A Bob        Christmas42
C         B        Smith     CBS               Claire    Receptionist Christmas42
Malcolm   Dudley   Duelittle Malcolm           Malcolm   Mr Danger    Christmas42
S         K        Masterly  SKM               Sylvester Data Team    Christmas42
```

Figure 3.30: Viewing users to be added to AD

When you import a CSV file, PowerShell converts the file into an array of the type System.Management.Automation.PSCustomObject. Each object is created with a NoteProperty representing each column in the CSV file. These properties are defined as being strings set to the appropriate values from the CSV file. You can view these details by piping the variable $Users to Get-Member.

Adding Users to AD

To add the users to AD, you just iterate over the array of users, and for each user you create a hash table of user properties and then call New-ADuser to add the user, as follows:

```
# 3. Add the users using the CSV
$Users |
  ForEach-Object -Parallel {
    $User = $_
    #  Create a hash table of properties to set on created user
    $Prop = @{}
    #  Fill in values
    $Prop.GivenName         = $User.Firstname
    $Prop.Initials          = $User.Initials
    $Prop.Surname           = $User.Lastname
    $Prop.UserPrincipalName = $User.UserPrincipalName + "@Reskit.Org"
    $Prop.Displayname       = $User.FirstName.Trim() + " " +
                              $User.LastName.Trim()
    $Prop.Description        = $User.Description
    $Prop.Name               = $User.Alias
    $PW = ConvertTo-SecureString -AsPlainText $User.Password -Force
    $Prop.AccountPassword    = $PW
    $Prop.ChangePasswordAtLogon = $true
    $Prop.Path               = 'OU=IT,DC=Reskit,DC=ORG'
    $Prop.Enabled            = $true
    #  Now Create the User
    New-ADUser @Prop
    # Finally, Display User Created
    "Created $($Prop.Name)"
  }
```

You can see the results of this step in Figure 3.31. The New-ADUser command does not produce output, so the output is generated by this snippet explicitly.

Viewing All Users in Reskit.Org

Having created some additional users, you can view all the users in the Reskit .Org domain, as follows:

```
# 4. Show All Users in AD (Reskit.Org)
Get-Aduser -Filter * |
  Format-Table -Property Name, UserPrincipalName
```

```
PS C:\Foo> # 3. Add the users using the CSV
PS C:\Foo> ForEach ($User in $Users) {
PS C:\Foo> #    Create a hash table of properties to set on created user
PS C:\Foo> $Prop = @{}
PS C:\Foo> #    Fill in values
PS C:\Foo> $Prop.GivenName          = $User.Firstname
PS C:\Foo> $Prop.Initials           = $User.Initials
PS C:\Foo> $Prop.Surname            = $User.Lastname
PS C:\Foo> $Prop.UserPrincipalName = $User.UserPrincipalName + "@Reskit.Org"
PS C:\Foo> $Prop.Displayname        = $User.FirstName.Trim() + " " +
                                      $User.LastName.Trim()
PS C:\Foo> $Prop.Description         = $User.Description
PS C:\Foo> $Prop.Name                = $User.Alias
PS C:\Foo> $PW = ConvertTo-SecureString -AsPlainText $User.Password -Force
PS C:\Foo> $Prop.AccountPassword     = $PW
PS C:\Foo> $Prop.ChangePasswordAtLogon = $true
PS C:\Foo> $Prop.Path                 = 'OU=IT,DC=Reskit,DC=ORG'
PS C:\Foo> $Prop.Enabled             = $true
PS C:\Foo> #    Now create the user
PS C:\Foo> New-ADUser @Prop
PS C:\Foo> #   Finally, display user created
PS C:\Foo> "Created $($Prop.Name)"
PS C:\Foo> }

Created BillyBob
Created Claire
Created Malcolm
Created Sylvester
```

Figure 3.31: Creating new users

You can view the output from this snippet in Figure 3.32.

```
PS C:\Foo> # 4. Show All Users in AD (Reskit.Org)
PS C:\Foo> Get-Aduser -Filter * |
             Format-Table -Property Name, UserPrincipalName

Name                UserPrincipalName
----                -----------------
Administrator
Guest
krbtgt
UK$
KAPOHO$
ThomasL             ThomasL@Reskit.Org
Rebecca Lee-Tanner  RLT@Reskit.Org
Jerry Garcia        jerryg@Reskit.Org
BillyBob            BBJB@Reskit.Org
Claire              CBS@Reskit.Org
Malcolm             Malcolm@Reskit.Org
Sylvester           SKM@Reskit.Org
```

Figure 3.32: Viewing all users

CSV files are flexible as input to scripts that manage AD objects. You can adopt the approach shown in this section when removing users such as a user who has left the organization. Create a file of users to be removed, and your script can remove them or move them to an "Ex-Employee" group as dictated by your policies. You can also use this technique for adding groups to the AD. Just create a CSV file of groups and then adjust this script to add the new AD groups.

This snippet uses an important new PowerShell 7 feature, which is the `-Parallel` parameter to `Foreach-Object`. This snippet runs user creation in parallel. In this case, where you are adding just four users to AD on the DC, using this construct is actually just a bit slower than not using `-Parallel`. However, this construct can be more useful were you to run this script on a client system where there were network latencies to consider, or where each iteration did more than just add a new user (such as adding the user to a group, creating files, and so on).

Configuring Just Enough Administration (JEA)

Managing rights and permissions can be complex even in smaller organizations. In all too many organizations, administrators of all sorts are just dropped into high-privilege groups such as Domain Administrators or Enterprise Administrators. That can make jobs easier, but it also opens up all sorts of potential security holes.

Just Enough Administration (JEA) is a tool to enable you to implement fine-grained administrative delegation, ensuring that a user has just enough privilege to do their job and not a bit more. JEA uses PowerShell remoting to define which users are in a specific role and what that role can do within a remoting session.

With JEA, for example, you can allow your DNS administrators to enter a remoting session on a domain controller and manage the DNS service (and very little more). Even though a user is in a remoting session on a DC, with JEA they would be unaware that other commands exist and would not be able to use them.

There are three distinct objects involved with JEA. To deploy JEA you need to develop each of these:

JEA role capabilities file: This file, essentially a PowerShell hash table stored with the extension `.PSRC`, defines a role in terms of the aliases, commands, functions, providers, and external programs an administrator can use within a JEA session. A PSRC files resembles a PowerShell module manifest.

JEA session configuration file: This file, stored with the extension `.PSSC`, defines how a JEA endpoint is configured. It states the users (groups) that can use the endpoint, a JEA session, and the roles to which they have access.

JEA-based remoting endpoint: This is a remoting endpoint that your restricted user accesses. The endpoint enables role users to access a constrained remoting endpoint based on the session configuration file.

Once you have the two files in place, you register the JEA-based endpoint to the server based on the session configuration.

A JEA user can enter a PowerShell remoting session or invoke commands in a remoting session specifying the constrained endpoint. PowerShell uses the user's group membership to determine the role involved and configures the PowerShell session based on the role capabilities file for that role.

Before You Start

In this example, you implement JEA on a domain controller, DC1, which you have used throughout this chapter. You created this host as a domain controller in "Establishing a Forest Root Domain."

You also need to create or use the AD user JerryG. You also need to make this user a member of the RKDnsAdmins group. You created the user and added the account to the group in "Managing AD Users, Groups, and Computers."

Creating a Transcript Folder

A useful feature of JEA is the use of PowerShell transcripts. With JEA, PowerShell can create a session transcript for any JEA session automatically. You first create a new folder to hold the transcripts, as follows:

```
# 1. Create transcripts folder
New-Item -Path C:\JEATranscripts -ItemType Directory | Out-Null
```

Creating a Role Capabilities Folder

The role capabilities file defines the capabilities of a role. While you can store that file anywhere, it's good security to store it in a specific folder, as follows:

```
# 2. Create capabilities folder
$JEACF = "C:\JEACapabilities"
New-Item -Path $JEACF -ItemType Directory | Out-Null
```

You might also want to restrict access to files in this folder.

Creating a Role Capabilities File

Next, you create a role capabilities file. The role capabilities file defines what a user in a role is allowed to do within a remoting session. You create a new JEA role capabilities file as follows:

```
# 3. Create Role Capabilities File
$RCF = Join-Path -Path $JEACF -ChildPath "RKDnsAsmins.psrc"
$RCHT = @{
  Path             = $RCF
  Author           = 'Reskit Administration'
  CompanyName      = 'Reskit.Org'
  Description      = 'Defines RKDnsAdmins role capabilities'
  AliasDefinition  = @{Name='gh';Value='Get-Help'}
  ModulesToImport  = 'Microsoft.PowerShell.Core','DnsServer'
  VisibleCmdlets   = ("Restart-Service",
```

Continues

continued

```
                        @{ Name       = "Restart-Computer";
                           Parameters = @{Name = "ComputerName"}
                           ValidateSet = 'DC1, DC2'},
                         'DNSSERVER\*')
    VisibleExternalCommands = ('C:\Windows\System32\whoami.exe')
    VisibleFunctions = 'Get-HW'
    FunctionDefinitions = @{
      Name = 'Get-HW'
      Scriptblock = {'Hello JEA World'}}
  }
  New-PSRoleCapabilityFile @RCHT
```

The role capabilities defined in this file enable a DNS admin to do all of the following:

- Use gh as an alias to Get-Help.
- Automatically have the remoting session started with the DNSServer module imported.
- Use the Restart-Service command (but not Get-Service).
- Use the Restart-Computer, but only to restart DC1 or DC1.
- Use any command in the DNSServer module.
- Use the console application whoami.exe.
- Use a new function called Get-HW (whose definition you can see in the role capabilities file).

Creating a JEA Session Configuration File

The JEA *session configuration* file is used by PowerShell to associate groups (such as the RKDnsAdmins group) whose members use a specific role (such as the RKDNSAdmins role). You can also configure some additional aspects of a JEA remoting session, as follows:

```
# 4. Create a JEA Session Configuration file
$SCF = 'C:\JEASessionConfiguration'
New-Item -Path $SCF -ItemType Directory | Out-Null
$P   = Join-Path -Path $SCF -ChildPath 'RKDnsAdmins.pssc'
$RDHT = @{
  'Reskit\RKDnsAdmins' = @{'RoleCapabilityFiles' =
                          'C:\JEACapabilities\RKDnsAsmins.psrc'}
}
$PSCHT= @{
  Author             = 'DoctorDNS@Gmail.Com'
  Description        = 'Session Definition for RKDnsAdmins'
  SessionType        = 'RestrictedRemoteServer'   # ie JEA!
  Path               = $P                         # the output file
  RunAsVirtualAccount = $true
```

```
        TranscriptDirectory = 'C:\ JeaTranscripts'
        RoleDefinitions     = $RDHT      # RKDnsAdmins role mapping
    }
    New-PSSessionConfigurationFile @PSCHT
```

The session configuration file's session type indicates that the remoting session is based on JEA. The configuration also tells PowerShell that the user identity in the session is based on a temporary account unique to a specific user and valid for only the duration of a JEA session.

For more details on the session configuration file, see docs.microsoft.com/ powershell/scripting/learn/remoting/jea/session-configurations.

This session configuration file also sets up a Transcripts folder. This enables PowerShell to create a transcript of all commands within a JEA session and store that in the specified folder. These transcripts are of the same type as created by the Start-Transcript command (see docs.microsoft.com/powershell/ module/microsoft.powershell.host/Start-Transcript?view=powershell-7 for more details on Start-Transcript). With JEA, PowerShell creates a transcript covering the entire JEA session.

Testing the Session Configuration File

It is useful to use Test-PSSessionConfiguration to test the session configuration file to ensure that it is properly formatted. This command ensures that you have valid keys in the session configuration file and that values are the correct type. You can do this as follows:

```
    # 5. Test the session configuration file
    Test-PSSessionConfigurationFile -Path $P
```

You can see the output of this command in Figure 3.33.

```
PS C:\Foo> # 5. Test the session configuration file
PS C:\Foo> Test-PSSessionConfigurationFile –Path $P
True
```

Figure 3.33: Testing the session configuration file

As you can see, Test-PSSessionConfigurationFile does not return a lot of information about what has been checked. However, if there are issues in the session configuration file, these are noted when you test the file.

Enabling Remoting and Creating the JEA Session Endpoint

Now that you have your JEA role and session configuration specified, you can create the JEA session endpoint. Before doing that, you enable PowerShell remoting explicitly using `Enable-PSRemoting`. Then you create the JEA endpoint using `Register-PSSessionConfiguration`, like this:

```
# 6. Enable Remoting and register the JEA Session Definition
Enable-PSRemoting -Force | Out-Null
$SCHT = @{
  Path  = $P
  Name  = 'RKDnsAdmins'
  Force = $true
}
Register-PSSessionConfiguration @SCHT
```

Figure 3.34 shows the output from running this snippet.

```
PS C:\Foo> # 6. Enable Remoting and Register the JEA Session Definition
PS C:\Foo> Enable-PSRemoting -Force |  Out-Null
WARNING: PowerShell remoting has been enabled only for PowerShell 6+ configurations
and does not affect Windows PowerShell remoting configurations. Run this cmdlet in
Windows PowerShell to affect all PowerShell remoting configurations.

PS C:\Foo> $SCHT = @{
            Path  = $P
            Name  = 'RKDnsAdmins'
            Force = $true
           }
PS C:\Foo> Register-PSSessionConfiguration @SCHT

  WSManConfig: Microsoft.WSMan.Management\WSMan::localhost\Plugin

Type       Keys                  Name
----       ----                  ----
Container  {Name=RKDnsAdmins}    RKDnsAdmins
```

Figure 3.34: Registering the session configuration file

This command creates a new remoting endpoint that provides a JEA environment for DNS administration.

Checking What the User Can Do

You can use the command `Get-PSSessionCapability` to determine what a user (in the `RKdnsAdmins` group) can do within a JEA remoting session, like this:

```
# 7. Check What the User Can Do
Get-PSSessionCapability -ConfigurationName RKDnsAdmins -Username
'Reskit\JerryG' |
  Sort-Object -Property Module
```

You can see the output from these commands in Figure 3.35.

```
PS C:\Foo> # 7. Check What The User Can Do
PS C:\Foo> Get-PSSessionCapability -ConfigurationName RKDnsAdmins -Username 'Reskit\JerryG' |
            Sort-Object -PropertyModule

CommandType    Name                              Version   Source
-----------    ----                              -------   ------
Alias          clear -> Clear-Hostcc
Function       Select-Object
Function       Restart-Computer
Function       Out-Default
Function       Measure-Object
Function       Get-HW
Function       Get-Help
Function       Get-FormatData
Cmdlet         Restart-Service                   7.0.0.0   Microsoft.PowerShell.Management
Function       Get-Command
Function       Exit-PSSession
Function       Clear-Host
Application    whoami.exe                        10.0.1776… C:\Windows\system32\whoami.exe
Alias          gh -> Get-Help
Alias          gcm -> Get-Command
Alias          measure -> Measure-Object
Alias          select -> Select-Object
Alias          exsn -> Exit-PSSession
Alias          cls -> Clear-Host
Function       Add-DnsServerRecursionScope       2.0.0.0   DnsServer
...   <Remainder of Commands from DnsServer module snipped for brevity>
```

Figure 3.35: Determining session capabilities

To save space in this book, the output shows only some of the commands available in the JEA session.

Creating Credentials for JerryG

With JEA set up, you can test it by running script blocks in a JEA session; but to do that, you need a credential object. You create credentials for a user who is in the RKDNSAdmins group using the following commands:

```
# 8. Create Credentials for user JerryG
$U    = 'JerryG@Reskit.Org'
$P    = ConvertTo-SecureString 'Pa$$w0rd' -AsPlainText -Force
$Cred = [PSCredential]::New($U,$P)
```

Creating Three Script Blocks to Test JEA

To test that JEA is delivering what you expected, you can try to run some simple scripts inside a JEA session, as follows:

```
# 9. Define Three Script Blocks and an Invocation Splatting Hash Table
$SB1   = {Get-Command}
$SB2   = {Get-HW}
$SB3   = {Get-Command -Module 'DNSSERVER'}
$ICMHT = @{
```

Continues

continued

```
ComputerName       = 'DC1.Reskit.Org'
Credential         = $Cred
ConfigurationName = 'RKDnsAdmins' }
```

This snippet creates three script blocks:

$SB1	This script block gets all the commands (that is, all the commands the JEA session provides to the user).
$SB2	This script block runs the Get-HW function.
$SB3	This block shows the commands that are in the DNSServer module and that are available to the JEA user.

These three script blocks test the capabilities that are provided to a DNS admin within the JEA session on DC1.

How Many Commands Exist in a JEA Session?

A test of JEA is to show the commands that are available within a JEA session. To achieve that, you execute the $SB1 script block within a remoting session using the newly created JEA endpoint. You can do that as follows:

```
# 10. Get commands available within the JEA session
Invoke-Command -ScriptBlock $SB1 @ICMHT |
  Sort-Object -Property Module |
    Select-Object -First 15
```

This snippet gets details of all the commands available within the JEA session, sorts them by module name, and then selects the first 15 commands. You can view the output in Figure 3.36.

```
PS C:\Foo> # 10. Get commands available within the JEA session
PS C:\Foo> Invoke-Command -ScriptBlock $SB1 @ICMHT |
            Sort-Object -Property Module |
            Select-Object -First 15


CommandType     Name                              Version    Source                          PSComputerName
-----------     ----                              -------    ------                          --------------
Function        Get-HW                                                                       DC1.Reskit.Org
Function        Select-Object                                                                DC1.Reskit.Org
Function        Restart-Computer                                                             DC1.Reskit.Org
Function        Out-Default                                                                  DC1.Reskit.Org
Function        Measure-Object                                                               DC1.Reskit.Org
Function        Get-Help                                                                     DC1.Reskit.Org
Function        Get-FormatData                                                               DC1.Reskit.Org
Function        Get-Command                                                                  DC1.Reskit.Org
Function        Exit-PSSession                                                               DC1.Reskit.Org
Function        Clear-Host                                                                   DC1.Reskit.Org
Cmdlet          Restart-Service                   7.0.0.0    Microsoft.PowerShell.Management  DC1.Reskit.Org
Function        Add-DnsServerResourceRecordDnsKey  2.0.0.0    DnsServer                       DC1.Reskit.Org
Function        Set-DnsServerDnsSecZoneSetting    2.0.0.0    DnsServer                       DC1.Reskit.Org
Function        Set-DnsServerDiagnostics          2.0.0.0    DnsServer                       DC1.Reskit.Org
Function        Set-DnsServerConditionalForwarderZone  2.0.0.0  DnsServer                    DC1.Reskit.Org
```

Figure 3.36: Checking on commands in the JEA session

You can see all the non-DNS commands available plus the first few from the DNSServer module. You can see in this list the Get-HW function defined only for this endpoint.

Invoking a JEA-Defined Function

In the role capabilities file, you defined a function, Get-HW, which is to be available within the JEA session. You can do this by invoking $SB2 in a JEA session, as follows:

```
# 11. Invoke a JEA Defined Function in a JEA Session as JerryG
Invoke-Command -ScriptBlock $SB2 @ICMHT
```

You can see the output in Figure 3.37.

```
PS C:\Foo> # 11. Invoke a JEA defined function in a JEA Ssession As JerryG
PS C:\Foo> Invoke-Command -ScriptBlock $SB2 @ICMHT
Hello JEA World
```

Figure 3.37: Invoking a JEA-defined function

Get the DNSServer Command Available in JEA Session

As a final test of JEA, you can obtain a count of how many commands are available in the JEA session and provided by the DNSServer module. You do that by invoking the $SB3 script block, as follows:

```
# 12. Get DNSServer commands available to JerryG
$C = Invoke-Command -ScriptBlock $SB3 @ICMHT
"$($C.Count) DNS commands available"
```

You can see the output of this command in Figure 3.38.

```
PS C:\Foo> # 12. Get DNSServer commands available to JerryG
PS C:\Foo> $C = Invoke-Command -ScriptBlock $SB3 @ICMHT
PS C:\Foo> "$($C.Count) DNS commands available"
131 DNS commands available
```

Figure 3.38: Counting DNS server commands available

Viewing the Transcripts Folder

In the session configuration file, you instructed PowerShell to create PowerShell transcripts for each JEA session. You can view the contents of the transcript folder as follows:

```
# 13. Examine the Contents of the Transcripts Folder:
Get-ChildItem -Path $PSCHT.TranscriptDirectory
```

You can view the output of this snippet in Figure 3.39.

```
PS C:\Foo> # 13. Examine the contents of the Transcripts folder:
PS C:\Foo> Get-ChildItem -Path $PSCHT.TranscriptDirectory

    Directory: C:\JEATranscripts

Mode          LastWriteTime  Length Name
----          -------------  ------ ----
-a---   17/03/2020    13:46     796 PowerShell_transcript.DC1.fmQ8QvFr.20200317134648.txt
-a---   17/03/2020    11:37   13175 PowerShell_transcript.DC1.tNpVHpEO.20200317113549.txt
-a---   17/03/2020    13:49   12836 PowerShell_transcript.DC1.W2L0ptea.20200317134802.txt
```

Figure 3.39: Viewing the JEA `Transcripts` folder

As you can see, there are three transcript files in the folder, one for each of the three script blocks you just ran. Because each session was short, these transcripts are also quite short. If users run long sessions, these transcript files can grow. If you are going to generate transcripts, you should ensure that older transcript files are removed.

Examining a JEA Transcript

Each transcript in the transcript folder holds details of everything that happens within the JEA session. You can examine the transcript generated when you ran the first script block, as follows:

```
# 14. Examine a transcript
Get-ChildItem -Path $PSCHT.TranscriptDirectory |
   Select-Object -First 1 |
      Get-Content
```

You can see the output of this snippet in Figure 3.40.

Depending on how many transcripts you have, you may need to adjust this snippet to ensure you are looking at the correct transcript.

In the figure, you see the results of running $SB2 in the JEA session. That script block called the Get-HW function, which in turn displayed the text Hello JEA World. In the transcript, you can see the start and end times for the session, the user who ran the script, and details about the environment and about every command run in the session.

If the JEA endpoint is used heavily, then the size of the transcript directory can grow. As with all logging, you should have a strategy for managing the JEA transcripts.

```
# 14. Examine a transcript

PS C:\Foo> Get-ChildItem -Path $PSCHT.TranscriptDirectory |
            Select-Object -First 1 |
                Get-Content
************************
PowerShell transcript start
Start time: 20200317134648
Username: RESKIT\JerryG
RunAs User: WinRM Virtual Users\WinRM VA_2_RESKIT_JerryG
Configuration Name: RKDnsAdmins
Machine: DC1 (Microsoft Windows NT 10.0.17763.0)
Host Application: C:\Windows\system32\wsmprovhost.exe -Embedding
Process ID: 5628
PSVersion: 7.0.0
PSEdition: Core
GitCommitId: 7.0.0
OS: Microsoft Windows 10.0.17763
Platform: Win32NT
PSCompatibleVersions: 1.0, 2.0, 3.0, 4.0, 5.0, 5.1.10032.0, 6.0.0, 6.1.0, 6.2.0, 7.0.0
PSRemotingProtocolVersion: 2.3
SerializationVersion: 1.1.0.1
WSManStackVersion: 3.0
************************
PS>CommandInvocation(Get-HW): "Get-HW"
Hello JEA World
************************
PowerShell transcript end
End time: 20200317134648
```

Figure 3.40: Viewing a JEA transcript

Summary

In this chapter, you examined some of the key AD-related actions you might need to perform using PowerShell 7. Two modules, Server Manager and the AD Deployment, both do not natively load PowerShell 7. Instead, you need to use the Windows PowerShell compatibility mechanism discussed in Chapter 2. You use `Import-Module` to load these two modules, allowing access to the commands they contain. The Active Directory module, on the other hand, works natively in PowerShell 7.

Managing Networking

Networking is fundamental to all organizations. Your servers and client systems communicate with each other via your network. Your users access a myriad of devices via your internal networks. Your internal networks connect to the Internet to help your users and customers interact. It is no surprise that PowerShell supports you in configuring and managing your network.

Networking has been built into Windows more or less since its beginning. Windows for Workgroups 3.11 contained built-in networking, as did Windows NT 3.1. But the later versions of NT (including Windows 10 and Windows Server 2019) come with a TCP/IP stack that supports both IPv4 and IPv6.

This chapter looks at how to use PowerShell to configure a network, how to test for network connectivity, and how to set up, configure, and manage both Dynamic Host Configuration Protocol (DHCP) and Domain Name Service (DNS).

- When you first install Windows on a computer, the setup program does a good job of detecting your network cards and setting default settings. By default, each NIC is configured to get its IP address via DHCP. This means you install Windows, plug the system into the network, and the DHCP clients configure IP addressing and DNS details automatically. But sometimes you need to set an IP address explicitly, as shown in the "Configuring IP Addressing" section.

- An important setup step for troubleshooting is to ensure that each host has full network connectivity to other systems either inside your network or externally. You should do this before adding applications and services to a server. In "Testing Network Connectivity," you see how to detect issues with connection to remote systems and services.

■ To simplify the connection of client computers and devices to the organization's network, you install a DHCP server. As you see in "Installing the DHCP Service," setting up DHCP is simple and straightforward.

■ Once your DHCP server is installed, you need to configure scopes, as described in "Configuring DHCP Scopes." A *scope* is a set of addresses your DHCP server can provide to the DHCP client along with a set of options and option values that you use to configure your DHCP clients. Options include a default gateway IP address and the address(es) of your DNS servers. You can configure options at the scope level (giving these option values to addresses provided within the scope) or at the server level (using the DHCP server to provide server options to any address the server provides), or a combination of both.

■ Because your clients rely on DHCP for obtaining IP network configuration details, any outage could stop those clients from networking. For larger organizations it might also be useful to have some performance load balancing to handle peak DHCP load. To support the load balancing and resiliency requirements, you use the DHCP server's failover and load balancing features, as described in "Configuring DHCP Failover."

■ After your systems get their IP configuration (either statically or via DHCP), to communicate with other hosts, you must provide a DNS service to do your name resolution, turning host names such as DC1.Reskit.Org into an IP address. Once the host resolves the IP address, the TCP/IP stack can connect to the remote system and interoperate with the remote host. As you see in "Implement a Standalone DNS Server," adding DNS to Windows Server 2019 is simple.

■ Likewise, configuring DNS zones and resource records is simple, as shown in "Configuring DNS Server Zones and Resource Records."

Systems Used in This Chapter

In this chapter, you use PowerShell 7 to manage various networking aspects. The scripts in this chapter make use of the following servers:

SRV2.Reskit.Org: You configure the IP address of this server with a static IP address. You also use this host to test DHCP IP address configuration.

DC1.Reskit.Org and DC2.Reskit.Org: You set up DHCP on these servers. In Chapter 3, DC1 provided DNS services for the Reskit.Org domain. This chapter extends the DNS service.

For the purposes of this chapter, you should ensure that DNS is set up and working on this server (Chapter 3, "Managing Active Directory," shows how to set up DNS Servers while installing Active Directory).

Figure 4.1 shows the systems in use in this chapter.

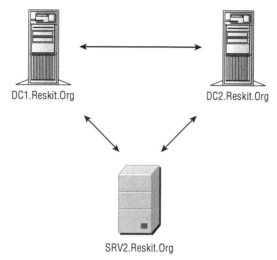

DC1.Reskit.Org   DC2.Reskit.Org

SRV2.Reskit.Org

Figure 4.1: Systems used in this chapter

You also need to have PowerShell 7 and, optionally, Visual Studio Code (VS Code) installed on each host. You can use the scripts shown in Chapter 1 for this purpose.

Configuring IP Addressing

The setup process you use when you install Windows on any host does a great job of detecting the network adapters built into your system's "hardware." That includes both the physical hardware components in your computer and any virtual hardware you provision inside a virtual machine. In both cases, after the setup process has completed, your NICs are detected and set to get their IP address and other configuration details via DHCP.

If you are installing client computers, this is a great default—install Windows, and networking just works. Server systems, however, generally need to be configured manually, as we do in this chapter's first example. Some organizations use DHCP to assign IP configuration to server systems but make use of a DHCP reservation. Each server gets its correct address with the configured DHCP options. This chapter does not show that approach.

Before You Start

You run the code in this section on SRV2.Reskit.Org, which you build using Windows Server 2019 installed with the Desktop Experience feature. As noted earlier, the default Windows Server Installation sets the server's single NIC to get IP address information from DHCP. If you created the SRV2 server using the Reskit build scripts on GitHub (github.com/doctordns/ReskitBuildScripts), then you would have set up SRV2 to have a static IP address. In this case, before running the following code, you can use ncpa.cpl to change the IPv4 settings to get an address from DHCP.

You also need to have PowerShell 7 and, optionally, VS Code installed on all systems.

Checking Adapter Details

Before updating your server's IP address, it is useful to check the current state of the network adapter. You can do this as follows:

```
# 1. Get the adapter, adapter Interface and Adapter Interface Index
#    for later use
$IPType = 'IPv4'
$Adapter = Get-NetAdapter |
  Where-Object Status -eq 'Up'
$Interface = $Adapter |
  Get-NetIPInterface -AddressFamily $IPType
$Index = $Interface.IfIndex
Get-NetIPAddress -InterfaceIndex $Index -AddressFamily $IPType |
  Format-Table -Property Interface*, IPAddress, PrefixLength
```

This code returns the IP address details shown in Figure 4.2. Note that with no DHCP server on the network and the VM configured to use any virtual switch but the default, the IP address for SRV2 is in the 169.254.0.0/16 network range (also known as automatic private IP addressing, or APIPA, range).

```
PS C:\Foo> # 1. Get the adapter, adapter Interface and Adapter Interface Index
PS C:\Foo> #    for later use
PS C:\Foo> $IPType  = 'IPv4'
PS C:\Foo> $Adapter = Get-NetAdapter |
             Where-Object Status -eq 'Up'
PS C:\Foo> $Interface = $Adapter |
             Get-NetIPInterface -AddressFamily $IPType
PS C:\Foo> $Index = $Interface.IfIndex
PS C:\Foo> Get-NetIPAddress -InterfaceIndex $Index -AddressFamily $IPType |
             Format-Table -Property Interface*, IPAddress, PrefixLength


InterfaceAlias InterfaceIndex IPAddress      PrefixLength
-------------- -------------- ---------      ------------
Ethernet                    6 169.254.175.44           16
```

Figure 4.2: IP address details returned after checking the current state

As mentioned earlier, by default the Windows setup process detects each NIC in the host and configures it to get IPv4 configuration via DHCP. And by default, when creating a new VM, Hyper-V adds a single NIC to the VM, which it sets to get an IPv4 address via DHCP. If you used the Reskit build scripts in GitHub (`github.com/doctordns/ReskitBuildScripts`), the scripts assign a static IPv4 address to this host. Consider using `ncpa.cpl` to reset the NIC to the default of getting IPv4 configuration details from DHCP.

Configuring an IP Address

Once you confirm that the server's NIC is set to DHCP, use the following code to configure the NIC to have a specific IPv4 address, subnet, and default gateway:

```
# 2. Set a new IP address for the NIC, and then check it
$IPHT = @{
  InterfaceIndex = $Index
  PrefixLength   = 24
  IPAddress      = '10.10.10.51'
  DefaultGateway = '10.10.10.254'
  AddressFamily  = $IPType    # IPv4
}
New-NetIPAddress @IPHT | Out-Null
```

This sets the NIC's IP address and subnet mask. It can take a few seconds to create this new address.

Verifying the New IP Address

You can use the `Get-NetIPAddress` command to verify the new IP address, as follows:

```
# 3. Verify the new IP address
Get-NetIPAddress -InterfaceIndex $Index -AddressFamily $IPType |
    Format-Table IPAddress, InterfaceIndex, PrefixLength
```

Figure 4.3 shows the output from this snippet.

```
PS C:\Foo> # 3. Verify the new IP Address
PS C:\Foo> Get-NetIPAddress -InterfaceIndex $Index -AddressFamily $IPType |
           Format-Table IPAddress, InterfaceIndex, PrefixLength

IPAddress    InterfaceIndex PrefixLength
---------    -------------- ------------
10.10.10.51               6           24
```

Figure 4.3: Verifying the NIC IP address

You should now see the specified IPv4 address of 10.10.10.51 and no longer an IP address in the APIPA range.

Setting DNS Server Details

Using the `New-NetIPAddress` cmdlet only sets the NIC's IP address, subnet mask, and default gateway. You also need to configure the NIC to use a specific IP address for the DNS server as follows:

```
# 4. Set DNS Server IP address
$CAHT = @{
    InterfaceIndex  = $Index
    ServerAddresses = '10.10.10.10'
}
Set-DnsClientServerAddress @CAHT
```

Validating the New IP Configuration

Once you complete these steps, you can validate your IP address settings as well as do some basic connectivity testing, with the following code:

```
# 5. Verify the New IP configuration
# Verify the IPv4 address is set as required
Get-NetIPAddress -InterfaceIndex $Index -AddressFamily IPv4
# Test that SRV2 can see the domain controller
Test-NetConnection -ComputerName DC1.Reskit.Org
# Test the DNS server on DC1.Reskit.Org correctly resolves
# the A record for SRV2.
Resolve-DnsName -Name SRV2.Reskit.Org -Server DC1.Reskit.Org -Type A
```

The output of these three steps looks like Figure 4.4.

```
PS C:\Foo> # 5. Verify the New IP configuration
PS C:\Foo> # Verify the IPv4 address is set as required
PS C:\Foo> Get-NetIPAddress -InterfaceIndex $Index -AddressFamily $IPType |
            Format-Table

ifIndex IPAddress    PrefixLength PrefixOrigin SuffixOrigin AddressState PolicyStore
------- ---------    ------------ ------------ ------------ ------------ -----------
6       10.10.10.51           24 Manual       Manual       Preferred    ActiveStore

PS C:\Foo> # Test that SRV2 can see the domain controller
Test-NetConnection -ComputerName DC1.Reskit.Org |
  Format-Table

ComputerName    RemotePort RemoteAddress PingSucceeded PingReplyDetails (RTT) TcpTestSucceeded
------------    ---------- ------------- ------------- ---------------------- ----------------
DC1.Reskit.Org 0           10.10.10.10   True          0 ms                   False

PS C:\Foo> # Test the DNS server on DC1.Reskit.Org correctly resolves
PS C:\Foo> # the A record for SRV2.
PS C:\Foo> Resolve-DnsName -Name SRV2.Reskit.Org -Server DC1.Reskit.Org -Type 'A'

Name            Type TTL  Section   IPAddress
----            ---- ---  -------   ---------
SRV2.Reskit.Org A    1200 Question  10.10.10.51
```

Figure 4.4: Verifying the new IP configuration

Testing Network Connectivity

Once you have configured networking and an IP address on a system, it is useful to test the connectivity to other servers and services on the network and indeed to the Internet.

Before PowerShell was available, we used tools such as `ipconfig.exe`, `tracert.exe`, `ping.exe`, and `pathping.exe` to test and verify network connectivity. Today, we can use two PowerShell commands: `Test-Connection` and `Test-NetConnection`. These newer commands return objects, which makes automation easier.

`Test-Connection` sends Internet Control Message Protocol (ICMP) Echo Request packets to a remote machine and looks for an ICMP Echo Reply response. The command-line tool `ping.exe` also uses ICMP Echo Request/Reply. This works well on most intranet LANs, but across the Internet or on more secure networks, it may not help because many routers, and hosts, simply drop ICMP Echo requests.

`Test-NetConnection` allows you to test an actual connection to a specific port on the remote server. While a web server or a router might drop ICMP packets, you should be able to connect to that server over specific service-related TCP ports. You can test the connection either with a "well-known" port name (such as SMB for testing SMB connectivity to the remote machine) or with a specific port number.

Before You Start

For this section, you need two systems up and running: `DC1.Reskit.Org` and `SRV2.Reskit.Org`. Note that `SRV2.Reskit.Org` is the system you are testing connectivity from. `DC1.Reskit.Org` is the system you are attempting to connect with. You configured `SRV2.Reskit.Org` with an IP address in "Configuring IP Addressing."

Note also that `SRV2.Reskit.Org` is a domain-joined server in the `Reskit.Org` domain and that `DC1.Reskit.Org` is both a DNS server and a domain controller.

Verifying That SRV2 and Loopback Are Working

One of the first things to verify is whether TCP/IP connectivity to the local loopback address is up and working, using `Test-Connection` and `Test-NetConnection`.

```
# 1. Verify SRV2 itself is up and that loopback is working
Test-Connection -ComputerName SRV2 -Count 1 -IPv4
Test-NetConnection -ComputerName SRV2 -CommonTCPPort WinRM
```

These commands check that the TCP/IP client is working and can connect via the loopback. The output of this step looks like Figure 4.5.

```
PS C:\Foo> # 1. Verify SRV2 itself is up and that loopback is working
PS C:\Foo> Test-Connection -ComputerName SRV2 -Count 1

   Destination: SRV2

Ping Source  Address      Latency BufferSize Status
                          (ms)       (B)
____ _____  _____      _____ _____ _____
   1 SRV2    10.10.10.51        0         32 Success

PS C:\Foo> Test-NetConnection -ComputerName SRV2 -CommonTCPPort WinRM

ComputerName     : SRV2
RemoteAddress    : fe80::99b7:6503:e702:af2c%6
RemotePort       : 5985
InterfaceAlias   : Ethernet
SourceAddress    : fe80::99b7:6503:e702:af2c%6
TcpTestSucceeded : True
```

Figure 4.5: Testing the TCP/IP stack

Note that both commands can, by default, use either IPv4 or IPv6 to test the connection. Test-Connection enables you to specify explicitly to use IPv4 (or IPV6).

Testing Connectivity to the DC

Because SRV2.Reskit.Org is joined to a domain, the next thing to check is that basic connectivity to the domain controller (DC1.Reskit.Org) exists, as follows:

```
# 2. Test Basic Connectivity to the DC
Test-Connection -ComputerName DC1.Reskit.Org -Count 1
```

Assuming the domain controller is up and running, the expected output from this command should resemble Figure 4.6.

```
PS C:\Foo> # 2. Test Basic Connectivity to DC1
PS C:\Foo> Test-Connection -ComputerName DC1.Reskit.Org -Count 1

   Destination: DC1.Reskit.Org

Ping Source  Address      Latency BufferSize Status
                          (ms)       (B)
____ _____  _____      _____ _____ _____
   1 SRV2    10.10.10.10        0         32 Success
```

Figure 4.6: Verifying connectivity to DC1

NOTE   You could configure the host firewall on the DC1.Reskit.Org server to drop ICMP Echo Request packets. Doing so would cause this step to fail (that is, no Echo Reply packets would be returned), even though the DC functions are unaffected.

Checking Connectivity to the SMB and LDAP Ports

For reliable domain operations, SRV2.Reskit.Org needs to be able to connect to the LDAP and SMB ports on the DC. A Windows host also needs SMB access to the domain controller to obtain Group Policy objects, including login scripts. LDAP access is also necessary to enable logon and other domain activities. You can test SMB and LDAP using Test-NetConnection.

```
# 3. Check Connectivity to SMB port and to LDAP port
Test-NetConnection -ComputerName DC1.Reskit.Org -CommonTCPPort SMB
Test-NetConnection -ComputerName DC1.Reskit.Org -Port 389
```

In Figure 4.7, you can see the expected output of these tests.

```
PS C:\Foo> # 3. Check Connectivity to SMP port and to LDAP port
PS C:\Foo> Test-NetConnection -ComputerName DC1.Reskit.Org -CommonTCPPort SMB

ComputerName     : DC1.Reskit.Org
RemoteAddress    : 10.10.10.10
RemotePort       : 445
InterfaceAlias   : Ethernet
SourceAddress    : 10.10.10.51
TcpTestSucceeded : True

PS C:\Foo> Test-NetConnection -ComputerName DC1.Reskit.Org -Port 389

ComputerName     : DC1.Reskit.Org
RemoteAddress    : 10.10.10.10
RemotePort       : 389
InterfaceAlias   : Ethernet
SourceAddress    : 10.10.10.51
TcpTestSucceeded : True
```

Figure 4.7: Verifying SMB/LDAP connectivity to DC1

Examining the Path to a Remote Server

A final test of network connectivity is to verify that the server can see the Internet. Whether or not a given server should be able to access systems on the Internet is a matter of your local policy. For many organizations, however, connectivity might be vital, and you can test using Test-NetConnection and specifying an address somewhere on the Internet. Assuming you have Internet access (an external network adapter) configured, you can test a path as follows:

```
# 4. Examine path to a remote server on the Internet
$NCHT = @{
  ComputerName     = 'WWW.Wiley.Com'
  TraceRoute       = $true
  InformationLevel = 'Detailed'
}
Test-NetConnection @ncht     # Check our wonderful publisher
```

The results of this command may vary significantly (particularly the traceroute section) depending on where you execute it from, but the output should look like Figure 4.8.

```
PS C:\Foo> # 4. Examine path to a remote server on the Internet
PS C:\Foo> $NCHT = @{
             ComputerName      = 'WWW.Wiley.Com'
             TraceRoute        = $true
             InformationLevel  = 'Detailed'
          }
PS C:\Foo> Test-NetConnection @NCHT     # Check our wonderful publisher

ComputerName            : WWW.Wiley.Com
RemoteAddress           : 13.227.170.93
NameResolutionResults   : 13.227.170.93  ←──────────────
                          13.227.170.25  ←──────────────
                          13.227.170.39  ←──────────────
                          13.227.170.61  ←──────────────
InterfaceAlias          : Ethernet 2
SourceAddress           : 10.10.10.51
NetRoute (NextHop)      : 10.10.10.254
PingSucceeded           : True
PingReplyDetails (RTT)  : 7 ms
TraceRoute              : 10.10.10.254
                          51.148.42.43
                          51.148.42.26
                          51.148.42.96
                          51.148.43.107
                          51.142.73.86
                          94.20.182.170
                          0.0.0.0
                          0.0.0.0
                          0.0.0.0
                          0.0.0.0
                          0.0.0.0
                          0.0.0.0
                          0.0.0.0
                          54.239.45.224
                          54.239.100.40
                          52.94.46.67
                          0.0.0.0
                          0.0.0.0
                          0.0.0.0
                          0.0.0.0
                          0.0.0.0
                          13.227.170.93  ←──────────────
```

Figure 4.8: Verifying access to an Internet server

In this figure, you can see that the site, www.wiley.com, resolves to four servers. The starting point and the path to www.wiley.com will vary depending where you are in the world. And given how often things change, it is entirely possible that the target IP addresses have changed.

The path taken from SRV2 through the Internet shows several hops where the ICMP Echo Request was dropped, but you can see that the final hop is to one of the four servers answering to WWW.Wiley.Com. This is not uncommon with some of the Internet's core routers that routinely drop ICMP Echo Requests. It is not relevant if an intermediate router, like those shown in Figure 4.8, fails to respond, so long as it is routing other packets properly, as is the case here. This is another reason PowerShell's `Test-NetConnection` cmdlet is an improvement over `ping.exe`.

It is worth noting that the `Test-NetConnection` cmdlet has been re-engineered in PowerShell 7. This command is now considerably quicker than in Windows PowerShell.

Installing the DHCP Service

The Dynamic Host Configuration Protocol (DHCP) allows hosts to discover IP address details at run time. Addresses and IP configuration options are specified on a DHCP server. Setting up a DHCP service is straightforward. DHCP is a Windows Server feature that you install with the `Install-WindowsFeature` cmdlet.

Once you install the DHCP Server service in Windows Server, you must authorize it explicitly within Active Directory. Authorization enables protection against rogue DHCP servers. The Windows DHCP Server service inside Windows Server 2019 checks to see whether it is authorized before starting up.

At the time of writing, the DHCP Server module is not supported natively in PowerShell 7. To get around this limitation, you use the Windows Compatibility feature described in Chapter 2.

Before You Start

You should have a Windows Server 2019 host, `DC1.Reskit.Org`, that you are going to set up to be a DHCP server. This host is also a domain controller in the `Reskit.Org` domain. You should have a second Windows 2019 host, `DC2.Reskit.Org`, that you use as part of a DHCP failover/load balancing implementation in "Configuring DHCP Failover."

You also need to ensure PowerShell 7 and, optionally, VS Code are up and running on these hosts as in previous sections.

Also, if you have added NICs to the VM, for example to enable Internet access, to test this section consider temporarily disabling those extra NICs to enable the server to get a DHCP address.

Installing the DHCP Feature

Installing the DHCP Server service is straightforward since it is a Windows feature. You install the DHCP service on the domain controller, `DC1`, by using the `Install-WindowsFeature` cmdlet.

```
# 1. Install the DHCP Feature on DC1 and add the Management tools
Import-Module -Name ServerManager -WarningAction SilentlyContinue
Install-WindowsFeature -Name DHCP -IncludeManagementTools
```

Once the Server Manager module is loaded, you can invoke the cmdlets, to produce the output shown in Figure 4.9.

```
PS C:\Foo> # 1. Install the DHCP Feature on DC1 and add the Management tools
PS C:\Foo> Import-Module -Name ServerManager -WarningAction SilentlyContinue
PS C:\Foo> Install-WindowsFeature -Name DHCP -IncludeManagementTools

Success Restart Needed Exit Code Feature Result
------- -------------- --------- --------------
True    No             Success   {DHCP Server, DHCP Server Tools}
```

Figure 4.9: Installing the DHCP service

In this case, you are installing the DHCP Server service on a domain controller that is also a DNS server. This is a best-practice configuration that minimizes network traffic between DNS, AD, and DHCP.

Authorizing the DHCP Server in the AD

Before your DHCP server can start the DHCP service, you must authorize the DHCP server explicitly in Active Directory. This prevents against the risk of a rogue DHCP server—one that curious users might decide to explore. A rogue DHCP could issue conflicting IP addresses or issue addresses to rogue gateways and/or DNS servers, thus compromising your network. If the DHCP service starts up (for example after you install it), the service checks whether it's been authorized in the AD and if not shuts down.

You also use the Add-DHCPSecurityGroup cmdlet to add a set of security groups. This cmdlet adds two domain groups: DHCP Users and DHCP Administrators as well as the DHCP Users local security groups on the DHCP server. You do this as follows:

```
# 2. Add DC1 to Trusted DHCP Servers and add the DHCP Security Group
Import-Module -Name DHCPServer -WarningAction SilentlyContinue
Add-DhcpServerInDC
Add-DHCPServerSecurityGroup
```

This snippet produces no output. Once you run this snippet, you can use the cmdlet Get-DHCPServerInDC to view the authorized DHCP server and the Get-LocalGroup cmdlet to view the local groups on the DHCP server.

Completing the DHCP Configuration

You complete the configuration of the DHCP service by updating the registry to indicate to Windows that the DHCP server is installed and ready to be used. The code to do this is as follows:

```
# 3. Let DHCP know it's all configured
$DHCPHT = @{
  Path  = 'HKLM:\SOFTWARE\Microsoft\ServerManager\Roles\12'
  Name  = 'ConfigurationState'
  Value = 2
}
Set-ItemProperty @DHCPHT
```

Setting registry values in this way produces no output.

Restarting the DHCP Service

With the DHCP service now configured, you can restart the service as follows:

```
# 4. Restart DHCP Server
Restart-Service -Name DHCPServer -Force
```

Restarting the server does not produce any output, although you may see warning messages as Windows stops and then restarts the DHCP service. When you restart the service, because the DHCP server has been authorized in the DHCP, it is ready to issue IP addresses once your DHCP scopes are created.

Checking the DHCP Service

Now that the DHCP Server service is authorized, restarting the service should show it up and running. Because you have not yet configured a DHCP scope, the service is not going to hand out addresses, so at this stage you simply check that the DHCP service is up and running and is set to start automatically. You can use the Get-Service command to return this information, as follows:

```
# 5. Test service availability
Get-Service -Name DHCPServer |
   Format-List -Property *
```

The output of this step looks like Figure 4.10.

You have installed DHCP and performed basic configuration. Your next step in deploying DHCP is to create one or more scopes.

```
PS C:\Foo> # 5. Test service availability
PS C:\Foo> Get-Service -Name DHCPServer |
            Format-List -Property *

UserName            : NT AUTHORITY\NetworkService
Description         : Performs TCP/IP configuration for DHCP clients, including dynamic
                      assignments of IP addresses, specification of the WINS and DNS
                      servers, and connection-specific DNS names. If this service is
                      stopped, the DHCP server will not perform TCP/IP configuration for
                      clients. If this service is disabled, any services that explicitly
                      depend on it will fail to start.
DelayedAutoStart    : False
BinaryPathName      : C:\Windows\system32\svchost.exe -k DHCPServer -p
StartupType         : Automatic
Name                : DHCPServer
RequiredServices    : {RpcSs, Tcpip, SamSs, EventLog, EventSystem}
CanPauseAndContinue : True
CanShutdown         : True
CanStop             : True
DisplayName         : DHCP Server
DependentServices   : {}
MachineName         : .
ServiceName         : DHCPServer
ServicesDependedOn  : {RpcSs, Tcpip, SamSs, EventLog, EventSystem}
StartType           : Automatic
ServiceHandle       : Microsoft.Win32.SafeHandles.SafeServiceHandle
Status              : Running
ServiceType         : Win32OwnProcess, Win32ShareProcess
Site                :
Container           :
```

Figure 4.10: Checking the DHCP service

Configuring DHCP Scopes

After you have the DHCP service authorized in AD and running, you need to configure your DHCP server with the IP address ranges and options to provide to DHCP clients.

To do this, you set up one or more scopes, configure the scopes with the appropriate option and options values, and then test to ensure that client computers can obtain IP addresses from this system.

A DHCP *scope* is a range of IP addresses within an IP network that the DHCP server can offer to DHCP clients. Its various configuration options are values that a DHCP client can request, such as the default gateway or DNS server IP address. Once configured, your DHCP server can issue these option values to any client that requests them.

You can define scope-specific options that apply only to IP addresses handed out with a specific DHCP scope. Alternatively, you can configure options at the server level, enabling the options to be supplied to all scopes defined on the server.

For more information about the deployment of DHCP, see docs.microsoft. com/en-us/windows-server/networking/technologies/dhcp/dhcp-deploy-wps.

Before You Start

This section assumes you have already installed and authorized the DHCP service on `DC1.Reskit.Org`, which is also the domain controller in the `Reskit.Org` domain.

Creating a DHCP Scope

You create an IPv4 DHCP scope by using the `Add-DhcpServerV4Scope` command. You specify the IP block in which the DHCP server is to provide IP addresses, as well as the subnet mask for the IP addresses in the scope, as follows:

```
# 1. Create an IPv4 Scope
Import-Module DHCPServer -WarningAction SilentlyContinue
$SCOPEHT = @{
  Name         = 'ReskitOrg'
  StartRange   = '10.10.10.150'
  EndRange     = '10.10.10.199'
  SubnetMask   = '255.255.255.0'
  ComputerName = 'DC1.Reskit.Org'
}
Add-DhcpServerV4Scope @SCOPEHT
```

The DHCP Server module is not supported natively in PowerShell 7. You access the commands using the Windows PowerShell compatibility mechanism described in Chapter 2.

In most cases, you configure your DHCP servers to hand out IPv4 addresses. With IPv6's autoconfiguration, if you have an IPv6-capable router serving a subnet, Windows hosts configure themselves with global (and local) addresses, including the router's address. Should you need more control over IPV6 addresses, you can create IPv6 scopes as needed.

Getting Scopes from the DHCP Server

Once you have a scope (or scopes) defined, you can view the scope information by using the `Get-DHCPServerv4Scope` command.

```
# 2. Get IPv4 Scopes from the server
Get-DhcpServerv4Scope -ComputerName DC1.Reskit.Org
```

In the output shown in Figure 4.11, you can see the scope you just created along with its IP address range (10.10.10.150 to 10.10.10.199) and the scope's subnet mask (255.255.255.0).

```
PS C:\Foo> # 2. Get IPV4 Scopes from the server
Get-DhcpServerv4Scope -ComputerName DC1.Reskit.Org

ScopeId       SubnetMask       Name       State    StartRange      EndRange       LeaseDuration
-------       ----------       ----       -----    ----------      --------       -------------
10.10.10.0    255.255.255.0    ReskitOrg  Active   10.10.10.150    10.10.10.199
```

Figure 4.11: Reviewing IPv4 scopes

Configuring Server-wide Options

Options are specific configuration items whose value can be requested by a DHCP client and provided by the DHCP Server. There is a large set of potential options—and almost all of them are only infrequently used. See www.iana. org/assignments/bootp-dhcp-parameters/bootp-dhcp-parameters.txt for the definitive list of options that can be set.

You can set DHCP options at the server level or the scope level. This allows you to have, for example, a single set of DNS servers provided to all DHCP clients in all scopes served by the server while you might have a scope-specific setting for the default gateway.

Two options you should specify are the IP addresses of your DNS servers and the DNS domain name for any DHCP clients. You can do this as follows:

```
# 3. Set Server Wide Option Values
$OPTION1HT = @{
  ComputerName = 'DC1.Reskit.Org' # DHCP Server to Configure
  DnsDomain    = 'Reskit.Org'     # Client DNS Domain
  DnsServer    = '10.10.10.10'    # Client DNS Server
}
Set-DhcpServerV4OptionValue @OPTION1HT
```

Configuring Scope-Specific Options

You can also set options at the scope level. A good example of a scope-specific option you might want to specify is the IP address of the default gateway (Router).

To set a scope-specific option value, you use the same Set-DHCPServerV4OptionsValue and specify the scope name (using the -ScopeId parameter).

```
# 4. Set a scope specific option
$OPTION2HT = @{
  ComputerName = 'DC1.Reskit.Org' # DHCP Server to Configure
  Router       = '10.10.10.254'
  ScopeID      = '10.10.10.0'
}
Set-DhcpServerV4OptionValue @OPTION2HT
```

Testing the DHCP Service in Operation

Now that you have the DHCP service installed, configured, and with a scope and options defined, you can begin to use it. You can test the DHCP service using the server SRV2.Reskit.Org. You used this server in "Configuring IP Addressing."

To do this you must first set the TCP/IP client on SRV2 to get IP address information from DHCP, as you see in the following code. In production, you should also test that your Windows 10 clients and other devices are getting the correct IP configuration. Once DHCP is seen to be providing an IP address, you can use the Resolve-DNSName command to ensure the new DHCP-provided IPv4 address is being resolved by DNS. These tests look like this:

```
# 5. Test the DHCP Service
#    Run on SRV2
$NICHT = @{
  InterfaceAlias = 'Ethernet'
  AddressFamily  = 'IPv4'
}
$NIC = Get-NetIPInterface @NICHT
Set-NetIPInterface -InterfaceAlias $NIC.ifALias -DHCP Enabled
Get-NetIPConfiguration
Resolve-DnsName -Name SRV2.Reskit.Org -Type A
```

This snippet sets the NIC in SRV2 to be DHCP-enabled. Running these commands produces the output shown in Figure 4.12, which shows that the server has a new IP address and related values. It can take a second or two to set this new address.

```
PS C:\Foo> # 5. Test the DHCP Service
PS C:\Foo> #    Run on SRV2
PS C:\Foo> $NICHT = @{
            InterfaceAlias = 'Ethernet'
            AddressFamily  = 'IPv4'
          }
PS C:\Foo> $NIC = Get-NetIPInterface @NICHT
PS C:\Foo> Set-NetIPInterface -InterfaceAlias $NIC.ifAlias -DHCP Enabled
PS C:\Foo> Get-NetIPConfiguration

InterfaceAlias       : Ethernet
InterfaceIndex       : 6
InterfaceDescription : Microsoft Hyper-V Network Adapter
NetProfile.Name      : Reskit.Org 2 (Unauthenticated)
IPv4Address          : 10.10.10.150
IPv6DefaultGateway   :
IPv4DefaultGateway   : 10.10.10.254
DNSServer            : 10.10.10.10
```

Figure 4.12: Checking DHCP operation

Configuring DHCP Failover

In early deployments of the Windows DHCP service, individual DHCP servers were standalone and did not communicate with other DHCP servers. If you wanted a measure of DHCP server failover, you would have had to create two DHCP servers and configure them to each offer IP addresses in the appropriate range (making sure the two servers did not issue the same address). A typical approach would be to configure the same DHCP scope on each DHCP server and then configure each server to issue only some of the addresses in the subnet block. With this approach, even if one server was down, clients could still get an IP address. This approach worked but was all too easy to misconfigure.

Later versions of Windows Server DHCP provided a better solution: built-in failover and load balancing. This involves installing two Windows Servers with the DHCP service running on both. Then after creating a scope on one server, you create a failover/load balancing relationship for that scope between the two servers. Once configured, the two servers share the scope and the responsibility of issuing an IP address and related configuration. You can configure the two DHCP servers to do load balancing of DHCP requests or just to provide failover support.

If you set up DHCP with just DHCP hot standby, you would need to configure how long the standby server should wait before servicing DHCP requests.

Before You Start

To implement DHCP failover, you first need two DHCP servers. The first one, DC1.Reskit.Org, was set up in "Configuring the DHCP Service." You also should have a second server, in this case DC2.Reskit.Org. This server is another domain controller in the Reskit.Org domain but without the DHCP feature loaded or configured. You can see how to do this in "Installing a Replica DC" in Chapter 3.

In this section, you run the PowerShell commands on the DC2.Reskit.Org server.

Installing the DHCP Server Feature on DC2

To implement a DHCP load balancing relationship you need to have installed DHCP on both the first server (which you did in "Installing the DHCP Service") and on the second server (DC2.Reskit.Org), which you do here. To install the DHCP feature on DC2.Reskit.Org, run the following code:

```
# 1. Install the DHCP Server feature on DC2
Import-Module -Name ServerManager -WarningAction SilentlyContinue
$FEATUREHT = @{
    Name            = 'DHCP'
```

```
        IncludeManagementTools = $True
    }
    Install-WindowsFeature @FEATUREHT
```

This command produces the output you see in Figure 4.13.

```
PS C:\Foo> # 1. Install the DHCP Server feature on DC2
PS C:\Foo> $FEATUREHT = @{
            Name                 = 'DHCP'
            IncludeManagementTools = $True
          }
PS C:\Foo> Install-WindowsFeature @FEATUREHT

Success Restart Needed Exit Code  Feature Result
------- -------------- ---------  --------------
True    No             Success    {DHCP Server, DHCP Server Tools}
```

Figure 4.13: Installing the DHCP feature

Letting DHCP Know It Is Fully Configured on DC2

As with the DHCP service on DC1.Reskit.Org, you need to tell Windows Server that DHCP is fully configured on DC2, which you do as follows:

```
# 2. Let DHCP Know It Is Fully Configured
$IPHT = @{
  Path  = 'HKLM:\SOFTWARE\Microsoft\ServerManager\Roles\12'
  Name  = 'ConfigurationState'
  Value = 2
}
Set-ItemProperty @IPHT
```

Authorizing the Second DHCP Server in AD

You also need to ensure that the DC2 DHCP server is authorized in AD, with the following code:

```
# 3. Authorize the DHCP Server in AD
Import-Module -Name DHCPServer -WarningAction 'SilentlyContinue'
Add-DhcpServerInDC -DnsName DC2.Reskit.Org
```

Viewing Authorized DHCP Servers

Once these steps are complete, you can use Get-DhcpServerInDC to test and view the DHCP servers you have authorized for the Reskit.Org domain:

```
# 4. View Authorized DHCP Servers
Get-DhcpServerInDC
```

In the output, shown in Figure 4.14, you can see the two authorized DHCP servers. The first, `DC1.Reskit.Org`, was created in "Installing the DHCP Service" earlier and the other here.

```
PS C:\Foo> # 4. View Authorized DHCP Servers
PS C:\Foo> Get-DhcpServerInDC

IPAddress     DnsName
---------     -------
10.10.10.10   dc1.reskit.org
10.10.10.11   dc2.reskit.org
```

Figure 4.14: Viewing authorized DHCP servers

Configuring DHCP Failover and Load Balancing

If you have two DHCP servers, you can configure a load-balancing relationship. The idea is to have the first DHCP server (in this case `DC1.Reskit.Org`) configured with one or more scopes defined and both server and scope options set as needed. Then, on a *new* DHCP server (`DC2.Reskit.Org`) to which you have just added the DHCP service, you create the relationship using the `Add-DhcpServerV4Failover` command.

With `DC2.Reskit.Org` now installed and configured as a DHCP server, you can configure DHCP failover/load balancing as follows:

```
# 5. Configure failover and load balancing:
$FAILOVERHT = @{
   ComputerName       = 'DC1.Reskit.Org'
   PartnerServer      = 'DC2.Reskit.Org'
   Name               = 'DC1-DC2'
   ScopeID            = '10.10.10.0'
   LoadBalancePercent = 60
   SharedSecret       = 'j3RryIsTheB3est'
   Force              = $true
}
Add-DhcpServerv4Failover @FAILOVERHT
```

After you run this command, the two DHCP servers are now in an active-active state. Both servers listen for and respond to DHCP client requests. If either DHCP server provides a lease for any configured scope, the DHCP service synchronizes the scopes automatically.

In this example, you created an active-active relationship, which is great for performance. To reduce the overall resource usage, you might want to set up an active standby. That allows one server to do all the work of managing leases and to synchronize with the second server. Should the first server become nonresponsive, the second can take over until the first server comes back online. You would use the `MaxClientLeadTime`, `AutoStateTransition`, and `StateSwitchInterval` parameters to configure the hot standby relationship. For more information on configuring hot standby, see `docs.microsoft.com/en-gb/archive/blogs/teamdhcp/dhcp-failover-using-powershell`. And as with other references to Windows Server documentation, this content is old but still accurate for the purposes of this chapter.

While all PowerShell cmdlets support the `-Verbose` parameter, some (many?) produce little or no useful output. Others, however, do produce a lot of valuable output that can be used for troubleshooting or debugging. If you use the `-Verbose` parameter with the `Add-DhcpServerv4Failover` command when creating a load-balancing relationship between the two servers, you see the verbose output as shown in Figure 4.15. This is informative and can be useful for troubleshooting.

```
VERBOSE: A new failover relationship will be created between servers DC1.Reskit.Org and DC2.Reskit.Org.
         The configuration of the specified scopes on server DC1.Reskit.Org will be replicated to the partner server.
VERBOSE: Add scopes on partner server DC2.Reskit.Org ...............................In progress.
VERBOSE: Update properties for scope 10.10.10.0 (1 of 1) on partner server DC2.Reskit.Org ......In progress.
VERBOSE: Update properties for scope 10.10.10.0 (1 of 1) on partner server DC2.Reskit.Org ......Successful.
VERBOSE: Update delay offer for scope 10.10.10.0 (1 of 1) on partner server DC2.Reskit.Org .....In progress.
VERBOSE: Update delay offer for scope 10.10.10.0 (1 of 1) on partner server DC2.Reskit.Org .....Successful.
VERBOSE: Update NAP properties for scope 10.10.10.0 (1 of 1) on partner server DC2.Reskit.Qrg ..In progress.
VERBOSE: Update NAP properties for scope 10.10.10.0 (1 of 1) on partner server DC2.Reskit.Org ..Successful.
VERBOSE: Update superscope for scope 10.10.10.0 (1 of 1) on partner server DC2.Reskit.Org ......In progress.
VERBOSE: Update superscope for scope 10.10.10.0 (1 of 1) on partner server DC2.Reskit.Org ......Successful.
VERBOSE: Update IP ranges for scope 10.10.10.0 (1 of 1) on partner server DC2.Reskit.Org .......In progress.
VERBOSE: Update IP ranges for scope 10.10.10.0 (1 of 1) on partner server DC2.Reskit.Org .......Successful.
VERBOSE: Update exclusions for scope 10.10.10.0 (1 of 1) on partner server DC2.Reskit.Org ......In progress.
VERBOSE: Update exclusions for scope 10.10.10.0 (1 of 1) on partner server DC2.Reskit.Org ......Successful.
VERBOSE: Update reservations for scope 10.10.10.0 (1 of 1) on partner server DC2.Reskit.Org ....In progress.
VERBOSE: Update reservations for scope 10.10.10.0 (1 of 1) on partner server DC2.Reskit.Org ....Successful.
VERBOSE: Update policies for scope 10.10.10.0 (1 of 1) on partner server DC2.Reskit.Org ........In progress.
VERBOSE: Update policies for scope 10.10.10.0 (1 of 1) on partner server DC2.Reskit.Org ........Successful.
VERBOSE: Update options for scope 10.10.10.0 (1 of 1) on partner server DC2.Reskit.Org .........In progress.
VERBOSE: Update options for scope 10.10.10.0 (1 of 1) on partner server DC2.Reskit.Org .........Successful.
VERBOSE: Add scopes on partner server DC2.Reskit.Org ...............................Successful.
VERBOSE: Disable scopes on partner server DC2.Reskit.Org ..........................In progress.
VERBOSE: Disable scopes on partner server DC2.Reskit.Org ..........................Successful.
VERBOSE: Creation of failover configuration on partner server DC2.Reskit.Org .........In progress.
VERBOSE: Creation of failover configuration on partner server DC2.Reskit.Org .........Successful.
VERBOSE: Creation of failover configuration on host server DC1.Reskit.Org ...........In progress.
VERBOSE: Creation of failover configuration on host server DC1.Reskit.Org ...........Successful.
VERBOSE: Activate scopes on partner server DC2.Reskit.Org .........................In progress.
VERBOSE: Activate scopes on partner server DC2.Reskit.Org .........................Successful
```

Figure 4.15: Verbose output when creating DHCP failover

Viewing Active Leases from Both DHCP Servers

With the DHCP installed and your DHCP scope (10.10.10.0) replicated, you can now view the DHCP server statistics, as follows:

```
# 6. Get active leases in the scope (from both servers!)
$DHCPServers = 'DC1.Reskit.Org', 'DC2.Reskit.Org'
$DHCPServers |
  ForEach-Object {
    "Server $_" | Format-Table
    Get-DhcpServerv4Scope -ComputerName $_ | Format-Table
  }
```

Once your DHCP clients are set up, they can use the DHCP service to obtain leases. The output, which you can see in Figure 4.16, shows the state of DHCP leases (after failover) on both servers.

```
PS C:\Foo> # 6. Get active leases in the scope (from both servers!)
$DHCPServers = 'DC1.Reskit.Org', 'DC2.Reskit.Org'
$DHCPServers |
  ForEach-Object {
    "Server $_" | Format-Table
    Get-DhcpServerv4Scope -ComputerName $_ | Format-Table
  }

Server DC1.Reskit.Org

ScopeId     SubnetMask      Name      State  StartRange     EndRange       LeaseDuration
-------     ----------      ----      -----  ----------     --------       -------------
10.10.10.0 255.255.255.0 ReskitOrg Active 10.10.10.150 10.10.10.199

Server DC2.Reskit.Org

ScopeId     SubnetMask      Name      State  StartRange     EndRange       LeaseDuration
-------     ----------      ----      -----  ----------     --------       -------------
10.10.10.0 255.255.255.0 ReskitOrg Active 10.10.10.150 10.10.10.119
```

Figure 4.16: Viewing active DHCP leases

As you can see, both servers have a copy of the scope, and both scopes have already had at least one DHCP client obtain an IP address lease from one or other of the DHCP servers. In this configuration, both servers are able to issue new IP address leases; and when one server does so, it coordinates the lease with the partner DHCP server.

Viewing DHCP Server Statistics

Finally, you can also view the scope statistics from each server, using the Get-DhcpServerv4ScopeStatistics command:

```
# 7. View DHCP Server Statistics from both DHCP Servers
$DHCPServers |
  ForEach-Object {
    "Server $_" | Format-Table
    Get-DhcpServerv4ScopeStatistics -ComputerName $_  | Format-Table
  }
```

As in the previous step, if you have a few DHCP clients using the DHCP server and zone, the output would resemble Figure 4.17.

Note that in this figure, you see just the IP address lease provided to SRV2. In your testing you may find different numbers of leases in use depending on what systems you have configured to have DHCP-based IP addressing. Note that both DHCP servers return this information, so it appears twice.

```
PS C:\Foo> # 7. View DHCP Server Statistics from both DHCP Servers
PS C:\Foo> $DHCPServers |
            ForEach-Object {
              "Server $_" | Format-Table
              Get-DhcpServerv4ScopeStatistics -ComputerName $_  | Format-Table
            }


Server DC1.Reskit.Org

ScopeId    Free InUse PercentageInUse Reserved Pending SuperscopeName
--------   ---- ----- --------------- -------- ------- --------------
10.10.10.0 49   1     2               0        0


Server DC2.Reskit.ORg

ScopeId    Free InUse PercentageInUse Reserved Pending SuperscopeName
--------   ---- ----- --------------- -------- ------- --------------
10.10.10.0 49   1     2               0        0
```

Figure 4.17: Viewing DHCP server statistics

Configuring the DNS Service

The DNS is a globally distributed name resolution service that converts DNS domain names into IP addresses. Once a DNS client resolves an IP address, the client can then initiate IP-related access to the remote server. An analogy is a telephone book: you look up someone's name to get a phone number and then dial that number.

DNS enables you to look up the IP address for a domain name, for example converting www.wiley.com into an IP address of 13.32.123.207. DNS also does reverse lookup, which involves resolving the IP address of 13.32.123.207 back to the server that hosts the www.wiley.com web site.

Windows included a DNS service with Windows NT and has included and improved the server with later releases of Windows Server. Microsoft also makes use of DNS to provide a domain locator service that enables clients and servers to discover domain controllers. Previously, that was done using NetBIOS.

With Windows, DNS is used for both name resolution and service location. A DNS client enables applications to communicate with remote hosts by name. The DNS client is also able to search for services such as LDAP (Active Directory), by way of SRV records.

This section assumes you have a good understanding of what DNS is and broadly how it works. For more information on the basics of DNS, see the DNS Technical Reference at docs.microsoft.com/en-us/previous-versions/windows/it-pro/windows-server-2003/cc779926(v=ws.10). For more information, see bookauthority.org/books/best-dns-books.

In Chapter 3, you installed several domain controllers to form three domains within two forests. There, all the domain controllers used a single DNS service on DC1, which you created in "Establishing a Forest Root Domain." After configuring AD, you can provide better resiliency for DNS by adding the DNS service to other DCs. Best practice is to have the DNS service on each domain controller and have the zones AD-integrated.

Like any DNS Service, Microsoft's DNS provides a number of configuration settings that allow you to deploy DNS as needed. PowerShell 7 provides the necessary cmdlets that configure DNS to meet your requirements.

In this section, you add the DNS service to a second DC, DC2, to ensure that zones are replicated between DCs and configure key DNS service settings.

Before You Start

This section adds and configures the DNS service on DC2, adds the DC2 DNS server to the DHCP Options you set in "Configuring DHCP Scopes," and sets other key DNS configuration options. You also need DC1 online. You run the snippets in this section from DC2.

Installing the DNS Feature on DC2

To set up a Windows Server host to be a DNS server, you install the DNS feature using the `Install-WindowsFeature` command.

```
# 1. Install the DNS Feature
Import-Module -Name ServerManager -WarningAction SilentlyContinue
Install-WindowsFeature -Name DNS -IncludeManagementTools
```

You can see the results of this command in Figure 4.18.

```
PS C:\Foo> # 1. Install the DNS Feature
PS C:\Foo> Import-Module ServerManager -WarningAction SilentlyContinue
PS C:\Foo> Add-WindowsFeature -Name DNS -ComputerName DC2 -IncludeManagementTools

Success Restart Needed Exit Code  Feature Result
------- -------------- ---------  --------------
True    No             Success    {DNS Server.DNS Server Tools}
```

Figure 4.18: Installing the DNS feature

Since PowerShell supports Server Manager via the compatibility mechanism described in Chapter 2, importing the module generates a warning message by default advising that the module is running in compatibility mode. You use the `-WarningAction` parameter to suppress this warning message.

Configuring the DNS Service

Once the DNS Server service is installed and active, you can configure some basic options. Depending on how and where you plan to deploy DNS, the DNS Server service's options you might need to configure include the following:

Disabling recursion: You may want to disable recursion to avoid clients forcing recursive queries (a potential denial-of-service attack vector for Internet-facing servers). For use within your organization, you would enable recursion.

Configuring the DNS Server local cache: You can set the maximum amount of memory that the DNS Server service can use for its local cache. For most Internet- or DMZ-based DNS servers, you can probably set this to 25MB and be OK. But monitor it carefully.

Configuring EDNS: Extended DNS (EDNS) is an extension mechanism that allows suitably configured DNS client systems to extend the DNS protocol while allowing older clients to work as previously. One example is to enable a larger DNS reply. This could be useful if you have larger numbers of resource records that can fit in a simple UDP datagram. EDNS is turned off by default, but there is no real downside to leaving this off.

Enabling the global name zone: The global name zone enables you to enable single-label DNS queries (for HRWEB, for example). This can be useful as a way of removing any lingering dependency on NetBIOS (or WINS) in an organization.

There are other options that you may need to configure less commonly, including these:

Configuring round robin: Round robin, which is enabled by default, returns resource records requested by a DNS query but in a random order. For situations where several servers all have the same domain name, this provides a degree of load balancing.

Configuring DNSSEC: DNS Security (DNSSEC) provides cryptographic assurance that DNS replies are valid. DNSSEC is complex but automatic in operation. Where possible, Internet-facing DNS servers, and the replies they generate, should be protected with DNSSEC. For more information about DNSSEC, see docs.microsoft.com/en-us/previous-versions/windows/ it-pro/windows-server-2012-r2-and-2012/jj200221(v%3Dws.11).

Configuring a DNS forwarder: In some cases, you might want to have your DNS server conditionally forward requests for certain domains to a specific server. You might, for example, want to route queries received at SRV2. Reskit.Org to DC1.Reskit.Org, but only for queries for the Reskit.Org zone. You set up forwarders in "Configuring a Cross-Forest Trust" in Chapter 3.

Specifying a zone data loading: For a standalone DNS server, you may want to save zone information in the registry or in a file. You can save it in AD, and have it automatically replicated within the forest or domain.

Configuring DNS debugging and event log logging: When you install the DNS server, by default the service does not perform diagnostic logging (logging either DNS requests or replies). You can turn this logging on. See docs.microsoft.com/en-us/previous-versions/windows/it-pro/windows-server-2012-r2-and-2012/dn800669(v%3Dws.11) for more information on DNS logging and diagnostics.

You can set key DNS server options as follows:

```
# 2. Set Key DNS Server Options
# Enable recursion on this server
Set-DnsServerRecursion -Enable $true
# Configure DNS Server cache maximum size
Set-DnsServerCache  -MaxKBSize 20480  # 20 MB
# Enable EDNS
$EDNSHT = @{
  EnableProbes    = $true
  EnableReception = $true
}
Set-DnsServerEDns @EDNSHT
# Enable Global Name Zone
Set-DnsServerGlobalNameZone -Enable $true
```

You would run this snippet on each DNS server in your organization, amended as appropriate for each server.

Viewing Key DNS Server Options

After configuring your server, it is prudent to check the server option settings. You can do this by using the Get-DNSServer command. This command on its own produces a lot of output, which would fill many pages of this book. However, the object that is returned from the Get-DNSServer command contains a number of expandable properties that contain details of your DNS server's overall configuration.

You use `Select-Object` to filter out the settings you want to view; the code looks like this:

```
# 3. View DNS Service and note the module
# Get DNS Server Settings
$WAHT = @{WarningAction='SilentlyContinue'}
$DNSRV = Get-DNSServer -ComputerName DC2.Reskit.Org @WAHT
# View Recursion settinngs
$DNSRV |
  Select-Object -ExpandProperty ServerRecursion
# View Server Cache settings
$DNSRV |
  Select-Object -ExpandProperty ServerCache
# View ENDS Settings
$DNSRV |
  Select-Object -ExpandProperty ServerEdns
```

You can see the output of this code in Figure 4.19.

```
PS C:\Foo> # 3. View DNS Service and note the module
PS C:\Foo> # Get DNS Server Settings
PS C:\Foo> $WAHT = @{WarningAction='SilentlyContinue'}
PS C:\Foo> $DNSRV = Get-DNSServer -ComputerName DC2.Reskit.Org @WAHT
PS C:\Foo> # View Recursion settinngs
PS C:\Foo> $DNSRV |
          Select-Object -ExpandProperty ServerRecursion


Enable               : True
AdditionalTimeout(s) : 4
RetryInterval(s)     : 3
Timeout(s)           : 8
SecureResponse       : True

PS C:\Foo> # View Server Cache settings
PS C:\Foo> $DNSRV |
          Select-Object -ExpandProperty ServerCache


MaxTTL                             : 1.00:00:00
MaxNegativeTTL                     : 00:15:00
MaxKBSize                          : 20480
EnablePollutionProtection          : True
LockingPercent                     : 100
StoreEmptyAuthenticationResponse   : True
IgnorePolicies                     : False

PS C:\Foo> $DNSRV |
          Select-Object -ExpandProperty ServerEdns

CacheTimeout EnableProbes EnableReception
------------ ------------ ---------------
00:15:00     True         True
```

Figure 4.19: Examining key DNS configuration settings

In the output produced by these commands, you can see that the maximum TTL is set to one day and the cache timeout is set to 15 minutes. For an internal DNS server, you might consider raising the maximum TTL and cache timeouts to higher values as appropriate in your environment. Increasing these values decreases DNS traffic but risks out-of-date records. On the internal network, this is not much of a risk as servers do not change IP addresses often. On Internet-facing DNS servers, erring on the side of accuracy is probably a good approach.

Configuring DNS Zones and Resource Records

Each DNS zone contains resource records (RRs), which the DNS service uses to return information. When a DNS client attempts to resolve a host name, such as DC1.Reskit.Org, the DNS server searches the zone to find the appropriate resource record or records to return them to the DNS client.

Many RRs are automatically added to your internal DNS servers using the DNS dynamic update feature whereby DNS clients update DNS with their IP address. If you have Internet-facing DNS servers, you are unlikely to want dynamic updates turned on.

The DNS records needed to support AD are updated in DNS each time a DC starts up and once every 24 hours thereafter. Likewise, Address (A) records for each host are written each time a host comes up and every 24 hours thereafter. For the most part, DNS is self-healing: you remove the records, and they are rewritten to DNS.

Other records, such as Mail Exchange (MX) or Sender Protected Framework (SPF) records, are *not* automatically added to DNS. You can add these records statically.

If you have a number of static RRs to configure, having a PowerShell script to create the zone and the RRs makes it easy to re-create the records should accidents happen. It's also great documentation as to what should be configured.

Before you can add RRs, you need to have the necessary zones defined on the server as well. A zone (such as Reskit.Org) holds RRs for that domain and possibly subdomains (e.g., UK.Reskit.Org). When the DNS client sends a DNS server a resolution request, the server can find the zone and relevant RRs and resolve the name.

A reverse lookup zone enables DNS to find a host name given its IP address—the reverse of forward lookup. Reverse lookup zones are generally not required but may be used by some services and applications. The older DNS lookup command, nslookup.exe, for example, uses the IP address configured for the DNS server and converts it to a friendly name via the server's PTR (reverse lookup) resource record when it starts up. You can see this in Figure 4.20 although you need to set up the reverse lookup zone first, which you do in "Creating a Reverse Lookup Zone."

```
PS C:\Foo> nslookup - 10.10.10.10
Default Server:  DC1.Reskit.Org
Address:  10.10.10.10
```

Figure 4.20: Starting NSLookup

If you do not create a reverse lookup zone, then `nslookup.exe` reports the default server is "UnKnown."

Before You Start

This section adds DNS RRs to the DNS Server you installed on `DC1.Reskit.Org`, which you created initially in "Establishing a Forest Root Domain" in Chapter 3.

Creating a DNS Forward Lookup Zone

A DNS forward lookup zone, for example `Cookham.Net`, is required before your DNS server can resolve a host name such as `Home.Cookham.Net` into an IP address such as `10.42.42.42`. You create a zone on `DC1` by doing the following:

```
# 1. Create a new primary forward DNS zone for Cookham.Net
Import-Module DNSServer
$ZHT1 = @{
  Name               = 'Cookham.Net'
  ResponsiblePerson  = 'dnsadmin.cookham.net.'
  ReplicationScope   = 'Forest'
  ComputerName       = 'DC1.Reskit.Org'
}
Add-DnsServerPrimaryZone @ZHT1
```

Although this snippet produces no output, you can see the results by using the DNS MMC console or by using DNS cmdlets. By default, this zone is AD integrated, meaning the zone information is stored in the AD. And, again by default, the zone is replicated to all DCs in the forest, which includes both DC1 and DC2.

Creating a Reverse Lookup Zone

You can also create reverse lookup zones that resolve IP addresses back into their respective host names. You use the `Add-DnsServerPrimaryZone` command to add a reverse lookup zone like this:

```
# 2. Create a reverse lookup zone
$ZHT2 = @{
  NetworkID          = '10.10.10.0/24'
  ResponsiblePerson  = 'dnsadmin.reskit.org.'
  ReplicationScope   = 'Forest'
```

Continues

continued

```
    ComputerName       = 'DC1.Reskit.Org'
}
Add-DnsServerPrimaryZone @ZHT2
```

In most cases, DNS clients register their reverse lookup information automatically using dynamic DNS update at the same time they register their forward lookup information. If you had an Internet-facing server offering DNS resolution for Internet-facing line-of-business (LOB) applications or systems, you would usually configure reverse lookups manually and turn off dynamic update. Allowing dynamic updates of Internet-facing DNS servers could be a security concern.

Registering DNS Records for DC1, DC2

By default, Windows hosts re-register their DNS resource records every 24 hours or when the system is rebooted. It can take time before the new zones work on all servers. To speed things up, you can force key systems to register their forward and reverse lookup records (A and PTR) using Register-DnsClient, as follows:

```
# 3. Register DNS for DC1, DC2
Register-DnsClient
Invoke-Command -ComputerName DC2 -ScriptBlock {Register-DnsClient}
```

These commands cause DC1 and DC2 to re-register their A and PRT records on their configured DNS Server, which is DC1.

Checking the DNS Zones on DC1

After creating two new zones, you verify that the zones are available. In this book, you have two forward lookup zones on the DC1 DNS server. The first holds the Reskit.Org information (which was created by the snippets in Chapter 3 that create the AD). The second zone is the one just added. You also have a reverse lookup zone for 10.10.10.0/24.

To view all the zones held in DC1, you can use Get-DNSServerZone and specify DC1 explicitly.

```
# 4. Check The DNS zones on DC1
Get-DNSServerZone -ComputerName DC1
```

The output, which you see in Figure 4.21, shows details of the zones held on DC1. As you see, there are two main forward lookup zones (for Reskit.Org and Cookham.Net), a forwarder (for Kapoho.Com) and a reverse-lookup zone for 10.10.10.0;/24. You see whether the zones were created manually, are AD-integrated, or are reverse lookup zones.

```
PS C:\Foo> # 4. Check The DNS zones on DC1
PS C:\Foo> Get-DNSServerZone -ComputerName DC1

ZoneName              ZoneType   IsAutoCreated  IsDsIntegrated  IsReverseLookupZone  IsSigned
--------              --------   -------------  --------------  -------------------  --------
_msdcs.Reskit.Org     Primary    False          True            False                False
0.in-addr.arpa        Primary    True           False           True                 False
10.10.10.in-addr.arpa Primary    False          True            True                 False
127.in-addr.arpa      Primary    True           False           True                 False
255.in-addr.arpa      Primary    True           False           True                 False
Cookham.Net           Primary    False          True            False                False
Kapoho.Com            Forwarder  False          False           False                False
Reskit.Org            Primary    False          True            False                False
TrustAnchors          Primary    False          True            False                False
```

Figure 4.21: Checking on recently created DNS zones

Adding DNS RR to the Cookham.Net Zone

With your zones created, you next need to add RRs for DNS to use when resolving names/addresses. There are many different RR types that you might want to add to a zone; the most important are these:

A record: This provides the IP address for a specific host name.

CNAME: This RR type provides an alias mechanism, enabling you to define an alias, such as WWW.Reskit.Org, and point that to another host, such as SRV2.Reskit.Org.

MX record: This tells email services where to send email for a particular domain.

You can add these RR types to the zone RR-specific commands, as follows:

```
# 5. Add Resource Record to Cookham.Net zone
# Add an A record
$RRHT1 = @{
  ZoneName      = 'Cookham.Net'
  A             = $true
  Name          = 'Home'
  AllowUpdateAny = $true
  IPv4Address   = '10.42.42.42'
  TimeToLive    = (30 * (24 * 60 * 60))  # 30 days in seconds
}
Add-DnsServerResourceRecord @RRHT1
# Add a Cname record
$RRHT2 = @{
  ZoneName      = 'Cookham.Net'
  Name          = 'MAIL'
  HostNameAlias = 'Home.Cookham.Net'
  TimeToLive    = (30 * (24 * 60 * 60))  # 30 days in seconds
}
```

Continues

continued

```
Add-DnsServerResourceRecordCName @RRHT2
# Add an MX record
$MXHT = @{
  Preference     = 10
  Name           = '.'
  TimeToLive     = '1:00:00'
  MailExchange   = 'Mail.Cookham.Net'
  ZoneName       = 'Cookham.Net'
}
Add-DnsServerResourceRecordMX @MXHT
```

The DNS Server module provides cmdlets that add specific RRs for most commonly used RR types with parameters suitable for that RR as used in this snippet. For other DNS resource records you might need to add, you can use the more generic `Add-DnsServerResourceRecord` command. For a deeper look at the range of RRs supported by Windows Server's DNS service, see `docs .microsoft.com/en-us/windows/win32/dns/managing-dns-resource-records`.

Restarting the DNS Service

The zones you have created so far were created on DC1 and were AD-integrated with forest-wide replication. That means that once DC1 has been updated, AD replicates the new zone and RR details to all DCs in the forest. If a DC runs the DNS Service, it finds the new zones automatically. With AD-integrated zones, a DNS client can register records on any DC (that runs a DNS service). AD then replicates those. The DNS service regularly updates its record information based on the newly replicated AD contents. While the replication and updating all happens fairly quickly, they can take some time. To speed things up you can restart the DNS service on DC1 and DC2, like this:

```
# 6. Restart DNS Service to ensure replication
Restart-Service -Name DNS
$SB = {Restart-Service -Name DNS}
Invoke-Command -ComputerName DC1 -ScriptBlock $SB
```

These commands have the side effect of clearing the DNS server's name cache. For busy intranet servers, that means losing cached RRs, which can lead to increased external traffic for a time. As a best practice, you should do maintenance like this during off-peak times or if possible, during a routine maintenance outage.

Checking the DNS RRs in the Cookham.Net Zone

After adding resource records to the Cookham.Net forward lookup zone, and restarting the DNS service, you can verify that the RRs are set up correctly.

```
# 7. Check results of RRs in Cookham.Net zone
Get-DnsServerResourceRecord -ZoneName 'Cookham.Net'
```

The output from these commands, in Figure 4.22, shows the RRs you just created (the MX, CNAME, and A records) plus two RRs created by the DNS server when you created the zone (the NS and SOA RRs).

```
PS C:\Foo> # 7. Check results of RRs in Cookham.Net zone
PS C:\Foo> Get-DnsServerResourceRecord -ZoneName 'Cookham.Net'

HostName  RecordType  Type  Timestamp  TimeToLive  RecordData
--------  ----------  ----  ---------  ----------  ----------
@         NS          2     0          01:00:00    dc2.reskit.org.
@         NS          2     0          01:00:00    dc1.reskit.org.
@         SOA         6     0          01:00:00    [5][dc2.reskit.org.][dnsadmin.cookha…
@         MX          15    0          01:00:00    [10][Mail.Cookham.Net.]
Home      A           1     0          00:00:00    10.42.42.42
MAIL      CNAME       5     0          00:00:00    Home.Cookham.Net.
```

Figure 4.22: Checking on DNS RRs

In this figure, the SOA record shows a version number of 5. Over time this version number increases as changes are made. This is normal.

Testing DNS Server Resolution

You should always test any DNS installation and changes to that installation carefully. Little mistakes can lead to huge consequences. An often-repeated bit of IT Pro humor suggests "The cause of your issue is DNS—now what was your issue?"

Besides the obvious checks that the DNS service is running and confirming key configuration values, such as recursion, server cache, and EDNS, you also need to test that key resource records are being resolved by all your DNS Servers (that is, DC1 and DC2). You can test the resolution on both DNS servers with code like this:

```
# 8. Test DNS Resolution on DC1, DC2
# Test the Cname
Resolve-DnsName -Server DC1.Reskit.Org -Name 'Mail.Cookham.Net'
# Test the MX
Resolve-DnsName -Server DC2.Reskit.Org -Name 'Cookham.Net' -Type MX
```

The testing produces the output you see in Figure 4.23.

As you can see in the figure, resolving the Mail.Cookham.Net domain name retrieves the CNAME record and the A record (for Home.Cookham.Net), which the CNAME points to. This DNS resolution was performed on DC1, and you verified that the MX record for the domain Cookham.Net points to the server Mail.Cookham.Net.

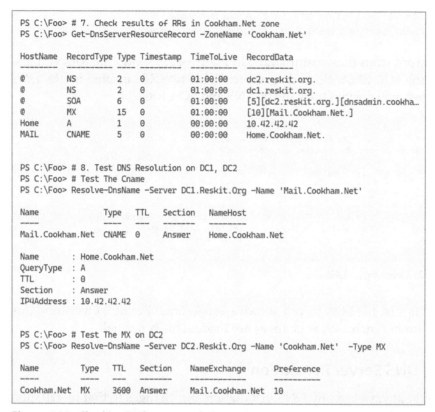

```
PS C:\Foo> # 7. Check results of RRs in Cookham.Net zone
PS C:\Foo> Get-DnsServerResourceRecord -ZoneName 'Cookham.Net'

HostName   RecordType Type Timestamp   TimeToLive   RecordData
--------   ---------- ---- ---------   ----------   ----------
@          NS         2    0           01:00:00     dc2.reskit.org.
@          NS         2    0           01:00:00     dc1.reskit.org.
@          SOA        6    0           01:00:00     [5][dc2.reskit.org.][dnsadmin.cookha…
@          MX         15   0           01:00:00     [10][Mail.Cookham.Net.]
Home       A          1    0           00:00:00     10.42.42.42
MAIL       CNAME      5    0           00:00:00     Home.Cookham.Net.


PS C:\Foo> # 8. Test DNS Resolution on DC1, DC2
PS C:\Foo> # Test The Cname
PS C:\Foo> Resolve-DnsName -Server DC1.Reskit.Org -Name 'Mail.Cookham.Net'

Name              Type   TTL   Section   NameHost
----              ----   ---   -------   --------
Mail.Cookham.Net  CNAME  0     Answer    Home.Cookham.Net

Name        : Home.Cookham.Net
QueryType   : A
TTL         : 0
Section     : Answer
IP4Address  : 10.42.42.42


PS C:\Foo> # Test The MX on DC2
PS C:\Foo> Resolve-DnsName -Server DC2.Reskit.Org -Name 'Cookham.Net'  -Type MX

Name          Type   TTL    Section   NameExchange       Preference
----          ----   ---    -------   ------------       ----------
Cookham.Net   MX     3600   Answer    Mail.Cookham.Net   10
```

Figure 4.23: Checking DNS name resolution on DC1

In this section you used a number of the core DNS server configuration commands. There are a number of advanced DNS features this book does not cover, such as DNS security (DNSSec), root hints, DNS server virtualization instances, DNS scavenging, and more. The DNS Server module has 134 commands to enable you to configure DNS as your needs dictate.

Summary

Networking is at the heart of every organization. In this chapter, you saw how to configure IP addressing and test network connectivity. You also looked at the installation and configuration of DHCP. With DHCP, you created a simple DHCP Server with one scope and then added a second failover/load-balancing DHCP server. In this chapter's final sections, you installed and configured your DNS server, and you configured and tested DNS zones and resource records.

Managing Storage

Since the dawn of IT, computer systems have supported a variety of mechanisms to store and retrieve data. Today, Windows supports a variety of physical storage and storage devices, including spinning disks, USB memory sticks, and SSD storage including Non-Volatile Memory Express (NVMe).

Before you can use a disk to store data, you need to first create a partition on the device. You want each physical storage device to contain one or more partitions or volumes. Once these are created, you format each volume with a filesystem that enables you to store and retrieve data.

Windows supports two different partitioning mechanisms: Master Boot Record (MBR) and GUID Partition Table (GPT). See www.howtogeek.com/193669/whats-the-difference-between-gptand-mbr-when-partitioning-a-drive/ for more information about the differences between these partitioning schemes. Disks formatted with MBR disks are limited to 2TB, which can be an issue in some cases.

You can use a number of different filesystems for a given volume or partition. The filesystems Windows supports include NTFS, exFAT, UDF, FAT32, and ReFS. In most cases the volumes you use are likely to be formatted with NTFS, but you have options. For details of the filesystems, see docs.microsoft.com/windows/win32/fileio/filesystem-functionality-comparison.

Note in particular that Windows Server supports the ReFS filesystem. Based on NFTS, this filesystem provides additional resiliency features, although it lacks some features you might need for certain roles. For example, it does not support file encryption by the filesystem. For a comparison between the ReFS and NTFS filesystems, see `www.iperiusbackup.net/en/refs-vs-ntfs-differences-and-performance-comparison-when-to-use/`.

Systems Used in This Chapter

This chapter demonstrates using PowerShell 7 to manage storage. Its example makes use of the following systems:

DC1.Reskit.Org: This is a domain controller in the domain `Reskit.Org`.

SRV1.Reskit.Org: This is a domain-joined server that you use for storage management.

SRV2.Reskit.Org: This is another domain-joined server that you use for storage management.

Figure 5.1 shows the systems you use in this chapter.

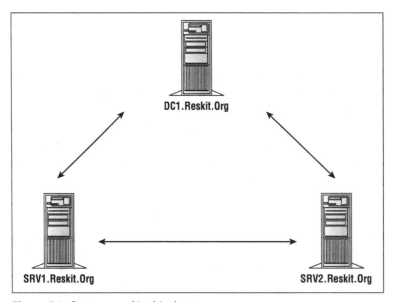

Figure 5.1: Systems used in this chapter

Note that all systems need PowerShell 7 loaded before starting. You can do that using the scripts from Chapter 1, "Setting Up a PowerShell 7 Environment."

Managing Disks and Volumes

A disk device on Windows needs to be partitioned into one or more individual volumes or drives. You also need to format each partition to add the appropriate filesystem.

You manage storage on Windows using the commands in the Storage module, whose 166 commands help you to manage disks, volumes, and partitions.

When creating new disk volumes (such as an NTFS-based F: drive from a newly added disk), you can create the volumes two ways, using either `New-Partition` or `New-Volume`. The latter command is also used for managing the Storage Spaces and Storage Spaces Direct technologies. For more details on Storage Spaces, see `docs` `.microsoft.com/en-us/windows-server/storage/storage-spaces/overview`, and for more information on Storage Spaces Direct, see `docs.microsoft.com/en-us/` `windows-server/storage/storage-spaces/storage-spaces-direct-overview`.

An important distinction between these commands is that `New-Volume` both creates a disk partition and formats the partition, whereas `New-Partition` just creates the partition, which you then need to format separately.

In this section, you use a server, SRV1, to which you have added two new disk devices. You then use the storage-related commands to bring these disks online, partition, and format them. You use these two disks on SRV1 in later sections of this chapter.

Before You Start

In this section you use a Window Server 2019 host, SRV1, a domain-joined system on which you have installed PowerShell 7, and, optionally, VS Code. You can use the scripts in Chapter 1 to do this.

After creating the server, you need to add two disks to this host. If you are using Hyper-V to implement SRV1, you can add these two drives by running the following:

```
# 0. Add 2 VHDs to SRV1 VM
#    Run this on the Hyper-V VM Host

# Stop the VM
Stop-VM -VMName SRV1

# Get File location for the disk in this VM
$VM = Get-VM -VMName SRV1
$Par = Split-Path -Path $VM.HardDrives[0].Path
```

Continues

continued

```
# Create two VHDx for F and G
$NewPath1 = Join-Path -Path $par -ChildPath FDrive.VHDX
$NewPath2 = Join-Path -Path $par -ChildPath GDrive.VHDX
$D1 = New-VHD -Path $NewPath1 -SizeBytes 128GB -Dynamic
$D2 = New-VHD -Path $NewPath2 -SizeBytes 128GB -Dynamic

# Add a new SCSI Controller to SRV1
$C = (Get-VMScsiController -VMName SRV1)
Add-VMScsiController -VMName SRV1

# Add first disk to VM
$HDHT = @{
  Path                = $NewPath1
  VMName              = 'SRV1'
  ControllerType      = 'SCSI'
  ControllerNumber    = $C.count
  ControllerLocation = 0
}
Add-VMHardDiskDrive @HDHT
# Add second disk to VM
$HDHT.Path = $NewPath2
$HDHT.ControllerLocation = 1
Add-VMHardDiskDrive @HDHT

# Start the VM
Start-VM -VMName SRV1
```

This snippet creates a new SCSI controller, along with two VHDX hard disk files on the VM host, and then it adds these VHDXs as SCSI disks to the SRV1 host. The two disks are attached to the net SCSI adapter in the VM and occupy the first two LUN values (0 and 1).

Getting Information about Physical Disks in SRV1

After you add the new disks to the SRV1 host and restart the host, log in to it as Reskit\Administrator. Use Get-Disk to examine the disk devices contained in SRV1, as follows:

```
# 1. Get physical disks on this system:
Get-Disk |
  Format-Table -AutoSize
```

Figure 5.2 shows the output from this snippet.

You can see that SRV1 has three disk drives. The VM sees the drive that you created when you built the VM either as an IDE drive by default, or, if the VM is created as a Generation 2 VM in Hyper-V, as a SCSI drive. You also see the two newly created disks, which are presented to Windows as SCSI drives. Because these two disk drives were just added to the host, Windows shows them as being offline.

```
PS C:\Foo> # 1. Get physical disks on this system:
PS C:\Foo> Get-Disk |
            Format-Table -AutoSize

Number Friendly Name     Serial Number HealthStatus OperationalStatus Total Size Partition Style
------ -------------     ------------- ------------ ----------------- ---------- ---------------
0      Virtual HD                      Healthy      Online            128 GB     MBR
1      Msft Virtual Disk               Healthy      Offline           128 GB     RAW
2      Msft Virtual Disk               Healthy      Offline           128 GB     RAW
```

Figure 5.2: Examining physical disks in `SRV1`

Initializing the New Disks

Before you can use these disks, which Windows shows as offline, you need to initialize them using `Initialize-Disk`. You can do this as follows:

```
# 2. Initialize the disks
Get-Disk |
  Where-Object PartitionStyle -eq Raw |
    Initialize-Disk -PartitionStyle GPT
```

This step gets the two new disks and initializes them. Each disk is now set up to use the GPT partitioning method noted earlier. Initializing the disks brings them online.

Viewing the Initialized Disks

Now that you have initialized the new disks, you can view their disk status again as follows:

```
# 3. Re-display disks
Get-Disk |
  Format-Table -AutoSize
```

Figure 5.3 shows the output from this snippet.

```
PS C:\Foo> # 3. Re-display disks
PS C:\Foo> Get-Disk |
            Format-Table -AutoSize

Number Friendly Name     Serial Number HealthStatus OperationalStatus Total Size Partition Style
------ -------------     ------------- ------------ ----------------- ---------- ---------------
0      Virtual HD                      Healthy      Online            128 GB     MBR
1      Msft Virtual Disk               Healthy      Online            128 GB     GPT
2      Msft Virtual Disk               Healthy      Online            128 GB     GPT
```

Figure 5.3: Examining the initialized disks in `SRV1`

As you see in the output, these two new disks are now healthy and online. Also note the disk number property of each disk. You use this disk number to perform disk-related activities.

Creating an F: Volume in Disk 1

One way you can create a new disk volume is to use the `New-Volume` command, which both creates the necessary partition and then formats the partition in a single operation. You create a new disk volume on the first of the two added disks, as follows:

```
# 4. Create an F: volume in Disk 1
$NVHT1 = @{
  DiskNumber   = 1
  FriendlyName = 'Storage(F)'
  FileSystem   = 'NTFS'
  DriveLetter  = 'F'
}
New-Volume @NVHT1
```

Figure 5.4 shows the output of this snippet.

```
PS C:\Foo> # 4. Create an F: volume in Disk 1
PS C:\Foo> $NVHT1 = @{
          DiskNumber   = 1
          FriendlyName = 'Storage(F)'
          FileSystem   = 'NTFS'
          DriveLetter  = 'F'
        }
PS C:\Foo> New-Volume @NVHT1

DriveLetter FriendlyName FileSystemType DriveType HealthStatus OperationalStatus SizeRemaining      Size
----------- ------------ -------------- --------- ------------ ----------------- -------------      ----
F           Storage(F)   NTFS           Fixed     Healthy      OK                127.88 GB 127.98 GB
```

Figure 5.4: Creating an F: volume

As you can see, you have created a new F: volume, formatted as NTFS, with 127.88GB of space remaining.

Creating a Partition in Disk 2

Whereas `New-Volume` both creates the disk partition and formats it, you can also perform these operations separately. To create a first small volume on disk 2 (the second of the two disks added to `SRV1`), you create a G: volume using the `New-Partition` command, as follows:

```
# 5. Now create a partition on Disk 2
New-Partition -DiskNumber 2  -DriveLetter G -Size 42gb
```

Figure 5.5 shows the output of this command. As you can see, the G: drive now exists and has 42GB of space available out of the 128GB total disk size.

```
PS C:\Foo> # 5. Now create a partition on Disk 2
PS C:\Foo> New-Partition -DiskNumber 2  -DriveLetter G -Size 42gb


   DiskPath: \\?\scsi#disk&ven_msft&prod_virtual_disk#000001#{53f56307-b6bf-11d0-94f2-00a0c91efb8b}

PartitionNumber  DriveLetter Offset         Size Type
---------------  ----------- ------         ---- ----
2                G           16777216      42 GB Basic
```

Figure 5.5: Creating a G: volume

You may see a pop-up window saying "You need to format the disk in drive G: before you can use it. Do you want to format it? Format disk/Cancel." Since you format it later in this example, you can ignore this pop-up (and just click Cancel).

Creating a Second Partition

If a disk has unallocated free space, you can create a new partition and use whatever space is available, with the New-Partition command.

```
# 6. Create a second partition H:
New-Partition -DiskNumber 2  -DriveLetter H -UseMaximumSize
```

Figure 5.6 shows the output of this command.

```
PS C:\Foo> # 6. Create a second partition H:
PS C:\Foo> New-Partition -DiskNumber 2  -DriveLetter H -UseMaximumSize


   DiskPath: \\?\scsi#disk&ven_msft&prod_virtual_disk#000001#{53f56307-b6bf-11d0-94f2-00a0c91efb8b}

PartitionNumber  DriveLetter Offset              Size Type
---------------  ----------- ------              ---- ----
3                H           45113933824   85.98 GB Basic
```

Figure 5.6: Creating an H: volume

As you can see, the command with these options creates an H: drive on disk 2 with 85.98GB of available space, using all the remaining free space on disk 2.

Viewing Volumes on SRV1

After creating several volumes, you can view them using the Get-Volume command, as follows:

```
# 7. View Volumes on SRV1
Get-Volume
```

The output from this command, shown in Figure 5.7, lists drives available to SRV1.

```
PS C:\Foo> # 10. Get Volumes on SRV1
PS C:\Foo> Get-Volume |
            Sort-Object -Property DriveLetter

DriveLetter FriendlyName FileSystemType DriveType HealthStatus OperationalStatus SizeRemaining      Size
----------- ------------ -------------- --------- ------------ ----------------- -------------      ----
A                        Unknown        Removable Healthy      Unknown                    0 B       0 B
C                        NTFS           Fixed     Healthy      OK                    116.34 GB    128 GB
D                        Unknown        CD-ROM    Healthy      Unknown                    0 B       0 B
F           Storage(F)   NTFS           Fixed     Healthy      OK                    127.88 GB 127.98 GB
G           Logs         NTFS           Fixed     Healthy      OK                     41.91 GB     42 GB
H           Music        NTFS           Fixed     Healthy      OK                     85.89 GB  85.98 GB
```

Figure 5.7: Viewing created volumes

As you can see, the volumes on SRV1 include an A: drive for a floppy disk—rarely used in real or virtual machines but available.

> **NOTE**   Hyper-V does not provide support for floppy disks in Hyper-V Generation 2 VMs. See blogs.technet.microsoft.com/jhoward/2013/11/04/hyper-v-generation-2-virtual-machines-part-7 for fuller details.

There is also the C: system drive, a CD/DVD drive (currently empty), and three drives created in the two prior sections (the F: , G:, and H: drives). Also, the F: drive (created with the New-Volume command) has been formatted with an NTFS filesystem, whereas you still need to format the G: and H: volumes before Windows can make use of them.

Formatting G: and H:

As noted in the previous section, the drives you created using New-Partition are not formatted. You can create and then format separate partitions as follows:

```
# 8. Format G: and H:
# Format G:
$NVHT1 = @{
   DriveLetter        = 'G'
   FileSystem         = 'NTFS'
   NewFileSystemLabel = 'Logs'
}
Format-Volume @NVHT1
# Format H:
$NVHT2 = @{
   DriveLetter        = 'H'
   FileSystem         = 'NTFS'
   NewFileSystemLabel = 'Music'
}
Format-Volume @NVHT2
```

The output in Figure 5.8 shows that these two partitions are now formatted using NTFS and have a friendly name. As you can see, the two partitions have different (maximum) size remaining and size values.

```
PS C:\Foo> # 8. Format G: and H:
PS C:\Foo> # Format G:
PS C:\Foo> $NVHT1 = @{
            DriveLetter       = 'G'
            FileSystem        = 'NTFS'
            NewFileSystemLabel = 'Logs'
          }
PS C:\Foo> Format-Volume @NVHT1

DriveLetter FriendlyName FileSystemType DriveType HealthStatus OperationalStatus SizeRemaining     Size
----------- ------------ -------------- --------- ------------ ----------------- -------------     ----
G           Logs         NTFS           Fixed     Healthy      OK                    41.91 GB     42 GB

PS C:\Foo> # Format H:
PS C:\Foo> $NVHT2 = @{
            DriveLetter       = 'H'
            FileSystem        = 'NTFS'
            NewFileSystemLabel = 'Music'
          }
PS C:\Foo> Format-Volume @NVHT2

DriveLetter FriendlyName FileSystemType DriveType HealthStatus OperationalStatus SizeRemaining     Size
----------- ------------ -------------- --------- ------------ ----------------- -------------     ----
H           Music        NTFS           Fixed     Healthy      OK                  85.89 GB  85.98 GB
```

Figure 5.8: Formatting volumes `G:` and `H:`

Getting Partitions on SRV1

Now that you have partitioned and formatted both new disk drives, you can review the partitions, as follows:

```
# 9. Get partitions on SRV1
Get-Partition |
  Sort-Object -Property DriveLetter |
    Format-Table -Property DriveLetter, Size, Type
```

Figure 5.9 shows the output from this command.

```
PS C:\Foo> # 9. Get partitions on SRV1
PS C:\Foo> Get-Partition |
          Sort-Object -Property DriveLetter |
            Format-Table -Property DriveLetter, Size, Type

DriveLetter        Size Type
-----------        ---- ----
            16759808 Reserved
            16759808 Reserved
C    137436856320 IFS
F    137421127680 Basic
G     45097156608 Basic
H     92323971072 Basic
```

Figure 5.9: Viewing partitions on SRV1

As you can see, after running the snippets in this section, SRV1 now has six partitions across three disk drives. Of those, four contain usable filesystems.

Getting Volumes on SRV1

Another way to look at the disk volumes available on SRV1 is to use the Get-Volume command, as follows:

```
# 10. Get Volumes on SRV1
Get-Volume |
   Sort-Object -Property DriveLetter
```

Figure 5.10 shows the output from this command.

```
PS C:\Foo> # 10. Get Volumes on SRV1
PS C:\Foo> Get-Volume |
           Sort-Object -Property DriveLetter

DriveLetter FriendlyName FileSystemType DriveType HealthStatus OperationalStatus SizeRemaining      Size
----------- ------------ -------------- --------- ------------ ----------------- -------------      ----
A                        Unknown        Removable Healthy      Unknown                      0 B       0 B
C                        NTFS           Fixed     Healthy      OK                      116.34 GB    128 GB
D                        Unknown        CD-ROM    Healthy      Unknown                      0 B       0 B
F           Storage(F)   NTFS           Fixed     Healthy      OK                      127.88 GB 127.98 GB
G           Logs         NTFS           Fixed     Healthy      OK                       41.91 GB    42 GB
H           Music        NTFS           Fixed     Healthy      OK                       85.89 GB 85.98 GB
```

Figure 5.10: Viewing partitions on SRV1

You have the option of using the Get-Partition and Get-Volume commands—either singly or together—to view the disk volumes available to you on SRV1. Each command produces somewhat different output. As ever with PowerShell, you have choices.

In this section you have seen how to manage disks, volumes, and partitions.

Managing NTFS Permissions

One prevalent issue with any filesystem and any operating system is ensuring that people see only what they are supposed to see and nothing else. Doing that requires a permissions mechanism to grant permissions to groups or users as your business requirements dictate.

The NTFS filesystem supports access control lists (ACLs) on files and folders. For each file or folder, the ACL describes who can have access to the resource and what kind of access is allowed. Each ACL contains one or more access control entries (ACEs) that define that a specific account (for example, a user or group) has a specific permission (such as Read-Only) to the resource. Permissions can include Deny, which explicitly denies a user access to the file/folder. If a user has no relevant ACEs in an ACL, they have no access to the resource implicitly.

Access control can also be inherited. If you have an ACE on, say, C:\Foo that allows a group full control of that folder, by default, that permission is inherited by lower-level folders (for example, C:\Foo\Test). Inheritance is provided by default, but you can turn it off.

With PowerShell, you can view the ACL of a file by using the Get-ACL cmdlet. You can also set an ACL (using Set-ACL). But there is no cmdlet available to create a new ACE; you would have to dip down into the .NET Framework to create the ACE that you could then set using Set-ACL. Managing inheritance is also not supported directly using the built-in commands.

As an alternative to managing ACLs using native .NET calls, you can leverage the NTFSSecurity module. This module works natively within PowerShell 7, and to use it, you download it from the PowerShell Gallery. This module makes it easier to manage ACLs and ACL inheritance with NTFS files and folders.

Before You Start

This section makes use of SRV1, a domain-joined server in the Reskit.Org domain. This server requires Internet access, and you should log on using the Reskit\ Administrator credentials. You also need to have the domain controller (DC1 .Reskit.Org) online.

Downloading and Installing the NTFSSecurity Module

The NTFSSecurity module is a third-party module, and Windows (and PowerShell) does not install it by default. For managing NTFS permissions on a server (SRV1), you might also need to update AD users/groups; and thus, the AD RSAT tools might be handy. You can add these modules as follows:

```
# 1. Download NTFSSecurity module from PSGallery
Install-Module -Name NTFSSecurity -Force
Import-Module ServerManager -WarningAction SilentlyContinue
Install-WindowsFeature -Name RSAT-AD-Tools -IncludeAllSubFeature |
   Out-Null
```

The NTFSSecurity module is community-developed, and you install it from the PowerShell Gallery. You can also obtain it directly from the GitHub page related to the module, here: github.com/raandree/NTFSSecurity.

The module and the source code are available for you to view, although downloading from the PS Gallery is simpler. The GitHub pages also provide two NTFSSecurity tutorials: one on basic permission management and the second on NTFS inheritance and privileges. These are worth exploring to learn more about the module's capabilities and usage.

This snippet also imports the Server Manager module and uses it to install the RSAT-AD tools. You use these tools to create a new AD in "Creating the Sales Group" shortly.

Finding Commands in the NTFSSecurity Module

With the NTFSSecurity module downloaded and installed, you can use `Get-Command` to discover the commands contained in the module, as follows:

```
# 2. Get commands in the module
Get-Command -Module NTFSSecurity
```

As shown in Figure 5.11, this command displays the cmdlets contained in the module. In the NTFSSecurity module (the latest version at the time of writing being 4.2.6), there were a total of 36 cmdlets that help you manage NTFS security.

```
PS C:\Foo> # 2. Get commands in the module
PS C:\Foo> Get-Command -Module NTFSSecurity

CommandType  Name                            Version  Source
-----------  ----                            -------  ------
Cmdlet       Add-NTFSAccess                  4.2.6    NTFSSecurity
Cmdlet       Add-NTFSAudit                   4.2.6    NTFSSecurity
Cmdlet       Clear-NTFSAccess                4.2.6    NTFSSecurity
Cmdlet       Clear-NTFSAudit                 4.2.6    NTFSSecurity
Cmdlet       Copy-Item2                      4.2.6    NTFSSecurity
Cmdlet       Disable-NTFSAccessInheritance   4.2.6    NTFSSecurity
Cmdlet       Disable-NTFSAuditInheritance    4.2.6    NTFSSecurity
Cmdlet       Disable-Privileges              4.2.6    NTFSSecurity
Cmdlet       Enable-NTFSAccessInheritance    4.2.6    NTFSSecurity
Cmdlet       Enable-NTFSAuditInheritance     4.2.6    NTFSSecurity
Cmdlet       Enable-Privileges               4.2.6    NTFSSecurity
Cmdlet       Get-ChildItem2                  4.2.6    NTFSSecurity
Cmdlet       Get-DiskSpace                   4.2.6    NTFSSecurity
Cmdlet       Get-FileHash2                   4.2.6    NTFSSecurity
Cmdlet       Get-Item2                       4.2.6    NTFSSecurity
Cmdlet       Get-NTFSAccess                  4.2.6    NTFSSecurity
Cmdlet       Get-NTFSAudit                   4.2.6    NTFSSecurity
Cmdlet       Get-NTFSEffectiveAccess         4.2.6    NTFSSecurity
Cmdlet       Get-NTFSHardLink                4.2.6    NTFSSecurity
Cmdlet       Get-NTFSInheritance             4.2.6    NTFSSecurity
Cmdlet       Get-NTFSOrphanedAccess          4.2.6    NTFSSecurity
Cmdlet       Get-NTFSOrphanedAudit           4.2.6    NTFSSecurity
Cmdlet       Get-NTFSOwner                   4.2.6    NTFSSecurity
Cmdlet       Get-NTFSSecurityDescriptor      4.2.6    NTFSSecurity
Cmdlet       Get-NTFSSimpleAccess            4.2.6    NTFSSecurity
Cmdlet       Get-Privileges                  4.2.6    NTFSSecurity
Cmdlet       Move-Item2                      4.2.6    NTFSSecurity
Cmdlet       New-NTFSHardLink                4.2.6    NTFSSecurity
Cmdlet       New-NTFSSymbolicLink            4.2.6    NTFSSecurity
Cmdlet       Remove-Item2                    4.2.6    NTFSSecurity
Cmdlet       Remove-NTFSAccess               4.2.6    NTFSSecurity
Cmdlet       Remove-NTFSAudit                4.2.6    NTFSSecurity
Cmdlet       Set-NTFSInheritance             4.2.6    NTFSSecurity
Cmdlet       Set-NTFSOwner                   4.2.6    NTFSSecurity
Cmdlet       Set-NTFSSecurityDescriptor      4.2.6    NTFSSecurity
Cmdlet       Test-Path2                      4.2.6    NTFSSecurity
```

Figure 5.11: Viewing cmdlets in the NTFSSecurity module

Some of the commands in this module improve on the cmdlets built into PowerShell 7. For example, the module includes the Get-Item2 cmdlet, which shows whether a file's ACL includes inherited ACEs.

Creating a New Folder and File

To demonstrate the use of the NFTSSecurity module, you create first a folder and then a file, as follows:

```
# 3. Create a new folder, and a file in the folder
New-Item -Path C:\Secure1 -ItemType Directory |
    Out-Null
'Secure' | Out-File -FilePath C:\Secure1\Secure.Txt
Get-ChildItem -Path C:\Secure1
```

Figure 5.12 shows the output of this snippet.

```
PS C:\Foo> # 3. Create a new folder, and a file in the folder
PS C:\Foo> New-Item -Path C:\Secure1 -ItemType Directory |
           Out-Null
PS C:\Foo> "Secure" | Out-File -FilePath C:\Secure1\Secure.Txt
PS C:\Foo> Get-ChildItem -Path C:\Secure1

    Directory: C:\Secure1

Mode           LastWriteTime    Length Name
----           -------------    ------ ----
-a---     26/01/2020    15:32        8 Secure.Txt
```

Figure 5.12: Creating a folder and file

Using this snippet, you created a new folder (C:\Secure1) and a new file within that folder (C:\Secure1\Secure.Txt). Since the C:\ drive is formatted as NTFS, both the folder and the file have ACLs, and by default the ACEs in the ACL for both contain inherited permissions.

Viewing the Default Folder ACL

When you created the folder, Windows assigned a default ACL. To see the specific permissions of the folder's default ACL, you can run the Get-NTFSAccess command as shown here:

```
# 4. View ACL of the folder
Get-NTFSAccess -Path C:\Secure1 |
  Format-Table -AutoSize
```

Figure 5.13 shows the output from this snippet.

```
PS C:\Foo> # 4. View ACL of the folder:
PS C:\Foo> Get-NTFSAccess -Path C:\Secure1 |
          Format-Table -AutoSize

   Path: C:\Secure1 (Inheritance enabled)

Account                  Access Rights                   Applies to                            Type  IsInherited InheritedFrom
-------                  -------------                   ----------                            ----  ----------- -------------
NT AUTHORITY\SYSTEM      FullControl                     ThisFolderSubfoldersAndFiles Allow True         C:
BUILTIN\Administrators   FullControl                     ThisFolderSubfoldersAndFiles Allow True         C:
BUILTIN\Users            ReadAndExecute, Synchronize ThisFolderSubfoldersAndFiles Allow True         C:
BUILTIN\Users            CreateDirectories               ThisFolderAndSubfolders      Allow True         C:
BUILTIN\Users            CreateFiles                     ThisFolderAndSubfolders      Allow True         C:
CREATOR OWNER            GenericAll                      SubfoldersAndFilesOnly       Allow True         C:
```

Figure 5.13: Viewing the ACL of the folder

The folder's ACL consists of six ACEs, all of which were inherited. The default ACL also gives wide permissions to the `Builtin\Users` group, which may not be appropriate. Naturally, you can refine the ACL for the folder as needed.

Viewing the Default ACL on File

When you created the file, Windows created a default ACL for the file as well, which you can view as follows:

```
# 5. View ACL of file
Get-NTFSAccess -Path C:\Secure1\Secure.Txt   |
   Format-Table -AutoSize
```

As you can see in the output, shown in Figure 5.14, the file has an ACL consisting of inherited permissions.

```
PS C:\Foo> # 5. View ACL of file
PS C:\Foo> Get-NTFSAccess C:\Secure1\Secure.Txt |
          Format-Table -AutoSize

   Path: C:\Secure1\Secure.Txt (Inheritance enabled)

Account                  Access Rights                   Applies to            Type  IsInherited InheritedFrom
-------                  -------------                   ----------            ----  ----------- -------------
NT AUTHORITY\SYSTEM      FullControl                     ThisFolderOnly Allow True         C:
BUILTIN\Administrators   FullControl                     ThisFolderOnly Allow True         C:
BUILTIN\Users            ReadAndExecute, Synchronize ThisFolderOnly Allow True         C:
```

Figure 5.14: Viewing the ACL of the file

In Windows, a folder and a file within that folder are separate objects. You control access to these objects by setting ACLs that match their underlying business need; for example, to define a Sales group that might contain Sales Team members from across your organization. You need to assign folder permissions to define what users can do in the folder (Can they create files? Can they create subfolders?) and what they can do to an individual file. Some files may be more "secure" than others and may need their ACLs adjusted as well.

Creating the Sales Group

To demonstrate using the NTFSSecurity module, you create an AD Universal group to hold the members of the organization-wide Sales group. To ensure that the group is created, you can do the following:

```
# 6. Create Sales group if it does not exist
try {
  Get-ADGroup -Identity 'Sales' -ErrorAction Stop
}
catch {
  New-ADGroup -Name Sales -GroupScope Universal |
    Out-Null
}
```

This snippet first checks to see whether the group already exists. If the group does not exist yet, the snippet creates it. The AD cmdlets run on SRV1 but access the domain database on DC1.Reskit.Org.

At first sight, this method of creating a new group looks long-winded. However, this is a good method of creating a group if the group does not exist. The Get-ADGroup cmdlet either returns the AD group or generates a nonterminating error (by default). You use the -ErrorAction parameter to turn the non-terminating error into a terminating error that is caught by the catch block.

This step creates a Universal group. Depending on your requirements, there are other group membership schemes you could adopt that are just variations on the steps shown here. In many larger organizations, an approach known as AGDLP (account, global, domain local permission) is used. See en.wikipedia .org/wiki/AGDLP for more details on this approach.

Displaying the Sales Group

To verify that the Sales group exists, you can do the following:

```
# 7. Displaying the Sales Group
Get-ADGroup -Identity Sales
```

Figure 5.15 shows the output from this command.

```
PS C:\Foo> # 7. Displaying the Sales Group
PS C:\Foo> Get-ADGroup -Identity Sales

DistinguishedName : CN=Sales,CN=Users,DC=Reskit,DC=Org
GroupCategory     : Security
GroupScope        : Universal
Name              : Sales
ObjectClass       : group
ObjectGUID        : bf735c90-d023-4e94-81a5-90b8e51d103c
SamAccountName    : Sales
SID               : S-1-5-21-629383343-2974153759-1939089791-1144
```

Figure 5.15: Checking the sales group

In this case, having previously loaded the RSAT-AD tools, you can use `Get-ADGroup`. Had you not loaded these tools, you could have used remoting to run that command on a DC or a host with the AD tools loaded.

Adding Full Control for Domain Admins

The folder and file you created is intended for use only by the Sales group. To achieve that, you need to remove the inherited permissions and add permissions for the Sales group. You begin this by first giving the domain administrators full control over the folder (and the files within) using the `Add-NTFSAccess` command, as follows:

```
# 8. Adding explicit full control for Domain Admins
$AHT1 = @{
  Path         = 'C:\Secure1'
  Account      = 'Reskit\Domain Admins'
  AccessRights = 'FullControl'
}
Add-NTFSAccess @AHT1
```

This snippet adds an explicit and non-inherited ACE onto the folder, providing full control for domain admins. This explicit ACE is, by default, inherited by files in the folders and any other subfolders in the `C:\Secure1` folder. Depending on your requirements, you may choose not to do this and instead simply restrict the files to members of the Sales group. Should admin access be required at some later date, a domain or enterprise could always take control of the folder or file and give itself access.

Removing the Default File ACE

When you created `Secure.Txt`, Windows assigned a default (inherited) ACE allowing all users to read and execute all files. Because this is not desirable in most cases, you need to remove this ACE from the file's ACL, using the `Remove-NTFSAccess` command.

```
# 9. Remove Builtin\Users access from Secure.Txt file
$AHT2 = @{
  Path         = 'C:\Secure1\Secure.Txt'
  Account      = 'Builtin\Users'
  AccessRights = 'FullControl'
}
Remove-NTFSAccess @AHT2
```

Removing a Folder's Inherited Rights

The next step in securing the folder is to remove all inherited rights so that the folder has only those permissions explicitly set, with no inherited permissions. You do this using `Disable-NTFSAccessInheritance`, as follows:

```
# 10. Remove inherited rights for the folder
$IRHT1 = @{
  Path                      = 'C:\Secure1'
  RemoveInheritedAccessRules = $True
}
Disable-NTFSAccessInheritance @IRHT1
```

Adding Sales Group Access to the Folder

The final step in securing the folder is to add an explicit permission on the folder to the appropriate users. In this case, that means giving the domain's Sales group access to the files and any subfolders below `C:\Secure1`.

You do this again using `Add-NTFSAccess`, as follows:

```
# 11. Add Sales group access to the folder
$AHT3 = @{
  Path         = 'C:\Secure1\'
  Account      = 'Reskit\Sales'
  AccessRights = 'FullControl'
}
Add-NTFSAccess @AHT3
```

Because the Sales group has full control over the folder, this permission is inherited.

Depending on the nature of the information being held, alternate permission schemes may be needed. Achieving the desired scheme may require some additional folders and more complex permission sets. You may also need some additional groups so as to segregate users based on the desired level of security. And rather than giving users Full Control access (which enables them to change permissions), granting them Modify permissions may be adequate for their business needs.

However you choose to implement permissions for folders like this, setting the necessary permissions is made much easier by the NTFSSecurity module.

Viewing Permissions on the Folder

With the folder and file ACLs configured, you can verify the ACLs that result from these configuration steps. You can check the ACL on the folder using `Get-NTFSAccess`, as follows:

```
# 12. Get ACL of folder

Get-NTFSAccess -Path C:\Secure1 |
  Format-Table -AutoSize
```

Figure 5.16 shows the output. As you can see, the folder now has no inherited permissions—only the permissions you have set explicitly.

```
PS C:\Foo> # 12. Get ACL of folder
PS C:\Foo> Get-NTFSAccess -Path C:\Secure1 |
          Format-Table -AutoSize

   Path: C:\Secure1 (Inheritance disabled)

Account                 Access Rights Applies to                       Type  IsInherited InheritedFrom
-------                 ------------- ----------                       ----  ----------- -------------
RESKIT\Domain Admins FullControl    ThisFolderSubfoldersAndFiles Allow False
RESKIT\Sales            FullControl    ThisFolderSubfoldersAndFiles Allow False
```

Figure 5.16: Viewing the ACL of the folder

Viewing Permissions on the File

As a final step, you can view the ACL on the file itself, as follows:

```
# 13. Get ACL of the file
Get-NTFSAccess -Path C:\Secure1\Secure.Txt |
  Format-Table -AutoSize
```

Figure 5.17 shows the output of this snippet.

```
PS C:\Foo> # 13. Get ACL on the file
PS C:\Foo> Get-NTFSAccess -Path C:\Secure1\Secure.Txt |
          Format-Table -AutoSize

   Path: C:\Secure1\Secure.Txt (Inheritance enabled)

Account                 Access Rights Applies to       Type  IsInherited InheritedFrom
-------                 ------------- ----------       ----  ----------- -------------
RESKIT\Domain Admins FullControl    ThisFolderOnly Allow True         C:\Secure1
RESKIT\Sales            FullControl    ThisFolderOnly Allow True         C:\Secure1
```

Figure 5.17: Viewing the ACL of the file

This output shows the ACLs you have configured in this section. These ACLs give the necessary permissions to both the Domain Admins and members of the Sales Universal group.

In this section, you created a file folder on SRV1 and a file in that folder on which you set explicit ACLs. To achieve this, you ensured that you had the relevant modules loaded on SRV1, and you created a Universal group that holds the members of the Sales group. The steps shown did not add any users to the Sales group; that is easy enough to do, as shown in Chapter 3, "Managing Active Directory."

Also, this section created a Universal user group. If you are to have multiple domains and especially if you are creating groups that utilize a cross-forest trust, you might consider using a Domain Local group.

The commands in the NTFSSecurity module make it easier to manage ACLs on NTFS files and folders.

Managing Storage Replica

Storage Replica (SR) is a feature of Windows Server that replicates storage volumes between servers to support disaster recovery. Both the Standard and Data Center editions of Windows Server 2019 support SR. However, with Windows Server 2019 Standard Edition, SR can replicate only a single volume of 2TB (or less). Data Center edition has no specific limitations.

SR can replicate from any storage type to any other storage type. You can replicate spinning disks, SSDs, and iSCSI and Fiber Channel LUNs. For an overview of Storage Replica, see docs.microsoft.com/en-us/windows-server/storage/storage-replica/storage-replica-overview.

Before You Start

In this example you use three hosts. SRV1 and SRV2 are domain-joined hosts. In "Managing Disk and Volumes," you added two disk drives to SRV1 and made them available for use. You also make use of DC1, the domain controller for the Reskit.Org domain.

To demonstrate SR, both SRV1 and SRV2 require extra disks. You added two disks and created the necessary volumes for SRV1 in "Managing Disks and Volumes." For SRV2, you can create the necessary disks, add them to the SRV2 virtual machine, and then format them as follows:

```
# 0. Add VHDs to SRV2 VM
#    Run this on the Hyper-V VM Host
# Stop the vm
Stop-VM -Name SRV2
# Get File location for the disk in this VM
$VM = Get-VM -VMName SRV2
$Par = Split-Path -Path $VM.HardDrives[0].Path

# Create two VHDx for G and H on SRV2
```

Continues

continued

```
$NewPath1 = Join-Path -Path $par -ChildPath FDrive.VHDX
$NewPath2 = Join-Path -Path $Par -ChildPath GDrive.VHDX
$D1 = New-VHD -Path $NewPath1 -SizeBytes 128GB -Dynamic
$D2 = New-VHD -Path $NewPath2 -SizeBytes 128GB -Dynamic

# Add a new SCSI Controller to SRV2
$C = (Get-VMScsiController -VMName SRV2).count
Add-VMScsiController -VMname SRV2

# Add first disk to SRV2 VM
$HDHT = @{
   Path                = $NewPath1
   VMName              = 'SRV2'
   ControllerType      = 'SCSI'
   ControllerNumber    = $C
   ControllerLocation = 0
}
Add-VMHardDiskDrive @HDHT   # Add 1st disk to vm
# Add Seconf disk to VM
$HDHT.Path               = $NewPath2
$HDHT.ControllerLocation = 1
Add-VMHardDiskDrive @HDHT   # Add 2nd disk to VM
Start-VM -VMName SRV2

# After restart, run this on SRV2 as reskit\administrator

Get-Disk |
   Where-Object PartitionStyle -eq Raw |
     Initialize-Disk -PartitionStyle GPT
$NVHT = @{
   DiskNumber   = 1
   FriendlyName = 'Storage(F)'
   FileSystem   = 'NTFS'
   DriveLetter  = 'F'
}
New-Volume @NVHT  # Add 1st new disk
$NVHT.DiskNumber   = 2
$NVHT.FriendlyName = 'Log'
$NVHT.DriveLetter  = 'G'
New-Volume @NVHT  # Add 2nd new disk

###
```

With this snippet, you add two new disks to SRV2 and format the disks. With this and the configuration you set in "Managing Disks and Volumes," you now have two VMs with two additional disk drives that you have formatted using the NTFS filesystem.

Creating Content on F:

You start this exploration of SR by logging on to SRV1 as a domain administrator. Then you create some content on SRV1, as follows:

```
# 1. Create Content on F:
1..100 | ForEach-Object -Parallel {
  $NF = "F:\CoolFolder$_"
  New-Item -Path $NF -ItemType Directory | Out-Null
  1..100 | ForEach-Object {
    $NF2 = "$NF\CoolFile$_"
    "Cool File" | Out-File -PSPath $NF2
  }
}
```

This snippet creates 100 folders within the recently created F: drive and inside each folder creates 100 files, each with a tiny bit of content. This creates some data to be replicated using Storage Replica—not a large amount of data but enough for basic testing. If you are considering deploying Storage Replica, you may want to do performance testing; in that case, you would create a source volume of the size appropriate for your environment.

This snippet uses a new PowerShell 7 feature, Foreach-Object's new parameter -Parallel. In testing, using this switch reduces the run time of this snippet from around 17 seconds to less than 10 seconds. By default, PowerShell 7 runs five parallel operations at once, but you can adjust that by using the -Throttlelimit parameter. On most modern multicore systems, the default throttle limit is probably a good starting point. Depending on your hardware, you might choose to increase the throttle limit for improved performance. On a dual processor (each with six cores), setting the throttle limit to 12 improves performance.

Measuring the New Content

Having created content on F:, you measure the files/folders contained in the created content, as follows:

```
# 2. Measuring New Content on F:
Get-ChildItem -Path F:\ -Recurse | Measure-Object
```

Figure 5.18 shows the output of this cmdlet.

This is useful to verify the created content. As you can see, there are 10,100 items on F:. This consists of 100 folders plus 10,000 files, or 100 files in each folder.

```
PS C:\Foo> # 2. Measuring New Content on F:
PS C:\Foo> Get-ChildItem -Path F:\ -Recurse | Measure-Object

Count              : 10100
Average            :
Sum                :
Maximum            :
Minimum            :
StandardDeviation  :
Property           :
```

Figure 5.18: Viewing the F: drive

Checking Content on the Target

In this exercise we plan to replicate data from SRV1 to SRV2, using SR. Before setting this up, check to see what is on the F: drive on SRV2, as follows:

```
# 3. Examine the same drives remotely on SRV2
$SB = {
  Get-ChildItem -Path F:\ -Recurse |
    Measure-Object
}
Invoke-Command -ComputerName SRV2 -ScriptBlock $SB
```

Figure 5.19 shows the output of this snippet. Since the drive on SRV2 has not been used, there are no files on the drive.

```
PS C:\Foo> # 3. Examine the same drives remotely on SRV2
$SB = {
  Get-ChildItem -Path F:\ -Recurse |
    Measure-Object
}
Invoke-Command -ComputerName SRV2 -ScriptBlock $SB

Count          : 0
Average        :
Sum            :
Maximum        :
Minimum        :
Property       :
PSComputerName : SRV2
```

Figure 5.19: Viewing the content of SRV2

Adding the Storage Replica Feature to the Source

The SR feature is not installed by default but is easy to install, as follows:

```
# 4. Add Storage Replica feature to SRV1
Import-Module ServerManager
Install-WindowsFeature -Name Storage-Replica -IncludeManagementTools
```

You can see the output of this command in Figure 5.20.

```
PS C:\Foo> # 4. Add storage replica feature to SRV1
PS C:\Foo> Import-Module ServerManager
WARNING: Module ServerManager is loaded in Windows PowerShell using WinPSCompatSession
remoting session; please note that all input and output of commands from this module
will be deserialized objects. If you want to load this module into PowerShell Core
please use 'Import-Module -SkipEditionCheck' syntax.

PS C:\Foo> $Features = 'fs-fileserver', 'storage-replica'
PS C:\Foo> Add-WindowsFeature -Name Storage-Replica -IncludeManagementTools

Success Restart Needed Exit Code      Feature Result
------- -------------- ----------     --------------
True    Yes            SuccessRestar… {Feature Administration Tools, Storage Repli…
```

Figure 5.20: The result of adding SR to `SRV1`

In the figure, you see a warning message that `Import-Module` produces when it loads any module using the Windows PowerShell compatibility mechanism described in Chapter 2, "PowerShell 7 Compatibility with Windows PowerShell." You can, as you see in other code fragments in this book, use the `-WarningAction` parameter to avoid seeing this warning.

Restarting the Source

With the installation of the SR feature completed, you need to reboot the server to finalize the installation, using `Restart-Computer` as follows:

```
# 5. Restart SRV1 to finish the installation process
Restart-Computer
```

Adding Storage Replica to the Target

When you set up a Storage Replica partnership, you need to have the Storage Replica feature installed on both the source and target systems, in this case `SRV1` and `SRV2`. You next add the feature, remotely, to `SRV2` with the `Install-WindowsFeature` command.

```
# 6. Add SR Feature to SRV2 Remotely
$SB = {
  Install-WindowsFeature -Name Storage-Replica | Out-Null
}
Invoke-Command -ComputerName SRV2 -ScriptBlock $SB
```

Restarting the Target

As with SRV1, you need to restart SRV2 to finalize the installation of SR on that server.

```
# 7. Restart SRV2 and wait for the restart
$RSHT = @{
  ComputerName = 'SRV2'
  Force        = $true
}
Restart-Computer @RSHT -Wait -For PowerShell
```

This snippet restarts SRV2 and waits until the reboot has completed and connectivity to the server is available (using PowerShell). In some cases, it appears that the Restart-Computer cmdlet takes a long time to complete (even though the reboot has been completed). If you can verify that the reboot is complete (for example, by logging into SRV2), then you can stop this command (using Ctrl+C) and move on to the next step.

Testing the Configuration of SR

You now have the Storage Replica feature installed on the two servers, the necessary disk volumes established, and the source disk populated with content. With this in place, you can test the validity of an SR partnership between these two servers. You can do this from SRV1 using the Test-SRTopology cmdlet, as follows:

```
# 8. Test Replica on SRV2 from SRV1
Import-WinModule -Name StorageReplica -WarningAction SilentlyContinue
$TSTHT = @{
  SourceComputerName        = 'SRV1.Reskit.Org'
  SourceVolumeName          = 'F:'
  SourceLogVolumeName       = 'G:'
  DestinationComputerName   = 'SRV2.Reskit.Org'
  DestinationVolumeName     = 'F:'
  DestinationLogVolumeName  = 'G'
  DurationInMinutes         = 15
  ResultPath                = 'C:\Foo'
  Verbose                   = $true
  IgnorePerfTests           = $true
}
Test-SRTopology @TSTHT
```

Figure 5.21 shows the output.

The Storage Replica module is among those that PowerShell 7 does not support natively. But the commands in the module work when used with the Windows PowerShell compatibility mechanism described in Chapter 2.

```
PS C:\Foo> # 8. Test Replica on SRV2 from SRV1
PS C:\Foo> Import-Module -Name StorageReplica -WarningAction SilentlyContinue
PS C:\Foo> $TSTHT = @{
            SourceComputerName        = 'SRV1.Reskit.Org'
            SourceVolumeName          = 'F:'
            SourceLogVolumeName       = 'G:'
            DestinationComputerName   = 'SRV2.Reskit.Org'
            DestinationVolumeName     = 'F:'
            DestinationLogVolumeName  = 'G'
            DurationInMinutes         = 15
            ResultPath                = 'C:\Foo'
            Verbose                   = $true
            IgnorePerfTests           = $true
          }
PS C:\Foo> Test-SRTopology @TSTHT

Validating data and log volumes...
Test completed. Result at C:\Foo\TestSrTopologyReport-2020-01-31-17-06-31.html
```

Figure 5.21: Testing the SR configuration

As you can see, `Test-SRTopology` performs the topology test and creates a report showing the test results. The report is generated as an HTML file in the `ResultPath` specified, in this case `C:\Foo`. The filename is created embedding the date and time of the test.

If you are using SR in production, it may be useful to perform routine testing of your SR infrastructure.

Viewing the Topology Test Report

You can view the report as follows:

```
# 9. View the Report
$File = Get-ChildItem C:\Foo\testsr* |
        Sort-Object -Property LastWriteTime -Descending |
          Select-Object -First 1
  Start-Process -Filepath $File
```

This snippet brings up the topology test report in a browser, as shown in Figure 5.22. The report consists of two parts. At the top of the report, you see an overview of results; in this case the overall topology test was successful. Then, you see detailed test results for each of the 20 specific tests that the command ran to diagnose the potential SR partnership. This snippet also displays only the most recent report.

One test that the `Test-SRTopology` command runs is to ensure you have adequate memory. If you created your SRV1 VM with low memory, you may see an error or warning. In that case, consider increasing the amount of memory allocated to the VM.

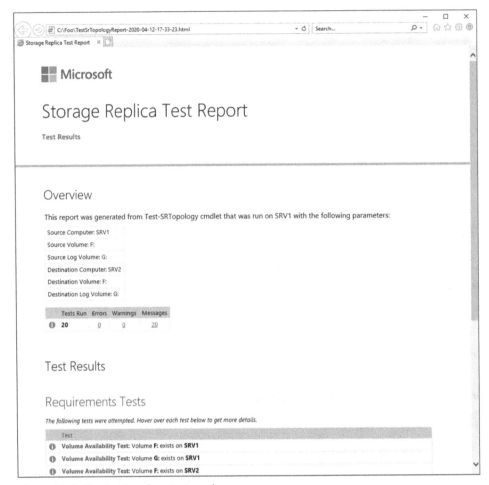

Figure 5.22: Viewing topology test results

The `Test-SRTopology` cmdlet can also evaluate the likely performance of the partnership, although in the snippet here, this test was omitted. If you are using Storage Replica to replicate volumes across a WAN, this testing should be done to ensure performance meets your requirements.

You might also consider running these topology tests on a frequent basis if Storage Replica forms a part of your disaster recovery strategy.

Creating a Storage Replica Partnership

Given that the test in the previous section was successful, you can now set up a Storage Replica partnership with the `New-SRPartnership` command as follows:

```
# 10. Create an SR Replica Partnership
$SRHT = @{
```

```
        SourceComputerName        = 'SRV1'
        SourceRGName              = 'SRV1RG'
        SourceVolumeName          = 'F:'
        SourceLogVolumeName       = 'G:'
        DestinationComputerName   = 'SRV2'
        DestinationRGName         = 'SRV2RG'
        DestinationVolumeName     = 'F:'
        DestinationLogVolumeName  = 'G:'
        LogSizeInBytes            = 2gb
    }
    New-SRPartnership @SRHT -Verbose
```

You can see the results of running this code in Figure 5.23.

```
PS C:\Foo> # 10. Create an SR Replica Partnership
PS C:\Foo> $SRHT = @{
            SourceComputerName       = 'SRV1'
            SourceRGName             = 'SRV1RG'
            SourceVolumeName         = 'F:'
            SourceLogVolumeName      = 'G:'
            DestinationComputerName  = 'SRV2'
            DestinationRGName        = 'SRV2RG'
            DestinationVolumeName    = 'F:'
            DestinationLogVolumeName = 'G:'
            LogSizeInBytes           = 2gb
         }
PS C:\Foo> New-SRPartnership @SRHT -Verbose

RunspaceId              : ef20f99f-879b-443a-88a7-c5b238aae776
DestinationComputerName : SRV2
DestinationRGName       : SRV2RG
Id                      : 62d513ab-6d0e-411d-9745-552c542959d5
SourceComputerName      : SRV1
SourceRGName            : SRV1RG
```

Figure 5.23: Creating an SR partnership

As you can see, there is not much information returned when an SR partnership is created successfully.

With the SR partnership in place, Storage Replica is now able to replicate the data from SRV1 to SRV2. The initial synchronization time is dependent on the total amount of data to be transferred. Once the drive is synchronized initially, any changes to the source volume are replicated to the target volume on the other server.

Viewing the Partnership

You can view the just-created SR partnership using Get-SRPartnership as follows:

```
# 11. View the SR partnership
Get-SRPartnership
```

Figure 5.24 shows the output of this command.

```
PS C:\Foo> # 11. View the SR partnership
PS C:\Foo> Get-SRPartnership

RunspaceId               : ef20f99f-879b-443a-88a7-c5b238aae776
DestinationComputerName  : SRV2
DestinationRGName        : SRV2RG
Id                       : 62d513ab-6d0e-411d-9745-552c542959d5
SourceComputerName       : SRV1
SourceRGName             : SRV1RG
```

Figure 5.24: Viewing the SR partnership

We can see the source and target systems and volumes in use in the partnership. The output from this step is essentially the same output you observed when creating the SR partnership.

Examining Volumes on the Target

With the SR partnership established, you can look to see what is on the F: volume on SRV2, as follows:

```
# 12. Examine the same drives remotely on SRV2
$SB = {
  Get-Volume |
    Sort-Object -Property DriveLetter |
      Format-Table
}
Invoke-Command -ComputerName SRV2 -ScriptBlock $SB
```

Figure 5.25 shows the output of this snippet.

```
PS C:\Foo> # 12. Examine the same drives remotely on SRV2
PS C:\Foo> $SB = {
            Get-Volume |
              Sort-Object -Property DriveLetter |
                Format-Table
          }
PS C:\Foo> Invoke-Command -ComputerName SRV2 -ScriptBlock $SB

DriveLetter FriendlyName FileSystemType DriveType HealthStatus OperationalStatus SizeRemaining      Size
----------- ------------ -------------- --------- ------------ ----------------- -------------      ----
A                        Unknown        Removable Healthy      Unknown                     0 B       0 B
C                        NTFS           Fixed     Healthy      OK                      116.01 GB    128 GB
D                        Unknown        CD-ROM    Healthy      Unknown                     0 B       0 B
F                        Unknown        Fixed     Healthy      Unknown                     0 B       0 B
G           Log          NTFS           Fixed     Healthy      OK                      125.88 GB 127.98 GB
```

Figure 5.25: Examining volumes on SRV2

As you can see, the F: partition/drive on SRV2 is not available as a volume. The partition is locked by Storage Replica, which means you cannot access it as a usable file storage volume so long as SR is using it as a replication target.

Even though you can't see any files, Storage Replica continues to monitor the F: partition/drive on SRV1 and replicate it to SRV2.

Reversing the Replication

Even though the target volume in an SR partnership is not viewable or accessible, Windows Server is constantly replicating any content update.

As part of recovering from a disaster, you may need to reverse the replication and have Windows replicate from SRV2 to SRV1. If you do this, Storage Replica makes the F: volume on SRV2 viewable while making the new target volume on SRV1 unviewable. You reverse the replication as follows:

```
# 13. Reverse the replication
$SRHT2 = @{
  NewSourceComputerName    = 'SRV2'
  SourceRGName             = 'SRV2RG'
  DestinationComputerName  = 'SRV1'
  DestinationRGName         = 'SRV1RG'
  Confirm                  = $false
}
Set-SRPartnership @SRHT2
```

Viewing Updated Replication Group Status

With the replication reversed, you can view the status of the replication partnership, as follows:

```
# 14. View SR Partnership on SRV1
Get-SRPartnership
```

You can see the results of this command in Figure 5.26.

```
PS C:\Foo> # 14. View SR Partnership on SRV1
PS C:\Foo> Get-SRPartnership

RunspaceId                 : ef20f99f-879b-443a-88a7-c5b238aae776
DestinationComputerName    : SRV1
DestinationRGName          : SRV1RG
Id                         : 62d513ab-6d0e-411d-9745-552c542959d5
SourceComputerName         : SRV2
SourceRGName               : SRV2RG
```

Figure 5.26: Examining updated RG status

This output shows that SR is now replicating from SRV2 to SRV1. This means the files are available on SRV2 but are not visible as files on SRV1.

Examining SRV2 Volumes

With the replication reversed, you can examine the disks and the replicated content available on SRV2, as follows:

```
# 15. Examine the same drives remotely on SRV2
$SB = {
  Get-Volume |
    Sort-Object -Property DriveLetter |
      Format-Table
    Get-ChildItem -Path F:\ -Recurse | Measure-Object |
      Format-List


}
Invoke-Command -ComputerName SRV2 -ScriptBlock $SB
```

You can see the output of this snippet in Figure 5.27.

```
PS C:\Foo> # 15. Examine the same drives remotely on SRV2
PS C:\Foo> $SB = {
            Get-Volume |
              Sort-Object -Property DriveLetter |
                Format-Table
              Get-ChildItem -Path F:\ -Recurse | Measure-Object |
                Format-List


            }
PS C:\Foo> Invoke-Command -ComputerName SRV2 -ScriptBlock $SB

DriveLetter FriendlyName FileSystemType DriveType HealthStatus OperationalStatus SizeRemaining      Size
----------- ------------ -------------- --------- ------------ ----------------- -------------      ----
A                        Unknown        Removable Healthy      Unknown                     0 B       0 B
C                        NTFS           Fixed     Healthy      OK                    116.01 GB    128 GB
D                        Unknown        CD-ROM    Healthy      Unknown                     0 B       0 B
F           Storage(F)   NTFS           Fixed     Healthy      OK                    127.87 GB 127.98 GB
G           Log          NTFS           Fixed     Healthy      OK                    125.88 GB 127.98 GB


Count    : 10100
Average  :
Sum      :
Maximum  :
Minimum  :
Property :
```

Figure 5.27: Examining volumes on SRV2

The F: drive is now available on SRV2 and healthy. Additionally, you can see that this drive now has the same 10,100 total items.

This section has demonstrated the ease with which you can use Storage Replica as part of a disaster-recovery implementation. As you have seen, you cannot use the data on the SR target while the SR is replicating (or able to replicate).

Managing Filestore Quotas

The File Server Resource Manager (FSRM) is a Windows Server feature that helps you to manage file servers. FSRM allows you to implement quotas on file stores, perform a variety of file management tasks, perform file screening, and offer in-depth reporting. For an overview of FSRM, see `docs.microsoft.com/ windows-server/storage/fsrm/fsrm-overview`.

In this section, you install the FSRM feature and use FSRM's quota management capability to set and test these quotas.

Before You Start

This section uses three servers (VMs), `SRV1`, `SRV2`, and `DC1`, which you have used in other sections of this chapter. You run the snippets in this section on `SRV1`. This Windows Server 2019 host has PowerShell 7 loaded.

FSRM features include the ability to send email, for example when a user has exceeded a filestore quota or has attempted to store a file of a particular file type (for example, an MP3 music file) prohibited via FSRM file screening.

To test FSRM email functionality, you need an SMTP server that FSRM uses to send email. In this section, you also use `SRV1` as the SMTP server (or relay).

For testing purposes in this chapter, you have alternatives with respect to the email server. If you have an internal SMTP server, then you can change the FSRM settings accordingly.

If you do not have access to an SMTP server, an option is to install IIS with the SMTP server on `SRV1` and use it as an SMTP relay to an SMTP smart host. One free relay service that many IT pros have used is offered by `SendGrid.com`. With the free service, you can send up to 100 emails per day, which should be more than adequate to test FSRM. To assist you in setting up this service, use `//tfl09.blogspot.com/2020/04/setting-up-smtp-relay-using-sendgrid.html`.

The example emails shown in this section were sent via the SMTP relay on `SRV1` to `SendGrid.com`, which then forwarded them onward. This is an excellent solution for testing. However, in production, you would configure FSRM with different settings to send mail to an internal mail server.

Installing the FS Resource Manager Feature

The FSRM feature is not deployed by default. You add it in the same way as other Windows Server features, as follows:

```
# 1. Install FS Resource Manager feature on SRV1
Import-Module -Name ServerManager -WarningAction 'SllentlyContinue'
```

Continues

continued

```
$IHT = @{
  Name                    = 'FS-Resource-Manager'
  IncludeManagementTools  = $True
  WarningActtion          = 'SilentlyContinue'
}
Install-WindowsFeature @IHT
```

Figure 5.28 shows the output from this step.

```
PS C:\Foo> # 1. Install FS Resource Manager feature on SRV1
PS C:\Foo> Import-module -Name ServerManager -WarningAction 'SllentlyContinue'
PS C:\Foo> $IHT = @{
             Name                   = 'FS-Resource-Manager'
             IncludeManagementTools = $True
             WarningAction          = 'SilentlyContinue'
           }
PS C:\Foo> Install-WindowsFeature @IHT

Success Restart Needed Exit Code  Feature Result
------- -------------- ---------  --------------
True    No             Success    {File and iSCSI Services, File Server, File …
```

Figure 5.28: Installing FSRM

Setting Up SMTP Settings for FSRM

FSRM can be configured to send email when important filesystem events occur.
Now that you have installed the FSRM feature, you configure the email settings
as follows:

```
# 2. Set SMTP settings in FSRM
$MHT = @{
  SmtpServer        = 'SRV1.Reskit.Org'
  FromEmailAddress  = 'FSRM@Reskit.Org'
  AdminEmailAddress = 'Doctordns@Gmail.Com'
}
Set-FsrmSetting @MHT
```

This snippet tells FSRM to send email to an SMTP server on SRV1. You should
adjust these details if you can send mail via another SMTP server. Ensure that
you are able to send email via your configured server before continuing.

Also, you should change the admin email address, unless you want to send
the book's author email.

Sending a Test Email

To check your SMTP settings, you can get FSRM to send a test email using the
email settings you just configured, using Send-FsrmTestEmail.

```
# 3. Send a test email to check the setup
$MHT = @{
  ToEmailAddress = 'DoctorDNS@gmail.com'
  Confirm        = $false
}
Send-FsrmTestEmail @MHT
```

This snippet sends a test email to the configured email address, using the SMTP server on SRV1.Reskit.Org. Although the snippet produces no visible output, you can see the email sent in Figure 5.29. If for some reason FSRM is not able to connect to the SMTP server, you would see an error 0x8004531c. In that case, you need to troubleshoot your SMTP server.

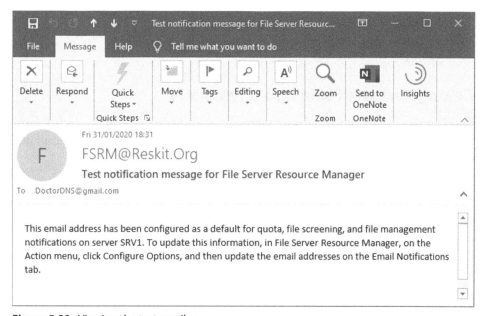

Figure 5.29: Viewing the test email

If you intend to utilize FSRM's email features, you need to ensure the FSRM email settings are working before proceeding. And you need to ensure that the remote SMTP server is online, is reachable, and is processing email. Some ISPs do not allow customers to use SMTP gateways such as SendGrid. Configuring and troubleshooting SMTP email is outside the scope of this book. If you get stuck, consider asking for help in the Spiceworks PowerShell forum at community.spiceworks.com/programming/powershell. Or just continue and omit using FSRM's email features.

Creating an FSRM Quota Template

FSRM implements templates for quotas that you can use to apply specific quota permissions. Several are built in, and you can create your own FSRM quota template that preconfigures some FSRM quota settings. Doing so allows you to create a filestore quota at any later time based on a template. You can create a new template as follows:

```
# 4. Create a new FSRM quota template for a 10MB hard limit
$QHT1 = @{
  Name        = '10 MB Reskit Quota'
  Description = 'Filestore Quota (10mb) For'
  Size        = 10MB
}
New-FsrmQuotaTemplate @QHT1
```

This snippet creates a new FSRM quota template.

Viewing Available FSRM Quota Templates

FSRM ships with a number of quota templates, and you can add or modify templates to suit your needs. You can view all the available FSRM quota templates with the Get-FsrmQuotaTemplate command.

```
# 5. View available FSRM quota templates
Get-FsrmQuotaTemplate |
    Format-Table -Property Name, Description, Size, SoftLimit
```

You can see the output of this snippet in Figure 5.30.

```
PS C:\Foo> # 5. View available FSRM quota templates

PS C:\Foo> Get-FsrmQuotaTemplate |
           Format-Table -Property Name, Description, Size, SoftLimit

Name                               Description                       Size SoftLimit
----                               -----------                       ---- ---------
100 MB Limit                                                    104857600     False
200 MB Limit Reports to User                                   209715200     False
Monitor 200 GB Volume Usage                                  214748364800      True
Monitor 500 MB Share                                           524288000      True
200 MB Limit with 50 MB Extension                              209715200     False
250 MB Extended Limit                                          262144000     False
2 GB Limit                                                    2147483648     False
5 GB Limit                                                    5368709120     False
10 GB Limit                                                  10737418240     False
Monitor 3 TB Volume Usage                                  3298534883328      True
Monitor 5 TB Volume Usage                                  5497558138880      True
Monitor 10 TB Volume Usage                                10995116277760      True
10 MB Reskit Quota                 Filestore Quota (10mb) For      10485760     False
```

Figure 5.30: Viewing quota templates

Creating a New Folder

To test FSRM quotas, you create a new folder, as follows:

```
# 6. Create a new folder on which to place quotas
If (-Not (Test-Path C:\Quota)) {
  New-Item -Path C:\Quota -ItemType Directory  |
    Out-Null
}
```

With this folder created, you can complete the actions necessary to protect the folder with an FSRM quota.

Building an FSRM Action

An FSRM *action* is an in-memory object that contains details of an action you want FSRM to take when a quota threshold is exceeded. You create an action before creating the FSRM quota, as follows:

```
# 7.  Build an FSRM Action
$Body = @'
User [Source Io Owner] has exceeded the [Quota Threshold]% quota
threshold for the quota on [Quota Path] on server [Server].
The quota limit is [Quota Limit MB] MB, and [Quota Used MB] MB
currently is in use ([Quota Used Percent]% of limit).
'@
$NAHT = @{
  Type      = 'Email'
  MailTo    = 'Doctordns@gmail.Com'
  Subject   = 'FSRM Over limit [Source Io Owner]'
  Body      = $Body
}
$Action1 = New-FsrmAction @NAHT
```

This FSRM action is used to send email to DoctorDNS@Gmail.Com with a body containing details of the quota exceeded. The email body contains a number of variables and is customizable. For details of the variables you can use in an Email body, see docs.microsoft.com/en-us/previous-versions/windows/it-pro/windows-server-2008-R2-and-2008/cc788122%28v%3dws.10%29#quota-notification-variables.

This action is created in memory and as such is not persisted anywhere. Also, there is no Get-FSRMAction cmdlet.

Create an FSRM Threshold

You next build an FSRM *threshold*. The threshold, which is another in-memory object, contains a threshold percentage and an action. You create the threshold object as follows:

```
# 8. Create an FSRM threshold
$Thresh = New-FsrmQuotaThreshold -Percentage 85 -Action $Action1
```

This threshold object, when later added to an FSRM quota, instructs FSRM to do the action in $action1 when the usage exceeds 85% of the quota.

Note that the FSRM threshold and the FSRM action are in-memory objects and do not persist across a reboot or into another PowerShell session. You use these objects as part of creating an FSRM quota.

Building an FSRM Quota

To build a persistent FSRM quota, you use the New-FSRMQuota cmdlet, like this:

```
# 9.  Build a quota for the folder
$NQHT1 = @{
  Path      = 'C:\Quota'
  Template  = '10 MB Reskit Quota'
  Threshold = $Thresh
}
New-FsrmQuota @NQHT1
```

You can view the output of this snippet in Figure 5.31.

```
PS C:\Foo> # 9.  Build a quota for the folder
PS C:\Foo> $NQHT1 = @{
          Path      = 'C:\Quota'
          Template  = '10 MB Reskit Quota'
          Threshold = $Thresh
        }
PS C:\Foo> New-FsrmQuota @NQHT1

Description    :
Disabled       : False
MatchesTemplate : False
Path           : C:\Quota
PeakUsage      : 1024
Size           : 10485760
SoftLimit      : False
Template       : 10 MB Reskit Quota
Threshold      : {MSFT_FSRMQuotaThreshold}
Usage          : 1024
PSComputerName :
```

Figure 5.31: Building a quota

This code tells FSRM to impose a 10MB quota on `C:\Quota`. Additionally, when the usage of the folder exceeds 85% (8.5MB), FSRM sends email to the user who exceeds the threshold. In this case, the quota uses the specified template, which provides you with flexibility. You could have just specified a limit (such as 10MB).

Test the 85% Quota Threshold

Now that you have set up an FSRM quota, based on a template, you can test the quota. Here is one way to test it:

```
# 10. Test the 85% SOFT quota limit on C:\Quota
Get-ChildItem -Path C:\Quota -Recurse |
  Remove-Item -Force # for testing purposes!
$S = '+'.PadRight(8MB)
# make a first file - under the soft quota
$S | Out-File -FilePath C:\Quota\Demo1.Txt
$S2 = '+'.PadRight(.66MB)
# Now create a second file to take the user over the soft quota
$S2 | Out-File -FilePath C:\Quota\Demo2.Txt
```

In this snippet, you first ensure that the folder is empty and then create a file (`Demo1.Txt`) that is smaller than the quota threshold. You then create a second file (`Demo2.txt`) that exceeds the soft quota threshold but does not use all of the quota. Because this snippet did not exceed the full 10MB quota limit, there is no direct output. Once a user exceeds a threshold, FSRM sends an email as you previously configured.

Examining the FSRM Email

In the previous step, you created two files. The first was within the threshold, but creating the second took you over the 85% soft quota threshold. Because you exceeded the soft threshold, FSRM sends an email, which you can see in Figure 5.32.

The output tells you which user has exceeded which quota. The mail also tells you the current maximum quota limit and how much is presently in use.

Testing the Hard Quota Limit

With a soft quota, a user can exceed the quota and save extra data. You can also create hard quota limits; for example, a hard quota limit on the `C:\Quota` folder of 10MB. With such a hard quota, any attempt to use more than the quota fails. You can test this by creating another large file in the `C:\Quota` folder, as follows:

```
# 11. Test hard limit quota
$S | Out-File -FilePath C:\Quota\Demo3.Txt
```

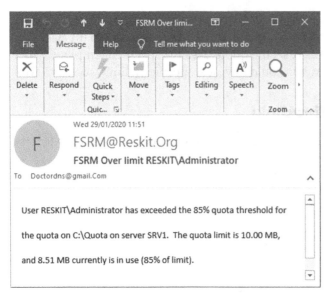

Figure 5.32: Examining the FSRM email

This step does two things. First FSRM generates an error message, shown in Figure 5.33.

```
PS C:\Foo> # 12. Test hard limit quota
PS C:\Foo> $S | Out-File –FilePath C:\Quota\demo3.Txt

out-lineoutput:
Line |
   2 |   $S | Out-File –FilePath C:\Quota\demo3.Txt

     | ┈┈┈┈┈┈┈┈┈┈┈┈┈┈┈┈┈┈┈┈┈┈┈┈┈┈┈┈┈┈┈┈┈┈┈┈┈┈┈┈┈┈┈┈┈┈┈┈┈┈
     | There is not enough space on the disk. : 'C:\Quota\demo3.Txt'
```

Figure 5.33: Testing the quota limit

The error message says that there is not enough space in the drive even though the actual error is that the quota has been fully used. If you are used to Windows PowerShell, the figure shows you PowerShell 7's new error reporting feature, which simplifies what you see when errors occur in your scripts or when running commands as in this case.

Note that error display in PowerShell differs from Windows PowerShell. You also get slightly different output if you run a line of code directly at the console or if you run it via a script file (or highlight the line of code with VS Code and run the selection). When run as a script, PowerShell provides details of where the error occurred.

The second thing that happens is that the Out-File option creates a new file, Demo3.Txt. But Windows only writes away contents that do not exceed the quota—the file is truncated to ensure that the folder does not exceed the hard quota.

Viewing the Folder Contents

Although you attempted to create Demo3.Txt to be the same size as Demo1.Txt, there is insufficient quota left. You can see the total size of all three files, as follows:

```
# 13. View Folder
Get-ChildItem -Path C:\Quota |
    Measure-Object -Sum -Property Length
```

Figure 5.34 shows the output from this step.

```
PS C:\Foo> # 13. View Folder
PS C:\Foo> Get-ChildItem -Path C:\Quota |
            Measure-Object -Sum -Property Length

Count             : 3
Average           :
Sum               : 10522464
Maximum           :
Minimum           :
StandardDeviation :
Property          : Length
```

Figure 5.34: Viewing the total size of the folder contents

As you can see, the total amount of space used by the three files you created in C:\Quota does not exceed the 10MB quota you assigned.

Managing File Screening

FSRM's file screening controls the types of files you allow to be stored on your file server. You could, for example, define a file screen to prohibit music files (files with the .FLAC or .MP3 extension) to be saved to your file server. If a user attempts to download and save a file such as GD71-02-18.T09.FLAC, FSRM stops the user from saving the file.

To configure FSRM file screening, you need to specify the folder to be screened and a file screen template that describes the file characteristics of files that FSRM should block. FSRM comes with five built-in file screen templates. You can create further templates to suit your requirements.

A file screen template contains a set of *file groups*, in which each file group defines a set of file extensions to block. FSRM comes with 11 built-in file groups that cover common content types and can be updated and extended.

One built-in FSRM file group is Audio and Video Files. This group, for example, includes a wide variety of audio and video file extensions, including .AAC, .MP3, .FLAC, and more. Interestingly, this built-in file group does not block .SHN (Shorten) files. Shorten is a lossless compression algorithm that was in effect replaced by .FLAC files but is much loved in music trading circles. You could easily add this extension to the relevant file group, should you wish.

Note that file screening works solely on the basis of file extensions. FSRM would block you saving a file such as GD71-02-18.T09.FLAC. However, if you stored that same file as GD71-02-18.T09.CALF, FSRM would allow the file to be stored. The FSRM file screening does not examine the file to ascertain the actual file type. A user who attempts to get around a corporate file screen ban using this technique can be disciplined more harshly for deliberately and willfully violating company security.

Before You Start

This section uses the domain-joined server SRV1.Reskit.Org, which has FSRM installed and configured. You set up FSRM on SRV1 in the "Managing Filestore Quotas" section.

Examining Existing FSRM File Groups

When you install FSRM (in "Managing Filestore Quotas"), the default installation creates a set of file groups you can use when you set up file screening. You can use Get-FsrmFileGroup to view the existing file groups.

```
# 1. Examine the existing file groups
Get-FsrmFileGroup |
    Format-Table -Property Name, IncludePattern
```

Figure 5.35 shows the output of this snippet.

As you can see, there is a useful set of file groups you can use to set up file screening.

There is a lot of information being output from this snippet, so you may need to adjust the width of your PowerShell console or VS Code to see the full output (and avoid PowerShell truncation). Also, consider changing the value of the default variable $PSFormatEnumerationLimit to see more of the file patterns.

Examining the Existing File Screen Templates

The default installation of FSRM also creates a number of file screening templates, which you can view using Get-FsrmFileScreenTemplate as follows:

```
# 2. Examine existing File Screen templates
Get-FsrmFileScreenTemplate |
    Format-Table -Property Name, IncludeGroup, Active
```

You can see the output in Figure 5.36.

```
PS C:\Foo> # 1. Examine the existing file groups
PS C:\Foo> Get-FsrmFileGroup |
           Format-Table -Property Name, IncludePattern

Name                     IncludePattern
----                     --------------
Audio and Video Files    {*.aac, *.aif, *.aiff, *.asf, *.asx, *.au, *.avi,
                          *.flac, *.m3u, *.mid, *.midi, *.mov, *.mp1, *.mp2,
                          *.mp3, *.mp4, *.mpa, *.mpe, *.mpeg, *.mpeg2, *.mpeg3,
                          *.mpg, *.ogg, *.qt, *.qtw, *.ram, *.rm, *.rmi, *.rmvb,
                          *.snd, *.swf, *.vob, *.wav, *.wax, *.wma, *.wmv, *.wvx}
Image Files              {*.bmp, *.dib, *.eps, *.gif, *.img, *.jfif, *.jpe,
                          *.jpeg, *.jpg, *.pcx, *.png, *.ps, *.psd, *.raw, *.rif,
                          *.spiff, *.tif, *.tiff}
Office Files             {*.accdb, *.accde, *.accdr, *.accdt, *.adn, *.adp,
                          *.doc, *.docm, *.docx, *.dot, *.dotm, *.dotx, *.grv,
                          *.gsa, *.gta, *.mad, *.maf, *.mda, *.mda, *.mda, *.mdb,
                          *.mde, *.mdf, *.mdf, *.mdm, *.mdt, *.mdw, *.mdw, *.mdw,
                          *.mdz, *.mpd, *.mpp, *.mpt, *.obt, *.odb, *.one,
                          *.onepkg, *.pot, *.potm, *.potx, *.ppa, *.ppam, *.pps,
                          *.ppsm, *.ppsx, *.ppt, *.pptm, *.pptx, *.pub, *.pwz,
                          *.rqy, *.rtf, *.rwz, *.sldm, *.sldx, *.slk, *.thmx,
                          *.vdx, *.vsd, *.vsl, *.vss, *.vst, *.vsu, *.vsw, *.vsx,
                          *.vtx, *.wbk, *.wri, *.xla, *.xlam, *.xlb, *.xlc,
                          *.xld, *.xlk, *.xll, *.xlm, *.xls, *.xlsb, *.xlsm,
                          *.xlsx, *.xlt, *.xltm, *.xltx, *.xlv, *.xlw, *.xsf,
                          *.xsn}
E-mail Files             {*.eml, *.idx, *.mbox, *.mbx, *.msg, *.oft, *.ost,
                          *.pab, *.pst}
Executable Files         {*.bat, *.cmd, *.com, *.cpl, *.exe, *.inf, *.js, *.jse,
                          *.msh, *.msi, *.msp, *.ocx, *.pif, *.pl, *.ps1, *.scr,
                          *.vb, *.vbs, *.wsf, *.wsh}
System Files             {*.acm, *.dll, *.ocx, *.sys, *.vxd}
Compressed Files         {*.ace, *.arc, *.arj, *.bhx, *.bz2, *.cab, *.gz,
                          *.gzip, *.hpk, *.hqx, *.jar, *.lha, *.lzh, *.lzx,
                          *.pak, *.pit, *.rar, *.sea, *.sit, *.sqz, *.tgz, *.uu,
                          *.uue, *.z, *.zip, *.zoo}
Web Page Files           {*.asp, *.aspx, *.cgi, *.css, *.dhtml, *.hta, *.htm,
                          *.html, *.mht, *.php, *.php3, *.shtml, *.url}
Text Files               {*.asc, *.text, *.txt}
Backup Files             {*.bak, *.bck, *.bkf, *.old}
Temporary Files          {*.temp, *.tmp, ~*}
```

Figure 5.35: Examining the existing file groups

```
PS C:\Foo> # 2. Examine existing File Screen templates
PS C:\Foo> Get-FsrmFileScreenTemplate |
           Format-Table -Property Name, IncludeGroup, Active

Name                               IncludeGroup                        Active
----                               ------------                        ------
Block Audio and Video Files        {Audio and Video Files}             True
Block Executable Files             {Executable Files}                  True
Block Image Files                  {Image Files}                       True
Block E-mail Files                 {E-mail Files}                      True
Monitor Executable and System Files {Executable Files, System Files}   False
```

Figure 5.36: Examining existing templates

This snippet shows you the name of each of the five built-in templates and, for each template, what file groups are included in the template and whether the screen template represents an active file screen.

Creating a New File Folder

To test file screening, you create a new folder, `C:\FileScreen`, as follows:

```
# 3. Create a new folder
$Path = 'C:\FileScreen'
If (-Not (Test-Path -Path $Path)) {
  New-Item -Path $Path -ItemType Directory  |
    Out-Null
}
```

If the folder does not exist, this snippet creates it.

Creating a New File Screen

You create a file screen that blocks executable files from being saved to the folder `C:\FileScreen`, as follows:

```
# 4. Create a new file screen
$FSHT =  @{
  Path         = $Path
  Description  = 'Block Executable Files'
  IncludeGroup = 'Executable Files'
}
New-FsrmFileScreen @FSHT
```

You can view the output of this snippet in Figure 5.37.

```
PS C:\Foo> # 4. Create a new file screen
PS C:\Foo> $FSHT =  @{
          Path         = $Path
          Description  = 'Block Executable Files'
          IncludeGroup = 'Executable Files'
        }
PS C:\Foo> New-FsrmFileScreen @FSHT

Active          : True
Description     : Block Executable Files
IncludeGroup    : {Executable Files}
MatchesTemplate : False
Notification    :
Path            : C:\FileScreen
Template        :
PSComputerName  :
```

Figure 5.37: Creating a file screen

The output indicates that this file screen is active and identifies what it is screening (executable files in C:\Filescreen).

Testing File Screening

Now that you have set up the file screening, you can test it. One simple way to test the screen is to copy an executable file (such as the Windows notepad.exe program) into the protected folder. You can test this as follows:

```
# 5. Test file screen by copying notepad.exe
$FSTHT = @{
  Path        = "$Env:windir\notepad.exe"
  Destination = 'C:\FileScreen\notepad.exe'
}
Copy-Item  @FSTHT
```

You can see the error output from this command in Figure 5.38.

```
PS C:\Foo> # 5. Test file screen by copying notepad.exe
PS C:\Foo> $FSTHT = @{
            Path        = "$Env:windir\notepad.exe"
            Destination = 'C:\FileScreen\notepad.exe'
          }
PS C:\Foo> Copy-Item @FSTHT

Copy-Item:
Line |
   6 |  Copy-Item  @FSTHT
     |  ~~~~~~~~~~~~~~~~~~
     |  Access to the path 'C:\FileScreen\notepad.exe' is denied.
```

Figure 5.38: Testing a file screen

As you can see, FSRM found that the extension of the file to be saved is one that has been blocked. As a result, Windows displays an error message and does not complete the file copy.

Setting Up an Active File Screen

An active file screen is one that carries out an action (in addition to blocking the "wrong" files). FSRM can, for example, allow you to send an email message when the file save fails.

You set up an active file screen as follows:

```
# 6. Setup Active Email Notification
$Body = "You attempted to save an executable program. " +
        "This is not allowed."
$FSRMA = @{
```

Continues

continued

```
    Type              = 'Email'
    MailTo            = "[Admin Email];[File Owner]"
    Subject           = "Warning: attempted to save an executable file"
    Body              = $Body
    RunLimitInterval  = 60
}
$Notification = New-FsrmAction @FSRMA
$FSFS = @{
    Path         = $Path
    Notification = $Notification
    IncludeGroup = 'Executable Files'
    Description  = 'Block any executable file'
    Active       = $true
}
Set-FsrmFileScreen @FSFS
```

In this snippet, you create an FSRM action to send an email message. Then you update the FSRM file screen to include the notification. The file screen now prevents executable files from being saved and sends an email message if a user attempts to save an executable file in the protected folder.

Viewing Notification Limits

Depending on how often screening or other limits are exceeded, the number of alerts and email can be an issue. On a busy FSRM file server, you could quickly generate large amounts of alerts or email. To minimize this, FSRM allows you to specify a period of time before another notification of the same type is sent. The default time is 60 minutes, but you can change that. To view the current limits, you can use the Get-FsrmSetting command.

```
# 7. Get-FSRM Notification Limits
Get-FsrmSetting |
    Format-List -Property "*NotificationLimit"
```

Figure 5.39 shows the output from this snippet.

```
PS C:\Foo> # 7. Get-FSRM Notification Limits
PS C:\Foo> Get-FsrmSetting |
            Format-List -Property "*NotificationLimit"


CommandNotificationLimit : 60
EmailNotificationLimit   : 60
EventNotificationLimit   : 60
ReportNotificationLimit  : 60
```

Figure 5.39: Viewing notification limits

Changing Notification Limits

To change any of these notification limits, you use the `Set-FSRMSetting` command, like this:

```
# 8. Changing FSRM notification limits
$FSRMSHT = @{
  CommandNotificationLimit = 1
  EmailNotificationLimit   = 1
  EventNotificationLimit   = 1
  ReportNotificationLimit  = 1
}
Set-FsrmSetting @FSRMSHT
```

This limit allows you to test your file screens and perhaps refine the email messages generated. In production, such low limits may result in an excessive number of emails, which may be undesirable.

Testing the Active File Screen

To test this file screen, you can repeat the attempt to save an executable file in the screened folder, as follows:

```
# 9. Re-test the file screen to check the action
Copy-Item @FSTHT
```

As in the earlier test of this file screen, FSRM prevents you from saving the executable file, as you can see in Figure 5.40.

```
PS C:\Foo> # 9. Re-test the file screen to check the the action
PS C:\Foo> Copy-Item @FSTHT

Copy-Item:
Line |
   2 |  Copy-Item @FSTHT
     |  ~~~~~~~~~~~~~~~~~
     |  Access to the path 'C:\FileScreen\notepad.exe' is denied.
```

Figure 5.40: Testing the active file screen

Viewing Active File Screen Email

You can see the file screen email sent by FSRM in the previous step in Figure 5.41.

The body of the message, as you have seen in "Managing Filestore Quotas," can be highly customized with a variety of additional FSRM variables to provide more information for both the user and the administrator.

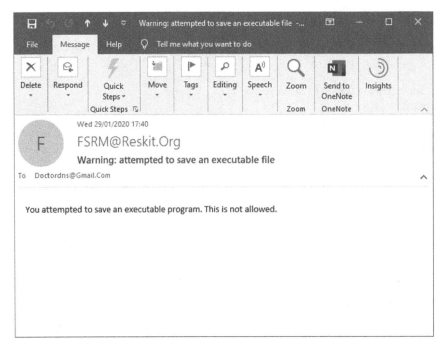

Figure 5.41: Viewing the screening email

Summary

PowerShell 7 enables you to manage disks and disk volumes on a variety of physical and virtual media. There are some built-in commands for managing NTFS permissions that can be supplemented with the community-developed NTFSSecurity module. For disaster recovery, PowerShell 7 supports and simplifies the use of the File System Resource Manager. FSRM provides a lot of assistance to customers using Windows Server to deliver file server features to users, and these are straightforward to use via PowerShell. They enable you to implement filestore quotas and filestore screening.

Some of the modules used in this chapter are not natively supported using PowerShell 7. As this chapter demonstrates, that does not provide a significant barrier to adoption.

Managing Shared Data

Sharing data between users and hosts is a core feature of every corporate network. In Chapter 5, "Managing Storage," you looked at managing disks and volumes/partitions. In this chapter, you examine the sharing of files between systems and some mechanisms for doing so.

The Server Message Block (SMB) file- and printer-sharing protocol has been in use since the late 1980s as a mechanism for storing data on a server and accessing it from client systems. All recent versions of Windows include an SMB client and SMB server feature, allowing users to share and use shared files.

Security of shared files is important. The SMB protocol has been around for a long time, and the first version, SMB1, is not considered safe for use so should be disabled. (Disabling SMB1 on a host can mean that older systems may not be able to connect to the host.)

When you share files, you can provide additional access controls over the share itself. The user of any shared folder or file is entitled to the lesser of the NTFS permissions and the share permissions. This can simplify the setting of permissions.

Windows Server comes with a number of file server features (each of which you can install using Install-WindowsFeature), which are organized as subfeatures of the FileAndStorage-Services role. The FileAndStorage-Services role, which enables some basic file sharing, is installed by default in Windows Server 2019. The subfeatures, which are not installed by default, include these:

FS-FileServer: This feature manages shared files and folders to enable users to access data on a server across the network.

FS-BranchCache: BranchCache is a WAN bandwidth optimization technology that caches content from a main office server on local systems. This avoids some WAN access.

FS-Data-Deduplication: This feature implements a single-instance storage feature. If a volume has multiple copies of the same file, this feature stores the data only once to save disk space.

FS-DFS-Namespace: DFS Namespace (DFSN) allows you to set up a logical file folder topology for data stored on different servers in your organization. DFSN also provides a level of fault tolerance by allowing you to store multiple copies of a given folder across multiple hosts. DFSN does not provide replication of data between the copies.

FS-DFS-Replication: DFS Replication (DFSR) is a multimaster replication engine that synchronizes folders in servers across your organization. Typically, you use DFSR to replicate data in DFSN-based folders.

FS-Resource-Manager: FSRM provides a number of features related to managing a file server. You used FSRM in Chapter 5 to provide file screening and file quotas.

FS-VSS-Agent: This feature enables you to create volume shadow copies of data on a server. Typically, you use this feature with backup applications.

FS-iSCSITarget-Server: This feature allows you to set up a Windows host to be an iSCSI target. The iSCSI initiator (client) service is installed on Windows hosts, although that service is stopped by default. You use the target server feature in "Creating and Using an iSCSI Target."

FS-NFS-Service: This feature enables the server to share files using the Network File System (NFS) protocol. NFS is used mainly in Linux/Unix environments. You can also use the NFS-Client Windows feature if you want to use NFS resources stored on other NFS servers (Windows or Linux/Unix-based).

FS-SyncShareService: This feature provides support for *work folders*. You can use work folders to host and synchronize user files.

All of these features can be used in any organization that needs to share files or data. Covering all these topics properly would take more space than is available. This chapter looks at the following:

Setting up and securing an SMB file server: Setting up a Windows Server–based file server is simple and straightforward. Securing it is also easy and something you should be doing on any file server.

Creating and securing SMB shares: Creating and securing shared folders is straightforward using the cmdlets in the SmbShare module augmented by the cmdlets in the downloadable NTFSSecurity module.

Using iSCSI: iSCSI is a mechanism for separating physical storage from a file server. You create an iSCSI disk on one server, a storage server, and use it on another, a file server. On the storage server, you implement an iSCSI target that you then use in the file server system. There are cmdlets for both creating and using iSCSI.

Creating a scale-out file server (SOFS): This feature leverages clustering to deliver a highly resilient and high-performance SMB3 file server.

Systems Used in This Chapter

In this chapter, you use the following systems:

DC1.Reskit.Org: This is a DC in the Reskit.Org domain. It also provides a DNS service for the Reskit.Org domain.

SRV2.Reskit.Org: You use this server to create an iSCSI target for use in a scale-out file server.

FS1.Reskit.Org, FS2.Reskit.Org: These are both domain-joined Windows Server 2019 hosts. You create an SMB server and share data from FS1 and then use the iSCSI initiator on FS1 to connect to the iSCSI target on SRV2. Finally, you also use FS1 and FS2 to deploy an SOFS.

Figure 6.1 shows the systems in use in this chapter.

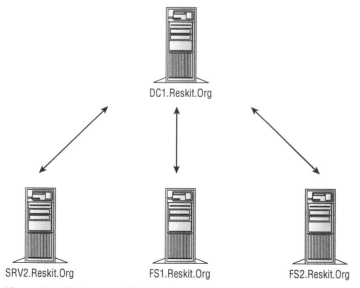

DC1.Reskit.Org

SRV2.Reskit.Org   FS1.Reskit.Org   FS2.Reskit.Org

Figure 6.1: Systems used in this chapter

Note that all systems need PowerShell 7 loaded before starting. You can do that manually, using the scripts from Chapter 1, "Establishing a PowerShell 7 Administrative Environment."

Setting Up and Securing an SMB File Server

The SMB protocol is a network protocol that runs on top of TCP/IP and is used to share access to files, printers, and other resources on your network. All currently supported versions of Windows (server and client) contain an SMB client and an SMB server.

In Windows, the SMB server is implemented by the `LanmanServer` service. In Linux and Unix, the Samba project (`www.samba.org`) provides an SMB server and client that interoperate with Windows clients/servers. For more information about the SMB protocol, see `docs.microsoft.com/en-us/windows/win32/fileio/microsoft-smb-protocol-and-cifs-protocol-overview`.

The SMB protocol has evolved significantly since it was first introduced with Microsoft's LAN Manager in the late 1980s, and SMB Version 1 is no longer considered safe for use. An important step in securing your file servers is to ensure you disable this version of the SMB protocol.

The latest version of the SMB protocol, SMB3, contains a number of significant improvements. These include SMB Scale-Out, SMB Multichannel, and SMB Direct, which all improve the performance and resilience of SMB and enable you to store SQL databases as well as Hyper-V virtual hard drives on an SMB3 file server. All current versions of Windows contain SMB3 support. For more details on SMB3, see `docs.microsoft.com/en-us/windows-server/storage/file-server/file-server-smb-overview`.

Before You Start

In this section, you use `FS1.Reskit.Org`, a domain-joined Windows Server 2019 host with no additional features installed (and with Internet access). To assist with DNS resolution, you must also have a DC in the `Reskit.Org` domain, `DC1 .Reskit.Org`, online. Also, ensure you have installed PowerShell 7 on this host (and optionally VS Code). You can use the scripts in Chapter 1 to do this.

Adding File Server Features to FS1

To create a file server using Windows Server 2019, you use the Server Manager module to add the necessary services and tools.

```
# 1. Add File Server features to FS1
  Import-Module -Name ServerManager -WarningAction SilentlyContinue
$Features = 'FileAndStorage-Services',
```

```
                    'File-Services',
                    'FS-FileServer'
    Install-WindowsFeature -Name $Features -IncludeManagementTools
```

You can view the output of this snippet in Figure 6.2.

```
PS C:\Foo> # 1. Add File Server features to FS1
PS C:\Foo> # Import-Module -Name ServerManager -WarningAction SilentlyContinue
PS C:\Foo> # $Features = 'FileAndStorage-Services',
                         'File-Services',
                         'FS-FileServer'
PS C:\Foo> # Install-WindowsFeature -Name $Features -IncludeManagementTools


Success Restart Needed Exit Code     Feature Result
------- -------------- ---------     --------------
True    No             Success       {File and iSCSI Services, File Server}
```

Figure 6.2: Installing file server features

With this snippet, you install the Windows Compatibility module, import the ServerManager module, and then install the file server features. Once this is complete, FS1 is capable of being a file server—you just need to configure the server and share folders.

Getting SMB Server Settings

You can use the Get-SmbServerConfiguration command to view the default configuration of the SMB service in FS1.

```
# 2. Get Default SMB Server Settings
Get-SmbServerConfiguration
```

The output, shown in Figure 6.3, shows the default property settings for the SMB service.

Before putting a file server into production, you should review the 43 properties of your file server. These default settings have changed over the different versions of Windows Server, so it's important that you check these properties and update them where needed.

Ensuring That SMB1 Is Disabled

Version 1 of the SMB protocol contains a vulnerability that enables an intruder to run arbitrary code. See cve.mitre.org/cgi-bin/cvename.cgi?name=CVE-2017-0144 for details of the vulnerability and the systems affected. The WannaCry ransomware, for example, exploited this weakness.

```
PS C:\Foo> # 2. Get SMB Server Settings
PS C:\Foo> Get-SmbServerConfiguration

AnnounceComment               :
AnnounceServer                : False
AsynchronousCredits           : 512
AuditSmb1Access               : False
AutoDisconnectTimeout         : 15
AutoShareServer               : True
AutoShareWorkstation          : True
CachedOpenLimit               : 10
DurableHandleV2TimeoutInSeconds : 180
EnableAuthenticateUserSharing : False
EnableDownlevelTimewarp       : False
EnableForcedLogoff            : True
EnableLeasing                 : True
EnableMultiChannel            : True
EnableOplocks                 : True
EnableSecuritySignature       : False
EnableSMB1Protocol            : False
EnableSMB2Protocol            : True
EnableStrictNameChecking      : True
EncryptData                   : False
IrpStackSize                  : 15
KeepAliveTime                 : 2
MaxChannelPerSession          : 32
MaxMpxCount                   : 50
MaxSessionPerConnection       : 16384
MaxThreadsPerQueue            : 20
MaxWorkItems                  : 1
NullSessionPipes              :
NullSessionShares             :
OplockBreakWait               : 35
PendingClientTimeoutInSeconds : 120
RejectUnencryptedAccess       : True
RequireSecuritySignature      : False
ServerHidden                  : True
Smb2CreditsMax                : 8192
Smb2CreditsMin                : 512
SmbServerNameHardeningLevel   : 0
TreatHostAsStableStorage      : False
ValidateAliasNotCircular      : True
ValidateShareScope            : True
ValidateShareScopeNotAliased  : True
ValidateTargetName            : True
```

Figure 6.3: Viewing SMB server settings

By default, Windows Server 2019 has SMB1 disabled. It is, though, a good thing to make sure this protocol is disabled explicitly.

```
# 3. Ensure SMB V1 is turned off
$CHT = @{
   EnableSMB1Protocol = $false
   Confirm            = $false
}
Set-SmbServerConfiguration @CHT
```

In this snippet, you explicitly disable the SMB1 protocol. Alternatively, you could have tested whether SMB1 was enabled and only then explicitly disable SMB1.

With Windows PowerShell, you could have used Desired State Configuration (DSC) to ensure that the SMB1 remains turned off. Unfortunately, as described in Chapter 2, "PowerShell 7 Compatibility with Windows PowerShell," DSC is not supported fully by PowerShell 7.

Enabling SMB Signing and SMB Encryption

The SMB protocol by default transfers all data unencrypted. On an internal network this may not matter, but it does represent a potential vulnerability. Two things you can do to improve network security are to encrypt any transferred data and sign each packet.

```
# 4. Turn on SMB signing and encryption
$SHT1 = @{
    RequireSecuritySignature = $true
    EnableSecuritySignature  = $true
    EncryptData              = $true
    Confirm                  = $false
}
Set-SmbServerConfiguration @SHT1
```

Signing and encrypting packets takes additional CPU time. This could be an issue on a busy file server serving hundreds of users simultaneously. If you are implementing file servers as virtual machines, you might consider adding one or more virtual CPUs to any file server VM if the VM shows a high CPU load (a CPU usage of 80% or more over a sustained time).

Encryption on the client side should not provide any significant performance issue.

Disabling Default Shares

Windows servers and clients create a number of default shares, also known as *administrative shares*. These shares are hidden and enable IT pros to have remote access to each disk volume on a network-connected system. You cannot delete these shares permanently, but you can disable them.

```
# 5. Turn off default server and workstations shares
$SHT2 = @{
    AutoShareServer      = $false
    AutoShareWorkstation = $false
    Confirm              = $false
}
Set-SmbServerConfiguration @SHT2
```

Turning Off Server Announcements

By default, SMB servers announce themselves on the network. This could be a potential security risk, but it is easy to stop.

```
# 6. Turn off server announcements
$SHT3 = @{
    ServerHidden    = $true
    AnnounceServer = $false
    Confirm         = $false
}
Set-SmbServerConfiguration @SHT3
```

Restarting the SMB Server Service

The SMB server settings you have set do not take effect until you restart the service.

```
# 7. Restart the service with the new configuration
Restart-Service -Name LanmanServer
```

Reviewing the Updated SMB Server Configuration

Once you have reconfigured the SMB server and restarted the service, you can review the SMB server settings and observe the updated configuration.

```
# 8. Review SMB Server Configuration
Get-SmbServerConfiguration
```

Figure 6.4 shows the results of the configuration changes.

As you can see from the figure, the settings you configured are now in operation on the running SMB service. There are many more settings you can set for an SMB server, although most of them remain not well documented.

Creating and Securing SMB Shares

SMB shares in Windows can be secured independently of any underlying file-system security. Irrespective of the filesystem you implement, you can provide ACLs to SMB shares to control access to the underlying data. With the NTFS filesystem, you are able to set share access permissions as well as filesystem permissions.

```
PS C:\Foo> # 8. Review SMB Server Configuration
PS C:\Foo> Get-SmbServerConfiguration

AnnounceComment                    :
AnnounceServer                     : False
AsynchronousCredits                : 512
AuditSmb1Access                    : False
AutoDisconnectTimeout              : 15
AutoShareServer                    : False
AutoShareWorkstation               : False
CachedOpenLimit                    : 10
DurableHandleV2TimeoutInSeconds    : 180
EnableAuthenticateUserSharing      : False
EnableDownlevelTimewarp            : False
EnableForcedLogoff                 : True
EnableLeasing                      : True
EnableMultiChannel                 : True
EnableOplocks                      : True
EnableSecuritySignature            : True
EnableSMB1Protocol                 : False
EnableSMB2Protocol                 : True
EnableStrictNameChecking           : True
EncryptData                        : True
IrpStackSize                       : 15
KeepAliveTime                      : 2
MaxChannelPerSession               : 32
MaxMpxCount                        : 50
MaxSessionPerConnection            : 16384
MaxThreadsPerQueue                 : 20
MaxWorkItems                       : 1
NullSessionPipes                   :
NullSessionShares                  :
OplockBreakWait                    : 35
PendingClientTimeoutInSeconds      : 120
RejectUnencryptedAccess            : True
RequireSecuritySignature           : True
ServerHidden                       : True
Smb2CreditsMax                     : 8192
Smb2CreditsMin                     : 512
SmbServerNameHardeningLevel        : 0
TreatHostAsStableStorage           : False
ValidateAliasNotCircular           : True
ValidateShareScope                 : True
ValidateShareScopeNotAliased       : True
ValidateTargetName                 : True
```

Figure 6.4: Viewing the reconfigured SMB server settings

Managing permissions for files (in an NTFS volume) is not fully supported by in-the-box cmdlets. You can use the Get-ACL and Set-ACL commands to update an ACL, but you have to use .NET Framework objects to create the individual ACEs you want to add to any ACL. The NTFSSecurity module makes updating ACLs much easier.

Before You Start

This section uses FS1, a server you set up in "Setting Up and Securing an SMB File Server." You also need the domain controller, DC1. This section also uses the AD group Sales created in "Managing NTFS Permissions" in Chapter 5.

Setting Up FS1

This section creates a new folder, C:\Sales. Later in this section, you also make use of commands in the NTFSSecurity module in this section, and you need to ensure you have it installed. You can do both tasks as follows:

```
# 1. Ensure folder exists and install NTFS Security module
$EAHT = @{Erroraction = 'SilentlyContinue' }
New-Item -Path C:\Sales1 -ItemType Directory @EAHT | Out-Null
Install-Module -Name NTFSSecurity -Force
```

This snippet ensures that the C:\Sales1 folder exists on FS1 and that the NTFSSecurity module is installed.

Discovering Existing SMB Shares

To discover the SMB shares available on your server, use the Get-SmbShare command.

```
# 2. Discover existing SMB shares on FS1
Get-SmbShare -Name *
```

You can see the output from this snippet in Figure 6.5.

```
PS C:\Foo> # 2. Discover existing SMB shares on FS1
PS C:\Foo> Get-SmbShare -Name *

Name ScopeName Path Description
---- --------- ---- -----------
IPC$ *             Remote IPC
```

Figure 6.5: Viewing shares on FS1

Notice that there is only one share on FS1, the IPC$ interprocess communication share. The IPC$ share is built into Windows and is used when performing remote administration of a computer or viewing a computer's shared resources.

You can see more information about the IPC$ share at support.microsoft.com/en-us/help/3034016/ipc-share-and-null-session-behavior-in-windows.

Creating an SMB Share

To create a new SMB share to the C:\Sales1 folder on FS1, you use the New-SmbShare command.

```
# 3. Creating a new share Sales1
New-SmbShare -Name Sales1 -Path C:\Sales1
```

Figure 6.6 shows the output of this command.

```
PS C:\Foo> # 3. Create a new share Sales1
PS C:\Foo> New-SmbShare -Name Sales1 -Path C:\Sales1

Name    ScopeName Path   Description
----    --------- ----   -----------
Sales1 Foo   *           C:\Sales1
```

Figure 6.6: Creating an SMB share

You could also have used the older Net.exe command, which has been part of Windows since Windows NT first shipped.

Setting a Share Description

It is useful to add a description to the share, which you can do with the Set-SmbShare command.

```
# 4. Set the share's Description
$CHT = @{Confirm=$False}
Set-SmbShare -Name Sales1 -Description 'Sales share on FS1' @CHT
```

The description field can help users find the correct share. You could also have created the description at the same time you created the share.

Setting the Folder Enumeration Mode

You can set the folder enumeration mode for a share to AccessBased. This tells Windows to not display any folders within a share that the user does not have access to.

```
# 5. Setting folder enumeration mode
$CHT = @{Confirm = $false}
Set-SmbShare -Name Sales1 -FolderEnumerationMode AccessBased @CHT
```

This is a useful approach as it helps to avoid questions from curious users who see folders in a share to which they have no access.

Requiring Encryption for a Share

As you saw in "Setting Up and Securing an SMB File Server," you can configure the system to always encrypt any shared data transmitted to/from an SMB share. You can configure Windows to always encrypt the traffic for that specific share with this Set-SmbShare command:

```
# 6. Require encryption on data transmistted to/from the share
Set-SmbShare -Name Sales1 -EncryptData $true @CHT
```

This ensures that data transferred to/from this share is to be encrypted. For more details about SMB encryption, see `docs.microsoft.com/en-us/windows-server/storage/file-server/smb-security#smb-encryption`.

Requiring encryption increases CPU usage on a file server. As noted on the SMB Security page, "... there is a notable performance operating cost with any end-to-end encryption protection when compared to non-encrypted."

As always with settings like this, you should be measuring the CPU utilization of your file server and take appropriate actions to minimize the impact of any performance bottlenecks. In Chapter 10, "Reporting," the section "Collecting Performance Data Using PLA" shows how to collect this information, and "Reporting on PLA Performance Data" shows how you can create a graph of server performance.

Removing All Access to Sales1 Share

By default, when you create a new share, Windows enables the Everyone group to have read access to the share. To restrict access to the share, you first remove that universal access, using `Revoke-SmbShareAccess`.

```
# 7. Removing all access to Sales1 share for the Everyone group
$AHT1 = @{
  Name        = 'Sales1'
  AccountName = 'Everyone'
  Confirm     = $false
}
Revoke-SmbShareAccess @AHT1 | Out-Null
```

This has the effect of, initially, denying everyone access to the data within the SMB share. Once you have revoked all access, you can set the specific permissions appropriate to the share to enable the security you need for the share.

Adding Reskit\Domain Admins to the Share

To enable administrator read access to the share, you can use the `Grant-Smb-ShareAccess` command.

```
# 8. Adding Reskit\Domain Admins to the share
$AHT2 = @{
    Name        = 'Sales1'
    AccessRight = 'Read'
    AccountName = 'Reskit\Domain Admins'
    ConFirm     = $false
}
Grant-SmbShareAccess @AHT2 | Out-Null
```

This snippet gives the domain's Domain Admins group read access to the share. By default, a domain or enterprise administrator can take ownership of a file and then give themselves more permissions should that ever become necessary. Giving domain admins only basic read access, as in this example, may or may not be appropriate in day-to-day operations.

Adding System Full Access

To ensure that Windows continues to have access to the folder, you can add another access control entry to the share's ACL.

```
# 9. Adding system full access
$AHT3 = @{
    Name          = 'Sales1'
    AccessRight   = 'Full'
    AccountName   = 'NT Authority\SYSTEM'
    Confirm       = $False
}
Grant-SmbShareAccess  @AHT3 | Out-Null
```

Giving the Creator/Owner Full Access

You also need to enable the owner or creator of a file to have full access to the files/folders they create.

```
# 10. Set Creator/Owner to Full Access
$AHT4 = @{
    Name          = 'Sales1'
    AccessRight   = 'Full'
    AccountName   = 'CREATOR OWNER'
    Confirm       = $False
}
Grant-SmbShareAccess @AHT4  | Out-Null
```

Granting the Sales Group Access

You can also grant the Sales group change access to the share.

```
# 11 Granting Sales group change access
$AHT5 = @{
    Name         = 'Sales1'
    AccessRight  = 'Full Control'
    AccountName  = 'Sales'
    Confirm      = $false
}
Grant-SmbShareAccess @AHT5 | Out-Null
```

In this snippet, you give all members of the Sales group change access over data in the share. This is a simple share permission to set, but it does mean that any member can make changes to any file.

You can, of course, limit access to data in the share by changing the ACL on the underlying NTFS files or folders. Although a user might have full control at the share level, you can set more restrictive NTFS permissions where that is appropriate.

Reviewing Share Access

With the configuration of this share completed, you can view the new access rights on the share.

```
# 12. Review Access to Sales1 sShare
Get-SmbShareAccess -Name Sales1 |
    Sort-Object AccessRight
```

Now that you have configured share access rights, you can view the share's resultant access rights, as shown in Figure 6.7.

```
PS C:\Foo> # 12. Review Access to Sales1 Share
PS C:\Foo> Get-SmbShareAccess -Name Sales1 |
            Sort-Object AccessRight


Name    ScopeName AccountName            AccessControlType AccessRight
----    --------- -----------            ----------------- -----------
Sales1 *          NT AUTHORITY\SYSTEM    Allow             Full
Sales1 *          CREATOR OWNER          Allow             Full
Sales1 *          RESKIT\Sales           Allow             Change
Sales1 *          RESKIT\Domain Admins   Allow             Read
```

Figure 6.7: Viewing share access

In this output, you can see that the share has an ACL that consists of the three explicit ACE entries.

It is important to note that these steps have reconfigured only the share's ACL. The NTFS filesystem holds a separate set of permissions that you can set independently from the share permissions. When accessing shared data, the user's effective permissions are the lesser of the NTFS and the share permissions. Thus far in this section, the NTFS permissions remain based on default Windows permissions and are probably overly generous. An important step in securing a file server is managing the default ACLs set by Windows.

Reviewing the NTFS Permissions

You can view the initial NTFS permissions on a folder by using the Get-NTFSAccess command from the NTFSSecurity module.

```
# 13. Review initial NTFS Permissions on the folder
Get-NTFSAccess -Path C:\Sales1
```

You can see the output in Figure 6.8, showing the current NTFS permissions on the C:\Sales1 folder.

```
PS C:\Foo> # 13. Review initial NTFS Permissions on the folder
PS C:\Foo> Get-NTFSAccess -Path C:\Sales1

    Path: C:\Sales1 (Inheritance enabled)


Account                  Access Rights         Applies to                 Type    IsInherited   InheritedFrom
-------                  -------------         ----------                 ----    -----------   -------------
NT AUTHORITY\SYSTEM      FullControl           ThisFolderSubfoldersAndF   Allow   True          C:
BUILTIN\Administrators   FullControl           ThisFolderSubfoldersAndF   Allow   True          C:
BUILTIN\Users            ReadAndExecute, Synch ThisFolderSubfoldersAndF   Allow   True          C:
BUILTIN\Users            CreateDirectories     ThisFolderAndSubfolders    Allow   True          C:
BUILTIN\Users            CreateFiles           ThisFolderAndSubfolders    Allow   True          C:
CREATOR OWNER            GenericAll            SubfoldersAndFilesOnly     Allow   True          C:
```

Figure 6.8: Reviewing NTFS permissions

An advantage of using Get-NTFSAccess is that you can also view inherited permissions. As you can see, the ACL for the C:\Sales1 folder is made up entirely of inherited permissions—as is normal for newly created folders. In many, and probably most, cases, this can be an overly permissive set of permissions. You can adjust this as needed.

Setting the NTFS ACL to Match the Share

A simple way to ensure that the share and the NTFS permissions are aligned is to use the Set-SmbPathAcl command, like this:

```
# 14. Setting the NTFS ACL to match share
Set-SmbPathAcl -ShareName 'Sales1'
```

This command makes the ACL for the C:\Sales1 folder match the share's ACL. This copies the explicit permissions on the share to the NTFS permissions on the folder.

Removing NTFS Inheritance

To complete securing the share and underlying data, you can also remove unwanted inherited ACLs, by removing the inheritance for the C:\Sales1 folder, like this:

```
# 15. Removing NTFS Inheritance
Set-NTFSInheritance -Path C:\Sales1 -AccessInheritanceEnabled:$False
```

Note that, currently, this command generates a spurious error stating "Nullable object must have a value." Despite the error, this snippet does turn off inheritance on the C:\Sales1 folder.

Viewing the Folder ACL

Now that you have configured the NTFS access to match only the share's access, you can view the NTFS access.

```
# 16. Viewing Folder ACL using Get-NTFSAccess
Get-NTFSAccess -Path C:\Sales1 |
  Format-Table -AutoSize
```

You can see the output in Figure 6.9.

```
PS C:\Foo> # 16. View folder ACL using Get-NTFSAccess
PS C:\Foo> Get-NTFSAccess -Path C:\Sales1
            Format-Table -AutoSize

   Path: C:\Sales1 (Inheritance disabled)

Account                Access Rights         Applies to               Type   IsInherited  InheritedFrom
-------                -------------         ----------               ----   -----------  -------------
NT AUTHORITY\SYSTEM    FullControl           ThisFolderSubfoldersAndF Allow  False
RESKIT\Domain Admins   ReadAndExecute, Synch ThisFolderSubfoldersAndF Allow  False
RESKIT\Sales           Modify, Synchronize   ThisFolderSubfoldersAndF Allow  False
```

Figure 6.9: Viewing folder ACL

As you can see from the output, the only ACEs remaining in the ACL for the C:\Sales1 folder are those you set explicitly on the share and then copied into the NTFS folder.

In this section, you add and configure a new share on FS1. The share you created is on a single host on a single volume and thus is not highly fault tolerant.

For departmental file sharing, as long as regular backups are performed, this configuration is, in many cases, cost-effective and generally acceptable, especially given the reliability of modern computer systems.

If you are less risk tolerant and have sufficient budget, you can improve the reliability and fault tolerance by ensuring the data volume is protected with some form of RAID and use failover clustering on your file server. "Setting Up a Clustered Scale-Out File Server" later in this chapter looks at clustering and creating a highly reliable file server solution.

Creating and Using an iSCSI Target

When you deploy a file server, you have a wide choice of storage technologies you can use to store your data. In "Creating and Securing SMB Shares," you deployed a new share, `Sales1`, based on a folder held locally on the `FS1` host. That share pointed to a local disk, which means there is a potential single point of failure—if a disk fails and you don't have a good backup, you may have lost user information.

Many organizations deploy a storage area network (SAN) to hold information. The SAN can provide great protection security for your organization's data. One popular method of attaching a host to data held on the SAN is to use iSCSI.

By way of background, Small Computer Systems Interface (SCSI) is a storage technology used to connect disk drives with host computers. SCSI provides faster bus speeds and also provides the ability to support larger numbers of disks than IDE/ATA drives. In larger enterprise servers, you typically use SCSI or serial attached SCSI (SAS) disks. These can include both spinning and solid-state drives.

iSCSI is a TCP/IP-based protocol that enables you to access what appear to be SCSI disks across TCP/IP networks. iSCSI is a client-server protocol. An iSCSI server effectively allows access to a disk (defined as a logical unit number, or LUN) on the server from the client. The virtual disk is known as an iSCSI *target*.

The iSCSI client, known as the iSCSI *initiator*, connects to the iSCSI target to use the data on the remote disk. The iSCSI initiator enables the client system (or systems) to access the iSCSI virtual disk as if it were local. After connecting to the iSCSI target, you could use the Disk Management application (`diskmgmt.msc`) and view the iSCSI disk as if it were a local disk.

Once you have connected to the iSCSI target, you can use the same commands you used in Chapter 5 to create a volume and manage the data on disk.

For a bit more background in iSCSI terminology, visit `lazywinadmin.com/2013/07/create-iscsi-target-using-powershell-on.html`.

To deploy an iSCSI target in Windows, you begin by adding some physical storage to your host and creating a local volume. Ideally, you should use hardware RAID to create a fault-tolerant local volume for your storage server. Within this local volume, you create a virtual iSCSI disk. Then, you expose this disk as an iSCSI target.

If you deploy a physical host, you can implement hardware RAID, create a local volume (using, for example, RAID 5 or RAID 20), and then create the virtual iSCSI disk in that volume.

If you deploy your iSCSI target in a VM, you store the iSCSI virtual disk inside a volume that is held within a VHDX in the Hyper-V host. This volume holding the VHDX file should also be protected using hardware RAID deployed on the VM host.

The iSCSI target in Windows Server has not been the subject of much development in recent times. It works and is a great solution for test labs or proof-of-concept deployments. In production, you may want to use other iSCSI vendors with more up-to-date and better-performing products. With third-party iSCSI products delivering your iSCSI targets, you should be able to use the iSCSI initiator in Windows to connect to any iSCSI target.

If you are to make heavy use of iSCSI, you might consider using TCP and/or iSCSI offload, moving some of the processing into hardware in your NICs. To check whether offloading is in operation on a host, you can use the `netstat -t` command to see which connections to your host are making use of any offload. TCP offloading has been an issue in some cases, so you need to check carefully that enabling a hardware-based offload solution works in your network. For more on performance tuning your network adapters, take a look at `docs.microsoft` `.com/en-us/windows-server/networking/technologies/network-subsystem/` `net-sub-performance-tuning-nics`.

In this section, you create an iSCSI target on `SRV2` and then use it via the iSCSI initiator on `FS1`.

Before You Start

This demonstration makes use of two servers: `FS1.Reskit.Org` and `SRV2.Reskit.` `Org`. You create an iSCSI virtual hard disk on `SRV2` and set up an iSCSI target for this virtual hard disk. You then use the iSCSI initiator on `FS1` to connect to the iSCSI target. You also want `DC1.Reskit.Org` online to enable DNS name resolution.

This section also makes use of a new physical disk within the `SRV2` host. Assuming you are using Hyper-V to host `SRV2`, adding a new disk is easy, as you saw in the Chapter 5's "Managing Disks and Volumes" section. If you are using Hyper-V, you can run the following code on your Hyper-V host:

```
# 0. Add additional disk to hold iSCSI VHD to SRV2 VM
#    Run this on the Hyper-V VM Host in an elevated console
# Stop the VM
Stop-VM -VMName SRV2 -Force
# Get File location for the disk in this VM
$VM = Get-VM -VMName SRV2
$Par = Split-Path -Path $VM.HardDrives[0].Path
# Create a new VHD for S drive
$NewPath3 = Join-Path -Path $Par -ChildPath SDrive.VHDX
$D4 = New-VHD -Path $NewPath3 -SizeBytes 128GB -Dynamic
# Work out next free slot on Controller 0
$Free = (Get-VMScsiController -VMName SRV2 |
```

```
              Select-Object -First 1 |
                Select-Object -ExpandProperty Drives).count
# Add new disk to VM
$HDHT = @{
  Path                = $NewPath3
  VMName              = 'SRV2'
  ControllerType      = 'SCSI'
  ControllerNumber    = 0
  ControllerLocation  = $Free
}
Add-VMHardDiskDrive @HDHT
# Start the VM
Start-VM -VMName SRV2
```

If you created your VM as a Type 2 Hyper-V VM, there is no need to start (or restart) it. If you created your VMs using the Reskit build scripts noted in Chapter 1, then the VM is of Type 1 and does need to be turned off to add more volumes.

Once you have added the virtual hard disk to the VM and restarted the VM, you need to log on to SRV2 and create a new volume in the new disk, as follows:

```
# Run on SRV2 once disk added
# Find the new disk
$NewDisk = Get-Disk |
            Where-Object PartitionStyle -eq Raw
$NewDisk |
    Initialize-Disk -PartitionStyle GPT

# Create a S: volume in newly added disk
$NVHT1 = @{
  DiskNumber    = $NewDisk.Number
  FriendlyName = 'iSCSI'
  FileSystem   = 'NTFS'
  DriveLetter  = 'S'
}
New-Volume @NVHT1
```

With these steps, you have added a new (virtual) hard disk to the SRV2 VM. You are now ready to create an iSCSI target on SRV2.

Installing the iSCSI Target Feature on SRV2

Because you are setting up SRV2 to expose an iSCSI target, you need to install the FS-ISCSITarget-Feature feature on SRV2, using the Install-WindowsFeature command.

```
# 1. Installing the iSCSI target feature on SRV2
Import-Module -Name ServerManager -WarningAction SilentlyContinue
```

```
$WFHT = @{
  Name                  = 'FS-iSCSITarget-Server'
  IncludeManagementTools = $true
}
Install-WindowsFeature @WFHT
```

You can see the output of this snippet in Figure 6.10.

```
PS C:\Foo> # 1. Installing the iSCSI target feature on SRV2
PS C:\Foo> Import-Module -Name ServerManager -WarningAction SilentlyContinue
PS C:\Foo> $WFHT = @{
             Name                  = 'FS-iSCSITarget-Server'
             IncludeManagementTools = $true
           }
PS C:\Foo> Install-WindowsFeature @WFHT

Success Restart Needed Exit Code  Feature Result
------- -------------- ---------  --------------
True    No             Success    {File and iSCSI Services, File Server, iSCSI...
```

Figure 6.10: Installing the iSCSI target feature

Exploring iSCSI Target Server Settings

With the iSCSI target feature installed, you can view the iSCSI target server settings on SRV2 by using `Get-IsciTargetServerSettings`.

```
# 2. Exploring default iSCSI target server settings
Import-Module -Name  IscsiTarget
Get-IscsiTargetServerSetting
```

Figure 6.11 shows the output from these commands.

```
PS C:\Foo> # 2. Exploring iSCSI target server settings:
PS C:\Foo> Import-Module -Name IscsiTarget -WarningAction SilentlyContinue
PS C:\Foo> Get-IscsiTargetServerSetting

RunspaceId              : 3057be01-50d0-49c9-8fe7-c9197ceb1e94
ComputerName            : SRV2.Reskit.Org
IsClustered             : False
Version                 : 10.0
DisableRemoteManagement : False
Portals                 : {+10.10.10.51:3260, -[fe80::552e:9047:1024:a199%7]:3260,
                          -[fe80::99b7:6503:e702:af2c%6]:3260}
```

Figure 6.11: Viewing iSCSI target server settings

As you can see, the target is currently not clustered and can be reached via both an IPv4 address and an IPv6 address. With more virtual NICs in your VM and with IPv6 enabled, you may see more portal addresses.

Creating a Folder on SRV2

You next need to create a folder on SRV2 to hold the iSCSI virtual disk, using the `New-Item` command.

```
# 3. Creating a folder on SRV2 to hold the iSCSI virtual disk
$NIHT = @{
  Path        = 'S:\iSCSI'
  ItemType    = 'Directory'
  ErrorAction = 'SilentlyContinue'
}
New-Item @NIHT | Out-Null
```

Creating an iSCSI Virtual Disk

To create the iSCSI virtual hard disk, you use the `New-IscsiVirtualDisk` command as follows:

```
# 4. Creating an iSCSI Virtual Disk
Import-WinModule -Name IscsiTarget
$LP  = 'S:\iSCSI\SalesData.Vhdx'
$LN  = 'SalesTarget'
$VDHT = @{
  Path        = $LP
  Description = 'LUN For Sales'
  SizeBytes   = 500MB
}
New-IscsiVirtualDisk @VDHT
```

You can view the output from this snippet in Figure 6.12.

```
PS C:\Foo> # 4. Creating an iSCSI virtual disk
PS C:\Foo> Import-Module -Name IscsiTarget -WarningAction SilentlyContinue
PS C:\Foo> $LP = 'S:\iSCSI\SalesData.Vhdx'
$LN = 'SalesTarget'
$VDHT = @{
          Path        = $LP
          Description = 'LUN For Sales'
          SizeBytes   = 500MB
        }
PS C:\Foo> New-IscsiVirtualDisk @VDHT

RunspaceId        : 3057be01-50d0-49c9-8fe7-c9197ceb1e94
ClusterGroupName  :
ComputerName      : SRV2.Reskit.Org
Description       : LUN For Sales
DiskType          : Dynamic
HostVolumeId      : {08A74429-F05B-4D7D-86CA-AD8B043C9801}
LocalMountDeviceId :
OriginalPath      :
ParentPath        :
Path              : S:\iSCSI\SalesData.Vhdx
SerialNumber      : E4D6F3A9-60B5-40BC-BA87-04BFE886C551
Size              : 524288000
SnapshotIds       :
Status            : NotConnected
VirtualDiskIndex  : 867953682
```

Figure 6.12: Creating an iSCSI virtual disk

With this snippet, you create a new iSCSI virtual disk of 500MB. In production, you would probably create much larger volumes. In most cases, you would probably configure the virtual disk to use all the space on the physical drive. In production, you would probably implement hardware Redundant Array of Independent Disks (RAID) on the storage server to enable the iSCSI target virtual disk to be fault tolerant.

Creating the iSCSI Target on SRV2

With the iSCSI virtual disk created, you create an iSCSI target on SRV2 by using `New-IscsiServerTarget`.

```
# 5. Creating the iSCSI target on SRV2
$THT = @{
  TargetName   = $LN
  InitiatorIds = 'IQN:*'
}
New-IscsiServerTarget @THT
```

You can see the output of this command in Figure 6.13.

```
PS C:\Foo> # 5. Creating the iSCSI target on SRV2
PS C:\Foo> $THT = @{
              TargetName   = $LN
              InitiatorIds = 'IQN:*'
           }
PS C:\Foo> New-IscsiServerTarget @THT

RunspaceId                   : 3057be01-50d0-49c9-8fe7-c9197ceb1e94
ChapUserName                 :
ClusterGroupName             :
ComputerName                 : SRV2.Reskit.Org
Description                  :
EnableChap                   : False
EnableReverseChap            : False
EnforceIdleTimeoutDetection  : True
FirstBurstLength             : 65536
IdleDuration                 : 00:00:00
InitiatorIds                 : {Iqn:*}
LastLogin                    :
LunMappings                  : {}
MaxBurstLength               : 262144
MaxReceiveDataSegmentLength  : 65536
ReceiveBufferCount           : 10
ReverseChapUserName          :
Sessions                     : {}
Status                       : NotConnected
TargetIqn                    : iqn.1991-05.com.microsoft:srv2-salestarget-target
TargetName                   : SalesTarget
```

Figure 6.13: Creating an iSCSI target

This command creates an iSCSI target, which points to the iSCSI virtual disk. In creating the target, you specify a wildcard initiator ID for initiators allowed to connect to this target. This allows any initiator to connect to the disk, which simplifies deployment. You can specify DNS host names or IP addresses allowed to connect.

Creating iSCSI Disk Target Mapping on SRV2

The final step in deploying the target is creating a mapping from the iSCSI target to the virtual iSCSI hard disk, with the command.

```
# 6. Creating iSCSI disk target mapping on SRV2
Add-IscsiVirtualDiskTargetMapping -TargetName $LN -Path $LP
```

With the mapping created, SRV2 is now configured as an iSCSI target server. It can allow any iSCSI initiator to connect to this new LUN. To demonstrate using this iSCSI target, you can use any iSCSI initiator.

To see the Windows Server iSCSI initiator in action, complete the remaining steps in this section on FS1.

Configuring the iSCSI Service on SRV2

With an iSCSI target created on SRV2, you can now access it using the built-in Windows iSCSI initiator on FS1. The iSCSI initiator service is installed in Windows Server 2019 by default, although the service is configured to not start. Enter the following commands to start the service and to set the service to start automatically after restarting the host:

```
# 7. Configuring the iSCSI service to auto start, then start the service
#    Run on FS1
Set-Service   -Name MSiSCSI -StartupType 'Automatic'
Start-Service -Name MSiSCSI
```

If your iSCSI initiator (client) is Windows 10, then feature updates can, and do, reset the MSiSCSI service's startup type to the default (not started). The startup type for servers does not change. Depending on your host, you may see the occasional warning message "Waiting for the Service 'Microsoft iSCSI Initiator Service (MSiSCSI)' to start...."

Setting Up the iSCSI Portal

To use the iSCSI target on FS1, you need to set up the iSCSI portal, which is the mechanism iSCSI uses to find iSCSI targets. To do this, use the `New-IscsiTargetPortal` command.

```
# 8. Setup portal to SRV2
Import-Module -Name Iscsi -WarningAction SilentlyContinue
$PHT = @{
  TargetPortalAddress    = 'SRV2.Reskit.Org'
  TargetPortalPortNumber = 3260
}
New-IscsiTargetPortal @PHT
```

Creating the iSCSI target portal produces the output you can see in Figure 6.14. An iSCSI initiator uses the portal to discover the iSCSI targets on the remote machine.

```
PS C:\Foo> # 8. Setup portal to SRV2
PS C:\Foo> Import-Module -Name Iscsi -WarningAction SilentlyContinue
PS C:\Foo> $PHT = @{
          TargetPortalAddress    = 'SRV2.Reskit.Org'
          TargetPortalPortNumber = 3260
        }
PS C:\Foo> New-IscsiTargetPortal @PHT

RunspaceId            : 3057be01-50d0-49c9-8fe7-c9197ceb1e94
InitiatorInstanceName :
InitiatorPortalAddress :
IsDataDigest          : False
IsHeaderDigest        : False
TargetPortalAddress   : SRV2.Reskit.Org
TargetPortalPortNumber : 3260
```

Figure 6.14: Creating the iSCSI target portal

Viewing the SalesTarget iSCSI Disk

Now that you have the iSCSI initiator set up, you can view the iSCSI target on SRV2.

```
# 9. Find and view the SalesTarget on portal
$Target  = Get-IscsiTarget
$Target
```

The output from this snippet, in Figure 6.15, shows the Sales Target LUN that is now available via the iSCSI portal.

```
PS C:\Foo> # 9. Find and view the SalesTarget on portal
PS C:\Foo> $Target = Get-IscsiTarget
PS C:\Foo> $Target

RunspaceId  : 884cc78d-66b4-4b5b-a77b-548281da6d0b
IsConnected : False
NodeAddress : iqn.1991-05.com.microsoft:srv2-salestarget-target
```

Figure 6.15: Viewing the SalesTarget

Connecting to the Target on SRV2

Connecting to the target enables FS1 to have access to the iSCSI disk on SRV2.

```
# 10. Connecting to the target on SRV2
$CHT = @{
  TargetPortalAddress = 'SRV2.Reskit.Org'
  NodeAddress         = $Target.NodeAddress
}
Connect-IscsiTarget  @CHT
```

This snippet connects FS1 to the iSCSI target held on SRV2. The output, in Figure 6.16, shows details of the iSCSI connection.

```
PS C:\Foo> # 10. Connecting to the target on SRV2
PS C:\Foo> $CHT = @{
           TargetPortalAddress = 'SRV2.Reskit.Org'
           NodeAddress         = $Target.NodeAddress
         }
PS C:\Foo> Connect-IscsiTarget  @CHT

RunspaceId            : 2e230664-1291-4320-9e44-b1429a775136
AuthenticationType    : NONE
InitiatorInstanceName : ROOT\ISCSIPRT\0000_0
InitiatorNodeAddress  : iqn.1991-05.com.microsoft:fs1.reskit.org
InitiatorPortalAddress : 0.0.0.0
InitiatorSideIdentifier : 400001370000
IsConnected           : True
IsDataDigest          : False
IsDiscovered          : False
IsHeaderDigest        : False
IsPersistent          : False
NumberOfConnections   : 1
SessionIdentifier     : ffff8e87f71fb010-4000013700000003
TargetNodeAddress     : iqn.1991-05.com.microsoft:srv2-salestarget-target
TargetSideIdentifier  : 0100
```

Figure 6.16: Connecting to the SalesTarget

You can see the iSCSI initiator and target address in the figure. Before proceeding, it is useful to check to ensure you have set up the target (and initiator) correctly.

Although it's not shown in these snippets, another feature you could add to the solution is Multipath IO (MPIO), which enables you to create multiple paths between your file server and the underlying iSCSI file server. For more details on MPIO, see whatis.techtarget.com/definition/Multipath-I-O-MPIO. And for more detail on using MPIO with the Windows iSCSI initiator, see petri.com/using-mpio-windows-server-iscsi-initiator.

Viewing the iSCSI Virtual Disk

Now that you have connected to the iSCSI target on SRV2, you can use Get-Disk to view the contents of the iSCSI virtual disk.

```
# 11. Viewing iSCSI disk from FS1 on SRV2
$ISD =  Get-Disk |
  Where-Object BusType -eq 'iscsi'
$ISD |
  Format-Table -AutoSize
```

Figure 6.17 shows the output of this snippet.

```
PS C:\Foo> # 11. Viewing iSCSI disk from FS1 on SRV2
PS C:\Foo> $ISD =  Get-Disk |
          Where-Object BusType -eq 'iscsi'
PS C:\Foo> $ISD |
          Format-Table -AutoSize

Number Friendly Name   Serial Number                      HealthStatus OperationalStatus Total Size Partition Style
------ -------------   -------------                      ------------ ----------------- ---------- ---------------
1      MSFT Virtual HD E4D6F3A9-60B5-40BC-BA87-04BFE886C551 Healthy      Offline            500 MB RAW
```

Figure 6.17: Viewing the disk

As you can see in the figure, this disk is raw (no partitions have yet been created on it). Additionally, the disk does not have a filesystem and is not online. This example demonstrates that the iSCSI virtual disk, exposed as an iSCSI target on SRV2, is seen in FS1 as just another disk.

Setting the Disk Online and Making It Read/Write

You use the Set-Disk command to ensure both that the disk is online and that it is read/write.

```
# 12. Turning disk online and make R/W
$ISD |
  Set-Disk -IsOffline  $False
$ISD |
  Set-Disk -IsReadOnly $False
```

This snippet sets the disk to be online and ensures that it is read/write. To verify this, you could repeat the previous step to view the properties of this disk.

Creating a Volume on FS1

The disk, when viewed from FS1, is now online and partitioned but has no volumes created. That is simple to do, as shown here:

```
# 13. Formatting the iSCSI volume on FS1
$NVHT = @{
```

```
    FriendlyName = 'SalesData'
    FileSystem   = 'NTFS'
    DriveLetter  = 'S'
  }
  $ISD |
    New-Volume @NVHT
```

You can see the output from this snippet in Figure 6.18.

```
# 13. Formatting the iSCSI volume on FS1
$NVHT = @{
  FriendlyName = 'SalesData'
  FileSystem   = 'NTFS'
  DriveLetter  = 'S'
}
$ISD |
  New-Volume @NVHT


DriveLetter FriendlyName FileSystemType DriveType HealthStatus OperationalStatus SizeRemaining      Size
----------- ------------ -------------- --------- ------------ ----------------- -------------      ----
S           SalesData    NTFS           Fixed     Healthy      OK                467.78 MB 483.93 MB
```

Figure 6.18: Creating an S: drive

With this step completed, the iSCSI disk on SRV2 is now formatted and available within FS1. From FS1, the iSCSI disk appears to be another disk on which you can format and create volumes. This disk is small: 500GB with a usable capacity of 467.78GB. In production, you would probably create much larger volumes.

Using the iSCSI Drive on FS1

With the steps so far, you have set up an S: drive on FS1, which is the iSCSI disk that you previously set up on SRV2. You can use this as if it were a locally attached disk on FS1.

```
# 14. Using the iSCSI drive on FS1
New-Item -Path S:\  -Name SalesData -ItemType Directory |
  Out-Null
'Testing iSCSI 1-2-3' | Out-File -FilePath S:\SalesData\Test.Txt
Get-ChildItem -Path S:\SalesData
```

You can see in Figure 6.19 that the S: volume is available, and you can use it just as if it were locally attached.

In the snippet, you created a file on the S: drive and then used Get-ChildItem to verify that the file now exists on the S: volume.

This completes the task of creating an iSCSI disk on SRV2 and using it from FS1. This section created a single iSCSI client, FS1, for the iSCSI target held on SRV2.

```
PS C:\Foo> # 14. Using the iSCSI drive from FS1
PS C:\Foo> New-Item -Path S:\  -Name SalesData -ItemType Directory |
            Out-Null
PS C:\Foo> 'Testing iSCSI 1-2-3' | Out-File -FilePath S:\SalesData\Test.Txt
PS C:\Foo> Get-ChildItem S:\SalesData


    Directory: S:\SalesData

Mode                 LastWriteTime        Length Name
----                 -------------        ------ ----
-a---          02/02/2020    20:10            21 Test.Txt
```

Figure 6.19: Using the iSCSI S: drive

Setting Up a Clustered Scale-Out File Server

In this section, you leverage the iSCSI disk you created in "Creating and Using an iSCSI Target" and create a clustered scale-out file server (SOFS) using both FS1 and FS2. You also create a continuously available SMB3 file share on the SOFS cluster.

Once you have both FS1 and FS2 set up and are able to view the iSCSI target on SRV2, you can cluster the two hosts and create the SOFS based on the cluster.

The Scale-Out File Server is based on Microsoft's Failover Clustering technology. Failover Clustering was first introduced with Windows NT4, where there was a very restricted Hardware Compatibility List (HCL). With the later versions, Microsoft created a cluster validation wizard to check the servers. As long as the cluster validation test is successful, the cluster is eligible for Microsoft support, and for large organizations, clustering and support are both important.

For some background on the SOFS feature, see docs.microsoft.com/en-us/ windows-server/failover-clustering/sofs-overview.

Once you create a failover cluster, you can build an SOFS on top. The SOFS relies on the clustering technology to deliver highly available and high-performance storage across your network.

Before You Start

This example uses three systems:

- **SRV2:** This is a domain-joined server hosting an iSCSI target (which you set up in "Creating and Using an iSCSI Target").

- **FS1:** This is a domain-joined server that is to be part of a two-node failover cluster.

- **FS2:** This is another domain-joined server that you add to the two-node cluster. You configure the cluster from this host. When you use this host, ensure you log in using credentials with domain administration privileges, Reskit\Administrator.

Since this section relies on Active Directory and DNS, you also need the domain controller and DNS server, DC1, online.

To set up the failover cluster, you also need to create the iSCSI environment on FS2. The setup for FS2 is similar to the setup of FS1 carried out in "Creating and Using an iSCSI Target."

Setting Up the iSCSI Portal for FS2

To set up the cluster, you need to configure FS2 to have access to the iSCSI shared disk. You set up FS2 as follows:

```
# 1. Setup FS2 to support ISCSI
# Adjust the iSCSI service to auto start, then start the service.
Set-Service MSiSCSI -StartupType 'Automatic'
Start-Service MSiSCSI
```

This snippet ensures that the iSCSI service on FS2 is started and configured to restart this service automatically whenever you restart the host.

Configuring the iSCSI Portal for FS2

With the iSCSI service started, configure the service on FS2, as follows:

```
# 2. Setup iSCSI portal to SRV2
$PHT = @{
  TargetPortalAddress     = 'SRV2.Reskit.Org'
  TargetPortalPortNumber  = 3260
}
New-IscsiTargetPortal @PHT
#  Get the SalesTarget on portal
$Target  = Get-IscsiTarget
# Connect to the target on SRV2
$CHT = @{
  TargetPortalAddress = 'SRV2.Reskit.Org'
  NodeAddress         = $Target.NodeAddress
}
Connect-IscsiTarget  @CHT
$ISD =  Get-Disk |
          Where-Object BusType -eq 'iscsi'
$ISD |
  Set-Disk -IsOffline  $False
$ISD |
  Set-Disk -Isreadonly $False
```

You can see the output of these commands in Figure 6.20. You may see different values for `TargetSideIdentifier`, but that is not significant.

```
PS C:\Foo> # 2. Setup iSCSI portal to SRV2
PS C:\Foo> $PHT = @{
  TargetPortalAddress     = 'SRV2.Reskit.Org'
  TargetPortalPortNumber  = 3260
}
New-IscsiTargetPortal @PHT

RunspaceId             : 318f089c-7ea5-4a40-ad15-bb6b3282c849
InitiatorInstanceName  :
InitiatorPortalAddress :
IsDataDigest           : False
IsHeaderDigest         : False
TargetPortalAddress    : SRV2.Reskit.Org
TargetPortalPortNumber : 3260

PS C:\Foo> $Target  = Get-IscsiTarget
PS C:\Foo> # Connect to the target on SRV2
PS C:\Foo> $CHT = @{
            TargetPortalAddress = 'SRV2.Reskit.Org'
            NodeAddress         = $Target.NodeAddress
          }
PS C:\Foo> Connect-IscsiTarget  @CHT

RunspaceId              : 318f089c-7ea5-4a40-ad15-bb6b3282c849
AuthenticationType      : NONE
InitiatorInstanceName   : ROOT\ISCSIPRT\0000_0
InitiatorNodeAddress    : iqn.1991-05.com.microsoft:fs2.reskit.org
InitiatorPortalAddress  : 0.0.0.0
InitiatorSideIdentifier : 400001370000
IsConnected             : True
IsDataDigest            : False
IsDiscovered            : False
IsHeaderDigest          : False
IsPersistent            : False
NumberOfConnections     : 1
SessionIdentifier       : ffffd70d62538010-4000013700000002
TargetNodeAddress       : iqn.1991-05.com.microsoft:srv2-salestarget-target
TargetSideIdentifier    : 0100

PS C:\Foo> $ISD =  Get-Disk |
            Where-Object BusType -eq 'iscsi'
PS C:\Foo> $ISD |
            Set-Disk -IsOffline $False
PS C:\Foo> $ISD |
            Set-Disk -Isreadonly $False
```

Figure 6.20: Setting up the iSCSI portal

These commands establish the iSCSI portal for FS2 and connect to the iSCSI disk, similarly to how you configured FS1 in the "Creating and Using an iSCSI Target" section earlier in this chapter.

Note that you had to use Set-Disk twice to ensure that the disk is both read/write and online. The Set-Disk command does not allow you to specify both parameters at the same time.

Adding the File Server Role to FS2

In "Adding File Server Features to FS1," you added key file server-related Windows features to FS1. Because you are creating a clustered file server, you add those same features to FS2, like this:

```
# 3. Add File Server features to FS2
Import-Module -Name ServerManager -WarningAction SilentlyContinue
$Features = 'FileAndStorage-Services',
            'File-Services',
            'FS-FileServer'
Install-WindowsFeature -Name $Features -IncludeManagementTools |
    Out-Null
```

Adding Clustering Features to FS1/FS2

When installing Windows Server, the setup process by default does not install the Failover Clustering feature. You use the Server Manager module's `Install-WindowsFeature` command to install the feature on both FS1 and FS2. Run this on FS2.

```
# 4. Adding clustering features to FS1/FS2
Import-Module -Name ServerManager -WarningAction SilentlyContinue
$IHT = @{
  Name                    = 'Failover-Clustering'
  IncludeManagementTools  = $true
}
Install-WindowsFeature -ComputerName FS2 @IHT
Install-WindowsFeature -ComputerName FS1 @IHT
```

Figure 6.21 shows the output from this snippet.

```
PS C:\Foo> # 4. Adding clustering features to FS1/FS1
PS C:\Foo> Import-Module ServerManager -WarningAction SilentlyContinue
PS C:\Foo> $IHT = @{
          Name                    = 'Failover-Clustering'
          IncludeManagementTools  = $true
          }
PS C:\Foo> Install-WindowsFeature -ComputerName FS2 @IHT

Success Restart Needed Exit Code     Feature Result
------- -------------- ---------     --------------
True    Yes            SuccessRestart {Failover Clustering, Remote Server Administ...
WARNING: You must restart this server to finish the installation process.

PS C:\Foo> Install-WindowsFeature -ComputerName FS1 @IHT

Success Restart Needed Exit Code     Feature Result
------- -------------- ---------     --------------
True    Yes            SuccessRestart {Failover Clustering, Remote Server Administ...
WARNING: You must restart this server to finish the installation process.
```

Figure 6.21: Installing clustering on FS1 and FS2

As you can see from the output, you need to restart Windows after you install the Failover Clustering feature.

Restarting FS1 and FS2

Adding the Failover Clustering feature to both hosts requires a reboot to complete the installation.

```
# 5. Restarting both FS1, FS2
Restart-Computer -ComputerName FS1 -Force
Restart-Computer -ComputerName FS2 -Force
```

Testing the Cluster Nodes

Microsoft added failover clustering with Windows NT4 but with a restricted set of supported hardware. Later, Microsoft created a cluster test tool—if your cluster passes the test, Microsoft can support it. Full Microsoft support is essential for many larger organizations that run mission-critical workloads based on failover clustering.

Before you create a failover cluster (using FS1 and FS2), you test the cluster members to determine whether the systems can be clustered in a supported fashion, using the Test-Cluster command.

```
# 6. Testing the Cluster Nodes
Import-Module -Name FailoverClusters -WarningAction SilentlyContinue
$CheckOutput = 'C:\Foo\Clustercheck'
Test-Cluster  -Node FS1, FS2  -ReportName $CheckOutput | Out-Null
```

This snippet, which produces no console output, tests the cluster. When setting up a cluster, you should ensure that the test is successful. If it is not, then you need to do some additional work to overcome any deficiencies that the Test-Cluster output shows.

With this snippet, you import the FailoverClusters module manually. This module is not supported natively in PowerShell 7, but its commands work well using the Windows PowerShell compatibility feature described in Chapter 2.

Viewing Cluster Validation Test Results

Once the tests are complete, you can view the results generated by the Test-Cluster command.

```
# 7. View the cluster validation test results
$COFILE = "$CheckOutput.htm"
Invoke-Item  -Path $COFILE
```

You can view some of the output from this command in Figure 6.22.

Figure 6.22: Viewing cluster test results

The cluster validation report is long—there are a large number of tests that Microsoft has specified are necessary in order to support the cluster. So long as the tests are all successful, you can proceed to create the cluster.

This snippet also omits any explicit storage testing. Depending on the disks you plan to add to your cluster, disk testing could mean some downtime, particularly if you are updating an existing cluster. To create the scale-out file server, you do not need to do any testing, so you can skip this testing.

For more information about cluster validation, see docs.microsoft.com/en-us/previous-versions/windows/it-pro/windows-server-2012-r2-and-2012/jj134244(v=ws.11).

As you can see, in this case, there were three tests carried out by the command, and all tests were successful. This means you are ready to create the cluster.

One issue that arises a lot when creating clusters is that the two nodes may not have the same set of updates. The Test-Cluster command makes the check to ensure that the hosts are up-to-date. You may find the PSWindowsUpdate module (available from the PowerShell Gallery; see www.powershellgallery.com/packages?q=pswindowsupdate) might be useful to help you to ensure that both FS1 and FS2 are up-to-date before proceeding to create a cluster.

A tip to simplify successful testing is to remove the Windows Defender service. Removing this service minimizes the issue of incompatible updates occurring while you are creating the cluster. If you do remove this service while you are creating the SOFS, be sure to re-enable it after you finish installing the cluster. As an alternative, you could use the -Ignore parameter and ignore the Validate Software Update Levels test, but that might miss other important updates.

Creating the Cluster

Once the cluster check is completed successfully, you can create the actual cluster, using the New-Cluster command.

```
# 8.  Creating the Cluster
$NCHT = @{
  Name          = 'FS'
  Node          = 'FS1.Reskit.Org', 'FS2.Reskit.Org'  StaticAddress =
'10.10.10.100'
}
New-Cluster @NCHT | Out-Null
```

This snippet creates a cluster with a cluster name of FS and a cluster address of 10.10.10.100.

Configuring a Quorum Share on DC1

Windows Failover Clustering provides high availability for your workloads. Cluster resources are highly available as long as the host is available.

You can configure a quorum witness to avoid issues that can arise with multiple nodes. To understand more about failover clustering and quorums, see docs.microsoft.com/windows-server/storage/storage-spaces/understand-quorum.

One approach is for you to configure your cluster to have a file share witness. To do this, you configure a file share witness, and to do that, you must first create a new file share on DC1, as follows:

```
# 9. Configure a share on DC1 to act as quorum
$SBDC1 = {
  New-Item -Path C:\Quorum -ItemType Directory
  New-SmbShare -Name Quorum -Path C:\Quorum -FullAccess Everyone
}
Invoke-Command -ComputerName DC1 -ScriptBlock $SBDC1 | Out-Null
```

Setting the Cluster Witness

With the share created on DC1, you can configure the cluster to use the file share as the quorum witness, as follows:

```
# 10. Set the cluster Witness
Set-ClusterQuorum -NodeAndFileShareMajority \\DC1\quorum | Out-Null
```

Ensuring that iSCSI Disks Are Connected

If and when you reboot both servers, it is useful to ensure that the iSCSI disks are connected to both cluster nodes, like this:

```
# 11. Ensuring iSCSI disks are connected
$SB = {
  Get-ISCSITarget |
    Connect-IscsiTarget -ErrorAction SilentlyContinue
}
Invoke-Command  -ComputerName FS1 -ScriptBlock $SB
Invoke-Command  -ComputerName FS2 -ScriptBlock $SB
```

Note that this snippet uses the `Invoke-Command` cmdlet. By default, the script block is executed using a Windows PowerShell 5.1 remoting endpoint. This works well for commands in the iSCSI module, since this module is not supported natively by PowerShell 7.

Adding the iSCSI Disk to the Cluster

Now you can add the iSCSI disk to the failover cluster.

```
# 12. Adding the iSCSI disk to the cluster
Get-Disk |
  Where-Object BusType -eq 'iSCSI'|
    Add-ClusterDisk
```

You can see the results of adding this iSCSI disk to your cluster in Figure 6.23.

```
PS C:\Foo> # 12. Adding iSCSI disk to the cluster
PS C:\Foo> Get-Disk |
           Where-Object BusType -eq 'iSCSI' |
           Add-ClusterDisk

Name              State OwnerGroup        ResourceType
----              ----- ----------        ------------
Cluster Disk 1          Available Storage Physical Disk
```

Figure 6.23: Adding an iSCSI disk to the cluster

Moving the iSCSI Disk into the CSV

For both nodes in the cluster to share data in the iSCSI disk, you must move the disk into the cluster shared volume (CSV), using the Add-ClusterSharedVolume command.

```
# 13. Move disk into CSV
Add-ClusterSharedVolume -Name 'Cluster Disk 1'
```

You can see the result of this snippet in Figure 6.24.

```
PS C:\Foo> # 13. Move disk into the CSV
PS C:\Foo> Add-ClusterSharedVolume -Name 'Cluster Disk 1'

Name              State Node
----              ----- ----
Cluster Disk 1          FS1
```

Figure 6.24: Adding the new disk to the CSV

Once you add the disk to the CSV, the iSCSI volume (which is stored physically on SRV2) is available to the cluster, and you can use it from both nodes. The CSV is, in effect, a filesystem that coordinates I/O from any cluster member.

Adding the SOFS Role to the Cluster

To create a clustered scale-out file server, you need to add the Cluster Scale-Out File Server role on FS2.

```
# 14. Add SOFS role to Cluster
Import-Module -Name ServerManager -WarningAction SilentlyContinue
Add-WindowsFeature File-Services -IncludeManagementTools | Out-Null
Add-ClusterScaleOutFileServerRole -Cluster RKFS
```

This snippet ensures that the File-Services feature is created and then adds the SOFS role to the FS cluster.

Creating a Folder

With the cluster set up and the iSCSI volume mounted in both nodes, you can use the storage as if it were local.

```
# 15. Create a folder and give Sales Access to the folder
Install-Module -Name NTFSSecurity -Force | Out-Null
$HvFolder = 'C:\ClusterStorage\Volume1\HVData'
New-Item -Path $HvFolder -ItemType Directory |
              Out-Null
$ACCHT = @{
  Path         = $HvFolder
  Account      = 'Reskit\Sales'
  AccessRights = 'FullControl'
}
Add-NTFSAccess   @ACCHT
```

Note that you created the Sales domain security group in "Managing NTFS Permissions" in Chapter 5.

Adding a Continuously Available Share

With the SOFS set up, you can add a continuously available share.

```
# 16. Adding a Continuously Available share to the entire cluster
$SMBSHT2 = @{
  Name                 = 'SalesHV'
  Path                 = $HvFolder
  Description          = 'Sales HV (CA)'
  FullAccess           = 'Reskit\Sales'
  ContinuouslyAvailable = $true
}
New-SmbShare   @SMBSHT2
```

Figure 6.25 shows the output of this snippet.

```
PS C:\Foo> # 16. Adding a Continuously Available share to the entire cluster
PS C:\Foo> $SMBSHT2 = @{
              Name                 = 'SalesHV'
              Path                 = $HvFolder
              Description          = 'Sales HV (CA)'
              FullAccess           = 'Reskit\Sales'
              ContinuouslyAvailable = $true
            }
PS C:\Foo> New-SMBShare   @SMBSHT2

Name     ScopeName Path                      Description
----     --------- ----                      -----------
SalesHA RKFSSOFS  C:\ClusterStorage\Volume1 Sales HA Share
```

Figure 6.25: Adding a continuously available share

Viewing Shares from FS1

With your SOFS set up and sharing a folder (held on the iSCSI target on SRV2), you can view the shares available from FS2.

```
# 17. View Shares on FS1 and FS2
Get-SmbShare    # FOR FS1
Invoke-Command -ComputerName FS2 -ScriptBlock {Get-SmbShare}
```

You can see the output of this command in Figure 6.26.

```
PS C:\Foo> # 17. View Shares on FS1 and FS2
PS C:\Foo> Get-SmbShare    # FOR FS2

Name               ScopeName Path                              Description
----               --------- ----                              -----------
ADMIN$             *         C:\Windows                        Remote Admin
C$                 *         C:\                               Default share
ClusterStorage$    FSSOFS    C:\ClusterStorage                 Cluster Shared Volumes Default Share
E$                 *         E:\                               Default share
IPC$               *                                           Remote IPC
SalesHV            FSSOFS    C:\ClusterStorage\Volume1\HVData   Sales HV (CA)

PS C:\Foo> Invoke-Command -ComputerName FS1 -ScriptBlock {Get-SmbShare }

Name               ScopeName Path                              Description                            PSComputerName
----               --------- ----                              -----------                            --------------
ADMIN$             *         C:\Windows                        Remote Admin                           FS2
C$                 *         C:\                               Default share                          FS2
ClusterStorage$    FSSOFS    C:\ClusterStorage                 Cluster Shared Volumes Default Share   FS2
E$                 *         E:\                               Default share                          FS2
IPC$               *                                           Remote IPC                             FS2
SalesHV            FSSOFS    C:\ClusterStorage\Volume1\HVData   Sales HV (CA)                          FS2
```

Figure 6.26: Viewing shares

As you can see in the output, the SalesHV share is set up on the cluster. You could view the shares using Net View \\FSSOFS, which would return the SalesHV share.

Now that you have the SOFS set up, you can use the Cluster Manager MMC console to pause the active node, and the file server continues to work. But note that the iSCSI target you created on SRV2 is a single point of failure (SPOF). To avoid SPOF issues, you could ensure that the drive created on SRV2 is based on hardware (or software) RAID.

In general, the iSCSI target is not a widely used feature of Windows Server 2019. However, many smaller organizations deploy low-cost third-party SANs that provide both fault tolerance in the box and an iSCSI interface.

Whether or not you are using a Windows Server iSCSI target, you may use the Windows iSCSI initiator to access an organization's SAN if it offers an iSCSI interface.

An example of such a SAN is from Synology; see `www.synology.com/ en-global/knowledgebase/DSM/tutorial/Virtualization/How_to_use_iSCSI_ Targets_on_a_Windows_Server` for details on how you set up iSCSI on this device. There are many other vendors that can offer lower-cost networked storage based on iSCSI.

Summary

In this chapter, you have examined setting up and configuring an SMB file server and how you can deploy an SOFS. The SOFS made use of an iSCSI target, which you also set up. Although in this case the actual target that you built on SRV2 was *not* fault tolerant, you could add a degree of fault tolerance (for example, by using RAID 5 on the underlying iSCSI partition in SRV2).

The use of the Windows-based iSCSI target in this chapter shows how easy it is to share data using SMB-based file services within Windows, controlled by PowerShell 7.

Managing Printing

Printing is a function of network infrastructure so basic to daily business operations that users just assume it is going to work the first time/every time. Meanwhile, IT pros have the challenge of making it so.

Although there has been no real change in the way users experience printing, its quality and speed have improved from the earliest days of the PC, when each application had its own set of printer drivers. The evolution of Windows has simplified printing significantly, although the printer server architecture in Windows Server 2019 is little changed from Windows Server 2012.

In Windows, the term *printer* refers to what is effectively a printer queue. Windows calls the physical printer a *print device*. When the application prints a document, it sends a print job to a print spooler. This spooler holds the individual print jobs, which may arrive faster than the print device can handle at any given time. The spooler then sends each print job to the printing device via a printer port, which can be either a physical port (such as LPT1:) or a network address.

With Windows Server 2019, the Print Services feature has three components.

Print server: This feature includes tools necessary to enable you to manage one or more print servers. It includes the Print Management MMC snap-in.

Internet printing: This provides the ability to connect and print to shared printers using the Internet Printing protocol (IPP).

LPD service: This feature installs the Line Printer Daemon (LPD) service. Linux/Unix users can use the Line Printer Remote (LPR) service to use shared printers via the LPD host.

This chapter covers only the Print Server feature. Neither the LPD service nor the Internet Printing feature in Windows Server is used widely in today's networks.

In this chapter, you explore the following tasks:

- "Installing and Sharing Printers" demonstrates the complete process of installing a physical printer on your network and sharing it.

- In "Publishing a Printer in AD," once you've installed a printer on the network, publishing it in Active Directory enables your users to find it.

- In "Changing the Spool Folder," following best practice, you move the print spooler file from the default temporary folder to one you configure here.

- "Printing a Test Page" uses Windows Management Instrumentation (WMI), discussed further in Chapter 9, "Using WMI and CIM cmdlets," to generate and print a test page.

- The "Creating a Printer Pool" section shows how to create a printer pool so that a single Windows printer can be associated with two or more physical print devices.

Systems Used in This Chapter

This chapter uses two hosts.

DC1.Reskit.Org: This is a domain controller in the Reskit.Org domain that you created in Chapter 3, "Managing Active Directory."

PSRV.Reskit.Org: This is a Windows Server 2019 host that is a member server in the Reskit.Org domain. In this chapter, you use this host and set it up as a print server.

This chapter also uses two networked printers, which you install using the chapter's scripts.

Figure 7.1 shows the systems (and printers) in use in this chapter.

Note that all systems used in this chapter need PowerShell 7 loaded before starting. You can do that manually, using the scripts from Chapter 1, or using the GitHub Gist at bit.ly/Pwsh-install-1 (or use the full URL shown in the introduction). Optionally, you can configure VS Code with the GitHub Gist at bit.ly/Pwsh-install-2 (or use the full URL shown in the introduction).

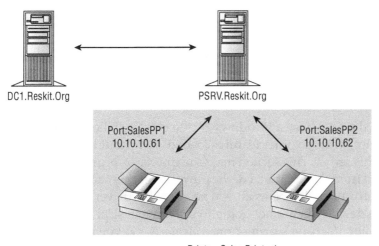

Port:SalesPP1
10.10.10.61

Port:SalesPP2
10.10.10.62

DC1.Reskit.Org   PSRV.Reskit.Org

Printer: Sales Printer1
10.10.10.61, 10.10.10.62

Figure 7.1: Systems used in this chapter

Installing and Sharing Printers

When you install Windows Server, the installation process sets up several printers on each system by default. These enable you to "print" to PDF or to Microsoft's XPS format. Adding applications can also add additional printers. For example, installing the Foxit PDF reader adds the entry `Foxit Reader PDF Printer`. Microsoft's Office product also installs a `OneNote` printer. These additional "printers" tend to be client-side and print to the respective document types. If you want to print to paper, you need to install, configure, and deploy further physical printers.

Deploying a new print device involves several steps.

1. Obtain and install the physical printer. You need to unpack it, turn it on, and connect it.

2. Obtain the print drivers for the print device and install them on the print server. Windows ships with a large number of printer drivers, but you can find, download, and install additional ones. The example begins with this step.

3. Configure a printer port to enable the print server to send data to the print device. This port is often a network address but can include printers attached physically to your print server.

4. Install the printer in Windows. This creates the printer queue and associates the queue with a driver and port.

5. Share the printer. You can share the printer to enable users to access it.

Before You Start

This section uses the PSRV host, a Windows 2019 server (installed with the full Desktop Experience), with no other features loaded. You should have installed PowerShell 7 on this server. This section makes use of Xerox printer drivers that you can download from the Internet. For the purposes of this chapter, you don't need an actual Xerox print device, as all you need are the driver files (although without the print device you are not going to see any physical output). If you have a different manufacturer's printer on your network, you may be able to modify the scripts to reflect your manufacturer and the driver URL(s) along with changes necessary to reflect how the drivers are packaged by the manufacturer.

Some printer manufacturers create installation programs that do the printer installation via a GUI. In that case, you could run the installation program on the printer server (for example, via RDP). Depending on the manufacturer and how it created the installation files, you may be able to install the drivers in a test machine and then extract the printer drivers and install them as shown here.

Installing the Print Server Feature on PSRV

You use the `Install-WindowsFeature` command to install the Print Server feature and the associated management tools.

```
# 1. Install the Print-Server feature on PSRV plus tools
Import-Module -Name ServerManager -WarningAction SilentlyContinue
Install-WindowsFeature -Name Print-Server -IncludeManagementTools
```

You can see the output of this code in Figure 7.2.

```
PS C:\Foo> # 1. Install the Print-Server feature on PSRV plus tools
PS C:\Foo> Import-Module -Name ServerManager -WarningAction SilentlyContinue
PS C:\Foo> Install-WindowsFeature -Name Print-Server -IncludeManagementTools


Success Restart Needed Exit Code  Feature Result
------- -------------- ---------  --------------
True    No             Success    {Print Server, Print and Document Services,...
```

Figure 7.2: Installing the Print Server feature

Creating a Folder for the Print Drivers

In preparation for installing a new printer, you need to create a temporary folder into which you can download the drivers. In this example, they are Xerox drivers. If you install printers from a different manufacturer, be sure to use an appropriate folder name.

```
# 2. Creating a folder for the Xerox printer drivers
$NIHT = @{
  Path        = 'C:\Xerox'
  ItemType    = 'Directory'
  Force       = $true
  ErrorAction = 'Silentlycontinue'
}
New-Item @NIHT | Out-Null
```

Downloading Printer Drivers

Different printing vendors provide their drives in a variety of channels. Xerox, for example, provides the drivers in a ZIP file that you can download using the Background Intelligent Transfer Service (BITS).

```
# 3. Downloading printer drivers for Xerox printers
$URL = 'http://bit.ly/XDrivers'
$Target='C:\Xerox\XDrivers.zip'
Start-BitsTransfer -Source $URL -Destination $Target
```

In many cases, you may use a web browser to navigate to your printer manufacturer's web site and search for the drivers you need.

In this example, you use a compressed URL to save space. The full URL for the driver package is download.support.xerox.com/pub/drivers/6510/drivers/win10x64/ar/6510_5.617.7.0_PCL6_x64.zip.

Expanding the ZIP File

In the previous step, you downloaded a ZIP file. In this step, you extract the Xerox drivers to C:\Xerox\Drivers, as follows:

```
# 4. Expand the zip file
$Drivers = 'C:\Xerox\Drivers'
Expand-Archive -Path $Target -DestinationPath $Drivers
```

Installing the Drivers

Once you have expanded the driver package, you install the drivers it contains. This specific driver package contains drivers for two Xerox printer models (Phaser 6510 and Phaser 6515) using `printui.dll`.

```
# 5. Installing the drivers
$M1 = 'Xerox Phaser 6510 PCL6'
$P =  'C:\Xerox\Drivers\6510_5.617.7.0_PCL6_x64_Driver.inf\x3NSURX.inf'
rundll32.exe printui.dll,PrintUIEntry /ia /m "$M1"  /f "$P"
$M2 = 'Xerox WorkCentre 6515 PCL6'
rundll32.exe printui.dll,PrintUIEntry /ia /m "$M2"  /f "$P"
```

The Print Management module does not provide a command to add printer drivers. You can, however, use the functionality in `printui.dll` to add the printers. This DLL is part of the Print Manager GUI. This GUI's underlying tool, `printmanagement.msc`, uses the DLL to perform printer-related administration. You use `rundll32.exe` to invoke the DLL, in this case to add drivers to the Windows driver store.

In some cases, you may find that these commands produce an error, calling `rundll32.exe`. If so, just rerun the command to resolve the issue.

The Xerox drivers you downloaded were contained in a ZIP file. Some printer drivers are built into Windows and do not require downloading. Other driver downloads may use other compression formats. Additionally, some drivers are delivered inside an installation program you run on the print server to install the drivers.

Adding a New Printer Port

In this example, the printer you are going to add is a networked printer. To enable the print spooler on PSRV to send data to the printer, you first define a new printer port.

```
# 6. Adding a new printer port
$PPHT = @{
  Name                = 'SalesPP'
  PrinterHostAddress = '10.10.10.61'
}
Add-PrinterPort @PPHT
```

In this case, you use the IP address 10.10.10.61. This is a hard-coded address you assign for the networked printing device. If the printer gets its IP address details via DHCP, ensure you create a reservation. This simplifies adding a new printer on the print server.

Adding a New Printer

With the drivers installed and a printer port created, you can use the `Add-Printer` command to add the printer to PSRV.

```
# 7. Adding a new printer
$PRHT = @{
  Name       = 'SalesPrinter1'
  DriverName = $M1
  PortName   = 'SalesPP'
}
Add-Printer @PRHT
```

Once this has completed, you should be able to print to the printer from PSRV.

Sharing the Printer

The steps thus far allow printing only from the print server. To enable users to access the printer remotely, you need to share it.

```
# 8. Sharing the printer
Set-Printer -Name SalesPrinter1 -Shared $True
```

Once you share a printer, users can begin to use it to print their documents. You can review the printer setup either using Net View \\PSRV (from an elevated PowerShell session) or using the printer commands.

Reviewing the Printer Configuration

The printer installation and configuration steps you have performed in this section produce no output. Once you have finished the installation of your new Xerox printer, you can use the relevant Get commands to review the printer port, printer driver, and printer settings, like this:

```
# 9. Review printer configuration
Get-PrinterPort -Name SalesPP |
    Format-Table -Autosize -Property Name, Description,
                            PrinterHostAddress, PortNumber
Get-PrinterDriver -Name Xerox* |
    Format-Table -Property Name, Manufacturer,
                            DriverVersion, PrinterEnvironment
Get-Printer -ComputerName PSRV -Name SalesPrinter1 |
    Format-Table -Property Name, ComputerName,
                            Type, PortName, Location, Shared
```

You can see the output of these commands in Figure 7.3.

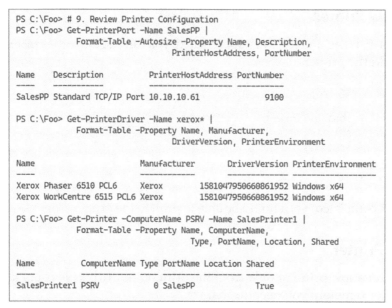

```
PS C:\Foo> # 9. Review Printer Configuration
PS C:\Foo> Get-PrinterPort -Name SalesPP |
           Format-Table -Autosize -Property Name, Description,
                               PrinterHostAddress, PortNumber

Name    Description           PrinterHostAddress PortNumber
----    -----------           ------------------ ----------
SalesPP Standard TCP/IP Port 10.10.10.61               9100

PS C:\Foo> Get-PrinterDriver -Name xerox* |
           Format-Table -Property Name, Manufacturer,
                               DriverVersion, PrinterEnvironment

Name                      Manufacturer      DriverVersion PrinterEnvironment
----                      ------------      ------------- ------------------
Xerox Phaser 6510 PCL6    Xerox       1581047950660861952 Windows x64
Xerox WorkCentre 6515 PCL6 Xerox      1581047950660861952 Windows x64

PS C:\Foo> Get-Printer -ComputerName PSRV -Name SalesPrinter1 |
           Format-Table -Property Name, ComputerName,
                               Type, PortName, Location, Shared

Name          ComputerName Type PortName Location Shared
----          ------------ ---- -------- -------- ------
SalesPrinter1 PSRV            0 SalesPP           True
```

Figure 7.3: Reviewing the setup of the new printer

In this section, you set up a new print server, created a printer port, and added/shared a new printer. Your printer is now available, and your users should be able to print to it.

Publishing a Printer in AD

Once you have a printer created and installed, you can also publish it to Active Directory. This helps your users find the printer. You can also specify a physical location for the printer to assist your users in finding the actual print device.

Once you publish the printer, your users can then search for published printers based on location, as well as on capabilities (such as color printers). In larger organizations this can be useful to enable users to find and use printers.

Before You Start

This example uses two hosts: PSRV and DC1. DC1 is a domain controller in the Reskit.Org domain. PSRV is a Windows 2019 server that you configured as a print server in "Installing and Sharing Printers."

Getting the Printer Object

To publish a printer in AD, you first must create a printer object for the printer.

```
# 1. Get the printer object
Import-Module -Name PrintManagement -WarningAction SilentlyContinue
$Printer = Get-Printer -Name SalesPrinter1
```

PowerShell 7 does not natively support the Print Management module, but the commands in the module work via the Windows PowerShell compatibility mechanism discussed in Chapter 2, "PowerShell 7 Compatibility with Windows PowerShell." By setting the -WarningAction parameter to SilentlyContinue, you avoid the warning message (warning that you are importing the module via the PowerShell compatibility mechanism).

Checking the Initial Publication Status

By default, printers are not published in AD. You can check the initial publication status by examining the printer object you just created.

```
# 2. Checking the initial publication status
$Printer | Format-Table -Property Name, Published
```

You can see, in the output in Figure 7.4, that the SalesPrinter1 printer is not currently shared in AD.

```
PS C:\Foo> # 2. Get the publication status
PS C:\Foo> $Printer | Format-Table –Property Name, Published

Name            Published
----            ---------
SalesPrinter1   False
```

Figure 7.4: Checking on the SalesPrinter1 printer

Publishing the Printer to AD

Publishing a printer is straightforward. Before you publish the printer, you should use the Set-Printer command to add a location to the printer information both held by PSRV and in AD, using the Set-Printer command, like this:

```
# 3. Publish and share the printer to AD
$Printer | Set-Printer -Location '10th floor 10E4'
$Printer | Set-Printer -Published $true
```

This code configures your printer with a Location value and then publishes it in AD.

Viewing the Printer Publication Status

Having set the printer details, you can use `Get-Printer` to observe the updated configuration.

```
# 4. View the updated publication status
Get-Printer -Name SalesPrinter1 |
    Format-Table -Property Name, Location, DriverName, Published
```

You can use the `Get-Printer` command to view the key settings for your new printer, as shown in Figure 7.5.

```
PS C:\Foo> # 4. View the updated publication status
Get-Printer -Name SalesPrinter1 |
  Format-Table -Property Name, Location, DriverName, Published, Shared


Name            Location        DriverName             Published Shared
----            --------        ----------             --------- ------
SalesPrinter1 10th floor 10E4 Xerox Phaser 6510 PCL6      True   True
```

Figure 7.5: Reviewing the setup of the new printer

As you can see, the Sales printer, `SalesPrinter1`, is now published to the AD.

Changing the Spool Folder

The Windows print spooler receives print jobs from printer users and sends the jobs to the print device. The print jobs that pass through the print server are stored temporarily in a spool folder on the print server. By default, Windows uses the folder `$Env:SystemRoot\system32\spool\PRINTERS`.

If you have a large print server handling a large number of printers, the potential size of this folder could become quite large. In turn, this could result in the system drive becoming full or full enough to affect the operation of your print server.

To avoid this issue, and as a best practice, you should move the spool file to another folder. This will allow you to keep your eye on the folder and possibly leverage Filesystem Resource Manager (FSRM) to generate reports on this folder. For a large print server, you might consider adding a disk to the server to hold the temporary spool files and updating the spool folder configuration to point to the new folder.

There are no PowerShell commands to enable you to change the spool folder. The .NET Framework includes the `System.Printing.PrintServer` class, which you use to set the spool folder location. By default, PowerShell does not load the `System.Printing` .NET namespace, which is necessary before you can change the spooler folder. Thus, you need to manually load the namespace and then use the classes to update the spool folder.

You can also configure the spool folder via the registry. Both methods work. The second method, via the registry, is probably a little faster than the first approach, but the difference is probably negligible in practice.

Before You Start

This section uses the printer server PSRV, which you created in "Installing and Sharing Printers."

Loading the System.Printing Namespace

As mentioned, you need to add the System.Printing namespace explicitly to load the classes that this namespace contains into the current PowerShell session; you do that using the Add-Type command.

```
# 1. Loading the System.Printing namespace and classes
Add-Type -AssemblyName System.Printing
```

Until you add this assembly, part of .NET Core, you cannot access the classes needed. If this assembly and the classes it contains are something you need to use on a regular basis, consider loading it as part of your PowerShell profile.

Displaying the Initial Spool Folder

Assuming you have not yet changed the configuration of the print server, you can use New-Object to observe the current, and default, spool folder.

```
# 2. Displaying the initial spool folder
New-Object -TypeName System.Printing.PrintServer |
   Format-Table -Property Name, DefaultSpoolDirectory
```

The output from this code, shown in Figure 7.6, shows the default spool folder on the PSRV print server.

```
PS C:\Foo> # 2. Displaying the initial spool folder
PS C:\Foo> New-Object -TypeName System.Printing.PrintServer |
              Format-Table -Property Name, DefaultSpoolDirectory

Name    DefaultSpoolDirectory
----    ---------------------
\\PSRV  C:\Windows\System32\spool\PRINTERS
```

Figure 7.6: Reviewing existing spool folder

As you can see, the default spool folder is C:\Windows\system32\spool\PRINTERS.

Defining Required Permissions

To administrate the printer, you have to create a print server object using administrative permissions. To do that, you first create an object that states the required permissions.

```
# 3. Define the required permissions—that is, the ability to
#    administrate the server
$Permissions =
    [System.Printing.PrintSystemDesiredAccess]::AdministrateServer
```

Creating a Print Server Object

Next, you create a print server object with administrative permissions.

```
# 4. Create a PrintServer object with the required permissions
$NOHT = @{
  TypeName     = 'System.Printing.PrintServer'
  ArgumentList = $Permissions
}
$PS = New-Object @NOHT   # Print Server object (as admin)
```

Creating a New Spool Folder

To illustrate the effect of changing the spool folder, you can use New-Item to create a new folder.

```
# 5. Create a new spool folder
$SP = 'C:\SpoolPath'
$NIHT = @{
  Path        = $SP
  ItemType    = 'Directory'
  Force       = $true
  ErrorAction = 'SilentlyContinue'
}
New-Item @NIHT | Out-Null
```

Changing the Spool Folder Path

You can now change the default spool folder by updating the appropriate property on the $PS object.

```
# 6. Changing the spool folder path
$PS.DefaultSpoolDirectory = $SP
```

Committing the Change

The updated $PS object next needs to be committed to save the change.

```
# 7. Committing the change
$PS.Commit()
```

The print server object is in-memory. To enable the Print Spooler service to use the updated settings, you need to commit the changed printer object as shown here.

Restarting the Spooler Service

Once you have updated the spool folder, use the `Restart-Service` command to restart the print spooler service. The PSRV server now spools all subsequent print jobs to the new spool folder.

```
# 8. Restart the Spooler Service to use the new folder
Restart-Service -Name Spooler
```

Depending on your system, you may see some warning messages. As long as the service starts, the messages are benign.

Reviewing the Spooler Folder

Once you have restarted the spooler, users can now print jobs, and Windows spools the print jobs to the newly specified folder. You can view this new folder:

```
# 9. Reviewing the spooler folder
New-Object -TypeName System.Printing.PrintServer |
    Format-Table -Property Name, DefaultSpoolDirectory
```

As you can see in the output, shown in Figure 7.7, your new spool folder is now in operation.

```
PS C:\Foo> # 9. Reviewing the spooler folder
PS C:\Foo> New-Object -TypeName System.Printing.PrintServer |
              Format-Table -Property Name, DefaultSpoolDirectory

Name    DefaultSpoolDirectory
----    ---------------------
\\PSRV  C:\SpoolPath
```

Figure 7.7: Reviewing the spool folder

Note that if there were unprinted printer jobs in the older spool folder, changing the folder name does not move those documents. You should ensure that the existing spool folder is empty before changing the spool folder.

Creating Another Spool Folder

As mentioned, there are two mechanisms for modifying the spooler folder, and you've just explored the first of them, using the System.Printing.PrintServer class. To demonstrate the second mechanism, using the registry, you need to create another new folder in the filesystem.

```
# 10. Creating a new/different spool folder
$SPL = 'C:\SpoolViaRegistry'  # different spool folder
$NIHT2 = @{
  Path        = $SPL
  Itemtype    = 'Directory'
  ErrorAction = 'SilentlyContinue'
}
New-Item  @NIHT2 | Out-Null
```

Stopping the Spooler Service

Before updating the registry, use Stop-Service to stop the spooler service.

```
# 11. Stopping the Spooler service
Stop-Service -Name Spooler
```

Configuring the New Spool Folder

Next, you update the appropriate registry value to configure the new printer spool folder, with Set-ItemProperty.

```
# 12. Configure the new spooler folder
$RPath = 'HKLM:\SYSTEM\CurrentControlSet\Control\Print\Printers'
$IP = @{
  Path     = $RPath
  Name     = 'DefaultSpoolDirectory'
  Value    = $SPL
}
Set-ItemProperty @IP
```

Restarting the Spooler

To complete the configuration of a new spool folder, you restart the spooler service.

```
# 13. Restarting the Spooler
Start-Service -Name Spooler
```

Viewing the Results

As you did previously, you can now review the updated spool directory by viewing the .NET `PrintServer` object.

```
# 14. Viewing the results
New-Object -TypeName System.Printing.PrintServer |
    Format-Table -Property Name, DefaultSpoolDirectory
```

As you can see in the output, shown in Figure 7.8, PSRV is now using the new spooler folder (`C:\SpoolViaRegistry`).

```
PS C:\Foo> # 14. View the results
PS C:\Foo> New-Object -TypeName System.Printing.PrintServer |
           Format-Table -Property Name, DefaultSpoolDirectory

Name    DefaultSpoolDirectory
----    ---------------------
\\PSRV  C:\SpoolViaRegistry
```

Figure 7.8: Reviewing the spool folder after the change

Printing a Test Page

After deploying a new printer or after changing printer consumables, it can be useful to print a test page. A test page shows that the printer and print server are working and demonstrates the quality of printing performed by the print device.

There is no PowerShell command support for creating a printer test page. However, Windows Management Instrumentation (WMI) provides a mechanism to print a test page.

WMI, discussed in more detail in Chapter 9, provides the IT professional with a great wealth of information via the hundreds of available classes. On a Windows system, the WMI class `WIN32_Printer` contains a WMI object for each printer in the system. This WMI object contains a method, `PrintTestPage`, that you use here to generate a test page.

Before You Start

This section uses the printer server PSRV, which you created in "Installing and Sharing Printers."

Getting Printer Objects from WMI

You retrieve the printers defined on this system by using WMI (and the `Get-CimInstance` command).

```
# 1. Get printer objects from WMI
$Printers = Get-CimInstance -ClassName Win32_Printer
```

This command returns an array of printer objects—one for each printer defined in the system. The command returns the same printers and the same number of printers you would see calling `Get-Printer`.

PowerShell 7 (and Windows PowerShell) uses a feature known as *cmdlet definition over XML*, which enables PowerShell to create commands based on WMI classes, combined with a small amount of XML. This incredibly useful technology enabled Microsoft to create a large number of new commands without a huge amount of effort. These commands, defined by XML contained in CDXML files, act just like cmdlets written in C#. The commands in the Print Management module are implemented using this technology.

The developers of the Print Management module chose which underlying properties and methods to expose. Not all the WMI printer object properties are exposed in the objects produced by `Get-Printer`. Also, there is no cmdlet to create a printer test page even though the underlying WMI class does provide a method to do that. You use that method in this section to create a test page.

Displaying the Number of Printers Defined

You can view the number of printers available on PSRV.

```
# 2. Display the number of printers defined on PSRV
'{0} Printers defined on this system' -f $Printers.Count
```

The output of this code, in Figure 7.9, shows seven printers defined on PSRV.

```
PS C:\Foo> # 2. Display the number of printers defined on PSRV:
PS C:\Foo> '{0} Printers defined on this system' -f $Printers.Count
7 Printers defined on this system
```

Figure 7.9: Displaying the number of printers

Getting the Sales Group Printer WMI Object

To print a test page, you first have to obtain the WMI object representing the `SalesPrinter1` printer, by using `Where-Object`.

```
# 3. Get the Sales Group printer WMI object
$Printer = $Printers |
  Where-Object Name -eq 'SalesPrinter1'
```

Display the Printer's Details

To view the printer's details, you can display the $Printer object.

```
# 4. Display the printer's details
$Printer | Format-Table -AutoSize
```

You can view the output of this command in Figure 7.10.

```
PS C:\Foo> # 4. Display the printer's details
PS C:\Foo> $Printer | Format-Table -AutoSize

Name          ShareName      SystemName PrinterState PrinterStatus Location
----          ---------      ---------- ------------ ------------- --------
SalesPrinter1 SalesPrinter1  PSRV          0             3         10th floor 10E4
```

Figure 7.10: Displaying the printer's details

Printing a Test Page

To print the printer test page, you invoke the PrintTestPage method.

```
# 5. Printing a test page
Invoke-CimMethod -InputObject $Printer -MethodName PrintTestPage
```

WMI objects can contain methods, which are commands that act on the underlying WMI object (or WMI class). You invoke these methods using the Invoke-CimMethod cmdlet. In this case, the printer object has a method, PrintTestPage, which creates a test page and sends it to the printer. Invoking the method produces some basic output, which you can see Figure 7.11 (in addition to printing the test page).

```
PS C:\Foo> # 5. Print a test page:
PS C:\Foo> Invoke-CimMethod -InputObject $Printer -MethodName PrintTestPage

ReturnValue PSComputerName
----------- --------------
          0
```

Figure 7.11: Printing a test page

In the output shown in Figure 7.11, the CIM method produces a ReturnValue of 0. This indicates the WMI method was successful. Of course, the actual test page output as rendered by the print device is the ultimate test. WMI might work successfully, but the printer might have issues preventing it from printing properly. To view the details of the print jobs waiting to be printed, including test pages, you can use the Print Manager GUI, printmanagement.msc.

Creating a Printer Pool

In Windows, a *printer pool* is a single printer associated with two or more printing devices (each of which is assigned to a different printer port). This can be useful in environments that generate a lot of printed output, for example a large legal practice printing lots of long documents.

This is one of those rare cases where there are no existing commands, WMI classes, or .NET classes that enable you to create a printer pool directly. However, the `printui.dll` library (added to the PSRV system when you added the print server feature) contains functionality to create the printer pool. You used this DLL to add a printer driver in "Installing and Sharing Printers."

Before You Start

This section uses the printer server PSRV, which you created in "Installing and Sharing Printers."

Adding a Printer Port

To create a printer pool, you need at least two print devices attached via different printer ports. You created the first port in "Installing and Sharing Printers" and now need to create a second port.

```
# 1. Add a printer port for the printer
$P   = 'SalesPrinter1'    # printer name
$PP2 = 'SalesPP2'         # new printer port name
Add-PrinterPort -Name $PP2 -PrinterHostAddress 10.10.10.62
```

Creating the Printer Pool for SalesPrinter1

To create the printer pool, you call `printui.dll` and tell it the printer and which ports to use.

```
# 2. Creating the printer pool for SalesPrinter1
$PP1='SalesPP'   # first port name
rundll32.exe printui.dll,PrintUIEntry /Xs /n $P Portname $P1,$P2
```

This code sets up a printer pool. The printer SalesPrinter1 is now served by two ports and two printing devices.

The `rundll32.exe` program runs the print utility DLL. In effect, `rundll` pretends to be the Printer Management GUI that uses the DLL to carry out some action. RunDLL allows you to pass parameters to the DLL and get the DLL to do things, such as creating a printer port.

For more details on how to use `rundll32` with `printui.dll`, see docs
.microsoft.com/en-us/windows-server/administration/windows-commands/
rundll32-printui.

Viewing Resulting Details

You can view the details for this printer using `Get-Printer`.

```
# 3. Viewing resultant details
Get-Printer $P |
   Format-Table -Property Name, Type, DriverName,
   PortName, Shared, Published
```

In the output of this code, shown in Figure 7.12, you can see that the
`SalesPrinter1` printer now has two ports associated and is set up in a printer
pool.

```
PS C:\Foo> # 3. View resultant details:
PS C:\Foo> Get-Printer Sales* |
           Format-Table -Property Name, Type, DriverName,
           PortName, Shared, Published

Name            Type DriverName           PortName          Shared Published
----            ---- ----------           --------          ------ ---------
SalesPrinter1      0 Xerox Phaser 6510 PCL6 SalesPP,SalesPP2  True      True
```

Figure 7.12: Viewing printer pool details

Summary

In this chapter, you have worked with Windows printing, using PowerShell
commands, WMI and .NET classes, and a Windows DLL.

You saw that the Printer Management module provided you the means to
perform common printer-related maintenance such as adding a printer. The
module, however, does not provide commands for all the activities you might
need to carry out, and therefore you need to use .NET objects and other command-line tools.

This chapter illustrates well that where there are no PowerShell 7 or Window
PowerShell commands to perform a task, you can often find other methods of
automating your environment.

Managing Hyper-V

OS virtualization is a process whereby you run an operating system instance inside another. Your host computer and its operating system can run multiple virtual machines, each with a different operating system and virtual hardware. Virtualization as a concept is not new. IBM used virtualization with its Time Sharing System OS (TSS) in the late 1960s, for example.

Microsoft's virtualization efforts began with the purchase of Connectix and the launch of two products: Microsoft Virtual PC and Microsoft Virtual Server. Both products enabled you to create and use virtual machines. Microsoft Virtual PC, version 2004, ran on Windows XP Professional and Windows 2000 Professional. Virtual Server was an enhanced product primarily for use on servers.

Hyper-V replaced these products, although initially, it was a server-only product. Microsoft shipped Hyper-V as a feature inside Windows Server 2008. Subsequently, Microsoft incorporated a client version of Hyper-V into Windows 8. Today, Microsoft supports Hyper-V in versions of Windows Server, Windows 8.1, and Windows 10 (Enterprise, Professional, and Education editions of Windows 10 only).

Microsoft also provides a free version of Hyper-V, the Microsoft Hyper-V Server. This product is a bare-metal hypervisor that only runs virtual machines and has no management GUI, very much like Windows Server installed without the Desktop Experience (aka Server Core). After installing the Hyper-V server, you perform some initial configuration using `sconfig.exe` and can then manage the server remotely using PowerShell or the Hyper-V management console `virgmgmt.msc`.

With Windows Server 2019 and Windows 10, Microsoft incorporated *nested virtualization*. This feature allows you to build a VM that can itself host VMs. Nested virtualization can be useful in cases such as training—you could provide each student a single VM on a large server dedicated to the class in which you create VMs as needed for lab work. Nested virtualization also provides an additional layer of security that might be useful when deploying VMs in multitenant scenarios. And for the geeks, it is pretty cool.

This chapter looks at Hyper-V running on Windows Server. If you are managing Hyper-V in Windows 10 or using Hyper-V Server, you can use the same tools discussed here. Some features, such as VM migration, are not available in Windows 10. You can use nested virtualization and create virtual machines running Windows Server 2019 and then use VM migration as shown in this chapter.

In this chapter, you examine the following topics:

- In "Installing and Configuring Hyper-V," you start to look at Hyper-V by installing and configuring the Hyper-V feature on Windows Server 2019.

- In "Creating a Hyper-V VM," you learn that once you have a VM host up and running, you can create a VM inside the host. You configure Hyper-V Virtual Machine Networking. Then you look at configuring the VM network.

- In "Using PowerShell Direct," you configure and use the PowerShell Direct (PS Direct) feature to manage a VM without network connectivity. PS Direct enables you to run scripts inside a VM even if the VM does not have networking configured. This is a useful part of setting up a VM.

- In "Configuring VM Networking," you configure Hyper-V Virtual Machine Networking. Then you look at configuring the VM network.

- In "Configuring VM Hardware," you learn that once you have a VM created, you can use commands in the Hyper-V Module to configure the virtual hardware on your VMs.

- In "Implementing Nested Virtualization," you learn that nested virtualization allows you to install Hyper-V inside a Hyper-V VM, running a VM inside another VM. In this chapter, you explore nested virtualization by enabling this feature on the HVDirect VM and then adding the Hyper-V role to the VM.

- In "Using VM Checkpoints," you learn that a checkpoint is a snapshot of a VM's state at a given time. You can create multiple checkpoints and move between them.

- In "Using VM Replication," you learn that Hyper-V Replica (HVR) is a feature of Hyper-V that creates a full replica of a VM for disaster recovery.

- In "Managing VM Movement," you learn that Hyper-V allows you to move either a VM or a VM's storage to a different location or onto a different host.

- In "Measuring VM Resource Usage," you look at monitoring resources used by a VM. In this final section, you learn how to monitor the resources that each VM uses.

Systems Used in This Chapter

This chapter uses three hosts:

DC1.Reskit.Org: This is a domain controller in the Reskit.Org domain, which you created in Chapter 3, "Managing Active Directory."

HV1.Reskit.Org, HV2.Reskit.Org: These are two Windows Server 2019 hosts—each is a member server in the Reskit.Org domain. In this chapter, you use these hosts to install and manage Hyper-V virtualization.

Figure 8.1 shows the systems in use in this chapter.

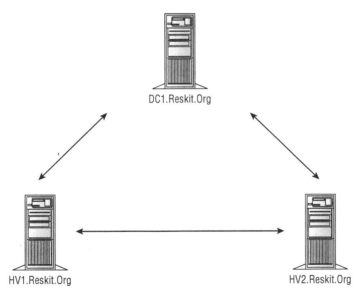

Figure 8.1: Systems used in this chapter

If you create HV1 and HV2 using the build scripts at github.com/doctordns/ ReskitBuildScripts, make sure you adjust the amount of virtual RAM to allocate to both HV1 and HV2. Having 4GB on each of these VMs is recommended, and more is preferable.

Note that all systems used in this chapter need PowerShell 7 (and VS Code) loaded before starting. You can do that manually using the scripts from Chapter 1, "Establishing a PowerShell 7 Administrative Environment."

Optionally, you can configure VS Code as shown in Chapter 1.

Installing and Configuring Hyper-V

Hyper-V is a Windows Server feature that you can install on Windows Server 2019 and Windows Server 2016. On supported editions of Windows 10, the Hyper-V client is an optional feature, and you install it differently.

You can install the Hyper-V management tools independently; doing so provides the ability for local and remote administration. And with the management tools, you have the choice of using the GUI or using PowerShell 7. If you choose to use Hyper-V with Windows 10, see docs.microsoft.com/virtualization/hyper-v-on-windows/quick-start/enable-hyper-v for more information on installing Hyper-V.

Before You Start

In this section, you install the Hyper-V feature on the HV1 server. HV1 is a Windows Server 2019 Datacenter host installed with the Desktop Experience. You should add PowerShell 7 and, optionally, VS Code to this host before proceeding.

Assuming you are using Hyper-V to host the HV1 VM, after you create DC1 as a basic, domain-joined host, you should then add PowerShell 7 and the Hyper-V feature. You can configure the HV1 VM as follows:

```
# 0. Configure HV1 VM
# Run on the Hyper-V Host running HV1
Stop-VM -VMName HV1
# Enable nested virtualization and set processor count for HV1
$VMHT = @{
    VMName                        = 'HV1'
    ExposeVirtualizationExtensions = $true
    Count                         = 4
}
Set-VMProcessor @VMHT
# Set VM Memory for HV1
$VMHT = [ordered] @{
    VMName               = 'HV1'
    DynamicMemoryEnabled = $true
    MinimumBytes         = 4GB
    StartupBytes         = 4GB
    MaximumBytes         = 6GB
}
Set-VMMemory @VMHT
Start-VM -VMName HV1
```

Installing the Hyper-V Feature on HV1

The first step in configuring a Windows Server 2019 host to support Hyper-V is to use `Install-WindowsFeature` to install both Hyper-V and the necessary management tools.

```
# 1. Install the Hyper-V feature on HV1
Import-Module -Name ServerManager -WarningAction SilentlyContinue
Install-WindowsFeature -Name Hyper-V -IncludeManagementTools
```

You can view the output of this code in Figure 8.2.

```
PS C:\Foo> # 1. Install the Hyper-V feature on HV1
PS C:\Foo> Import-Module -Name ServerManager -WarningAction SilentlyContinue
PS C:\Foo> Install-WindowsFeature -Name Hyper-V -IncludeManagementTools


Success Restart Needed Exit Code     Feature Result
------- -------------- ---------     --------------
True    Yes            SuccessRestar… {Hyper-V, Hyper-V Module for Windows PowerSh…
WARNING: You must restart this server to finish the installation process.
```

Figure 8.2: Installing Hyper-V on `HV1`

In most cases, you want to install both the feature and the tools on each Hyper-V host. You can also install the management tools separately where you need them by installing the Hyper-V RSAT tools.

Rebooting HV1

As you can see in the output in Figure 8.2, you need to reboot `HV1` to complete the installation of Hyper-V.

```
# 2. Reboot HV1 to complete the installation
Restart-Computer
```

Creating Folders to Hold VM Disks and VM Details

Hyper-V provides control over where to store VM configuration details and VM hard disks. To see this for yourself, create some new folders using `New-Item`.

```
# 3. Create new folders to hold VM details and disks
$VMS  = 'C:\VM\VMS'
$VHDS = 'C:\VM\VHDS\'
New-Item -Path $VMS  -ItemType Directory -Force | Out-Null
New-Item -Path $VHDS -ItemType Directory -force | Out-Null
```

If you use the -Force parameter when creating a new folder, PowerShell automatically creates any intermediate folders in the path. In this case, you are creating C:\VM\VMS, and using -Force creates both the C:\VM and C:\VM\VMS folders.

Building a Configuration Hash Table

You can set a number of separate configuration items on your Hyper-V host. You use Set-VMHost to apply these settings and begin by creating a splatting hash table with some of the configuration options given nondefault values. Then you pass the hash table to Set-VMHost to configure the options specified there. The complete snippet looks like this:

```
# 4. Build Hash Table to configure the VM Host
$VMCHT = @{
# Where to store VM configuration files
  VirtualMachinePath  = $VMS
# Where to store VHDx files
  VirtualHardDiskPath = $VHDS
# Enable NUMA spanning
  NumaSpanningEnabled = $true
# Enable Enhanced Session Mode
  EnableEnhancedSessionMode = $true
# Specify Resource metering save interval
  ResourceMeteringSaveInterval  = (New-TimeSpan -Hours 2 )
}
Set-VMHost @VMCHT
```

There are 15 configuration settings you can update using the Set-VMHost command. For more details on the command and the options you can set, see docs.microsoft.com/powershell/module/hyper-v/set-vmhost. For Microsoft's explanation of splatting in PowerShell 7, see docs.microsoft.com/powershell/module/microsoft.powershell.core/about/about_splatting?view=powershell-7.

Reviewing Key VM Host Settings

You can review some of the VM host settings using the GUI, or you can review or you can review them all using all using Get-VMHost. To see the updated settings for your host, you can use this syntax:

```
# 5. Review key VMHost settings
Get-VMHost  |
  Format-Table -Property 'Name', 'V*Path','Numasp*', 'Ena*','RES*'
```

This code produces the output you can see in Figure 8.3.

```
PS C:\Foo> # 5. Review key VMHost settings
PS C:\Foo> Get-VMHost |
           Format-Table -Property 'Name', 'V*Path','Numasp*', 'Ena*','RES*'

Name VirtualHardDiskPath VirtualMachinePath NumaSpanningEnabled EnableEnhancedSessionMode ResourceMeteringSaveInterval
---- ------------------- ------------------ ------------------ ------------------------- ---------------------------
HV1  C:\VM\VHDS\         C:\VM\VMS                        True                      True 02:00:00
```

Figure 8.3: Reviewing VM host settings

With some objects, selecting properties can be challenging, especially when you have long property names. As shown in the output, you can "cheat" a bit when specifying the property names with wildcards. As an alternative, you could create a string array holding the full names of all the properties to display and pass that to `Format-Table`. For production scripts, you may want to spell out explicitly the name of the properties to view.

Creating a Hyper-V VM

Once you have a VM host up and running, you can create a VM inside the host. To create a Hyper-V VM and install an operating system as part of the process, you need a bootable OS installation ISO file. You can download an ISO image for Window Server 2019 from the Microsoft Evaluation Center web site at microsoft.com/evalcenter/evaluate-windows-server-2019.

This section uses a Windows Server ISO image. As an alternative, Microsoft's Evaluation Center also provides a virtual disk file you can use to build a preconfigured VM.

Before You Start

This section uses the `HV1` host, which you configured in "Installing and Configuring Hyper-V." It also uses an ISO image of Windows Server, a 180-day evaluation edition downloaded from the Microsoft Evaluation Center.

The filename of the ISO can (and often does) vary depending on your particular image source and when you download it. You can use the same ISO image in this section that you used to create the other VMs used throughout this book. For the purposes of this chapter, a specific filename for the ISO image is used. After downloading the ISO image, you store the image as `C:\ISO\WinSrv2019.ISO`.

Creating Variables

You start this section by setting values for key variables to be used later in this section, as follows:

```
# 1. Set up the VM name and paths
$VMname      = 'HVDirect'
```

```
$VMLocation   = 'C:\VM\VMs'
$VHDlocation = 'C:\VM\Vhds'
$VHDPath      = "$VHDlocation\HVDirect.Vhdx"
$ISOPath      = 'C:\ISO\WinSrv2019.ISO'
```

These variables are used in creating a VM. $ISOPath is the path name for the Windows Server 2019. This section assumes a specific filename, although the actual name of the file you download may vary depending on your source and when you do the download. You can either change the file name of the ISO image or change the value you assigned to $ISOPath to match your actual filename.

Verifying That the ISO Image Exists

To verify that the ISO image is available, you can use Test-Path.

```
# 2. Verify drive contents
If (-Not (Test-Path -Path $ISOPath)) {
    Throw "ISO Image [$ISOPath] NOT found"
}
```

The Test-Path cmdlet returns a value of True (if the file exists) or False. If for some reason the ISO file is not there, the code throws an exception. If the file is there, this code produces no output, and you move on to the next step.

Importing the DISM Module

Microsoft's Windows Deployment Image Servicing and Management (DISM) module is a set of tools that help you to manage Windows images as part of deployment. In this section, you use DISM to obtain the versions of Windows that can be installed from your ISO image. A typical ISO image contains Windows Server Standard and Windows Server Datacenter, with and without the Desktop Experience. This book uses Windows Server Datacenter with Desktop Experience.

The DISM module is one of the older Windows PowerShell modules that is not natively supported within PowerShell 7. Nevertheless, you can use the module based on the Windows PowerShell compatibility feature described in Chapter 2. The Import-Module statement looks like this:

```
# 3. Import the DISM Module
Import-Module -Name DISM -WarningAction SilentlyContinue
```

Running this command normally produces a warning message that the module has been loaded using a compatibility remoting session (as described in Chapter 2, "PowerShell 7 Compatibility with Windows PowerShell"). To avoid this warning, you can use the -WarningAction parameter to tell PowerShell not to display it.

Mounting the ISO Image

An ISO image represents a bootable DVD containing the Windows Installation media. You could burn the image to a physical CD or put the image on a USB stick for use in installing Windows on physical hardware. You can also mount the ISO image within Windows as if it were an actual DVD. You use the Mount-DiskImage command to mount the ISO image on HV1 as follows:

```
# 4. Mount ISO Image
Mount-DiskImage -ImagePath $ISOPath
```

This command mounts the ISO image onto your host computer and produces the output you can see in Figure 8.4.

```
PS C:\Foo> # 4. Mount ISO Image
PS C:\Foo> Mount-DiskImage -ImagePath $ISOPath

Attached          : True
BlockSize         : 0
DevicePath        : \\.\CDROM2
FileSize          : 5296713728
ImagePath         : C:\ISO\WinSrv2019.iso
LogicalSectorSize : 2048
Number            : 2
Size              : 5296713728
StorageType       : 1
PSComputerName    :
```

Figure 8.4: Mounting the ISO disk image

Viewing ISO Image Contents

When you mount the ISO image, Windows gives it a drive letter and enables read-only access to all the files/folders within the image. With Windows Server 2019, the Windows installation ISO contains a file called <dvddrive>:\sources\install.wim. This file contains one or more specific images that you can install using this image. To see what version of Windows Server you can install, you use the Get-WindowsImage cmdlet, as shown here:

```
# 5. Get details and Display ISO image contents and Dismount the ISO
$ISOImage = Get-DiskImage -ImagePath $ISOPath | Get-Volume
$ISODrive = [string] $ISOImage.DriveLetter + ":"
Get-WindowsImage -ImagePath $ISODrive\sources\install.wim |
  Format-Table -Property ImageIndex, Imagename, Imagedescription -Wrap
Dismount-DiskImage -ImagePath $ISOPath | Out-Null
```

These commands provide you with details of the versions of Windows Server you can install from the ISO image, after which you dismount the image.

Depending on the source of your ISO image, the output from this step looks like Figure 8.5.

```
PS C:\Foo> # 5. Get details and Display ISO image contents and Dismount the ISO
PS C:\Foo> $ISOImage = Get-DiskImage -ImagePath $ISOPath | Get-Volume
PS C:\Foo> $ISODrive = [string] $ISOImage.DriveLetter + ":"
PS C:\Foo> Get-WindowsImage -ImagePath $ISODrive\sources\install.wim |
            Format-Table -Property ImageIndex, Imagename, Imagedescription -Wrap

ImageIndex ImageName                                                 ImageDescription
---------- ---------                                                 ----------------
         1 Windows Server 2019 Standard Evaluation                   (Recommended) This option omits most of the Windows graphical
                                                                     environment. Manage with a command prompt and PowerShell, or
                                                                     remotely with Windows Admin Center or other tools.
         2 Windows Server 2019 Standard Evaluation (Desktop Experience) This option installs the full Windows graphical environment,
                                                                     consuming extra drive space. It can be useful if you want to
                                                                     use the Windows desktop or have an app that requires it.
         3 Windows Server 2019 Datacenter Evaluation                 (Recommended) This option omits most of the Windows graphical
                                                                     environment. Manage with a command prompt and PowerShell, or
                                                                     remotely with Windows Admin Center or other tools.
         4 Windows Server 2019 Datacenter Evaluation (Desktop Experience) This option installs the full Windows graphical environment,
                                                                     consuming extra drive space. It can be useful if you want to
                                                                     use the Windows desktop or have an app that requires it.
PS C:\Foo> Dismount-DiskImage -ImagePath $ISOPath | Out-Null
```

Figure 8.5: Viewing the contents of `install.wim`

Before proceeding, you should ensure that the ISO contains an image for Windows Server 2019 Datacenter with Desktop Experience.

Creating a New VM in HV1

To create a VM, you use the New-VM command, as shown here:

```
# 6.   Create a new VM
New-VM -Name $VMname -Path $VMLocation -MemoryStartupBytes 1GB
```

This creates a new Hyper-V VM, although at this point it is not usable yet. You can see the output from this command in Figure 8.6.

```
PS C:\Foo> # 6.   Create a new VM
PS C:\Foo> New-VM -Name $VMname -Path $VMLocation -MemoryStartupBytes 1GB

Name     State CPUUsage(%) MemoryAssigned(M) Uptime   Status            Version
----     ----- ----------- ----------------- ------   ------            -------
HVDirect Off   0           0                 00:00:00 Operating normally 9.0
```

Figure 8.6: Creating a new VM

Creating a VHDX File for the VM

Every VM needs at least one virtual disk on which you install the OS. You use the New-VHD command to create this file for the new VM, as follows:

```
# 7. Create a virtual disk file for the VM
New-VHD -Path $VhdPath -SizeBytes 128GB -Dynamic | Out-Null
```

Adding the VHD to the VM

You use the `Add-VMHardDiskDrive` command to add a disk to a VM:

```
# 8. Add the virtual hard drive to the VM
Add-VMHardDiskDrive -VMName $VMname -Path $VhdPath
```

By default, a Hyper-V VM has two IDE controllers that both have two locations that can contain virtual disks or virtual CDs. This command adds the newly created (and empty) disk in the first location on the first controller, which Windows creates as the C: drive.

Adding the ISO Image to the VM

You next use the `Set-VMDvdDrive` command to set the ISO image in the VM's virtual DVD drive.

```
# 9. Set ISO image in the VM's DVD drive
$IHT = @{
  VMName          = $VMName
  ControllerNumber = 1
  Path            = $ISOPath
}
Set-VMDvdDrive @IHT
```

This inserts the ISO image into the virtual DVD drive. The `$ISOPath` variable holds the full path for the ISO image file.

Starting the VM

With the disk drive and DVD added to the VM, you can now start the VM. By default, Hyper-V boots from the DVD image to begin the process of installing Windows Server 2019. You use the `Start-VM` command to start the VM as follows:

```
# 10. Start the VM
Start-VM -VMName $VMName
```

Installing Windows Server 2019

Now that you have started the VM, you should use the Hyper-V Virtual Machine Connection tool (`vmconnect.exe`) to connect to it. You can run this tool directly from the command line or via the Hyper-V Manager MMC (`wbadmin.msc`). After connecting to the newly created VM, you can complete the manual installation of Windows Server. This includes creating the Administrator user and specifying the password. For the examples in this chapter, be sure to use the book's general-use password (Pa$$w0rd). Alternatively, use a different password (and remember to use that password in later sections of this chapter).

Viewing the Results

Once you complete the installation process, you can view the VM details using Get-VM, as follows:

```
# 12. View the results
Get-VM -VMName $VMName
```

You can see the output from this command in Figure 8.7.

```
PS C:\Foo> # 12. View the results
PS C:\Foo> Get-VM -VMName $VMName

Name      State    CPUUsage(%) MemoryAssigned(M) Uptime              Status             Version
----      -----    ----------- ----------------- ------              ------             -------
HVDirect  Running  0           1024              00:07:32.5670000    Operating normally 9.0
```

Figure 8.7: Viewing newly created VM details

Using PowerShell Direct

PowerShell Direct is a Hyper-V feature that allows you to use a VM that does not have a working network stack. Without a working network stack, you cannot, for example, use the Remote Desktop application to connect to the VM. Instead, you can use PowerShell and just specify the VM name. Using the feature means you do need to have the credentials for the VM. PS Direct enables you to use the VM, often to configure networking within the VM.

Before You Start

You run the code in this section on HV1, which you set up in "Installing and Configuring Hyper-V," and after you have created the HVDirect VM in "Creating a Hyper-V VM."

Creating Variables for Use in This Section

To begin this section, you create a number of variables, as follows:

```
# 1. Create a credential object for local Administrator
$LHAN    = 'Localhost\Administrator'
$PS      = 'Pa$$w0rd'
```

```
$LHP    = ConvertTo-SecureString -String $PS -AsPlainText -Force
$CREDHT = @{
            TypeName     = 'System.Management.Automation.PSCredential'
            Argumentlist = $LHAN, $LHP
}
$LHCred = New-Object @CREDHT
$VMNAME = 'HVDirect'
```

This code first creates a new credential object for the HVDirect VM. Note that you use the hostname Localhost. Then you set the variable $VMNAME to the VM name. By default, the VM's hostname was assigned by the Windows Server setup process and so is different from the VM name.

Displaying Details of HVDirect VM

Before using the HVDirect VM, check to ensure the VM is up and running, using Get-VM as follows:

```
# 2. Display the details of the HVDirect VM
Get-VM -Name $VMNAME
```

This command produces the output shown in Figure 8.8.

```
PS C:\Foo> # 2. Display the details of the HVDirect VM
PS C:\Foo> Get-VM –Name $VMNAME

Name     State   CPUUsage(%) MemoryAssigned(M) Uptime              Status             Version
----     -----   ----------- ----------------- ------              ------             -------
HVDirect Running 0           1024              02:28:57.1970000 Operating normally 9.0
```

Figure 8.8: Displaying VM details

Invoking a Command using VMName

To demonstrate using PS Direct, you can use Invoke-Command to run a command inside the VM, as follows:

```
# 3. Invoke a command on the VM, specifying VM name
$SBHT = @{
  VMName      = $VMNAME
  Credential  = $LHCred
  ScriptBlock = {hostname}
}
Invoke-Command @SBHT
```

The `Invoke-Command` cmdlet runs the script block inside the `HVDirect` VM and produces the output you can see in Figure 8.9.

```
PS C:\Foo> # 3. Invoke a command on the VM, specifying VM name
PS C:\Foo> $SBHT = @{
             VMName      = $VMNAME
             Credential  = $LHCred
             ScriptBlock = {hostname}
           }
PS C:\Foo> Invoke-Command @SBHT
WIN-DIDLT555LM3
```

Figure 8.9: Getting the VM host name

The output confirms the host name as, in this case, WIN-DIDLT555LM3. This host name was assigned by the Windows Setup process automatically when you created the VM. This is probably not a host name you want to retain and is easy to change.

Invoking a Command Based on VM ID

In the previous step, you ran a command on a VM based on the Hyper-V VM name. Another way to identify the VM is based on the internal Hyper-V VM ID. This is a GUID created by Hyper-V when you create the VM and, unlike the VM name itself, never changes. You can use the VM ID in conjunction with `Invoke-Command` as follows:

```
# 4. Invoke a command based on VMID
$VMID = (Get-VM -VMName $VMNAME).VMId.Guid
Invoke-Command -VMid $VMID -Credential $LHCred -ScriptBlock {ipconfig}
```

You can see the output from this command in Figure 8.10.

```
PS C:\Foo> # 4. Invoke a command based on VMID
PS C:\Foo> $VMID = (Get-VM -VMName $VMNAME).VMId.Guid
PS C:\Foo> Invoke-Command -VMid $VMID -Credential $LHCred  -ScriptBlock {ipconfig}

Windows IP Configuration

Ethernet adapter Ethernet:

   Media State . . . . . . . . . . . : Media disconnected
   Connection-specific DNS Suffix  . :
```

Figure 8.10: Displaying VM details using VM ID

As you can see in Figure 8.10, the network inside `HVDirect` is not connected to a working network. This is expected, given that you created this VM as shown in "Creating a Hyper-V VM," and it is easy to resolve as you see in "Configuring VM Networking."

Configuring VM Networking

With Hyper-V, you can configure a VM to have one or more virtual NICs associated with different virtual switches. To enable VMs to communicate with each other, with the VM host, and with the wider Internet, you also need to implement one or more VM switches. Once you create a virtual switch, you assign a VM's virtual NIC to the switch to enable communication with other systems using the same switch. For more details on planning Hyper-V networking, see docs.microsoft.com/en-gb/windows-server/virtualization/hyper-v/plan/plan-hyper-v-networking-in-windows-server.

Before You Start

In this section, you configure networking for the VM you created in "Creating a Hyper-V VM." This VM, HVDirect, runs on the HV1 host, which you set up in "Installing and Configuring Hyper-V."

In "Creating a Hyper-V VM," you created a VM with a host name of HVDirect. In this section, you create a new external switch on HV1 and configure the HVDirect VM to be connected to that switch.

Once you have networking for this VM configured fully, you can join the VM to the Reskit domain and change the host name in the process. In this section you assign a new host name, Tiger, to this VM.

Getting Virtual NIC Details from HVDirect

You start this section by getting details of the virtual NIC inside the HVDirect VM.

```
# 1. Get NIC details and any IP Address from the HVDirect VM
$VMNAME = 'HVDirect'
Get-VMNetworkAdapter -VMName $VMNAME
```

Figure 8.11 shows the output from this command.

```
PS C:\Foo> # 1. Get NIC details and any IP Address from the PSDirect VM
PS C:\Foo> $VMName = 'HVDirect'
PS C:\Foo> Get-VMNetworkAdapter -VMName $VMName

Name             IsManagementOs VMName    SwitchName MacAddress    Status IPAddresses
----             -------------- ------    ---------- ----------    ------ -----------
Network Adapter  False          HVDirect             00155D0AC900  {Ok}   {169.254.32.79, fe80::9d5c:b263:8fcd:204f}
```

Figure 8.11: Viewing NIC details

Creating a Credential for the VM

You need to create a credential object for this VM, which you can do using `New-Object` as follows:

```
# 2. Create a credential
$LHAN   = 'Localhost\Administrator'
$PS     = 'Pa$$w0rd'
$LHP    = ConvertTo-SecureString -String $PS -AsPlainText -Force
$T      = 'System.Management.Automation.PSCredential'
$LHCred = New-Object -TypeName $T -ArgumentList $LHAN, $LHP
```

This credential object is for the VM host's administrator account.

This snippet shows one of the many methods you can use to create a PowerShell account credentials object.

Getting NIC Details

You use the `Get-NetIPConfiguration` command run inside the VM to get the IP address configuration, as follows:

```
# 3. Get NIC Details from inside the VM
$VMHT = @{
    VMName      = $VMName
    ScriptBlock = {Get-NetIPConfiguration |
                    Format-List }
    Credential  = $LHCred
}
Invoke-Command @VMHT
```

When you use `Invoke-Command` in this way, PowerShell runs the script block within the VM. This produces the output you see in Figure 8.12.

```
PS C:\Foo> # 3. Get NIC Details from inside the VM
PS C:\Foo> $VMHT = @{
    VMName      = $VMName
    ScriptBlock = {Get-NetIPConfiguration |
                    Format-List }
    Credential  = $LHCred
}
Invoke-Command @VMHT

InterfaceAlias       : Ethernet
InterfaceIndex       : 4
InterfaceDescription : Microsoft Hyper-V Network Adapter
NetAdapter.Status    : Disconnected
```

Figure 8.12: Viewing the NIC configuration

In the output, you can see that the network adapter is shown as being disconnected. Given the way you created the VM (by using the code in "Creating a Hyper-V VM"), this is to be expected.

Creating a Virtual Switch

By default, when you install Hyper-V, the installation process does not create any virtual switches. You can create a simple external switch using `New-VMSwitch`, as follows:

```
# 4. Create a virtual switch on HV1
$VSHT = @{
    Name            = 'External'
    NetAdapterName  = 'Ethernet'
    Notes           = 'Created on HV1'
}
New-VMSwitch @VSHT
```

Figure 8.13 shows the output.

```
PS C:\Foo> # 4. Create a virtual switch on HV1
PS C:\Foo> $VSHT = @{
    Name            = 'External'
    NetAdapterName  = 'Ethernet'
    Notes           = 'Created on HV1'
}
New-VMSwitch @VSHT

Name      SwitchType NetAdapterInterfaceDescription
----      ---------- ------------------------------
External  External   Microsoft Hyper-V Network Adapter
```

Figure 8.13: Creating a virtual switch

Connecting the VM to the Switch

Now that you have an external virtual switch defined, you can connect the NIC inside the `HVDirect` VM to the switch, using the `Connect-VMNetworkAdapter` command.

```
# 5. Connect HVDirect to the switch
Connect-VMNetworkAdapter -VMName $VMNAME -SwitchName External
```

This command connects the virtual NIC to the external switch, which enables networking.

Enabling MAC Spoofing

The examples in this chapter make use of the nested virtualization feature you examine later, in "Implementing Nested Virtualization." If you are using Hyper-V and have implemented HV1 as a VM, you need to update HV1's NIC configuration to enable MAC address spoofing, using the Set-VMNetworkAdapter command, as follows:

```
# 6. Enable spoofing From VM Host
#    Run this command on the VM Host that hosts HV1
Get-VMNetworkAdapter -VMName HV1 |
   Set-VMNetworkAdapter -MacAddressSpoofing On
```

With this command, the virtual NIC inside the VM now appears to be on the local network. Since the VM was created, by default, with a single NIC that is set to get its address by DHCP, if you have a DHCP server on the network, DHCP allocates IP address details to the VM.

Viewing VM Network Information

Now that you have set up networking for the HVDirect VM, you can view the results by using Get-VMNetworkAdapter from your VM host.

```
# 7. Get VM networking information
Get-VMNetworkAdapter -VMName $VMName
```

You can see the output from this command in Figure 8.14.

```
PS C:\Foo> # 7. Get VM networking information
PS C:\Foo> Get-VMNetworkAdapter -VMName $VMName

Name              IsManagementOs VMName    SwitchName MacAddress    Status IPAddresses
----              -------------- ------    ---------- ----------    ------ -----------
Network Adapter False           HVDirect  External   00155D0AC900  {Ok}   {10.10.10.154, fe80::9d5c:b263:8fcd:204f}
```

Figure 8.14: Viewing the virtual NIC configuration

Viewing IP Address Inside HVDirect

In Chapter 4, "Managing Networking," you installed a DHCP server ("Installing the DHCP Service") and created a DHCP scope (in "Configuring DHCP Scopes") on DC1. If you have the DHCP service running on DC1, then after you connect the virtual NIC to the network, Windows assigns a new DHCP-supplied IP address to the NIC. You can view this IP address by running Get-NetIPConfiguration as follows:

```
# 8. With HVDirect now in the network, observe the IP address in the VM
$NCHT = @{
    VMName      = $VMName
```

```
        ScriptBlock = {Get-NetIPConfiguration | Format-List}
        Credential  = $LHCred
    }
    Invoke-Command @NCHT
```

You can see the output from this command in Figure 8.15.

```
PS C:\Foo> # 8. With HVDirect now in the network, observe the IP address in the VM
PS C:\Foo> $NCHT = @{
            VMName      = $VMNAME
            ScriptBlock = {Get-NetIPConfiguration | Format-List}
            Credential  = $LHCred
          }
PS C:\Foo> Invoke-Command @NCHT

InterfaceAlias       : Ethernet
InterfaceIndex       : 4
InterfaceDescription : Microsoft Hyper-V Network Adapter
NetProfile.Name      : Reskit.Org
IPv4Address          : 10.10.10.154
IPv6DefaultGateway   :
IPv4DefaultGateway   : 10.10.10.254
DNSServer            : 10.10.10.10
```

Figure 8.15: Viewing the NIC IP address

In this command, you retrieved the IP address information for the NIC inside the VM using PowerShell remoting. Since there is a DHCP server (on DC1) in your network, the VM obtains IP configuration from the DHCP server.

By default, the objects that PowerShell creates within a remoting session are serialized when returned. In this case, PowerShell does not have access to the display XML that was in the remote session, which results in output that is much harder to read. A way around this is to pipe the network details to Format-List inside the remote session, which produces easier-to-use output.

If, for any reason, there is no DHCP server in the network, you need to configure HVDirect to have a working IP address so that it can connect to the domain controller (to join the domain).

Joining the Reskit Domain

In the steps in this section so far, you have configured the HVDirect VM to obtain a working IP address configuration. You can now join this host to the Reskit domain by using the Add-Computer command, as shown here:

```
# 9. Join the Reskit Domain
# Update the script block
$NCHT.ScriptBlock = {
  $RKAdmin = 'Reskit\Administrator'
  $PS      = 'Pa$$w0rd'
  $RKPW    = ConvertTo-SecureString -String $PS -AsPlainText -Force
```

```
$T = 'System.Management.Automation.PSCredential'
$DomCred = New-Object -TypeName $T -ArgumentList $RKAdmin, $RKPW
$JCHT = @{
   Domain      = 'Reskit.Org'
   Credential = $DomCred
   NewName     = 'Tiger'
}
Add-Computer @JCHT
}
Invoke-Command @NCHT
```

These commands produce the output you can see in Figure 8.16.

```
PS C:\Foo> # 9. Join the Reskit Domain
PS C:\Foo> # Update the script block
PS C:\Foo> $NCHT.ScriptBlock = {
         $RKAdmin = 'Reskit\Administrator'
         $PS      = 'Pa$$w0rd'
         $RKPW    = ConvertTo-SecureString -String $PS -AsPlainText -Force
         $T = 'System.Management.Automation.PSCredential'
         $DomCred = New-Object -TypeName $T -ArgumentList $RKAdmin, $RKPW
         $JCHT = @{
            Domain      = 'Reskit.Org'
            Credential = $DomCred
            NewName     = 'Tiger'
         }
         Add-Computer @JCHT
         }
PS C:\Foo> Invoke-Command @NCHT
WARNING: The changes will take effect after you restart the computer WIN-DIDLT555LM3.
```

Figure 8.16: Joining the domain

In this code fragment, you first created a script block that contains the commands necessary to join the Reskit domain and to change the host name. Then
you use PowerShell remoting to run that script block inside the HVDirect VM.
This has the effect of joining the Reskit domain and changing the host name
from the name Windows created for you to Tiger. As the output shows, you
have to restart the system for these changes to take effect.

Once you reboot and these changes take effect, you have a VM with a VM
name of HVDirect and a host name of Tiger.

Rebooting the VM

To complete the renaming of the host and join the host to the domain, you
need to restart the host. To do this, you use the Restart-VM command from the
Hyper-V host.

```
# 10. Reboot and wait for the restarted VM
Restart-VM -VMName $VMName -Wait -For IPAddress -Force
```

This command reboots the VM and waits for it to restart and get an IP address. This illustrates how you can use PowerShell to reboot another host and wait until the host has fully restarted and can accept incoming network connections. After the VM has rebooted, its FQDN is now Tiger.Reskit.Org.

Getting the Host Name of the HVDirect VM

Once the VM has restarted the HVDirect VM, you can check inside the VM to get the host name (which was changed to Tiger in "Configuring VM Networking"). Also, since the host has been joined to the domain, you use domain credentials to invoke commands inside the VM.

You can check the host name using the hostname command. But since the VM credentials have changed, you need to recreate a credential object, as follows:

```
# 11. Get hostname of the HVDirect VM
$RKAdmin           = 'Reskit\Administrator'
$PS                = 'Pa$$w0rd'
$RKPW              = ConvertTo-SecureString -String $PS -AsPlainText
                     -Force
$T                 = 'System.Management.Automation.PSCredential'
$DomCred           = New-Object -TypeName $T -ArgumentList $RKAdmin,
                     $RKPW
$NCHT.Credential   = $DomCred
$NCHT.ScriptBlock = {hostname}
Invoke-Command @NCHT
```

This set of commands produces the output you see in Figure 8.17.

```
PS C:\Foo> # 11. Get hostname of the HVDirect VM
PS C:\Foo> $RKAdmin           = 'Reskit\Administrator'
PS C:\Foo> $PS                = 'Pa$$w0rd'
PS C:\Foo> $RKPW              = ConvertTo-SecureString -String $PS -AsPlainText -Force
PS C:\Foo> $T                 = 'System.Management.Automation.PSCredential'
PS C:\Foo> $DomCred           = New-Object -TypeName $T -ArgumentList $RKAdmin, $RKPW
PS C:\Foo> $NCHT.Credential   = $DomCred
PS C:\Foo> $NCHT.ScriptBlock = {hostname}
PS C:\Foo> Invoke-Command @NCHT
Tiger
```

Figure 8.17: Obtaining the host name

Now that you have joined the HVDirect VM to the Reskit domain, you can use the domain credentials when running a remote session. In this case you saw that the HVDirect VM has the host name Tiger.

Configuring VM Hardware

With Hyper-V, your VMs contain virtual hardware—virtual NICs, virtual CPUs, virtual disk controllers, virtual disks, virtual memory, and so on. Once you have a VM created, you can use commands in the Hyper-V module to configure the virtual hardware on your VMs.

Before You Start

This section uses the Hyper-V Server HV1 (created in "Installing and Configuring Hyper-V") and the HVDirect VM you created in "Creating a Hyper-V VM" and updated in "Configuring VM Networking."

Turning Off the HVDirect VM

Depending on the VM generation on your VMs, some hardware can be hot-added/removed. Some changes to virtual hardware, for example, changing the number of virtual processors in a VM, can be done only while the VM is turned off.

```
# 1. Turn off the HVDirect VM
$VMName = 'HVDirect'
Stop-VM -VMName $VMName
Get-VM -VMName $VMName
```

You can see the output from these commands in Figure 8.18.

```
PS C:\Foo> # 1. Turn off the HVDirect VM
PS C:\Foo> $VMName = 'HVDirect'
PS C:\Foo> Stop-VM –VMName $VMName
PS C:\Foo> Get-VM –VMName VMName

Name      State CPUUsage(%) MemoryAssigned(M) Uptime   Status             Version
----      ----- ----------- ----------------- ------   ------             -------
HVDirect  Off   0           0                 00:00:00 Operating normally 9.0
```

Figure 8.18: Shutting down a VM

To update the virtual hardware in a VM, you need to turn off the VM before adjusting the hardware. Some hardware changes can, however, be made while the VM is running.

With Windows Server 2019 and Generation 1 VMs, you can adjust the amount of virtual memory for a hard drive. Additionally, for Generation 2 VMs, you can add or remove network adapters while the VM is running. Both VM generations support hot-add hot-adding of SCSI disks of SCSI disks.

Setting the Hardware Startup Order

With a Hyper-V VM, you can specify the startup order, using the `Set-VMBios` command as follows:

```
# 2. Set the StartupOrder in the VM's BIOS
$Order = 'IDE','CD','LegacyNetworkAdapter','Floppy'
Set-VMBios -VmName $VMName -StartupOrder $Order
Get-VMBios $VMName
```

This produces the output you see in Figure 8.19.

```
PS C:\Foo> # 2. Set the StartupOrder in the VM's BIOS
PS C:\Foo> $Order = 'IDE','CD','LegacyNetworkAdapter','Floppy'
PS C:\Foo> Set-VMBios -VmName $VMName -StartupOrder $Order
PS C:\Foo> Get-VMBios $VMName

VMName    StartupOrder                                    NumLockEnabled
------    ------------                                    --------------
HVDirect {IDE, CD, LegacyNetworkAdapter, Floppy} False
```

Figure 8.19: Updating VM BIOS

When you next attempt to start the VM, Hyper-V attempts to boot from the first volume in the first IDE controller (which is where Hyper-V inserted the C: drive for your VM). Changing the BIOS startup order means when you start up a VM, Hyper-V does not attempt to boot from a DVD image but boots from the system drive.

Setting Socket Count

Like a physical machine, Hyper-V allows you to add virtual processors to the VM, using the `Set-VMProcessor` command.

```
# 3. Set CPU count for HVDirect
Set-VMProcessor -VMName $VMName -Count 2
Get-VMProcessor -VMName $VMName |
   Format-Table VMName, Count
```

This produces the output you see in Figure 8.20.

```
PS C:\Foo> # 3. Set CPU count for HVDirect
PS C:\Foo> Set-VMProcessor -VMName $VMName -Count 2
PS C:\Foo> Get-VMProcessor -VMName $VMName |
           Format-Table VMName, Count

VMName    Count
------    -----
HVDirect    2
```

Figure 8.20: Changing the VM processor count

This code gives the `HVDirect` VM a total of two virtual processors. When Windows is running inside the VM, it sees that the virtual hardware has two CPUs and uses both.

If you have multiple cores in your Hyper-V Host, then you can allocate larger numbers of virtual processors to VMs. You might, for example, devote eight cores or more to a Microsoft SQL Server VM.

Setting VM Memory

You can also vary the memory allocated for the VM by using the `Set-VMMemory` command, as follows:

```
# 4. Set VM memory
$VMHT = [ordered] @{
  VMName                = $VMName
  DynamicMemoryEnabled  = $true
  MinimumBytes          = 768MB
  StartupBytes          = 960MB
  MaximumBytes          = 1GB
}
Set-VMMemory @VMHT
Get-VMMemory -VMName $VMName
```

This produces the output you see in Figure 8.21.

```
PS C:\Foo> # 4. Set VM memory
PS C:\Foo> $VMHT = [ordered] @{
            VMName                = $VMName
            DynamicMemoryEnabled  = $true
            MinimumBytes          = 768MB
            StartupBytes          = 960MB
            MaximumBytes          = 1GB
          }
PS C:\Foo> Set-VMMemory @VMHT
PS C:\Foo> Get-VMMemory -VMName $VMName


VMName    DynamicMemoryEnabled Minimum(M) Startup(M) Maximum(M)
-------   -------------------- ---------- ---------- ----------
HVDirect  True                        768        960       1024
```

Figure 8.21: Changing the VM memory allocation

You can specify any amount of memory you want, but Hyper-V needs to have sufficient free memory on the VM host to allocate, in this case, a 1GB maximum amount of virtual RAM for this VM.

In setting VM memory, you can only start VMs that, in total, use less RAM than you have available on your host.

Adding an SCSI Controller

Larger VMs frequently need multiple disks. Hyper-V's IDE controllers enable you to support a maximum of four virtual disk drives (or three if you are using a DVD). To support more disks, you can add additional virtual SCSI controllers to the VM, each of which can contain many VHD drives. To add an SCSI controller, you use the `Add-VMScsiController` command as follows:

```
# 5. Add an ScsiController to the VM
Add-VMScsiController -VMName $VMName
Get-VMScsiController -VMName $VMName
```

This produces the output you see in Figure 8.22.

```
PS C:\Foo> # 5. Add a ScsiController to the VM
PS C:\Foo> Add-VMScsiController -VMName $VMName
PS C:\Foo> Get-VMScsiController -VMName $VMName

VMName    ControllerNumber Drives
------    ---------------- ------
HVDirect  0                {}
HVDirect  1                {}
```

Figure 8.22: Adding an SCSI controller

As you can see in the output, the `HVDirect` VM now has two SCSI controllers you can use.

Restarting the VM

With the changes to the virtual hardware made, you use the `Start-VM` command to start the `HVDirect` VM.

```
# 6. Restart the HVDirect VM
Start-VM -VMName $VMName
Wait-VM -VMName $VMName -For IPAddress
```

When you run these commands from `HV1`, Hyper-V starts up the `HVDirect` VM. You can use the `Wait-VM` command to wait until the VM is up and running and has an IP address with which you can connect.

Creating a New Virtual Disk

To demonstrate adding a virtual disk to a VM, first you use `New-VHD` from `HV1` to create a new VHD, as follows:

```
# 7. Create a new VHDX file
$VHDPath = 'C:\Vm\Vhds\HVDirect-D.VHDX'
New-VHD -Path $VHDPath -SizeBytes 8GB -Dynamic
```

This command creates a new virtual disk drive and produces the output shown in Figure 8.23.

```
PS C:\Foo> # 7. Create a new VHDX file
PS C:\Foo> $VHDPath = 'C:\Vm\Vhds\HVDirect-D.VHDX'
PS C:\Foo> New-VHD -Path $VHDPath -SizeBytes 8GB -Dynamic

ComputerName              : HV1
Path                      : C:\Vm\Vhds\HVDirect-D.VHDX
VhdFormat                 : VHDX
VhdType                   : Dynamic
FileSize                  : 4194304
Size                      : 8589934592
MinimumSize               :
LogicalSectorSize         : 512
PhysicalSectorSize        : 4096
BlockSize                 : 33554432
ParentPath                :
DiskIdentifier            : 86B8B2DD-D219-48F2-A221-2917D7119B3F
FragmentationPercentage   : 0
Alignment                 : 1
Attached                  : False
DiskNumber                :
IsPMEMCompatible          : False
AddressAbstractionType    : None
Number                    :
```

Figure 8.23: Creating a new virtual disk

Because this is for demonstration and not production use, you define a maximum size of 8GB.

Adding a Disk to a VM

You can now use the Add-VMHardDiskdrive command to add the newly created VHDX to the HV1 VM.

```
# 8. Add the VHD to the ScsiController
$VHDHT = @{
    VMName              = $VMName
    ControllerType      = 'SCSI'
    ControllerNumber    = 0
    ControllerLocation  = 0
    Path                = $VHDPath
}
Add-VMHardDiskDrive @VHDHT
```

This command immediately adds the VHDX to the virtual SCSI controller, and you can now begin to use it. You can use the scripts shown in Chapter 5 "Managing Windows Storage," including the ones in "Managing Disks and Volumes" and "Managing NTFS Permissions."

Viewing SCSI Disks inside HVDirect

You use the `Get-VMScsiController` command to see details of the virtual SCSI disks within the VM, as follows:

```
# 9. Get SCSI Disks in the VM
Get-VMScsiController -VMName $VMName |
  Select-Object -ExpandProperty Drives
```

Figure 8.24 shows the SCSI virtual disk drives contained in the `HVDirect` VM.

```
PS C:\Foo> # 9. Get SCSI Volumes in the VM
PS C:\Foo> Get-VMScsiController –VMName $VMName |
           Select-Object –ExpandProperty Drives

VMName    ControllerType ControllerNumber ControllerLocation DiskNumber Path
------    -------------- ---------------- ------------------ ---------- ----
HVDirect SCSI            0                0                              C:\Vm\Vhds\HVDirect-D.VHDX
```

Figure 8.24: Viewing SCSI disks

Implementing Nested Virtualization

Nested virtualization is a feature that allows you to install Hyper-V inside a Hyper-V VM, running a VM inside another VM. This nesting has a number of use cases. The VMs used in writing this book are all based on nested virtualization, for example. To learn more about nested virtualization, see docs.microsoft.com/en-us/virtualization/hyper-v-on-windows/user-guide/nested-virtualization.

In this section you explore nested virtualization by enabling this feature on the `HVDirect` VM and then adding the Hyper-V role to the VM. Without nested virtualization, the installation of Hyper-V in the `HVDirect` VM would not succeed. Once nested virtualization has been enabled, you can install Hyper-V inside the nested VM.

Before You Start

This section uses the `HVDirect` VM, which you set up in "Creating a Hyper-V VM."

Stopping HVDirect VM

To configure nested virtualization in a VM, you must first shut down the VM, using `Stop-VM`.

```
#  1. Stop HVDirect VM
$VMName = 'HVDIRECT'
Stop-VM -VMName $VMName
```

Configuring Virtual Processor

With the VM stopped, you can now configure nested virtualization (and add an extra virtual processor for this VM) using the `Set-VMProcessor` command as follows:

```
# 2. Change the VM's processor to support virtualization
$VMName = 'HVDIRECT'
$VMHT = @{
  VMName                        = $VMName
  ExposeVirtualizationExtensions = $true
  Count                         = 2
}
Set-VMProcessor @VMHT
Get-VMProcessor -VMName $VMName |
    Format-Table -Property Name, Count,
                           ExposeVirtualizationExtensions
```

You can see the output of these commands in Figure 8.25.

```
PS C:\Foo> # 2. Change the VM's processor to support virtualization
PS C:\Foo> $VMName = 'HVDIRECT'
PS C:\Foo> $VMHT = @{
            VMName                        = $VMName
            ExposeVirtualizationExtensions = $true
            Count                         = 2
          }
PS C:\Foo> Set-VMProcessor @VMHT
PS C:\Foo> Get-VMProcessor -VMName $VMName |
            Format-Table -Property Name, Count,
                           ExposeVirtualizationExtensions


Name       Count ExposeVirtualizationExtensions
----       ----- ------------------------------
Processor    2                             True
```

Figure 8.25: Configuring the VM processor

These commands expose hardware virtualization features to this VM and add a second virtual processor to the VM.

Enabling MAC Address Spoofing

Because you are going to be running VMs inside this VM, you need to enable MAC address spoofing on the virtual NIC inside the `HVDirect` VM, using `Set-VMNetworkAdapter`. The code looks like this:

```
# 3. Enable MAC Address spoofing on the virtual NIC
Get-VM -VMName $VMName |
  Get-VMNetworkAdapter |
    Set-VMNetworkAdapter -MacAddressSpoofing On
```

MAC address spoofing is one approach to networking of nested VMs. Using Network Address Translation is an alternative. Using NAT, you would create a new internal virtual switch and configure the switch to support NAT. For more information on supporting NAT, see docs.microsoft.com/en-us/virtualization/hyper-v-on-windows/user-guide/nested-virtualization.

Restarting the VM

You restart the VM and view the VM status by using the following commands:

```
# 4. Restart the VM
Start-VM -VMName $VMName
Wait-VM  -VMName $VMName -For Heartbeat
Get-VM   -VMName $VMName
```

You can see the output from these commands in Figure 8.26.

```
PS C:\Foo> # 4. Restart the VM
PS C:\Foo> Start-VM -VMName $VMName
PS C:\Foo> Wait-VM  -VMName $VMName -For Heartbeat
PS C:\Foo> Get-VM   -VMName $VMName

Name     State   CPUUsage(%) MemoryAssigned(M) Uptime        Status             Version
----     -----   ----------- ----------------- ------        ------             -------
HVDirect Running 14          960               00:00:45.9750000 Operating normally 9.0
```

Figure 8.26: Restarting HVDirect

Creating Credentials

You need a credentials object to run commands in a remoting session. You create the credentials object using New-Object.

```
# 5. Create credentials for HVDirect
$User = 'Reskit\Administrator'
$PHT = @{
  String      = 'Pa$$w0rd'
  AsPlainText = $true
  Force       = $true
}
$PSS     = ConvertTo-SecureString @PHT
$Type    = 'System.Management.Automation.PSCredential'
$CredRK = New-Object -TypeName $Type -ArgumentList $User,$PSS
```

Installing Hyper-V in HVDirect VM

Now that the VM is running, as a test of nested virtualization, you can attempt to install the Hyper-V Windows feature inside the VM, using the following commands:

```
# 6.  Install Hyper-V inside the HVDirect VM
$SB = {
   Install-WindowsFeature -Name Hyper-V -IncludeManagementTools
}
$IHT  = @{
   VMName       = $VMName
   ScriptBlock  = $SB
   Credential   = $CredRK
}
Invoke-Command @IHT
```

These commands use PowerShell remoting to install the Hyper-V Windows feature and produce the output shown in Figure 8.27.

```
PS C:\Foo> # 6. Install Hyper-V inside the HVDirect VM
PS C:\Foo> $SB = {
             Install-WindowsFeature -Name Hyper-V -IncludeManagementTools
           }
PS C:\Foo> $IHT  = @{
             VMName       = $VMName
             ScriptBlock  = $SB
             Credential   = $CredRK
           }
PS C:\Foo> Invoke-Command @IHT

PSComputerName : HVDirect
RunspaceId     : 77a19a70-e4c0-4c88-bd0b-f8cc370623d8
Success        : True
RestartNeeded  : Yes
FeatureResult  : {Hyper-V, Hyper-V Module for Windows PowerShell, Hyper-V GUI Management Tools,
                 Remote Server Administration Tools, Hyper-V Management Tools,
                 Role Administration Tools}
ExitCode       : SuccessRestartRequired

WARNING: You must restart this server to finish the installation process.
```

Figure 8.27: Installing Hyper-V in HVDirect

As indicated in the output, you need to restart the VM to complete the installation of Hyper-V.

Restarting the VM

To restart the VM, you need to stop and then restart the VM, using the following commands:

```
# 7. Restart the VM to finish adding Hyper-V
Stop-VM  -VMName $VMName
```

```
Start-VM  -VMName $VMName
Wait-VM   -VMName $VMName -For IPAddress
Get-VM    -VMName $VMName
```

These commands produce the output shown in Figure 8.28.

```
PS C:\Foo> # 7. Restart the VM to finish adding Hyper-V
PS C:\Foo> Stop-VM   -VMName $VMName
PS C:\Foo> Start-VM -VMName $VMName
PS C:\Foo> Wait-VM   -VMName $VMName -For IPAddress
PS C:\Foo> Get-VM    -VMName $VMName


Name      State    CPUUsage(%) MemoryAssigned(M) Uptime         Status              Version
----      -----    ----------- ----------------- ------         ------              -------
HVDirect Running 19            960               00:00:50.4490000 Operating normally 9.0
```

Figure 8.28: Restarting HVDirect

As you can see from the output, the VM has restarted. As an alternative to using the Stop-VM and Start-VM commands, you could have used Restart-Computer and specified the VM's host name.

Checking Hyper-V in HVDirect

To complete your look at nested virtualization, you can examine the Hyper-V feature that you just installed in the VM and the Hyper-V services that support Hyper-V. You use the following commands to view these details:

```
# 8. Check Hyper-V inside HVDirect VM
$SB = {
  Get-WindowsFeature *Hyper* |
    Format-Table Name, InstallState
  Get-Service VM*
}
Invoke-Command -VMName $VMName -ScriptBlock $SB -Credential $CredRK
```

You can view the output produced from these commands in Figure 8.29.

As you can see from the output, Hyper-V and related features are installed. Additionally, you can see that the key Hyper-V integration services are installed and the needed services are all running. Without nested virtualization, none of these services would have been installed or running.

To find out more about these services, see docs.microsoft.com/en-us/virtualization/hyper-v-on-windows/reference/integration-services.

```
PS C:\Foo> # 8. Check Hyper-V inside HVDirect VM
PS C:\Foo> $SB = {
            Get-WindowsFeature *Hyper* |
              Format-Table Name, InstallState
            Get-Service VM*
          }
PS C:\Foo> Invoke-Command -VMName $VMName -ScriptBlock $SB -Credential $CredRK

Name                InstallState
----                ------------

Hyper-V                 Installed
RSAT-Hyper-V-Tools      Installed
Hyper-V-Tools           Installed
Hyper-V-PowerShell      Installed


Status  Name                    DisplayName                                     PSComputerName
------  ----                    -----------                                     --------------
Running vmcompute              Hyper-V Host Compute Service                     HVDirect
Stopped vmicguestinterface     Hyper-V Guest Service Interface                  HVDirect
Running vmicheartbeat          Hyper-V Heartbeat Service                        HVDirect
Running vmickvpexchange        Hyper-V Data Exchange Service                    HVDirect
Running vmicrdv                Hyper-V Remote Desktop Virtualization Service    HVDirect
Running vmicshutdown           Hyper-V Guest Shutdown Service                   HVDirect
Running vmictimesync           Hyper-V Time Synchronization Service             HVDirect
Running vmicvmsession          Hyper-V PowerShell Direct Service                HVDirect
Running vmicvss                Hyper-V Volume Shadow Copy Requestor             HVDirect
Running vmms                   Hyper-V Virtual Machine Management               HVDirect
```

Figure 8.29: Examining Hyper-V within HVDirect

Using VM Checkpoints

A benefit of Hyper-V, and any virtualization solution, is the ability to save a state and later revert to that state. You might take a checkpoint for a VM just prior to adding an application that you can later revert back to.

Hyper-V supports two types of checkpoints: standard and production. A *standard* checkpoint is a snapshot of a VM and its system memory at the moment that the checkpoint is initiated. A *production* checkpoint uses the Volume Shadow Copy Service (or File System Freeze in Linux VMs) to create a data-consistent backup of the VM. Production checkpoints do not take a snapshot of system memory. For more details on Hyper-V checkpoints, see `docs.microsoft.com/en-us/virtualization/hyper-v-on-windows/user-guide/checkpoints`.

In this section you create checkpoints and examine the results of taking and reverting to a checkpoint.

Before You Start

This section uses the `HVDirect` VM you created in "Creating a Hyper-V VM." You run the commands in this section on `HV1`, the Hyper-V host you set up in "Installing and Configuring Hyper-V." You must run these commands in an elevated console (or in VS Code that you run as Administrator).

Creating Credentials

In this section you run numerous commands within the HVDirect VM, and for that you need to create a credential object for the Reskit Administrator user. You create the credential object using New-Object as follows:

```
# 1. Create credentials for HVDirect VM
$RKUN   = 'Reskit\Administrator'
$PS     = 'Pa$$w0rd'
$RKP    = ConvertTo-SecureString -String $PS -AsPlainText -Force
$T      = 'System.Management.Automation.PSCredential'
$RKCred = New-Object -TypeName $T -ArgumentList $RKUN,$RKP
```

Examining C: in the HVDirect VM

In this section you create checkpoints and files within the C: drive for the HVDirect VM to observe the effect of taking and reverting to checkpoints. Before doing this, you look at the contents of C: in the HVDirect VM, using Invoke-Command.

```
# 2. Look at C:\ in HVDirect before starting
$VMName = 'HVDirect'
$ICHT = @{
  VMName      = $VMName
  ScriptBlock = {Get-ChildItem -Path C:\ | Format-Table}
  Credential  = $RKCred
}
Invoke-Command @ICHT
```

These commands produce the output you see in Figure 8.30.

```
PS C:\Foo> # 2. Look at C: in HVDirect before starting
PS C:\Foo> $VMName = 'HVDirect'
PS C:\Foo> $ICHT = @{
            VMName      = $VMName
            ScriptBlock = {Get-ChildItem -Path C:\ | Format-Table}
            Credential  = $RKCred
          }
PS C:\Foo> Invoke-Command @ICHT

    Directory: C:\

Mode            LastWriteTime    Length Name
----            -------------    ------ ----
d-----    15/09/2018    08:19           PerfLogs
d-r---    15/02/2020    17:15           Program Files
d-----    13/02/2020    16:23           Program Files (x86)
d-r---    15/02/2020    14:11           Users
d-----    15/02/2020    14:06           Windows
```

Figure 8.30: Examining the HVDirect C: drive

Creating a Checkpoint

You use the `Checkpoint-VM` command to create a Hyper-V checkpoint as follows:

```
# 3. Create a checkpoint of HVDirect
$CPHT = @{
  VMName        = $VMName
  SnapshotName = 'Checkpoint1'
}
Checkpoint-VM @CPHT
```

This command creates a VM checkpoint for the `HVDirect` VM. For each virtual disk drive in the VM, Hyper-V creates a differencing disk each time you create a new checkpoint. When Hyper-V takes the checkpoint, the previous base disk is frozen, and Hyper-V makes any changes to the differencing disk(s). Each additional checkpoint you take creates further differencing disks.

This means in a case where you have a large number of checkpoints, a disk read being performed by a VM might have to read all of the differencing disks to carry out the I/O operation. Unless there is a good reason, you should avoid having excessive checkpoints as it can affect disk performance.

Examining the Checkpoint Files

Having taken a first checkpoint, you can view the supporting checkpoint files using `Get-ChildItem`.

```
# 4. Look at the files created to support checkpoints
$Parent = Split-Path -Parent (Get-VM -Name $VMName |
            Select-Object -ExpandProperty HardDrives).Path |
              Select-Object -First 1
Get-ChildItem -Path $Parent
```

Figure 8.31 shows the output from these commands.

```
PS C:\Foo> $Parent = Split-Path -Parent (Get-VM -Name $VMName |
              Select-Object -ExpandProperty HardDrives).Path |
              Select-Object -First 1
PS C:\Foo> Get-ChildItem -Path $Parent


    Directory: C:\VM\VHDS


Mode          LastWriteTime       Length Name
----          -------------       ------ ----
-a----  15/02/2020   19:28  10573840384 HVDirect.Vhdx
-a----  15/02/2020   19:29    171966464 HVDirect_66E4CEA9-EB53-42CE-A7F7-C053457D1285.avhdx
-a----  15/02/2020   17:07      4194304 HVDirect-D.VHDX
-a----  15/02/2020   19:28      4194304 HVDirect-D_1B8202C8-D509-4E7D-BB65-477088669B42.avhdx
```

Figure 8.31: Examining the checkpoint files

These commands discover the folder name that Hyper-V uses to store the VM's virtual hard drives and then get the files stored in that folder. As you can see in the output, there are two base virtual disks.

You see four files in this output. The first is the VM's C: drive with the second the VM's D: drive. The two additional files are the differencing disks Hyper-V creates when you create the checkpoint.

Creating Content in HVDirect

To illustrate the effects of checkpoints, you can create some content on the HVDirect VM. This content is created *after* you created the first checkpoint.

```
# 5. Create some content in a file on HVDirect and display it
$SB = {
    $FileName1 = 'C:\File_After_Checkpoint_1'
    'After Checkpoint 1' |
      Out-File -FilePath $FileName1
    Get-Content -Path $FileName1
}
$ICHT = @{
  VMName      = $VMName
  ScriptBlock = $SB
  Credential  = $RKCred
}
Invoke-Command @ICHT
```

These commands create a file in the C: drive in HVDirect and then view the content of this file, producing the output you see in Figure 8.32.

```
PS C:\Foo> # 5. Create some content in a file on HVDirect and display it
PS C:\Foo> $SB = {
            $FileName1 = 'C:\File_After_Checkpoint_1'
            'After Checkpoint 1' |
              Out-File -FilePath $FileName1
            Get-Content -Path $FileName1
          }
PS C:\Foo> $ICHT = @{
            VMName      = $VMName
            ScriptBlock = $SB
            Credential  = $RKCred
          }
PS C:\Foo> Invoke-Command @ICHT
After Checkpoint 1
```

Figure 8.32: Creating content on HVDirect

Taking a Second Checkpoint

After creating a file in C:, you can take a further checkpoint using `Checkpoint-VM`.

```
# 6. Take a second checkpoint
$SNHT = @{
  VMName          = $VMName
  SnapshotName  = 'Checkpoint2'
}
Checkpoint-VM @SNHT
```

Viewing Checkpoint Details for HVDirect

After taking the two checkpoints, you can again view the existing checkpoints by using the `Get-VMCheckPoint` alias.

```
# 7. Get the VM checkpoint details for HVDirect
Get-VMCheckPoint -VMName $VMName
```

This command produces the output shown in Figure 8.33.

```
PS C:\Foo> # 7. Get the VM checkpoint details for HVDirect
PS C:\Foo> Get-VMCheckpoint -VMName $VMName

VMName    Name        SnapshotType CreationTime          ParentSnapshotName
------    ----        ------------ ------------          ------------------
HVDirect  Checkpoint1 Standard     15/02/2020 19:29:00
HVDirect  Checkpoint2 Standard     15/02/2020 19:34:00   Checkpoint1
```

Figure 8.33: Viewing Hyper-V checkpoints

The `Get-VMCheckpoint` command is an alias to `Get-VMSnapShot`. In early versions of Hyper-V, the terminology for this technology was inconsistent. System Center VM Manager, for example, used the term *checkpoint*, while Hyper-V called it a *snapshot*. Additionally, the term snapshot was often confused with the Volume Shadow Copy Service snapshots that backup programs use. In Hyper-V with Server 2012 R2, the Hyper-V team renamed the term. Thus, the command that creates the snapshot/checkpoint is now named `Checkpoint-VM`. However, instead of renaming the other VM snapshot cmdlets, the team chose to keep the existing cmdlet names, such as `Get-VMSnapshot`, and instead created aliases such as `Get-VMCheckpoint`.

Examining Files Supporting Checkpoints

With two checkpoints taken for the HVDirect VM, you can look at the files that Hyper-V is using to support the two virtual disks in the VM.

```
# 8. Look at the files supporting the two checkpoints
Get-ChildItem -Path $Parent
```

You can view the output from this command in Figure 8.34.

```
PS C:\Foo> # 8. Look at the files supporting the two checkpoints
PS C:\Foo> Get-ChildItem -Path $Parent

    Directory: C:\VM\VHDS

Mode          LastWriteTime       Length Name
----          -------------       ------ ----
-a---   15/02/2020    19:28   10573840384 HVDirect.Vhdx
-a---   15/02/2020    19:33     252706816 HVDirect_66E4CEA9-EB53-42CE-A7F7-C053457D1285.avhdx
-a---   15/02/2020    19:34      71303168 HVDirect_ED4AF601-8C28-4EBD-8AE8-C5174A273911.avhdx
-a---   15/02/2020    17:07       4194304 HVDirect-D.VHDX
-a---   15/02/2020    19:33       4194304 HVDirect-D_1B8202C8-D509-4E7D-BB65-477088669B42.avhdx
-a---   15/02/2020    19:33       4194304 HVDirect-D_AF350BAA-D04E-4B2B-ACE6-B6C43E6C0AEF.avhdx
```

Figure 8.34: Viewing checkpoint files

As you can see, there are now two differencing disks for each of the original VHDX files.

Creating Another File in HVDirect

With two checkpoints taken, you create a new file in the HVDirect VM to demonstrate the content that is created after you take the second checkpoint. You then view the contents of that file, as follows:

```
# 9. Create and display another file in HVDirect
#     (after you have taken Checkpoint2)
$SB = {
  $FileName2 = 'C:\File_After_Checkpoint_2'
  'After Checkpoint 2' |
    Out-File -FilePath $FileName2
  Get-ChildItem -Path C:\ -File | Format-Table
}
$ICHT = @{
  VMName      = $VMName
  ScriptBlock = $SB
  Credential  = $RKCred
}
Invoke-Command @ICHT
```

These commands display the two files you created in the C: drive. You can view the output from these commands in Figure 8.35.

Reverting to Checkpoint1

You have, thus far, created two checkpoints of the VM and have added some content beyond the second checkpoint. You can now use the Restore-VMCheckpoint command to revert the VM to the first checkpoint.

```
# 10. Restore the VM back to the checkpoint named Checkpoint1
$CP1 = Get-VMCheckpoint -VMName $VMName -Name Checkpoint1
Restore-VMCheckpoint -VMSnapshot $CP1 -Confirm:$false
Start-VM -Name $VMName
Wait-VM -For IPAddress -Name $VMName
```

```
PS C:\Foo> # 9. Create and display another file in HVDirect
PS C:\Foo> #    (after you have taken Checkpoint2)
PS C:\Foo> $SB = {
            $FileName2 = 'C:\File_After_Checkpoint_2'
            'After Checkpoint 2' |
              Out-File -FilePath $FileName2
            Get-ChildItem -Path C:\ -File | Format-Table
          }
PS C:\Foo> $ICHT = @{
            VMName      = $VMName
            ScriptBlock = $SB
            Credential  = $RKCred
          }
PS C:\Foo> Invoke-Command @ICHT


    Directory: C:\

Mode             LastWriteTime  Length Name
----             -------------  ------ ----
-a----    15/02/2020     19:32     42 File_After_Checkpoint_1
-a----    15/02/2020     19:38     42 File_After_Checkpoint_2
```

Figure 8.35: Viewing checkpoint files after the second checkpoint

These commands first find Checkpoint1 and then revert the HVDirect VM to the earlier checkpoint. Once it is reverted, you start the VM, waiting until it has fully started.

Viewing VM Files

With the VM reverted to the point at which you took the first checkpoint, you can observe the files available in the C: drive in HVDirect using Get-ChildItem.

```
# 11. See what files we have now in the VM
$ICHT = @{
  VMName      = $VMName
  ScriptBlock = {Get-ChildItem -Path C:\ |
                    Format-Table }
  Credential  = $RKCred
}
Invoke-Command @ICHT
```

You can see the output from these commands in Figure 8.36.

```
PS C:\Foo> # 11. See what files we have now in the VM
PS C:\Foo> $ICHT = @{
            VMName      = $VMName
            ScriptBlock = {Get-ChildItem -Path C:\ |
                            Format-Table }
            Credential  = $RKCred
          }
PS C:\Foo> Invoke-Command @ICHT


    Directory: C:\


Mode                LastWriteTime         Length Name
----                -------------         ------ ----
d-----        15/09/2018     08:19               PerfLogs
d-r---        15/02/2020     17:15               Program Files
d-----        13/02/2020     16:23               Program Files (x86)
d-r---        15/02/2020     14:11               Users
d-----        15/02/2020     14:06               Windows
```

Figure 8.36: Viewing files in the VM

In this output, you can see that neither of the two files you created after taking the first checkpoint is missing. This is to be expected.

Rolling Forward to Checkpoint2

Hyper-V enables you to roll forward and apply a checkpoint you made previously. You can do this by using the `Restore-VMCheckpoint` command.

```
# 12. Roll forward to Checkpoint2
$Checkpoint2 = Get-VMCheckpoint -VMName $VMName -Name Checkpoint2
Restore-VMCheckpoint -VMSnapshot $Checkpoint2 -Confirm:$false
Start-VM -Name $VMName
Wait-VM -For IPAddress -Name $VMName
```

These commands find the second checkpoint and roll the VM forward to the state that existed when you took the second checkpoint.

Viewing VM Files After Rolling Forward

Now that you have rolled the VM forward to the state that existed when you created the second checkpoint, you can look at the files that exist inside the HVDirect VM, using `Get-ChildItem` (remotely), as shown here:

```
# 13. Observe the files you now have on HVDirect VM
$ICHT = @{
  VMName      = $VMName
  ScriptBlock = {Get-ChildItem -Path C:\ |
                Format-Table }
  Credential  = $RKCred
}
Invoke-Command @ICHT
```

Figure 8.37 shows the output from these commands.

```
PS C:\Foo> # 13. Observe the files you now have on HVDirect VM
PS C:\Foo> $ICHT = @{
              VMName      = $VMName
              ScriptBlock = {Get-ChildItem -Path C:\ |
                                    Format-Table }
              Credential  = $RKCred
          }
PS C:\Foo> Invoke-Command @ICHT


    Directory: C:\


Mode                LastWriteTime     Length Name
----                -------------     ------ ----
d-----       15/09/2018     08:19            PerfLogs
d-r---       15/02/2020     17:15            Program Files
d-----       13/02/2020     16:23            Program Files (x86)
d-r---       15/02/2020     14:11            Users
d-----       15/02/2020     14:06            Windows
-a----       15/02/2020     19:32         42 File_After_Checkpoint_1
```

Figure 8.37: Viewing files in the VM after rolling forward

As you can see in this output, the file you created after Checkpoint1 is available. However, as is to be expected, the file you created after you took the *second checkpoint* is lost.

This illustrates a key point about checkpoints. If you do have to revert to an earlier checkpoint, consider carefully what state your VM is in before reverting. If you revert a VM but want to keep any data modified after the last checkpoint, you should take an additional checkpoint (Checkpoint3) before reverting. You can always remove the checkpoints later.

Viewing Checkpoints in the VM

With two checkpoints taken, you can view the Hyper-V checkpoint details using Get-VMCheckpoint, as shown here:

```
# 14. View checkpoints for HVDirect
Get-VMCheckpoint -VMName $VMName
```

You can view the output of this command in Figure 8.38, where you can see the two checkpoints you have taken thus far for the HVDirect VM.

```
PS C:\Foo> # 14. Check checkpoints for HVDirect
PS C:\Foo> Get-VMCheckpoint -VMName $VMName

VMName    Name        SnapshotType CreationTime             ParentSnapshotName
------    ----        ------------ ------------             ------------------
HVDirect  Checkpoint1 Standard     16/02/2020 12:20:49
HVDirect  Checkpoint2 Standard     16/02/2020 12:21:34 Checkpoint1
```

Figure 8.38: Viewing checkpoints for HVDirect

Removing Checkpoints

You can use the `Remove-VMSnapshot` command to remove the checkpoints for the `HVDirect` VM.

```
# 15. Remove all the checkpoints for HVDirect
Get-VMCheckpoint -VMName $VMName |
  Remove-VMSnapshot
```

These commands use both cmdlet name (`Remove-VMSnapshot`) and an alias name (`Get-VMCheckpoint`). If you are writing scripts to manage VM backups, you should be consistent with which commands, or cmdlet nouns, you use.

Checking VM Data Files after Removing Checkpoints

Now that you have removed all the checkpoints, you can reexamine the files supporting the `HVDirect` VM, using `Get-ChildItem`.

```
# 16. Check VM data files again
Get-ChildItem -Path $Parent
```

You can see the output from this command in Figure 8.39.

```
PS C:\Foo> # 16. Check VM data files again
PS C:\Foo> Get-ChildItem -Path $Parent


    Directory: C:\VM\VHDS


Mode            LastWriteTime         Length Name
----            -------------         ------ ----
-a---     15/02/2020     20:25   105738403B4 HVDirect.Vhdx
-a---     15/02/2020     20:25       4194304 HVDirect-D.VHDX
```

Figure 8.39: Viewing virtual hard disks

With all the checkpoints removed, you now just have a single VHDX file for each virtual disk. The state of the VM, however, is that of the second checkpoint.

Using VM Replication

Hyper-V Replica (HVR) is a feature of Hyper-V that creates a full replica of a VM for disaster recovery. HVR takes a running VM, such as the `HVDirect` VM you used in earlier sections of this chapter, running on the `HV1` VM host, and replicates it to a second host, `HV2`. In the case of a disaster affecting `HV1`, `HV2` has an up-to-date copy of the `HVDirect` VM, which you could then use.

With HVR, you can co-locate the replica source and target in another nearby Hyper-V host, for example, in the same rack in your computer suite. Alternatively, you can locate the target across a WAN. The Hyper-V hosts whose VMs you replicate can be any combination of workgroup, domain-joined, or clustered hosts. Additionally, there is no specific dependency on AD. This provides simple and easy disaster recovery across a range of scenarios.

HVR uses change tracking with asynchronous replication. This means that, initially, HVR creates a full duplicate of the VM's data on the replication target's host. Then, as changes are made on the source VM, HVR writes the changes to a log file and replays them on the replica target's VM host.

HVR also allows for extended replication, that is, from the replication target to a second extended target. You might use this to create basic VM replication within a single data center and create a third replica in your off-site DR location. This provides quick failover in the case of relatively minor hardware issues and full disaster recovery via the extended replicas.

Before You Start

This section makes use of two Hyper-V servers: HV1 and HV2. You created HV1 in "Installing and Configuring Hyper-V" and updated it in later sections in this chapter. Before you work with the code in this section, you need a second Hyper-V host, HV2. This host is another domain-joined Windows Server 2019 Enterprise.

After installing Windows Server 2019 Enterprise edition onto HV2, you need to configure the host to support virtualization. If HV2 is a VM, then you can configure the VM from the VM host, as follows:

```
# 0.1 Configure HV2 VM from the VM host
# If HV2 is a VM, configure it on the Hyper-V Host running HV2
# Stop the VM
Stop-VM -VMName HV2
# Enable nested virtualization and set processor count for HV2
$VMHT = @{
  VMName                          = 'HV2'
  ExposeVirtualizationExtensions = $true
  Count                           = 4
}
Set-VMProcessor @VMHT
# Set VM Memory for HV2
$VMHT = [ordered] @{
  VMName              = 'HV2'
  DynamicMemoryEnabled = $true
  MinimumBytes        = 768MB
  StartupBytes        = 2GB
  MaximumBytes        = 4GB
}
```

```
Set-VMMemory @VMHT

# Restart HV2 VM
Start-VM -VMName HV2
Wait-VM -VMName HV2 -For IPAddress
```

After HV2, newly configured to support virtualization and related features, has rebooted, log into it as Domain Admin and then add the Hyper-V Windows feature using Install-WindowsFeature.

```
# 0.2 Login to HV2 to add Hyper-V feature to HV2
# Install the Hyper-V feature on HV2
Import-Module -Name Servermanager -WarningAction SilentlyContinue
Install-WindowsFeature -Name Hyper-V -IncludeManagementTools
# Reboot HV2 to complete the installation of Hyper-V
Restart-Computer
# Login to HV2 again and configure Hyper-V Host on HV2
# Create folders to hold VM details and disks
$VMS  = 'C:\VM\VMS'
$VHDS = 'C:\VM\VHDS\'
New-Item -Path $VMS  -ItemType Directory -Force | Out-Null
New-Item -Path $VHDS -ItemType Directory -force | Out-Null
# Build Hash Table to Configure the VM Host
$VMCHT = @{
# Where to store VM configuration files on
  VirtualMachinePath  = $VMS
# Where to store VHDx files
  VirtualHardDiskPath = $VHDS
# Enable NUMA spanning
  NumaSpanningEnabled = $true
# Enable Enhanced Session Mode
  EnableEnhancedSessionMode = $true
# Specify Resource metering save interval
  ResourceMeteringSaveInterval  = (New-TimeSpan -Hours 2 )
}
Set-VMHost @VMCHT
# Create new External Switch
$NIC = Get-NetIPConfiguration | Select-Object -First 1
New-VMSwitch -Name External -NetAdapterName $NIC.InterfaceAlias
```

This snippet also creates an external switch in the HV2 VM. That virtual switch enables HV1 and HV2 to communicate.

Configuring HV1 and HV2 for Delegation

To simplify security of HVR, you set each VM host to enable delegation, using Set-ADComputer as follows:

```
# 1. Configure HV1 and HV2 to be trusted for delegation in AD on DC1
$SB1 = {
```

```
    Set-ADComputer -Identity HV1 -TrustedForDelegation $True
}
Invoke-Command -ComputerName DC1 -ScriptBlock $SB1
$SB2 = {
    Set-ADComputer -Identity HV2 -TrustedForDelegation $True
}
Invoke-Command -ComputerName DC1 -ScriptBlock $SB2
```

These commands enable Kerberos delegation for the two Hyper-V servers. You can read a bit more about delegation in argonsys.com/microsoft-cloud/library/live-migration-via-constrained-delegation-with-kerberos-in-windows-server-2016/.

Rebooting HV1 and HV2

To complete the configuration of delegation you need to restart both hosts using `Restart-Computer`.

```
# 2. Reboot the HV1 and HV2
Restart-Computer -ComputerName HV1 -Force
Restart-Computer -ComputerName HV2 -Force
```

Setting VMReplication

You begin the setup of HVR using the command `Set-VMReplicationServer` as follows:

```
# 3. Once both systems are restarted, logon back to HV2,
#     set up both servers as a replication server
$VMRHT = @{
    ReplicationEnabled            = $true
    AllowedAuthenticationType     = 'Kerberos'
    KerberosAuthenticationPort    = 42000
    DefaultStorageLocation        = 'C:\Replicas'
    ReplicationAllowedFromAnyServer = $true
    ComputerName                  = 'HV1', 'HV2'
}
Set-VMReplicationServer @VMRHT
```

Enabling Replication from the Source VM

Before you can replicate a VM between Hyper-V hosts, you need to use `Enable-VMReplication` to configure the replication as follows:

```
# 4. Enable HVDirect on HV1 to be a replica source with HV2 the target
$VMRHT = @{
```

```
    VMName              = 'HVDirect'
    Computer            = 'HV1'
    ReplicaServerName   = 'HV2'
    ReplicaServerPort   = 42000
  AuthenticationType    = 'Kerberos'
 CompressionEnabled     = $true
 RecoveryHistory        = 5
}
Enable-VMReplication  @VMRHT
```

This command initializes the replication of the HVDirect VM. The HVR replica source VM is on HV1, and the target is on HV2.

This command specifies that Kerberos is to be used to authenticate the two hosts involved in VM replication. Since both HV1 and HV2 are members of the Reskit domain (and you have configured them for Kerberos delegation), this is straightforward to configure.

If the source and target Hyper-V hosts are in different security realms, then you can use certificate authentication. For a look at how you can set up replication using self-signed certificates, see medium.com/@pbengert/setup-2-hyper-v-2016-servers-enable-hyper-v-replica-with-self-created-certificates-and-connect-to-fceef21c8b8e.

Viewing VM Replication Status

Now that you have enabled replication, you can view the replication status of each Hyper-V host using Get-VMReplicationServer.

```
# 5. View the replication status of HV1 and HV2
Get-VMReplicationServer -ComputerName HV1
Get-VMReplicationServer -ComputerName HV2
```

You can see the output from these commands in Figure 8.40.

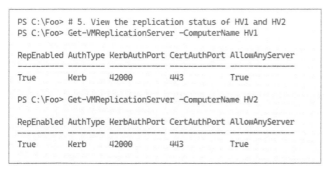

Figure 8.40: Viewing replication status

Viewing VM Status

Before initiating the replication, use Get-VM to ensure that the VM is running on HV1.

```
# 6. Check HVDirect on HV1
Get-VM -ComputerName HV1 -VMName HVDirect
```

As you can see in the output, shown in Figure 8.41, the HVDirect VM is up and running on HV1.

```
PS C:\Foo> # 6. Check HVDirect on HV1
PS C:\Foo> Get-VM -ComputerName HV1 -VMName HVDirect

Name      State    CPUUsage(%) MemoryAssigned(M) Uptime            Status             Version
----      -----    ----------- ----------------- ------            ------             -------
HVDirect  Running 1            960               00:42:04.2000000  Operating normally 9.0
```

Figure 8.41: Viewing VM status

Initiating Replication

Having previously defined the replication source and target for HVDirect, you are ready to initiate replication. To do that, use Start-VMInitialReplication.

```
# 7. Start the initial replication from HV1 to HV2
Start-VMInitialReplication -VMName HVDirect -ComputerName HV1
```

This command starts the creation of a replica. Hyper-V first has to make a copy on HV2 of the VM hard drives, which can take some time.

Examining Initial Replication State

To view the state of the replication of HVDirect, you can use the Measure-VMReplication command.

```
# 8. Examine the initial replication state on HV1 just after
#    you start the initial replication
Measure-VMReplication -ComputerName HV2
```

Figure 8.42 shows the output of this command, issued shortly after the initial replication began.

```
PS C:\Foo> # 8. Examine the initial replication state on HV1 just after
PS C:\Foo> #    you start the initial replication
PS C:\Foo> Measure-VMReplication -ComputerName HV2

VMName    State                      Health  LReplTime PReplSize(M) AvgLatency AvgReplSize(M) Relationship
------    -----                      ------  --------- ------------ ---------- -------------- ------------
HVDirect  WaitingForInitialReplication Warning          0.00                    0.00          Simple
```

Figure 8.42: Examining the replication status

The initial replication can take some time; this depends on the available bandwidth between HV1 and HV2, the size of the VM, and the workload on each Hyper-V host. On a fast network, the initial replication of the HVDirect VM you created in this chapter should take two to three minutes.

Viewing Replication

You can use Measure-VMReplication repeatedly to watch the progress of the initial replication.

```
# 9. Wait for replication to finish, then examine the
#    replication status on HV2
Measure-VMReplication -ComputerName HV2
```

Figure 8.43 shows the output of this command after the initial replication has completed.

```
PS C:\Foo> # 9. Wait for replication to finish, then examine the
PS C:\Foo> #    replication status on HV2
PS C:\Foo> Measure-VMReplication -ComputerName HV2

VMName    State       Health LReplTime               PReplSize(M) AvgLatency AvgReplSize(M) Relationship
------    -----       ------ ---------               ------------ ---------- -------------- ------------
HVDirect Replicating Normal 17/02/2020 13:08:19 0.00              00:02:42   1,896.00       Simple
```

Figure 8.43: Viewing the progress of replication

You can run this command multiple times to observe the progress until you see, as in the output from this step, that Hyper-V has completed the initial replication.

Testing Replica Failover

Once initial replication has completed, Hyper-V detects changes to the VM on HV1 and replicates them to HV2.

You can test the failover by using the Start-VMFailOver command.

```
# 10. Test HVDirect failover from HV1 to HV2
$VM = Start-VMFailover -AsTest -VMName HVDirect -Confirm:$false
Start-VM $VM
```

This snippet initiates a test of the replica failover. When you test an HVR replica failover, Hyper-V creates a new VM on the replication target host with a new name. This VM is, in effect, the replica of the VM, running but with a different Hyper-V-generated VM name.

During the test, the original VM on HV1 continues to run and Hyper-V continues to replicate any changes.

Viewing VM Status on HV2 after Failover

Use `Get-VM` to see the VMs that are now running on HV2, as follows:

```
# 11. View the status of VMs on HV2
Get-VM -ComputerName HV2
```

The output, shown in Figure 8.44, shows the VMs now running on HV2.

```
PS C:\Foo> # 11. View the status of VMs on HV2
PS C:\Foo> Get-VM -ComputerName HV2

Name              State   CPUUsage(%) MemoryAssigned(M) Uptime            Status             Version
----              -----   ----------- ----------------- ------            ------             -------
HVDirect          Off     0           0                 00:00:00          Operating normally 9.0
HVDirect - Test   Running 19          960               00:00:30.7750000  Operating normally 9.0
```

Figure 8.44: Viewing the VMs running on HV2

The first VM you see in this output is the replica target for the HVDirect VM. The second is the VM failover test. Note that the replication test VM name has `-Test` appended to the replicated VM's name. Thus, the test VM's name is HVDirect - Test.

Getting VM Details from HV1

To test replication, you first run some commands on the HVDirect VM running on HV1.

```
# 12. Get VM Details in replica source
$RKUN    = 'Reskit\Administrator'
$PS      = 'Pa$$w0rd'
$RKP     = ConvertTo-SecureString -String $PS -AsPlainText -Force
$CREDHT = @{
  TypeName      = 'System.Management.Automation.PSCredential'
  Argumentlist = $RKUN, $RKP
}
$RKCred = New-Object @CREDHT
$SB1 = {
  $SB1a = @{
    VMName        = 'HVDirect'
    ScriptBlock   = {hostname;ipconfig}
    Credential    = $using:RKCred
  }
  Invoke-Command @SB1a
}
Invoke-Command -Computer HV1 -Script $SB1
```

You can see the output from this command in Figure 8.45.

```
PS C:\Foo> # 12. Get VM Hostname in replica source
PS C:\Foo> $RKUN   = 'Reskit\Administrator'
PS C:\Foo> $PS     = 'Pa$$w0rd'
PS C:\Foo> $RKP    = ConvertTo-SecureString -String $PS -AsPlainText -Force
PS C:\Foo> $CREDHT = @{
              TypeName     = 'System.Management.Automation.PSCredential'
              ArgumentList = $RKUN, $RKP
           }
PS C:\Foo> $RKCred = New-Object @CREDHT
PS C:\Foo> $SB1 = {
              $SB1a = @{
                VMName      = 'HVDirect'
                ScriptBlock = {hostname;ipconfig}
                Credential  = $using:RKCred
              }
              Invoke-Command @SB1a
           }
PS C:\Foo> Invoke-Command -Computer HV1 -Script $SB1
Tiger

Windows IP Configuration


Ethernet adapter Ethernet:

   Connection-specific DNS Suffix  . : Reskit.Org
   Link-local IPv6 Address . . . . . : fe80::9d5c:b263:8fcd:204f%4
   IPv4 Address. . . . . . . . . . . : 10.10.10.154
   Subnet Mask . . . . . . . . . . . : 255.255.255.0
   Default Gateway . . . . . . . . . : 10.10.10.254
```

Figure 8.45: Getting the VM details on the replica source

The output from these commands shows that the HVDirect VM is up and running normally on HV1. This VM has an IP address and network details provided by the DHCP server you created on DC1.

Getting VM Details from HV2

Once the failover test VM has started, you can also examine it using the same commands.

```
# 13. Get VM details in replica test VM on HV2
$SB2 = {
  $SB2a = @{
    VMName      = 'HVDirect - Test'
    ScriptBlock = {hostname;ipconfig}
    Credential  = $using:RKCred
  }
  Invoke-Command @SB2a
}
Invoke-Command -Computer HV2 -Script $SB2
```

You can see the output from these commands in Figure 8.46.

```
PS C:\Foo> # 13. Get VM details in replica test VM on HV2
PS C:\Foo> $SB2 = {
              $SB2a = @{
                VMName       = 'HVDirect - Test'
                ScriptBlock  = {hostname;ipconfig}
                Credential   = $using:RKCred
              }
              Invoke-Command @SB2a
          }
PS C:\Foo> Invoke-Command -Computer HV2 -Script $SB2
Tiger

Windows IP Configuration


Ethernet adapter Ethernet:

   Media State . . . . . . . . . . . : Media disconnected
   Connection-specific DNS Suffix  . : Reskit.Org
```

Figure 8.46: Testing the replica VM

The output shows that the test VM is up and running and can process commands. Note that the host name of the test VM is `Tiger`. This is also the host name for the `HVDirect` VM (running on `HV1`). You created this host name when you joined the VM to the domain in "Configuring VM Networking." But you also see that there is no TCP/IP networking configured. Given how you have configured `HV2` so far, this is to be expected.

This step also illustrates sending a script block to a host (`HV2`) and then having that script invoke a second script block inside a VM. If you are managing many Hyper-V servers, which each run multiple VMs, this can be a useful technique to target a particular VM running on a particular Hyper-V host.

You can now test the failover VM, possibly using PowerShell to investigate the VM. In production, you should ensure that relevant services are up and running and that, if needed, the failover VM could be used to recover from a disaster befalling `HV1`.

Stopping the Failover Test

Once you have ensured that the failover test has succeeded and that the test VM is up and running (all but the networking), you can stop it using the `Stop-VMFailover` command.

```
# 14. Stop the failover test
Stop-VMFailover -VMName HVDirect
```

Prior to the failover test, you had the working `HVDirect` VM on `HV1` plus the replica on `HV2`. The failover test created a new and temporary VM on `HV2`, which Hyper-V removes when you stop the failover test.

Viewing VM Status

With the failover test stopped, you can again view the status of the two VM hosts, using `Get-VM`.

```
# 15. View the status of VMs on HV1 and HV2 after failover stopped
Get-VM -ComputerName HV1
Get-VM -ComputerName HV2
```

You can see the output from these commands in Figure 8.47.

```
PS C:\Foo> # 15. View the status of VMs on HV1 and HV2 after failover stopped
PS C:\Foo> Get-VM —ComputerName HV1

Name      State    CPUUsage(%) MemoryAssigned(M) Uptime              Status             Version
----      -----    ----------- ----------------- ------              ------             -------
HVDirect  Running  1           960               04:06:12.2070000    Operating normally 9.0

PS C:\Foo> Get-VM —ComputerName HV2

Name      State    CPUUsage(%) MemoryAssigned(M) Uptime              Status             Version
----      -----    ----------- ----------------- ------              ------             -------
HVDirect  Off      0           0                 00:00:00            Operating normally 9.0
```

Figure 8.47: Viewing VM status

The output shows that all traces of the failover VM on HV2 are now gone from HV2. As you can see, the two Hyper-V hosts are back to the pre-failover test state where HV1 continues to run the HVDirect VM with Hyper-V replicating any changes from HV1 to the replica on HV2.

Setting Failover IP Address for VM Failover

When you performed the failover test of HVDirect, you notice that the test VM (HVDirect - Test) had no networking setup. As noted, this is normal. If you want specific network address details (such as IP address and subnet mask), you can set them using the Set-VMNetworkadapterFailoverConfiguration command.

```
# 16. Set Failover IP address for HVDirect on HV2
$NAHT = @{
  IPv4Address          = '10.10.10.142'
  IPv4SubnetMask       = '255.255.255.0'
  IPv4PreferredDNSServer = '10.10.10.10'
}
Get-VMNetworkAdapter -VMName HVDirect -ComputerName HV2 |
  Set-VMNetworkAdapterFailoverConfiguration @NAHT
Connect-VMNetworkAdapter -VMName HVDirect -SwitchName External
```

This snippet obtains the network details of the HVDirect replica VM as currently residing on HV2. This VM is not active and is the target of Hyper-V VM replication—but the VM does have a virtual NIC.

You can use the commands shown previously to set IP address configuration in the event of any failover. These commands also ensure that the virtual NIC is associated with a switch. The result of these commands is to set up the replica to have a different network configuration and to attach to a virtual switch in the case of further failover. With this configured, when you fail over the HVDirect VM to HV2, Hyper-V connects the NIC in the VM to a switch and configures the virtual NIC with an appropriate IP address configuration.

Stopping HVDirect on HV1

With the steps so far, you have configured HVR to maintain a replica on a second Hyper-V host so that Hyper-V replicates all changes from HV1 to the replica on HV2.

To simulate a real-life failover, you first stop the HVDirect VM on HV1.

```
# 17. Stop HVDirect on HV1 prior to performing a failover
Stop-VM HVDirect -ComputerName HV1
```

This simulates the failure of the VM on HV1. However, failover is not automatic. If you wanted automatic failover, you could use failover clustering and cluster the Hyper-V role.

Starting Failover from HV1 to HV2

Using HVR, failover is not automatic but something you need to do in two steps (as noted if you want automatic failover, you should deploy failover clustering).

To start the failover, you use the Start-VMFailover on HV2. This tells Hyper-V to begin a failover.

```
# 18. Start VM failover from HV1
Start-VMFailover -VMName HVDirect -Confirm:$false
```

You can use the Start-VMFailover for several purposes.

- To start a planned failover of a VM
- To create a test virtual machine on a replica virtual machine
- To failover a replica virtual machine to a chosen recovery point

In effect, this command tells Hyper-V what kind of a failover it is to perform. By using the -Confirm:$false, you ensure that Start-VmFailover does not prompt for confirmation.

Completing the Failover of HVDirect

Once you have started the failover, you can complete it using `Complete-VMFailover`, like so:

```
# 19. Complete the failover
$CHT = @{
  VMName        = 'HVDirect'
  ComputerName  = 'HV2'
  Confirm       = $false
}
Complete-VMFailover @CHT
```

This command completes the failover. Note that this command also removes all recovery points on the VM that Hyper-V has failed over.

Note that in this case you used a hash table to specify the parameters for `Complete-VMFailOver`—another way to invoke a cmdlet.

Starting the Failover VM

Once the VM failover has completed, you have a working VM on HV2, although it is not running. To start the VM, you use the `Start-VM` command and then wait until the VM is up and running on HV2.

```
# 20. Start the replicated VM on HV2
Start-VM -VMname HVDirect -ComputerName HV2
Wait-VM -VMName HVDirect -For IPAddress
```

These commands start the failover replica on HV2. As it takes some time for the VM to start, you can use the `Wait-VM` command to wait until the HVDirect VM is up and running on HV2 and has a working IP address.

One reason to use this two-step approach is to enable you to make a good decision as to when to start the replica.

Checking VM Status After Failover

You can repeat the use of `Get-VM` on both Hyper-V servers to view the VMs on the two virtualization hosts.

```
# 21. See VMs on HV1 and HV2 after the planned failover
Get-VM -ComputerName HV1
Get-VM -ComputerName HV2
```

You can see the output from these commands in Figure 8.48.

As the output shows, the HVDirect VM is running on HV2 but stopped on HV1.

```
PS C:\Foo> # 21. See VMs on HV1 and HV2 after the planned failover
PS C:\Foo> Get-VM –ComputerName HV1

Name      State CPUUsage(%) MemoryAssigned(M) Uptime    Status               Version
----      ----- ----------- ----------------- ------    ------               -------
HVDirect  Off   0           0                 00:00:00  Operating normally 9.0


PS C:\Foo> Get-VM –ComputerName HV2

Name      State   CPUUsage(%)  MemoryAssigned(M) Uptime             Status             Version
----      -----   -----------  ----------------- ------             ------             -------
HVDirect  Running 1            960               00:09:35.1750000 Operating normally 9.0
```

Figure 8.48: Checking VM status after failover

Testing Failover VM Networking

With the steps so far, you have set up and initiated a failover of the HVDirect
VM from HV1 to HV2. Having set up failover network details, you can verify the
networking configuration by running the following commands:

```
# 22. Retest Migrated HVDirect VM
$SB4 =@{
   VMName      = 'HVDirect'
   ScriptBlock = {hostname; ipconfig}
   Credential  = $rkcred
}
Invoke-Command @SB4
```

You can see the output from these commands in Figure 8.49.

```
PS C:\Foo> # 22. Retest Migrated HVDirect VM
PS C:\Foo> $SB4 =@{
  VMName      = 'HVDirect'
  ScriptBlock = {hostname; ipconfig}
  Credential  = $rkcred
}
PS C:\Foo> Invoke-Command @SB4
Tiger

Windows IP Configuration

Ethernet adapter Ethernet:

   Connection-specific DNS Suffix  . :
   Link-local IPv6 Address . . . . . : fe80::9d5c:b263:8fcd:204f%4
   IPv4 Address. . . . . . . . . . . : 10.10.10.142
   Subnet Mask . . . . . . . . . . . : 255.255.255.0
   Default Gateway . . . . . . . . . :
```

Figure 8.49: Verifying the VM networking configuration

The output shows that the VM has the host name Tiger and has a new IP
configuration (the one that you set using Set-VMNetworkAdapterFailoverConfiguration in "Setting Failover IP Address for VM Failover").

In this section you have configured and tested HVR and VM failover. You now have the HVDirect VM up and running on HV2.

Managing VM Movement

Hyper-V provides you with the ability to move both a VM and its virtual disk drives to other systems with the VM up and running—live migration.

Before You Start

This section uses the two Hyper-V hosts you have used in this chapter. This section assumes you have created the HVDirect VM and that it's running on HV1.

In the previous section, you ended up with the HVDirect VM running on HV2. You can revert the running of HVDirect back to HV1 with this syntax:

```
# 0. Revert VMs before starting
Stop-VM -Name HVDirect -ComputerName HV2 -Force
Remove-VM -Name HVDirect -ComputerName HV2 -Force
Start-VM HVDirect -ComputerName HV1
```

Viewing the HVDirect VM

You start this section by examining the state of the HVDirect nested VM on HV1, using the Get-VM command.

```
# 1. View the HVDirect VM on HV1 and verify that it is running and not
saved
Get-VM -Name HVDirect
```

You can see the results of this command in Figure 8.50.

```
PS C:\Foo> # 1. View the HVDirect VM on HV1 and verify that it is turned off and not saved
PS C:\Foo> Get-VM –Name HVDirect

Name      State    CPUUsage(%) MemoryAssigned(M) Uptime         Status              Version
----      -----    ----------- ----------------- ------         ------              -------
HVDirect  Running 1            4096              00:03:11.0230000 Operating normally 9.0
```

Figure 8.50: Viewing HVDirect VM

You should see the HVDirect VM, which you created in "Creating a Hyper-V VM." Depending on how you have configured the VM, your output might be slightly different—for example you might see a different amount of memory.

Getting VM Configuration Location

Next, you need to see the folder that Hyper-V is currently using to hold the configuration information for the HVDirect VM. Do that using the Get-VM command.

```
# 2. Get the VM configuration location
(Get-VM -Name HVDirect).ConfigurationLocation
```

You can see the output of this command in Figure 8.51.

```
PS C:\Foo> # 2. Get the VM configuration location
PS C:\Foo> (Get-VM -Name HVDirect).ConfigurationLocation
C:\VM\VMS\HVDirect
```

Figure 8.51: Viewing the VM configuration path

If you have run the code in "Managing VM Replication," you may see a different path. Irrespective of where Hyper-V stores this information, later steps in this section change the location.

In an enterprise deployment of Hyper-V, you would typically hold the virtual hard drives on a SAN or via an SMB3 scale-out file server. In production, the VM details and the virtual hard drives are on separate hosts connected by a fast network.

Getting VM Hard Drive Locations

You use the Get-VMHardDiskDrive command to get details of the virtual hard drives contained in the HVDirect VM.

```
# 3. Get Hard Drive locations
Get-VMHardDiskDrive -VMName HVDirect |
    Format-Table -Property VMName, ControllerType, Path
```

You can see the output of this command in Figure 8.52.

```
PS C:\Foo> # 3. Get Hard Drive locations
PS C:\Foo> Get-VMHardDiskDrive -VMName HVDirect |
             Format-Table -Property VMName, ControllerType, Path

VMName    ControllerType Path
------    -------------- ----
HVDirect             IDE C:\VM\VHDS\HVDirect.Vhdx
HVDirect            SCSI C:\VM\VHDS\HVDirect-D.VHDX
```

Figure 8.52: Getting the VM hard drive locations for HVDirect

If you have run the commands in "Managing VM Replication," you may see a different file paths, but the virtual drive name is the same. And as with the

VM details location, what is important is where the files are now since they change using the later steps in this section.

Migrating VM Storage

You can move the virtual disk drives used by a running VM using the Move-VMStorage command.

```
# 4. Move the VMs to the C:\HVD_NEW folder
$MHT = @{
  Name                = 'HVDirect'
  DestinationStoragePath = 'C:\HVD_NEW'
}
Move-VMStorage @MHT
```

This command moves the files to the path you specify. In this case, you are just moving the virtual disks on a local hard drive. Instead of storing the VHD files on the local hard disk, you could store them on a remote host or your SAN.

It is important to also note that moving files did not require the VM to be stopped—this was a "live" storage migration.

Viewing Configuration Details

After you have moved the VM's storage, you can view the configuration details again using the Get-VM and Get-VMHardDiskDrive commands.

```
# 5. View the configuration details after moving the VM's storage
(Get-VM -Name HVDirect).ConfigurationLocation
Get-VMHardDiskDrive -VMName HVDirect |
  Format-Table -Property VMName, ControllerType, Path
```

Figure 8.53 shows the output from these commands.

```
PS C:\Foo> # 5. View the configuration details after moving the VM's storage
PS C:\Foo> (Get-VM -Name HVDirect).ConfigurationLocation
C:\HVD_NEW

PS C:\Foo> Get-VMHardDiskDrive -VMName HVDirect |
           Format-Table -Property VMName, ControllerType, Path

VMName    ControllerType Path
------    -------------- ----
HVDirect             IDE C:\HVD_NEW\Virtual Hard Disks\HVDirect.Vhdx
HVDirect            SCSI C:\HVD_NEW\Virtual Hard Disks\HVDirect-D.VHDX
```

Figure 8.53: Viewing the VM configuration path

As you can see in the output, the virtual disk drives for the `HVDirect` VM are now in a different location. Had you been running applications inside the VM, they would continue running as normal.

Viewing VMs on HV2

Prior to migrating an entire VM, you should first look at the VMs currently running on HV2, using `Get-VM`.

```
# 6. Get the VM details for VMs from HV2
Get-VM -ComputerName HV2
```

This command produces no output—there are no VMs running on HV2.

Enabling VM Migration

Installing Hyper-V does not enable VM replication by default. But that is easy to change using `Enable-VMMigration`.

```
# 7. Enable VM migration on both HV1 and HV2
Enable-VMMigration -ComputerName HV1, HV2
```

This command enables VM replication on both HV1 and HV2.

Configuring VM Migration

Hyper-V provides a number of options for configuring migration. These allow for the different deployment scenarios you might find in production. You might run VMs in production on domain-joined hosts but need to migrate VMs to a host in a work group or a separate domain. In this case, you use Kerberos authentication and configure the replication using `Set-VMHost`, as follows:

```
# 8. Configure VM Migration on both hosts
$SVHT = @{
  UseAnyNetworkForMigration                 = $true
  ComputerName                              = 'HV1', 'HV2'
  VirtualMachineMigrationAuthenticationType = 'Kerberos'
  VirtualMachineMigrationPerformanceOption  = 'Compression'
}
Set-VMHost @SVHT
```

Because both HV1 and HV2 are in the Reskit domain, you can use Kerberos for authentication between the two hosts. Were these hosts in different security realms (for example, with one Hyper-V host in your network and the other in a disaster recovery partner's network), then you could use certificate authentication.

Migrating a VM Between Hosts

To migrate a running VM from one host (HV1) to another (HV2), you use the Move-VM command.

```
# 9. Move the VM to HV2
$Start = Get-Date
$VMHT = @{
    Name                   = 'HVDirect'
    ComputerName           = 'HV1'
    DestinationHost        = 'HV2'
    IncludeStorage         = $true
    DestinationStoragePath = 'C:\HVDirect' # on HV2
}
Move-VM @VMHT
$Finish = Get-Date
```

Hyper-V performs the migration as fast as it can, but the migration time depends on several factors, including the load on the two Hyper-V servers and the quality of the network.

Displaying Migration Time

After the migration has completed, you can subtract the two date/time objects to calculate how long it took Hyper-V to migrate the VM from HV1 to HV2.

```
# 10. Display the time taken to migrate
$OS = "Migration took: [{0:n2}] minutes"
$OS -f ($($Finish-$Start).TotalMinutes)
```

You can see the output of these commands in Figure 8.54.

```
PS C:\Foo> # 10. Display the time taken to migrate
PS C:\Foo> $OS = "Migration took: [{0:n2}] minutes"
PS C:\Foo> $OS -f ($($Finish-$Start).TotalMinutes)
Migration took: [3.11] minutes
```

Figure 8.54: Displaying migration time

The migration time shown in this figure came from running this step on a high-speed multiprocessor system. In production, the time taken to migrate a VM will vary depending on the size of the virtual hard drives and CPU load on both the two VM hosts. You also need to factor in the load on the network(s) connecting the two Hyper-V hosts. If you migrate a large production VM across a suboptimal WAN, migration times are likely to be a lot longer. If you plan to use migration often, it might be useful to test the migration time to inform future planning.

Live migration using Move-VM is an easy way to move a VM to a new home (and back again as needed). But for large VMs, the time it takes to copy the virtual hard disks may be an issue. If you are regularly moving VMs around, the Hyper-V Replica tool, as you saw in "Using VM Replication," might be more useful.

Checking VMs on HV1

Now that you have migrated your HVDirect VM to HV2, you can use Get-VM to look at the VMs on HV1.

```
# 11. Check the VMs on HV1
Get-VM -ComputerName HV1
```

Assuming that the migration was successful, you should see no output from this command—there are no VMs running on HV1.

Checking VMs on HV2

You can also use Get-VM to look at the VMs on HV2.

```
# 12. Check the VMs on HV2
Get-VM -ComputerName HV2
```

You can see the output from this command in Figure 8.55.

```
PS C:\Foo> # 12. Check the VMs on HV2
PS C:\Foo> Get-VM –ComputerName HV2

Name      State   CPUUsage(%) MemoryAssigned(M) Uptime            Status            Version
----      -----   ----------- ----------------- ------            ------            -------
HVDirect  Running 1           4096              00:05:09.5150000  Operating normally 9.0
```

Figure 8.55: Viewing the VMs on HV2

In this case, you should see the HVDirect VM is now running on HV2.

Examining Virtual Disk Details

You can also get the details of where Hyper-V now stores the VM configuration details for the HVDirect VM and the details of the virtual drives used in this VM, like so:

```
# 13. Look at the details of the moved VM
(Get-VM -Name HVDirect -Computer HV2).ConfigurationLocation
Get-VMHardDiskDrive -VMName HVDirect -Computer HV2   |
  Format-Table -Property VMName, Path
```

You can see the output from these commands in Figure 8.56.

```
PS C:\Foo> # 13. Look at the details of the moved VM
PS C:\Foo> (Get-VM -Name HVDirect -Computer HV2).ConfigurationLocation
C:\HVDirect

PS C:\Foo> Get-VMHardDiskDrive -VMName HVDirect -Computer HV2  |
            Format-Table -Property VMName, Path

VMName    Path
------    ----
HVDirect  C:\HVDirect\Virtual Hard Disks\HVDirect.VHDX
HVDirect  C:\HVDirect\Virtual Hard Disks\HVDirect-D.VHDX
```

Figure 8.56: Examining VM details

As you can see, the VM configuration details are now stored in C:\HVDirect, and the virtual hard drives are held in C:\HVDirect\Virtual Hard Disks.

Measuring VM Resource Usage

If you deploy Hyper-V in production, you may find you are running different VMs that belong to different cost centers and you need to measure resource usage of VMs for chargeback. You can use Hyper-V *resource metering* to determine the resources used by a given VM. In turn, this can enable you to measure accurately both the assigned capacity and current usage of key resources (such as CPU). This Hyper-V feature removes the need to develop chargeback solutions, which can be complex and expensive to develop, depending on your requirements.

With resource metering, Hyper-V enables you to measure the following key resources:

- Average CPU usage
- Average physical memory usage
- Minimum memory usage
- Maximum memory usage
- Maximum amount of disk space allocated to a virtual machine
- Total incoming network traffic
- Total outgoing network traffic

Before You Start

This section uses the Hyper-V VM (HVDirect) and the two Hyper-V hosts (HV1, HV2) that you have used throughout this chapter. The section assumes that HVDirect VM is running on HV2 (that is, the state after you've completed "Managing VM Movement").

Getting VM Details

You can ensure that you have at least one VM running on HV2, using Get-VM.

```
# 1. Get-VMs on HV2
$VM = Get-VM
$VM
```

You can see the output from these two commands in Figure 8.57.

```
PS C:\Foo> # 1. Get-VMs on HV2
PS C:\Foo> $VM = Get-VM
PS C:\Foo> $VM

Name      State CPUUsage(%) MemoryAssigned(M) Uptime   Status            Version
----      ----- ----------- ----------------- ------   ------            -------
HVDirect Off    0           0                 00:00:00 Operating normally 9.0
```

Figure 8.57: Examining VM details

You should see, in this figure, just one VM, HVDirect.

Enabling VM Resource Monitoring

You use the Enable-VMResourcedMetering command to enable Hyper-V to do resource monitoring for the HVDirect VM.

```
# 2. Enable resource monitoring of HVDirect
Enable-VMResourceMetering -VM $VM
```

This command directs Hyper-V to do the resource monitoring for just one VM. In general, you will probably want to enable resource monitoring on all your VMs.

Starting the HVDirect VM

If the VM is not running, you can use the Start-VM command to start the VM.

```
# 3. Start VM if needed
If ($VM.State -ne 'Running') {
  Start-VM $VM
  Wait-VM -VM $VM -FOR IPAddress
}
```

This ensures the VM is up and running.

Creating Credentials for HVDirect

You need a credential object for the HVDirect VM, which you can create as follows:

```
# 4. Create Credentials for HVDirect
$User = 'Tiger\Administrator'
$PHT = @{
  String      = 'Pa$$w0rd'
  AsPlainText = $true
  Force       = $true
}
$PSS     = ConvertTo-SecureString @PHT
$Type    = 'System.Management.Automation.PSCredential'
$CredHVD = New-Object -TypeName $Type -ArgumentList $User,$PSS
```

These commands create a credential object for the VM. In this case, you are creating credentials for the administrator of the host.

Getting Initial Resource Measurements

With the HVDirect VM running and with Hyper-V measuring resource usage, you can get an initial set of measurements by using Measure-VM.

```
# 5. Get Initial Measurements
Measure-VM -VM $VM
```

You can see the output from this command in Figure 8.58.

```
PS C:\Foo> # 5. Get Initial Measurements
PS C:\Foo> Measure-VM -VM $VM

VMName    AvgCPU(MHz) AvgRAM(M) MaxRAM(M) MinRAM(M) TotalDisk(M) NetworkInbound(M) NetworkOutbound(M)
------    ----------- --------- --------- --------- ------------ ----------------- ------------------
HVDirect  372         2876      4096      4096      139264       2                 2
```

Figure 8.58: Measuring VM resource usage

Performing Compute Work

To get the VM to do some compute work (and increase the CPU usage of the HVDirect VM), you can invoke a simple compute-bound script block inside the VM.

```
# 6. Do some Compute Work in the VM
$SB ={
    1..10000000 | ForEach-Object {$I++;$I--}
}
Invoke-Command -VMName HVDirect -ScriptBlock $SB -Cred $CredHVD
```

These commands, which produce no output, increment and then decrement the value of the $I variable within a PowerShell session running on the VM. These operations primarily use CPU time in the VM.

Measuring VM Resource Usage Again

After starting and running some compute work in the VM, you can re-measure the resources used by HVDirect with the Measure-VM command.

```
# 7. Get Additional Measurements
Measure-VM -VM $VM
```

You can see the output in Figure 8.59.

```
PS C:\Foo> # 7. Get Additional Measurements
PS C:\Foo> Measure-VM -VM $VM

VMName     AvgCPU(MHz) AvgRAM(M) MaxRAM(M) MinRAM(M) TotalDisk(M) NetworkInbound(M) NetworkOutbound(M)
--------   ----------- --------- --------- --------- ------------ ----------------- ------------------
HVDirect 628          3102      4096      4096      139264       2                 2
```

Figure 8.59: Remeasuring VM resource usage after computation

As you can see in the output, the amount of average CPU usage has gone up based on the compute work you just carried out.

The exact numbers that Measure-VM produces for you are highly likely to differ from those shown in this chapter. The key thing to note is that after doing some computation within a VM, the measurements show an increased use of CPU within the VM. In a chargeback scenario, the extra work might attract additional costs to the VM owner.

Summary

In this chapter, you examined numerous aspects of Hyper-V, including installing Hyper-V, creating and managing VMs, configuring and using nested virtualization, and using VM replication and VM (and VM storage) migration. You also saw how to measure VM resource usage on the VM host.

Using WMI with CIM Cmdlets

Windows Management Instrumentation (WMI) is Microsoft's implementation of Web-Based Enterprise Management (WBEM) and the Common Information Model (CIM). WBEM is a standards-based management tool that unifies the management of distributed computing environments. The CIM is a standard for defining how device and application characteristics are represented. The Distributed Management Task Force (DMTF) created both standards with considerable industry input.

> **NOTE** Work on WBEM began in 1996. BMC Software, Cisco Systems, Compaq Computer, Intel, and Microsoft sponsored the early work. Microsoft provided an initial implementation of WBEM with WMI for Windows NT 4 and Windows 95. WMI has evolved significantly ever since. WMI is a fundamental Windows component used by a variety of Windows features and applications. PowerShell leverages WMI and provides the IT professional with easy access to the rich capabilities of WMI.

WBEM was originally designed to use web-based protocols, such as HTTP, to communicate. The Microsoft implementation was WMI, based instead on using the Component Object Model (COM) and Distributed COM (DCOM). Both COM and DCOM were popular and relatively fast at the time. Later versions of PowerShell and WMI incorporated Windows Remote Management (WinRM) remoting for WMI. This enabled you to access WMI on remote systems.

Internally, WMI is based on COM and not .NET. The .NET Framework provides applications with a way to access and leverage COM components. When the WMI subsystem returns data, .NET encapsulates it in .NET objects. When the literature talks about WMI objects with respect to PowerShell, technically they are talking about WMI data returned in a .NET object.

The great thing about this is that you use WMI objects (aka WMI data wrapped in a .NET object) the same way that you use other .NET objects. Invoking WMI methods is a little different than invoking .NET methods, as explained in "Invoking Static and Dynamic Methods."

PowerShell 7 is based on .NET. Cmdlets such as `Get-Process` are little more than wrappers around objects provided by the .NET Framework. When you call `Get-Process`, for example, the cmdlet uses the `System.Diagnostics.Process` class to obtain the Windows process details via the `GetProcesses()` method. For details about the class, you can view `docs.microsoft.com/dotnet/api/system.diagnostics.process?view=netcore-3.0`.

In this book so far, you have dealt with a large number of .NET objects. You looked at the AD-related objects in Chapter 3, "Managing Active Directory," and at the various objects used by Hyper-V in Chapter 8, "Managing Hyper-V." The terminology for WMI is similar to that for .NET objects but with some small differences. This chapter covers the following topics:

- In "Exploring WMI Namespaces," you learn WMI data is stored in classes that reside in namespaces. You look at the namespaces that exist on the local and remote hosts.

- In "Exploring WMI Classes," you discover the members of WMI classes and examine how to discover details about WMI objects.

- In "Getting Local and Remote WMI Objects," you retrieve WMI information from local and remote hosts.

- In "Invoking WMI Methods," you invoke a WMI method to create and remove an SMB share.

- In "Managing WMI Events," you look at creating event handlers using PowerShell. To demonstrate WMI's power, you create a WMI permanent event handler to protect AD groups from being "accidentally improved" by unauthorized users being added into high privilege groups by persons unknown.

WMI is a complex subject, and this chapter does not have the space to go into a lot of detail. You can read more about WMI in Richard Siddaway's *PowerShell and WMI* (Manning, 2012). Note that this book goes into depth about WMI, and all of its code examples use the WMI cmdlets rather than the CIM cmdlets we use here. That being said, much of its discussion of WMI features and functions is still relevant even if you now access them via different cmdlets.

Reviewing WMI Architecture in Windows

Before proceeding, it's useful to have a better understanding of the WMI architecture, which you can view in Figure 9.1.

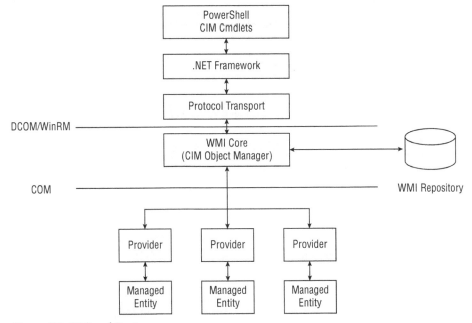

Figure 9.1: WMI architecture

The WMI architecture comprises multiple components:

CIM cmdlets: The CIM cmdlets provide access to the functions and features of WMI. The CIM cmdlets shipped initially with PowerShell 3 as an alternative to the WMI cmdlets that shipped with PowerShell 1. With PowerShell 7, the earlier WMI cmdlets are no longer available or supported, so all WMI access is via the CIM cmdlets.

.NET Framework: PowerShell cmdlets, including the CIM cmdlets, make use of the .NET Framework, which provides a mechanism to access COM and interact with WMI.

Protocol Transport: WMI needs some mechanism to communicate between the various components. The WBEM specification used HTTP/S as a transport layer. However, Microsoft implemented WMI using COM (and DCOM) to enable individual WMI components to communicate and interoperate. WMI is, in effect, a large multicomponent application built in

COM. The WMI COM API enables .NET applications such as PowerShell to access this COM application. For remote access, the CIM cmdlets use WinRM by default as a transport but can work with DCOM for interoperability reasons.

CIM Object Manager (CIMOM): At the heart of WMI is the CIMOM, which manages access to the objects within WMI. Some objects are stored in the CIM database, while others are synthesized via WMI providers. The CIM cmdlets communicate with the CIMOM to manage access to data in the CIM database.

CIM Database (CIMDB): WMI stores information about WMI-Managed objects in the CIMDB, also known as the WMI repository. The CIM cmdlets allow you to query and update this repository. This database is, in effect, a hierarchical database based on namespaces and classes.

Provider: A provider manages entities in WMI. It implements class methods and events (see "Managing WMI Events" and "Implementing Permanent WMI Event Handling" later in this chapter). A provider enables WMI to interoperate with various Windows components and subsystems (including AD, networking, and more). A provider can also create WMI objects dynamically as an alternative to storing them in the CIMDB. For more details on the providers built into Windows, see `docs.microsoft.com/en-us/windows/win32/wmisdk/wmi-providers`.

Managed Entity: This refers to any component that WMI exposes to the CIM cmdlets, such as the BIOS, a network card, or the operating system running at the time. Each managed entity is represented by one or more WMI classes. You use the CIM cmdlets to manage these entities.

In WMI, you use the CIM cmdlets to interact with managed entities. The cmdlets enable you to add, update, and remove information from the CIMDB (and react to events that occur within a Windows system). WMI providers do much of the actual work involved, with the other layers just part of the plumbing.

Obtaining WMI Data

The CIMDB is a hierarchical database, which WMI uses as its data store. It consists of a hierarchy of namespaces and classes. A WMI *namespace* is a container object that can contain child namespaces and classes. The root WMI namespace is named `root`. The CIM cmdlets use the namespace `root\CIMV2` as a default namespace.

A WMI *class* is a definition of a WMI-Managed object. A WMI class, which lives in a namespace, contains members including properties and methods. One example is the `Win32_Share` class, which defines an SMB share. Although you can use WMI to manage SMB shares, you are more likely to use the SMB cmdlets described in Chapter 6, "Managing Shared Data."

> **NOTE**   Best practice is to use SMB cmdlets rather than the CIM cmdlets to manage SMB shares. The SMB cmdlets in the SMB share module are often easier to use and are far easier to understand/modify when that becomes necessary. The `Win32_Share` WMI class, nevertheless, is useful as an introduction to WMI.

A *property* is an attribute of a WMI class. A `Win32_Share` has a property `Name`, which is the name of the SMB share. Each property has a data type, such as `String` or `Int`. The `Name` property in the `Win32_Share` class is `String`. Some classes (and properties) have names that begin with two underscore characters (__). These are system classes and properties and generally are not of much use to IT professionals, with some exceptions.

A *method* is some action that a WMI object or class is able to carry out. There are two method types you can use: dynamic and static. A *dynamic* method is one based on an occurrence of a class. For example, the `Delete()` method in the `Win32_Share` class deletes the SMB share related to a specific share object. A *static* method is one that is carried out by the class itself. The `Win32_Share` class has a static method `Create()`, which you could use to create an SMB share.

A WMI *event* is created, or fired, whenever a specific event occurs within Windows. You can subscribe to events and view the information provided. The `__ClassOperationEvent`, for example, is fired whenever an occurrence of a class is added, changed, or removed within a namespace. Events in WMI are powerful, as you can see in "Managing WMI Events."

When you use the CIM cmdlets to retrieve class instances, PowerShell returns the data wrapped in a .NET object. For example, when you retrieve the SMB share objects from the `Win32_Share` class, the data representing each SMB share is returned contained in an object of the type `Microsoft.Management.Infrastructure.CimInstance`. This approach simplifies retrieving data from WMI, as the objects are basically the same as the .NET objects you have used throughout this book.

Using the CIM Cmdlets

With the first version of Windows PowerShell, Microsoft shipped a set of WMI cmdlets that enabled basic access into WMI, although they were not functionally complete and could be hard to use. The WMI cmdlets also relied on DCOM for accessing WMI on remote machines. Although these initial cmdlets were not complete, workarounds were available for the functionality gaps.

With version 3 of Windows PowerShell, Microsoft did some reengineering of WMI. This simplified the implementation of WMI providers, created a new set of cmdlets, and led a drive to push WMI (WBEM) into Linux.

The CIM cmdlets were introduced with PowerShell 3 and provided greatly improved feature coverage. The CIM cmdlets also use different .NET class wrappers, which are smaller. This can reduce the bandwidth when accessing WMI remotely.

Another major improvement is that the CIM cmdlets use WinRM for remote communications. WinRM is easier to secure and can be more lightweight than using DCOM. WinRM is also standards-based, opening up interoperation with Linux and Macintosh hosts. The Open Management Infrastructure project has created an open source version of WMI for Linux.

With the CIM cmdlets, you can create a CIM session with a remote machine. Once the session is established, you can run multiple WMI operations on the remote machine without incurring the relatively large setup costs. If necessary, you can create a CIM session using DCOM, which allows you to use the newer commands against older hosts that do not support WinRM.

Systems Used in This Chapter

This chapter uses several hosts: DC1 and DC2, which are domain controllers in the Reskit.Org domain, and SRV2, which is a member server in the domain. You have used all these servers in previous chapters in this book.

Exploring WMI Namespaces

As mentioned in the chapter introduction, WMI data comes from instances within WMI classes that reside in WMI namespaces. In WMI, the root namespace is named ROOT. This root namespace contains both classes and additional namespaces. In every namespace, WMI has an internal class __NAMESPACE that contains the names of namespaces below the current one. This enables you to discover the namespaces available in WMI. Although there are a number of namespaces, not all of them are overly useful to the IT professional.

Viewing Classes in the Root Namespace

You can begin your exploration of WMI data by looking at the classes that WMI contains in the root namespace, using Get-CimClass like this:

```
# 1. View CIM classes in the root namespace
Get-CimClass -Namespace 'root' | Select-Object -First 20
```

You can see the output from this command in Figure 9.2.

This output shows the first 20 classes in the root WMI namespace. As you can see, many these classes begin with __ (two underline characters). These are internal or system classes used by WMI and typically contain little of use for the IT professional. From a structural point of view, WMI applications can use the __NAMESPACE class as the key to building a complete hierarchy of namespaces within WMI, as you will see shortly.

```
PS C:\Foo> # 1. View CIM classes in the root namespace
PS C:\Foo> Get-CimClass -Namespace 'root' | Select-Object -First 20

   NameSpace: ROOT

CimClassName                          CimClassMethods CimClassProperties
------------                          --------------- ------------------
__SystemClass                         {}              {}
__thisNAMESPACE                       {}              {SECURITY_DESCRIPTOR}
__CacheControl                        {}              {}
__EventConsumerProviderCacheControl   {}              {ClearAfter}
__EventProviderCacheControl           {}              {ClearAfter}
__EventSinkCacheControl               {}              {ClearAfter}
__ObjectProviderCacheControl          {}              {ClearAfter}
__PropertyProviderCacheControl        {}              {ClearAfter}
__ArbitratorConfiguration             {}              {OutstandingTasksPerUser, OutstandingTasksTotal, Pe
__CIMOMIdentification                 {}              {SetupDateTime, VersionCurrentlyRunning, VersionUse
__NAMESPACE                           {}              {Name}
__ProviderHostQuotaConfiguration      {}              {HandlesPerHost, MemoryAllHosts, MemoryPerHost, Pro
__Provider                            {}              {Name}
__Win32Provider                       {}              {Name, ClientLoadableCLSID, CLSID, Concurrency, Def
__ProviderRegistration                {}              {provider}
__EventProviderRegistration           {}              {provider, EventQueryList}
__ObjectProviderRegistration          {}              {provider, InteractionType, QuerySupportLevels, Sup
__ClassProviderRegistration           {}              {provider, InteractionType, QuerySupportLevels, Sup
__InstanceProviderRegistration        {}              {provider, InteractionType, QuerySupportLevels, Sup
__MethodProviderRegistration          {}              {provider}
```

Figure 9.2: Viewing classes in root namespace

Viewing Namespaces Below the Root

The WMI root namespace is named `root`. The namespaces directly below `root` are contained in the WMI class `__NAMESPACE`. You can view the top-level namespaces—that is, the namespaces that are children of `root`—by getting the occurrences of this class, as follows:

```
# 2. Look in __NAMESPACE in Root
Get-CimInstance -Namespace 'root' -ClassName __NAMESPACE |
   Sort-Object -Property Name
```

You can see the output from this command in Figure 9.3.

Enumerating Classes in root\CIMV2

The classes in the `root\CIMV2` namespace are the ones that are most useful for IT professionals. To simplify access to the most commonly used classes, WMI uses the `root\CIMV2` as the default namespace for scripting.

You could use the `WmiMgmt.msc` management console to change this default. If you are using classes in non-default namespaces from the command line, this might be convenient, but that could be dangerous if you have production scripts that assume the default; changing the default could break those scripts. So make sure you test any changes to the default carefully—or just leave the default as is.

```
PS C:\Foo> # 2. Look in __NAMESPACE in Root
PS C:\Foo> Get-CimInstance -Namespace 'root' -ClassName __NAMESPACE |
            Sort-Object -Property Name


Name                        PSComputerName
----                        --------------
AccessLogging
Appv
CIMV2
Cli
DEFAULT
directory
Hardware
Interop
InventoryLogging
Microsoft
MicrosoftActiveDirectory
MicrosoftDfs
MicrosoftDNS
msdtc
PEH
Policy
RSOP
SECURITY
ServiceModel
StandardCimv2
subscription
WMI
```

Figure 9.3: Viewing namespaces in root

To get and count all the classes in this important WMI namespace, you can use the `Get-CimClass` cmdlet, like this:

```
# 3. Get and count classes in root\CIMV2
$Classes = Get-CimClass -Namespace 'root\CIMV2'
"There are $($Classes.Count) classes in root\CIMV2"
```

You can view the number of classes in the root\CIMV2 namespace in Figure 9.4.

```
PS C:\Foo> # 3. Get and count classes in root\CIMV2
PS C:\Foo> $Classes = Get-CimClass -Namespace 'root\CIMV2'
PS C:\Foo> "There are $($Classes.Count) classes in root\CIMV2"
There are 1212 classes in root\CIMV2
```

Figure 9.4: Getting classes in the root \ CIMV2 namespace

Depending on the features you have installed, the exact number of classes could vary. There are around 400 classes that might be of use to the IT professional. The root\CIMV2 namespace contains around 350 performance-related classes, which you examine later in this chapter and in Chapter 10, "Reporting."

Discovering All Namespaces in WMI

Since every namespace contains a __NAMESPACE class containing the names of child namespaces, you can discover the names of all the namespaces within WMI, as follows:

```
# 4. Discovering ALL namespaces on DC1
Function Get-WMINamespaceEnum {
  [CmdletBinding()]
  Param($NS)
  Write-Output $NS
  Get-CimInstance "__Namespace" -Namespace $NS -ErrorAction
SilentlyContinue |
  ForEach-Object { Get-WMINamespaceEnum "$ns\$($_.name)"   }
}  # End of function
$Namespaces = Get-WMINamespaceEnum 'root' | Sort-Object
"There are $($Namespaces.Count) WMI namespaces on this host"
```

You can see the output from these commands in Figure 9.5.

```
PS C:\Foo> # 4. Discovering ALL namespaces on DC1
PS C:\Foo> Function Get-WMINamespaceEnum {
            [CmdletBinding()]
            Param($NS)
            Write-Output $NS
            Get-CimInstance "__Namespace" -Namespace $NS -ErrorAction SilentlyContinue |
            ForEach-Object { Get-WMINamespaceEnum "$ns\$($_.name)"   }
          }  # End of function
PS C:\Foo> $Namespaces = Get-WMINamespaceEnum 'root' | Sort-Object
PS C:\Foo> "There are $($Namespaces.Count) WMI namespaces on this host"

There are 108 WMI namespaces on this host
```

Figure 9.5: Getting all namespaces

This code snippet, which was originally written by Alan Renouf (see akaplan .com/2019/02/get-wmi-namespaces-with-powershell/), defines a recursive function, Get-WMINameSpaceEnum, which initially gets all the namespaces in the root namespace, and then calls the function recursively to get all the namespaces within each child namespace. This produces a complete set of namespaces, which is then sorted in alphabetic order.

As you can see, there are 108 namespaces on DC1. Adding applications or Windows features can add additional WMI namespaces as well as adding classes to existing namespaces.

Viewing Some WMI Namespaces

You can view some of the namespaces in WMI on DC1 with this syntax:

```
# 5. View some of the namespaces
$Namespaces |
  Select-Object -First 20
```

You can see the first 20 namespaces on WMI in Figure 9.6.

```
PS C:\Foo> # 5. View some of the namespaces
PS C:\Foo> $Namespaces |
             Select-Object -First 20
root
root\AccessLogging
root\Appv
root\CIMV2
root\CIMV2\mdm
root\CIMV2\mdm\dmmap
root\CIMV2\mdm\MS_409
root\CIMV2\MS_409
root\CIMV2\power
root\CIMV2\power\ms_409
root\CIMV2\Security
root\CIMV2\Security\MicrosoftTpm
root\CIMV2\TerminalServices
root\CIMV2\TerminalServices\ms_409
root\Cli
root\Cli\MS_409
root\DEFAULT
root\DEFAULT\ms_409
root\directory
root\directory\LDAP
```

Figure 9.6: Viewing some namespaces

Most of these namespaces are of little interest, but a few are useful as you see later in this chapter. In particular, you use the root\CIMV2 and root\directory\ LDAP namespaces in later exercises.

Counting WMI Classes

You can use the set of namespaces, combined with Get-CimClass, to display a count of all the classes within WMI on DC1 using this snippet:

```
# 6. Counting WMI classes on DC1
$WMIClasses = @()
Foreach ($Namespace in $Namespaces) {
  $WMIClasses += Get-CimClass -Namespace $Namespace
}
"There are $($WMIClasses.count) classes on $(hostname)"
```

As shown in Figure 9.7, this displays a count of all the WMI classes on DC1. This count of available WMI classes demonstrates the richness of WMI. Once you have retrieved all the WMI classes, you can use PowerShell to find classes that might be useful. You could pipe $WMIClasses to Where-Object, looking for class names that might be of interest.

```
PS C:\Foo> # 6. Counting WMI classes on DC1
PS C:\Foo> $WMIClasses = @()
PS C:\Foo> Foreach ($Namespace in $Namespaces) {
            $WMIClasses += Get-CimClass -Namespace $Namespace
       }
PS C:\Foo> "There are $($WMIClasses.count) classes on $(hostname)"

There are 15511 classes on DC1
```

Figure 9.7: Counting classes

Viewing Namespaces on a Remote Server

The CIM commands also work well across the network. It's easy to discover the namespaces on a remote host, such as SRV2, with this syntax:

```
# 7. View namespaces on SRV2
Get-CimInstance -Namespace root -ClassName __NAMESPACE -CimSession SRV2
```

In Figure 9.8 you can see the results of this command, namely, the top-level WMI namespaces on SRV2.

```
PS C:\Foo> # 7. View namespaces on SRV2
PS C:\Foo> Get-CimInstance -Namespace root -ClassName __NAMESPACE -CimSession SRV2

Name                PSComputerName
----                --------------
subscription        SRV2
DEFAULT             SRV2
CIMV2               SRV2
msdtc               SRV2
Cli                 SRV2
SECURITY            SRV2
RSOP                SRV2
PEH                 SRV2
StandardCimv2       SRV2
WMI                 SRV2
AccessLogging       SRV2
directory           SRV2
Policy              SRV2
InventoryLogging    SRV2
interop             SRV2
Hardware            SRV2
ServiceModel        SRV2
Microsoft           SRV2
Appv                SRV2
```

Figure 9.8: Viewing namespaces on SRV2

The -CimSession parameter accepts either a CIM session (that is, one that you previously created) or a computer name. If you pass a computer name, Get-CimInstance creates a CIM session with the remote host, runs the command over that session, and then destroys the session.

As you can see, the namespaces are not listed in alphabetic order. You can pipe the output of this command to Sort-Object to sort the list into alphabetic order.

Counting Namespaces/Classes on SRV2

To show how easy it is to use the CIM cmdlets across a network and to show the differences in available CIM classes, you can count the total number of WMI namespaces and classes on a remote host. To do that, you can combine some of the earlier code snippets into a script block and then run that script block on a remote host, like this:

```
# 8. Enumerate all namespaces and Classes on SRV2
$SB = {
  Function Get-WMINamespaceEnum {
    [CmdletBinding()]
    Param(
      $NS
    )
    Write-Output $NS
    Get-CimInstance "__Namespace" -Namespace $NS -ErrorAction
SilentlyContinue |
      ForEach-Object { Get-WMINamespaceEnum "$ns\$($_.name)" }
  } # End of function
  $Namespaces = Get-WMINamespaceEnum 'root' | Sort-Object
  $WMIClasses = @()
  Foreach ($Namespace in $Namespaces) {
  $WMIClasses += Get-CimClass -Namespace $Namespace
  }
  "There are $($Namespaces.count) WMI namespaces on $(hostname)"
  "There are $($WMIClasses.count) classes on $(hostname)"
}
Invoke-Command -ComputerName SRV2 -ScriptBlock $SB
```

You can see, from the output shown in Figure 9.9, that there are 104 WMI namespaces and 14,120 WMI classes on SRV2.

When you add features or applications to a Windows host, you can find added WMI namespaces and classes. It is normal that the number of classes differs between systems.

```
PS C:\Foo> # 8 Enumerate all namespaces and Classes on SRV2
PS C:\Foo> $SB = {
          Function Get-WMINamespaceEnum {
            [CmdletBinding()]
            Param(
              $NS
              )
            Write-Output $NS
            Get-CimInstance "__Namespace" -Namespace $NS -ErrorAction SilentlyContinue |
              ForEach-Object { Get-WMINamespaceEnum "$ns\$($_.name)"   }
            }  # End of function
            $Namespaces = Get-WMINamespaceEnum 'root' | Sort-Object
            $WMIClasses = @()
            Foreach ($Namespace in $Namespaces) {
            $WMIClasses += Get-CimClass -Namespace $Namespace
           }
          "There are $($Namespaces.count) WMI namespaces on $(hostname)"
          "There are $($WMIClasses.count) classes on $(hostname)"
        }
PS C:\Foo> Invoke-Command -ComputerName SRV2 -ScriptBlock $SB
There are 104 WMI namespaces on SRV2
There are 14120 classes on SRV2
```

Figure 9.9: Counting namespaces and classes on SRV2

Counting Namespaces/Classes on DC2

You can also run this script block on the other domain controller in the Reskit.Org domain (DC2), like this:

```
# 9. Run the script block on DC2
Invoke-Command -ComputerName DC2 -ScriptBlock $SB
```

You can see the output from this command in Figure 9.10.

```
PS C:\Foo> Run the script block on DC2
PS C:\Foo> Invoke-Command -ComputerName DC2 -ScriptBlock $SB
There are 108 WMI namespaces on DC2
There are 15511 classes on DC2
```

Figure 9.10: Counting namespaces and classes on DC2

As you can see from the figures in this section, the number of namespaces and classes on the three servers varies. This is to be expected. You have installed AD on both DC1 and DC2, which adds namespaces and classes to WMI. SRV2 has other Windows features loaded (including FSRM), which likewise adds classes. Many of the features in Windows come with WMI providers that add namespaces and classes. The classes in WMI provide IT professionals with more options for managing Windows systems.

There is no central registry of all WMI namespaces and classes within a Windows host. Documentation for many namespaces and classes is thin or non-existent. The Win32 WMI provider, which provides many of the classes in the `root\CIMV2` namespace, is covered by some documentation on `docs.microsoft.com`, although it is developer-focused. Your search engine is a good source of information on useful WMI classes.

Exploring WMI Classes

As you discovered in the previous section, WMI on a Windows Server 2019 host contains more than 15,000 WMI classes. Each of those WMI classes can have zero, one, or more than one occurrence. Each occurrence of a class is a separate WMI object, which you can manage using the CIM cmdlets. Before looking at the occurrences, it's useful to explore the WMI class.

The vast majority of the classes in WMI today are of limited or no use to IT professionals. But many can be useful. You use the `Get-CimClass` cmdlet to discover what classes exist in a namespace as well as obtaining details about any given WMI class. Details include the WMI methods supported by the class and the properties on WMI objects.

Examining the Win32_Share Class

You can use the `Get-CimClass` cmdlet to discover the details of the `Win32_Share` class. This class, which is in the `root\CIMV2` namespace, represents the print and file shares offered by the Windows Server service. Each WMI object in this class represents a single share.

While most IT professionals use the SMB share module to manage these shares, as you did in Chapter 6, WMI is an alternative.

To find out more about this class, you use the `Get-CimClass` cmdlet.

```
# 1. View Win32_Share class
Get-CimClass -ClassName Win32_Share
```

Figure 9.11 shows the output from this command.

```
PS C:\Foo> # 1. View Win32_Share class
PS C:\Foo> Get-CimClass -ClassName Win32_Share

   NameSpace: ROOT/cimv2

CimClassName   CimClassMethods       CimClassProperties
------------   ---------------       ------------------
Win32_Share    {Create, SetShareIn… {Caption, Description, Inst…
```

Figure 9.11: Viewing the `Win32_Share` WMI class

Viewing Class Properties

You can use the `Get-CimClass` cmdlet to retrieve details of occurrences of a class. This allows you to see the properties of a given WMI object as well as to discover the data type for each property. You can use the `Select-Object` cmdlet to retrieve property details.

```
# 2. Get Win32_Share class properties
Get-CimClass -ClassName Win32_Share |
  Select-Object -ExpandProperty CimClassProperties |
    Sort-Object -Property Name |
      Format-Table -Property Name, CimType
```

Figure 9.12 shows the output, consisting of the property and data type for the properties of an object of the class `Win32_Share`.

```
PS C:\Foo> # 2. Get Win32_Share class properties
PS C:\Foo> Get-CimClass -ClassName Win32_Share |
            Select-Object -ExpandProperty CimClassProperties |
              Sort-Object -Property Name |
                Format-Table -Property Name, CimType

Name            CimType
----            -------
AccessMask      UInt32
AllowMaximum    Boolean
Caption         String
Description     String
InstallDate     DateTime
MaximumAllowed  UInt32
Name            String
Path            String
Status          String
Type            UInt32
```

Figure 9.12: Counting namespaces and classes on DC1

Viewing Class Methods

Methods are actions that WMI can perform on either a class or a WMI object (an occurrence of a WMI class). WMI methods are generally implemented by WMI providers. You can use the `Get-CimClass` cmdlet to explore details of the methods for a given WMI class.

```
# 3. Get class methods
Get-CimClass -ClassName Win32_Share |
  Select-Object -ExpandProperty CimClassMethods
```

You can see the methods supported by the `Win32_Share` class in Figure 9.13. When you use `Get-CimClass` and do not specify a namespace, WMI assumes the namespace in which to find the specified class is `root\CIMv2`.

```
PS C:\Foo> # 3. Get class methods
PS C:\Foo> Get-CimClass -ClassName Win32_Share |
            Select-Object -ExpandProperty CimClassMethods

Name           ReturnType Parameters                                              Qualifiers
----           ---------- ----------                                              ----------
Create         UInt32     {Access, Description, MaximumAllowed, Name, Password, Path, Type} {Constructor, Implemented, MappingStrings, Static}
SetShareInfo   UInt32     {Access, Description, MaximumAllowed}                    {Implemented, MappingStrings}
GetAccessMask  UInt32     {}                                                      {Implemented, MappingStrings}
Delete         UInt32     {}                                                      {Destructor, Implemented, MappingStrings}
```

Figure 9.13: Viewing the methods supported by the `Win32_Share` class

For each method returned, you can see the names of the parameters (where the methods have any). You can see that the `Delete()` method takes no parameters, whereas the `Create` method takes seven. You can use the previous command to confirm the data type for each parameter.

Viewing Class Details in a Specified Namespace

If you want to view details of a class in a namespace other than the default, you specify it with the `-Namespace` parameter.

```
# 4. Get classes in a non-default namespace
Get-CimClass -Namespace root\directory\LDAP |
    Where-Object CimClassName -match '^ds_Group'
```

You can see the class details in Figure 9.14.

```
PS C:\Foo> # 4. Get classes in a non-default namespace
PS C:\Foo> Get-CimClass -Namespace root\directory\LDAP |
            Where-Object CimClassName -match '^ds_p'

   NameSpace: ROOT/directory/LDAP

CimClassName              CimClassMethods  CimClassProperties
------------              ---------------  ------------------
ds_groupofuniquenames     {}               {ADSIPath, DS_adminDescription, DS_adminDisplayN...
ds_groupofnames           {}               {ADSIPath, DS_adminDescription, DS_adminDisplayN...
ds_group                  {}               {ADSIPath, DS_adminDescription, DS_adminDisplayN...
ds_grouppolicycontainer   {}               {ADSIPath, DS_adminDescription, DS_adminDisplayN...
```

Figure 9.14: Viewing class details with a specified namespace

The AD WMI provider implements the `ds_Group` class in the `\root\directory\LDAP` namespace. Each instance of this class represents an AD group, complete with all the properties you can retrieve using the `Get-ADGroup` command.

Getting Local and Remote Objects

As you have seen, WMI contains a large number of namespaces and classes. While most of the classes are of little or no use to the IT professional, many contain information that can be useful. You use the `Get-CimInstance` cmdlet to return instances of a WMI class.

This cmdlet gets the relevant rows from WMI and returns that information wrapped in a .NET object.

Using Get-CimInstance

You use the `Get-CimInstance` cmdlet to retrieve WMI objects within a given WMI class, like this:

```
# 1. Using Get-CimInstance in default Namespace
Get-CimInstance -ClassName Win32_Share
```

As shown in Figure 9.15, this command returns the objects in the `Win32_Share` class.

```
PS C:\Foo> # 1. Using Get-CimInstance in default Namespace
PS C:\Foo> Get-CimInstance -ClassName Win32_Share

Name      Path                                            Description
----      ----                                            -----------
ADMIN$    C:\Windows                                      Remote Admin
C$        C:\                                             Default share
IPC$                                                      Remote IPC
NETLOGON  C:\Windows\SYSVOL\sysvol\Reskit.Org\SCRIPTS Logon server share
Quorum    C:\Quorum
SYSVOL    C:\Windows\SYSVOL\sysvol                        Logon server share
```

Figure 9.15: Viewing details of the `Win32_Share` class

Each WMI object returned represents a single SMB share on the host.

Getting Objects from a Non-default Namespace

To retrieve the WMI objects from any class that is not in the default `root\WIN32` namespace, you must also specify the namespace, as shown here:

```
# 2. Get WMI objects from non-default namespace
$GCIMHT1 = @{
    Namespace = 'root\directory\LDAP'
    ClassName = 'ds_group'
}
Get-CimInstance @GCIMHT1 |
  Sort-Object -Property Name |
    Select-Object -First 10 |
      Format-Table -Property DS_name, DS_distinguishedName
```

The output from these commands, which is similar to the previous step, is shown in Figure 9.16.

As you can see, retrieving objects from any non-default namespace is pretty simple; you just specify the namespace.

```
PS C:\Foo> # 2. Get WMI objects from non-default namespace
PS C:\Foo> $GCIMHT1 = @{
            Namespace = 'root\directory\LDAP'
            ClassName = 'ds_group'
         }
PS C:\Foo> Get-CimInstance @GCIMHT1 |
            Sort-Object -Property Name |
              Select-Object -First 10 |
                Format-Table -Property DS_name, DS_distinguishedName

DS_name                                 DS_distinguishedName
-------                                 --------------------
Administrators                          CN=Administrators,CN=Builtin,DC=Reskit,DC=Org
Domain Users                            CN=Domain Users,CN=Users,DC=Reskit,DC=Org
Domain Guests                           CN=Domain Guests,CN=Users,DC=Reskit,DC=Org
Group Policy Creator Owners             CN=Group Policy Creator Owners,CN=Users,DC=Reskit,DC=Org
RAS and IAS Servers                     CN=RAS and IAS Servers,CN=Users,DC=Reskit,DC=Org
Server Operators                        CN=Server Operators,CN=Builtin,DC=Reskit,DC=Org
Account Operators                       CN=Account Operators,CN=Builtin,DC=Reskit,DC=Org
Pre-Windows 2000 Compatible Access      CN=Pre-Windows 2000 Compatible Access,CN=Builtin,DC=Reskit,DC=Org
Incoming Forest Trust Builders          CN=Incoming Forest Trust Builders,CN=Builtin,DC=Reskit,DC=Org
Windows Authorization Access Group      CN=Windows Authorization Access Group,CN=Builtin,DC=Reskit,DC=Org
```

Figure 9.16: Viewing details of a class in a non-default namespace

Using a WMI Filter

A WMI *filter* is an expression that filters the objects returned from commands such as Get-CimInstance. A filter is similar to the -FilterScript parameter to the Where-Object cmdlet, but it uses a different syntax, based on the ANSI SQL query language. An important difference between WMI filters and Where-Object is that a WMI filter controls occurrences at the source rather than instantiating them and dropping the ones you are not interested in. This is known as early filtering and is more efficient.

You apply a WMI filter to Get-CimInstance.

```
# 3. Using -Filter
$Filter = "ds_Name LIKE '%operator%' "
Get-CimInstance @GCIMHT1  -Filter $Filter |
   Format-Table -Property ds_Name
```

You can see the output of these commands in Figure 9.17.

```
PS C:\Foo> # 3. Using -Filter
PS C:\Foo> $Filter = "ds_Name like '%operator%' "
PS C:\Foo> Get-CimInstance @GCIMHT1  -Filter $Filter |
            Format-Table -Property ds_Name

ds_Name
-------
Print Operators
Backup Operators
Network Configuration Operators
Cryptographic Operators
Access Control Assistance Operators
Server Operators
Account Operators
```

Figure 9.17: Using the -Filter parameter

In this example, you use the WMI filter to return only those objects where the ds_Name property contains the string "operator."

Note that with the LIKE clause, WQL uses % to match one or more characters, unlike PowerShell's -Like operator, which uses *.

Using a WMI Query

As mentioned, WMI contains a specialized query language, WMI Query Language (WQL), which is, in effect, a limited subset of the ANSI SQL language. WQL contains just a single command (SELECT), which has a few useful clauses. A full WQL query enables you to specify conditions on which instances are returned and which specific properties are returned, which can reduce the bandwidth used when you retrieve remote WMI objects.

You can specify a WMI query to the Get-CimInstance command like this:

```
# 4. Use a WMI Query
$Q = @"
  SELECT * from ds_group
    WHERE ds_Name like '%operator%'
"@
Get-CimInstance -Query $q -Namespace 'root\directory\LDAP' |
  Format-Table ds_Name
```

You can see the output of these commands, the CIM classes from this non-standard namespace that contain "operator" in their names, in Figure 9.18.

```
PS C:\Foo> # 4. Use a WMI Query
PS C:\Foo> $Q = @"
            SELECT * from ds_group
                WHERE ds_Name like '%operator%'
            "@
PS C:\Foo> Get-CimInstance -Query $q -Namespace 'root\directory\LDAP' |
  Format-Table ds_Name

ds_Name
-------
Print Operators
Backup Operators
Network Configuration Operators
Cryptographic Operators
Access Control Assistance Operators
Server Operators
Account Operators
```

Figure 9.18: Using a WQL query

There are two important advantages of using WMI queries, especially when querying remote hosts. First, the SELECT command instructs WMO to return only specific properties of each class occurrence. In a large WMI class, this can improve performance by not passing unneeded properties. You can also use the WHERE clause to specify a filter. The filter specified in the WHERE clause is the same as you specified in the Filter parameter. The WHERE clause is similar in concept to Where-Object, except that the filtering is done by WMI when the objects are being returned. This is known as early filtering. Additionally, the syntax of the WHERE clause is *not* the same as you use with PowerShell and the -LIKE operator.

Getting Remote WMI Objects

With the CIM cmdlets, you can get WMI objects from a remote machine. You use the same cmdlet (Get-CimInstance) and use the -ComputerName property. You can get class instances from a remote system with this syntax:

```
# 5. Get WMI Object from a remote system
Get-CimInstance -CimSession SRV2 -ClassName Win32_ComputerSystem
```

You can see the output of these commands in Figure 9.19.

```
PS C:\Foo> # 5. Get WMI Object from a remote system
PS C:\Foo> Get-CimInstance -CimSession SRV2 -ClassName Win32_ComputerSystem

Name  PrimaryOwnerName      Domain      TotalPhysicalMemory  Model            Manufacturer          PSComputerName
----  ----------------      ------      -------------------  -----            ------------          --------------
SRV2  PSMC Class Attendees  Reskit.Org  1624821760                  Virtual Machine  Microsoft Corporation SRV2
```

Figure 9.19: Getting remote WMI objects

As you can see, getting remote CIM objects is straightforward.

Invoking WMI Methods

A *method*, in many programming languages, is an action that an object (or class) is able to perform. In WMI in Windows, methods are generally implemented by WMI providers. In many cases, these methods duplicate functionality provided to the IT professional via PowerShell commands.

WMI has two types of method: *static* and *instance*. A static method is one that WMI performs based on the class, while an instance method is one that WMI performs on an instance. As you saw in "Viewing Class Methods," the Win32_Share class has a static method Create, which creates a new SMB share. WMI objects that are instances of this class have a Delete method, which deletes the specific SMB share. The Delete method is an instance method. In general, you use static methods to create WMI instances and instance methods to act on instances once they are created.

Reviewing Static Methods of a Class

As you have already seen, the `Get-CimClass` cmdlet provides useful information about a WMI class, including the methods available and the parameters that those methods use. The object returned by the `Get-CimClass` cmdlet has a property, `CimClassMethods`, which describes each available method, including each one's parameter names and whether the method is static or instance-based. You can use `Select-Object` to expand and then view the method's details.

```
# 1. Review methods of Win32_Share Class
Get-CimClass -ClassName Win32_Share |
    Select-Object -ExpandProperty CimClassMethods
```

You can see the output from these commands, the methods provided by the `Win32_Share` class, in Figure 9.20.

```
PS C:\Foo> # 1. Review methods of Win32_Share class
PS C:\Foo> Get-CimClass -ClassName Win32_Share |
            Select-Object -ExpandProperty CimClassMethods

Name          ReturnType Parameters                                                            Qualifiers
----          ---------- ----------                                                            ----------
Create        UInt32     {Access, Description, MaximumAllowed, Name, Password, Path, Type}     {Constructor, Implemented, MappingStrings, Static}
SetShareInfo  UInt32     {Access, Description, MaximumAllowed}                                  {Implemented, MappingStrings}
GetAccessMask UInt32     {}                                                                    {Implemented, MappingStrings}
Delete        UInt32     {}                                                                    {Destructor, Implemented, MappingStrings}
```

Figure 9.20: Viewing methods of the `Win32_Share` class

In WMI, both classes and methods can have qualifiers, which provide information about the class or method. The `Constructor` qualifier shows that the `Create` method creates instances of this class, while the `Destructor` qualifier documents that the `Delete` method deletes instances of this class. Finally, the `Implemented` qualifier notes that this method is implemented. During the development of a WMI provider, you might find that some parts of a WMI object are defined but not fully implemented. But this is not something you normally see in released versions of Windows. The qualifiers shown for the `Create` method include the `Static` and `Constructor` qualifiers. This tells you that the `Create` method is a static method used to construct new instances of the class.

For more details on WMI qualifiers, see docs.microsoft.com/windows/win32/wmisdk/wmi-qualifiers.

Reviewing Properties of a Class

You can use the `Get-CimClass` cmdlet to provide details of the properties of the class. Each WMI object has one or more properties that are, like .NET objects, of different types. For example, you can view the properties of an instance of the `Win32_Share` class with this code:

```
# 2. Review properties of Win32_Share class
Get-CimClass -ClassName Win32_Share |
  Select-Object -ExpandProperty CimClassProperties |
    Format-Table -Property Name, CimType
```

Figure 9.21 shows the output from these commands, detailing the properties of an instance of the `Win32_Share` class.

```
PS C:\Foo> # 2. Review properties of Win32_Share class
PS C:\Foo> Get-CimClass -ClassName Win32_Share |
              Select-Object -ExpandProperty CimClassProperties |
                Format-Table -Property Name, CimType


Name             CimType
----             -------
Caption          String
Description      String
InstallDate      DateTime
Name             String
Status           String
AccessMask       UInt32
AllowMaximum     Boolean
MaximumAllowed   UInt32
Path             String
Type             UInt32
```

Figure 9.21: Viewing methods of the `Win32_Share` class

As you can see in this output, the properties of this class are similar to the properties of the objects returned from the `Get-SMBShare` command. Knowing the data types of the parameters can be important for interoperation and when you invoke CIM methods.

Creating a New Share

To create a new SMB share via WMI, you use the `Invoke-CimMethod` cmdlet to invoke the `Create` method.

```
# 3. Create Hash Table of new share properties using static method
$NSHT = @{
  Name        = 'TestShare1'
  Path        = 'C:\Foo'
  Description = 'Test Share'
  Type        = [uint32] 0 # disk
}
Invoke-CimMethod -ClassName Win32_Share -MethodName Create -Arguments
$NSHT
```

As you can see in Figure 9.22, the only output from these commands is a result code, where zero means success.

```
PS C:\Foo> # 3. Create Hash Table of new share properties using static method
PS C:\Foo> $NSHT = @{
            Name        = 'TestShare1'
            Path        = 'C:\Foo'
            Description = 'Test Share'
            Type        = [uint32] 0 # disk
          }
PS C:\Foo> Invoke-CimMethod -ClassName Win32_Share -MethodName Create -Arguments $NSHT

ReturnValue PSComputerName
----------- --------------
          0
```

Figure 9.22: Invoking a WMI method

When you invoke a WMI method, you pass the parameters via a hash table. In the hash table, the keys represent the names of the class properties and the values are those you want the new class occurrence to have. In this case, you specify the SMB share name, path, description, and type. To create a disk share, you specify `Type` with a value of 0 (zero).

Note that in this snippet, you pass the method arguments (that is, the details of the share that the cmdlet is to create) as a hash table. This is different from using a hash table to splat parameter values, so you use the notation `$NSHT` to pass the method parameters.

Viewing the SMB Share Using Get-SMBShare

Now that you have created the share using the WMI method, you can use the `Get-SMBShare` command to view the details of the share.

```
# 4. View the new SMB Share
Get-SMBShare -Name 'TestShare1'
```

Figure 9.23 shows the output from this command, the properties of an instance of the `Win32_Share` class.

```
PS C:\Foo> # 4. View the new SMB Share
PS C:\Foo> Get-SMBShare -Name 'TestShare1'

Name        ScopeName Path   Description
----        --------- ----   -----------
TestShare1 *          C:\Foo Test Share
```

Figure 9.23: Viewing the SMB share

Viewing the SMB Share Using Get-CimInstance

You can also view the newly created SMB share by using a WMI filter.

```
# 5. View the new SMB Share using Get-CimInstance
Get-CimInstance -Class Win32_Share -Filter "Name = 'TestShare1'"
```

You can see the output from this command, showing details about this newly created share, in Figure 9.24.

```
PS C:\Foo> # 5. View the new SMB Share using Get-CimInstance
PS C:\Foo> Get-CimInstance -Class Win32_Share -Filter "Name = 'TestShare1'"

Name       Path    Description
----       ----    -----------
TestShare1 C:\Foo  Test Share
```

Figure 9.24: Viewing an SMB share

Note that the syntax for the filter is based on the ANSI SQL language and does not adopt normal PowerShell patterns.

Removing an SMB Share

You used the `Create` static method to create an SMB share. Each SMB share instance has an instance method, `Delete`, which deletes a share. You can remove the newly created share with this code:

```
# 6. Remove the share
Get-CimInstance -Class Win32_Share -Filter "Name = 'TestShare1'" |
    Invoke-CimMethod -MethodName Delete
```

You can see the output of these commands in Figure 9.25. As you saw when creating a new share with WMI, the output indicates only that WMI has removed the share successfully from WMI (and Windows).

```
PS C:\Foo> # 6. Remove the share
PS C:\Foo> Get-CimInstance -Class Win32_Share -Filter "Name = 'TestShare1'" |
       Invoke-CimMethod -MethodName Delete

ReturnValue PSComputerName
----------- --------------
          0
```

Figure 9.25: Removing an SMB share

This snippet first gets the WMI object related to the new share and then pipes that to `Invoke-CimMethod`. WMI then removes the share instance from the `Win32_Share` class.

As you have seen, you can use WMI to create and remove various objects, in this case an SMB share. A final reminder: although you can use WMI to manage SMB shares, it is easier to use the native cmdlets, in this case the SMB cmdlets.

Managing WMI Events

WMI has rich event-management functionality. WMI and its providers implement a range of event classes that enable you to detect and handle the wide range of events that occur in a Windows computer.

WMI itself can raise events whenever any WMI object—that is, any underlying data in the CIM database—is added, modified, or removed. This includes any changes to a namespace, changes to classes within a namespace, and changes to class occurrences. Such events are known as *intrinsic* events. An example would be Windows starting a new process and creating a new instance of the `Win32_Process` class.

WMI providers also implement provider-specific events, known as *extrinsic* events. The WMI registry provider offers events that detect changes to the registry. The Active Directory WMI provider has events that fire whenever objects, such as an AD group, are changed.

With WMI event handling, you need to create an event subscription that tells WMI which event you are interested in. Additionally, you can define an event handler that performs some action(s) when the event occurs. For more information on the kinds of events that WMI can generate, see `docs.microsoft` `.com/en-us/windows/win32/wmisdk/determining-the-type-of-event-to-receive`.

WMI provides two kinds of event handling you can use. The first, temporary event handling, makes use of `Register-CimEvent` to subscribe to a specific event such as a change to the registry. The second is permanent eventing, which you'll explore in "Implementing Permanent WMI Event Handling." In both cases, you must first register for the event, sometimes referred to as *subscribing* to the event.

With temporary eventing, when you register for an event, you can also specify a script block, which you specify using the `-Action` parameter to `Register-CimIndicationEvent`. As long as you keep the PowerShell session open, when the event occurs, PowerShell executes the action block. The script inside the action block runs inside a background PowerShell job. PowerShell creates the job when you register for the event. PowerShell runs the job in the background and buffers any output from the script block. You can view that output by using `Receive-Job`. Also, if the script block contains `Write-Host` statements, PowerShell writes the output directly to the console and not to the background job output. The first time this happens, it can be a bit confusing since the output from the `Write-Host` statement(s) just appears in the console.

If you do not specify an action block when registering for the event, Power-Shell queues any events that occur in the event log. You use the `Get-WinEvent` cmdlet to retrieve the event records and process them accordingly.

When any WMI event occurs, WMI creates an event record that contains details of the event. However, the information included in the event record is often less than IT professionals might like. For example, WMI can detect when someone changes the membership of an AD group, but WMI does not record who made the change or the IP address of the host they used to make the change. Similarly, the Registry WMI provider can raise an event when a Registry key value is changed, but the event record does not contain the before and after values (or who made the change). WMI eventing, combined with your use of other tools, can be extremely powerful as part of troubleshooting.

Registering for an Event

You use the `Register-CimIndicationEvent` cmdlet to tell WMI what event you want to register for, as shown here:

```
# 1. Register for an intrinsic event
$Query1 = "SELECT * FROM __InstanceCreationEvent WITHIN 2
          WHERE TargetInstance ISA 'Win32_Process'"
$CEHT = @{
  Query            = $Query1
  SourceIdentifier = 'NewProcessEvent'
}
Register-CimIndicationEvent @CEHT
```

These commands specify a WQL query that describes the event you want to subscribe to. The query tells WMI to generate an event any time a new WMI object is added to the `Win32_Process` class. Any time you run a process, WMI raises this event.

After you register for this event, WMI writes to a PowerShell event queue each time Windows starts a new process (that is, runs some program).

Running a Windows Process

You can test the event subscription by running a Windows program.

```
# 2. Run Notepad
notepad.exe
```

This command runs the Notepad Windows application, and you see the application open. At this point, WMI has raised the event and has queued the event details in the PowerShell event queue.

Getting the WMI Event

To retrieve details of this event from the event queue, you use the `Get-Event` command like this:

```
# 3. Get Event
$Event = Get-Event -SourceIdentifier 'NewProcessEvent' |
            Select -Last 1
```

This command returns any event in the event queue with the identifier `NewProcessEvent`. Depending on how busy your system is and what you have running on it, the command may return many events, so we select the most recent one. Depending on how long you leave this query running, Windows may start up several processes as part of normal operation. Each time this happens, WMI writes a further entry to the event queue.

Displaying Event Details

The WMI event, held in the `$Event` variable, is a complex object with a lot of properties. Most of those properties are not overly useful for the IT professional. If you view `$Event.SourceEventArgs.NewEvent.TargetInstance`, you get the information WMI recorded about the event, like this:

```
# 4. Display event details
$Event.SourceEventArgs.NewEvent.TargetInstance
```

You can see the output in Figure 9.26.

```
PS C:\Foo> # 4. Display event details
PS C:\Foo> $Event.SourceEventArgs.NewEvent.TargetInstance

ProcessId Name        HandleCount WorkingSetSize VirtualSize
--------- ----        ----------- -------------- -----------
7596      notepad.exe 245            17969152     2203511496704
```

Figure 9.26: Viewing WMI event details

As you can see in the output, the event details show that Windows started a `notepad.exe` process.

Unregistering for a WMI Event

Once you have completed looking at a given event, there are two ways to remove the event and clean up the environment. The simplest way is to just close PowerShell, which removes all temporary event subscriptions. You can also explicitly deregister for the event by using the `Unregister-Event` command, like this:

```
# 5. Unregister Event
Unregister-Event -SourceIdentifier 'NewProcessEvent'
```

Creating an Extrinsic Event Registration

An extrinsic WMI event is one raised by a WMI provider. The WMI registry provider can raise an event whenever the registry changes. As noted earlier, you can also specify an action block—a script block that WMI executes whenever the event occurs, as follows:

```
# 6. Create and Register Extrinsic event query - handled by provider
New-Item -Path 'HKLM:\SOFTWARE\Wiley' | Out-Null
$Query2 = "SELECT * FROM RegistryValueChangeEvent
            WHERE Hive='HKEY_LOCAL_MACHINE'
              AND KeyPath='SOFTWARE\\Wiley' AND ValueName='MOLTUAE'"
$Action2 = {
  Write-Host -Object "Registry Value Change Event Occurred"
    $Global:RegEvent = $Event }
Register-CimIndicationEvent -Query $Query2 -Action $Action2 -Source
RegChange
```

Figure 9.27 shows the output from these commands.

```
PS C:\Foo> # 6. Create and Register Extrinsic event query - handled by provider
PS C:\Foo> New-Item -Path 'HKLM:\SOFTWARE\Wiley' | Out-Null
PS C:\Foo> $Query2 = "SELECT * FROM RegistryValueChangeEvent
           WHERE Hive='HKEY_LOCAL_MACHINE'
             AND KeyPath='SOFTWARE\\Wiley' AND ValueName='MOLTUAE'"
PS C:\Foo> $Action2 = {
           Write-Host -Object "Registry Value Change Event Occured"
             $Global:RegEvent = $Event }
PS C:\Foo> Register-CimIndicationEvent -Query $Query2 -Action $Action2 -Source RegChange

Id   Name       PSJobTypeName    State       HasMoreData  Location   Command
--   ----       -------------    -----       -----------  --------   -------
1    RegChange                   NotStarted  False                   ...
```

Figure 9.27: Creating an extrinsic event subscription

These commands first create a new registry key. Then you define a WQL query that looks for a change in any registry value. You create an action block, which is a PowerShell script block that you want WMI to run when the event occurs. You then register for this event, specifying the action block. The output you see is the summary of the new background job, which PowerShell uses to invoke the code in the action block. The action block has two commands: the first uses `Write-Host` to write a message to the PowerShell host, and the other sets a global PowerShell variable to hold the event details.

Modifying the Registry

Now that you have the new registry key created and have registered the event, you can test this event registration. To do that, you update a value entry on the registry key being watched, using the following commands:

```
# 7. Create a new registry key and change a value entry
$Q2HT = [ordered] @{
  Type  = 'DWord'
  Name  = 'MOLTUAE'
  Path  = 'HKLM:\Software\Wiley'
  Value = 42
}
Set-ItemProperty @Q2HT
Get-ItemProperty -Path HKLM:\SOFTWARE\Wiley
```

These commands update a registry value and create the output you can see in Figure 9.28.

```
PS C:\Foo> # 7. Create a new registry key and change a value entry
PS C:\Foo> $Q2HT = [ordered] @{
            Type  = 'DWord'
            Name  = 'MOLTUAE'
            Path  = 'HKLM:\Software\Wiley'
            Value = 42
          }
PS C:\Foo> Set-ItemProperty @Q2HT
PS C:\Foo> Get-ItemProperty -Path HKLM:\SOFTWARE\Wiley

MOLTUAE      : 42
PSPath       : Microsoft.PowerShell.Core\Registry::HKEY_LOCAL_MACHINE\SOFTWARE\Wiley
PSParentPath : Microsoft.PowerShell.Core\Registry::HKEY_LOCAL_MACHINE\SOFTWARE
PSChildName  : Wiley
PSDrive      : HKLM
PSProvider   : Microsoft.PowerShell.Core\Registry


Registry Value Change Event Occurred
```

Figure 9.28: Updating a registry value

You can see the updated registry value in the figure. A few seconds after using `Set-ItemProperty`, the WMI event handler sends the message to the console that "Registry Value Change Event Occurred."

Unregister the Registry Event

To remove the event registration, you can use the `Unregister-Event` command.

```
# 8. Unregister for the event
Unregister-Event -SourceIdentifier 'RegChange'
```

This command removes the registration, and no further events are raised for this subscription.

Examining Result Details

Because the action block saved the results of the most recent event in the `$RegEvent` variable, you can examine this variable to see details of the event, like this:

```
# 9. Look at result details
$RegEvent.SourceEventArgs.NewEvent
```

You can see the output from this command in Figure 9.29.

```
PS C:\Foo> # 9. Look at result details
PS C:\Foo> $RegEvent.SourceEventArgs.NewEvent

SECURITY_DESCRIPTOR :
TIME_CREATED        : 132321357486764279
Hive                : HKEY_LOCAL_MACHINE
KeyPath             : SOFTWARE\Wiley
ValueName           : MOLTUAE
PSComputerName      :
```

Figure 9.29: Viewing event details

Defining a WQL Event Query

The WQL query you create monitors any changes to the `ds_group` WMI class.

```
# 10. Create WQL Event Query
$Group = 'Enterprise Admins'
$Query1 = @"
  Select * From __InstanceModificationEvent Within 5
    Where TargetInstance ISA 'ds_group' AND
          TargetInstance.ds_name = '$Group'
"@
```

In this query, you are asking WMI to generate the event any time there is any change to an object in the `ds_group` class (that is, any time a change to the group occurs). This query also tells WMI how often to look for the event.

Creating a Temporary WMI Event Subscription

Now that you have the WQL query, you can create the event subscription by using `Register-CimIndicationEvent`.

```
# 11. Create a temporary WMI event indication
$Event = @{
  Namespace =  'root\directory\LDAP'
  SourceID  = 'DSGroupChange'
  Query     = $Query1
  Action    = {
    $Global:ADEvent = $Event
    Write-Host 'We have a group change'
  }
}
Register-CimIndicationEvent @Event
```

Since you specified an action block, PowerShell runs a batch job to perform the script block. You can see the job details in Figure 9.30.

```
PS C:\Foo> # 11. Create a temporary WMI event indication
PS C:\Foo> $Event = @{
          Namespace =  'root\directory\LDAP'
          SourceID  = 'DSGroupChange'
          Query     = $Query1
          Action    = {
            $Global:ADEvent = $Event
            Write-Host 'We have a group change'
          }
        }
PS C:\Foo> Register-CimIndicationEvent @Event

Id   Name            PSJobTypeName  State      HasMoreData  Location  Command
--   ----            -------------  -----      -----------  --------  -------
3    DSGroupChange                  NotStarted False                 ...
```

Figure 9.30: Creating a temporary WMI event subscription

Adding to the Enterprise Admins Group

To test the subscription, you need to add a user to the Enterprise Admins group, using `Add-ADGroupMember`.

```
# 12. Add a user to the Enterprise Admins group
Add-ADGroupMember -Identity 'Enterprise Admins' -Members Sylvester
```

This command adds the user Sylvester to the Enterprise Admins group. You created this user in Chapter 3. The command itself does not produce any output. But when WMI detects the event, it outputs the message "We have a group change" to the console, as you can see in Figure 9.31.

```
PS C:\Foo> # 12. Add a user to the Enterprise Admins group
PS C:\Foo> Add-ADGroupMember -Identity 'Enterprise Admins' -Members Sylvester
PS C:\Foo> We have a group change
```

Figure 9.31: Adding a user to an AD group

Viewing the Event

Once WMI has detected the group change and generated an event, it executes the action block. In addition to emitting the message to the console, this block saved details of the event to the $ADEvent variable. You can view the details of the event by examining the variable, as shown here:

```
# 13. View who was added
$ADEvent.SourceEventArgs.NewEvent.TargetInstance |
   Format-Table -Property DS_sAMAccountName,DS_Member
```

You can see the event information in Figure 9.32.

```
PS C:\Foo> # 13. View who was added
PS C:\Foo> $ADEvent.SourceEventArgs.NewEvent.TargetInstance |
           Format-Table -Property DS_sAMAccountName,DS_Member

DS_sAMAccountName DS_Member
----------------- ---------
Enterprise Admins {CN=Sylvester,OU=IT,DC=Reskit,DC=Org, CN=Administrator,CN=Users,DC=Reskit,DC=Org}
```

Figure 9.32: Viewing event details

Although you can see the user added to the AD, WMI does not capture which user made the change or details that might help you determine who made the change.

Unregistering the WMI Event

To complete this section, you remove the WMI event subscription as follows:

```
# 15. Unregister for the event
Unregister-Event -SourceIdentifier 'DSGroupChange'
```

This removed the event registration. As an alternative, you could have just exited from PowerShell.

In this section, you examined temporary WMI event handling. You set up an intrinsic query and two extrinsic queries and observed how WMI handles events.

Implementing Permanent WMI Event Handling

In the previous section, you saw how to make use of temporary event handling with WMI. You created a subscription, with or without an action block, and are able to consume and handle events when they occur. This event handling is temporary in that when you exit from PowerShell, the event subscription is removed, and no further events are generated.

Temporary event handling works only in a given PowerShell session, which makes it a great diagnostic tool as part of troubleshooting. Cleanup is also simple—just close the PowerShell session. This means you might need to open, and keep open, a PowerShell console with which to carry out WMI event monitoring. To avoid this, you can use *permanent* event handling.

With permanent event handling, you configure WMI to both subscribe to an event and then perform some predefined action when that event occurs. You first store details of the specific event and how to respond to it as new instances in the WMI CIM database by adding objects to two WMI classes. Then you bind these two new instances, which tells WMI to run the action whenever the event occurs.

WMI in Windows provides five built-in permanent event handlers:

Active Script Consumer: You use this to run a specific VBS script.

Log File Consumer: This handler writes details of events to your own log files.

NT Event Log Consumer: This consumer writes event details into the Windows Event Log.

SMTP Event Consumer: You can use this consumer to send an SMTP email message when an event occurs.

Command Line Consumer: You use this consumer to run a program, such as PowerShell 7, and pass a script filename. When the event occurs, the script has access to the event details and can do pretty much anything.

Microsoft developed the Active Script consumer in the days of Visual Basic and VBS scripts. Unfortunately, the consumer does not support PowerShell scripts.

The Log File consumer enables you to write information to a log file of your choice. You specify the message you want to write and can ask WMI to add information about the event to the entry. See `docs.microsoft.com/windows/win32/wmisdk/writing-to-a-log-file-based-on-an-event` for more information on how to do this.

The NT Log File consumer writes details to the Windows Event log. This is useful if you have a tool such as System Center Operations Manager that tracks event logs and responds to events.

The Command Line consumer enables you to run any program, with parameters. You can specify `pwsh.exe` as the command to run and pass the name of a script file that WMI runs each time the event fires. This section uses this consumer.

To implement permanent event handling, you must do three things:

- **Define an event filter:** This involves adding an instance to an event class. The event filter tells WMI which specific event it should look for. The event filter is basically the same as you used in "Managing WMI Events," but you save the query in the WMI database.

- **Define an event consumer:** This involves defining the action you want to take when an event occurs.

- **Bind the event filter and event consumer:** This tells WMI that whenever the event occurs, it should perform the action defined by an event consumer. You do this by adding a further occurrence to another WMI class.

When you create the event filter, you define a WQL query that directs WMI to watch for events of a particular event class. For example, you can specify you want the event to fire whenever the Enterprise Admins group changes. You also specify a polling or refresh interval—how often WMI should look for that event. The shorter the refresh interval, the higher the load on the system. A change to a high-privilege group like this could be a precursor to an attack on the server, but at the same time, you do not cripple your DCs looking for changes every second.

The AD WMI provider implements a wide range of events you can subscribe to. In WMI, every namespace provides events that fire whenever any class instance is added, modified, or removed in that namespace. For example, the class `__InstanceModificationEvent` in the namespace `root/directory/LDAP` detects changes to any AD group.

Creating a permanent event subscription, therefore, requires you to add three WMI objects to three WMI classes. Once you have bound the event handler to the action, WMI monitors events and invokes the action accordingly. This event handling continues even after a reboot.

A word of caution: be careful when experimenting with permanent event handling. Before you add permanent event handlers (that is, add a new object to each of the three WMI event classes), you should understand how to remove those objects to remove the event handler. Unless you remove a WMI permanent event handler (that is, remove the three related WMI objects), WMI continues to watch and handle the permanent event, consuming host resources. It is also useful to generate two functions that display the event subscription and that delete it.

Finally, be careful when changing an event filter's refresh time. As you decrease the refresh time, you add load (mainly CPU and memory) to the host. For the most part, checking more often than every five seconds is probably overkill.

Specifying Valid Users

In this section, you detect an attempt to add an unauthorized user to the Enterprise Admins group. You begin by creating a file of authorized users and save that into a file named C:\Foo\OKUsers.Txt, as follows:

```
# 1. Create a list of valid users for Enterprise Admins
$OKUsersFile = 'C:\Foo\OKUsers.Txt'
$OKUsers      = 'Administrator'
$OKUsers | Out-File -FilePath $OKUsersFile
```

In practice, the file of valid users would most likely contain more users. You can adjust the file accordingly.

Defining Helper Functions

Implementing a permanent event handler means that WMI carries out the filtering and action-invoking until you remove the handler. Unlike the filters you used in "Managing WMI Events," these items (or at least the bindings) must be removed to stop WMI from handling the event.

It is useful to create functions to show the details of the WMI permanent event filter—that is, the WMI objects that make up this filter—and to delete the relevant records, especially for testing. You define the two functions as follows:

```
# 2. Define two helper functions
Function Get-WMIPE {
  Write-Output -InputObject '***Event Filters Defined:'
  Get-CimInstance -Namespace root\subscription -ClassName __EventFilter  |
    Where-Object Name -eq "EventFilter1" |
      Format-Table Name, Query
  Write-Output -InputObject '***Consumer Defined:'
  $NS = 'root\subscription'
  $CN = 'CommandLineEventConsumer'
  Get-CimInstance -Namespace $NS -Classname  $CN |
    Where-Object {$_.name -eq "EventConsumer1"}  |
      Format-Table Name, Commandlinetemplate
  Write-Output -InputObject'***Bindings Defined:'
  Get-CimInstance -Namespace root\subscription -ClassName __
FilterToConsumerBinding |
    Where-Object -FilterScript {$_.Filter.Name -eq "EventFilter1"} |
      Format-Table Filter, Consumer
}
Function Remove-WMIPE {
  Get-CimInstance -Namespace root\subscription __EventFilter |
    Where-Object Name -eq "EventFilter1" |
      Remove-CimInstance
```

```
Get-CimInstance -Namespace root\subscription CommandLineEventConsumer |
  Where-Object Name -eq 'EventConsumer1' |
    Remove-CimInstance
Get-CimInstance -Namespace root\subscription __FilterToConsumerBinding |
  Where-Object -FilterScript {$_.Filter.Name -eq 'EventFilter1'} |
    Remove-CimInstance
}
```

The first function, `Get-WMIPE`, gets the details of the specific permanent event hander (that is, the event filter, event consumer, and binding), while the second, `Remove-WMIPE`, removes the relevant records. These commands create two functions and set an alias for each one. If you are creating a WMI permanent event filter, you should create these functions, if only for testing.

Creating an Event Query

The event query is a WQL SELECT statement, as shown here:

```
# 3. Create an event filter query
$Group = 'Enterprise Admins'
$Query = @"
  SELECT  * From __InstanceModificationEvent WITHIN 10
   WHERE TargetInstance ISA 'ds_group' AND
         TargetInstance.ds_name = '$Group'
"@
```

These commands define a WMI event query, which is similar to the query you created in "Managing WMI Events."

Creating an Event Filter

You next add the event filter details into the CIM database, with this code:

```
# 4. Create an event filter
$Param = @{
  QueryLanguage =  'WQL'
  Query         = $Query
  Name          = "EventFilter1"
  EventNameSpace = "root/directory/LDAP"
}
$IHT = @{
  ClassName = '__EventFilter'
  Namespace = 'root/subscription'
  Property  = $Param
}
$InstanceFilter = New-CimInstance @IHT
```

These commands add a new item to the `__EventFilter` class in the `root/subscription` WMI namespace. You store the details of the new CIM instance in a variable for use later.

Creating a Script for the Event Handler to Run: Monitor.ps1

With this permanent event handler, you want WMI to run a script whenever the event occurs. You can create a simple script and save it, like this:

```
# 5. Create Monitor.ps1 that is to run each time
#    the Enterprise Admins group membership changes
$MONITOR = @'
$LogFile    = 'C:\Foo\Grouplog.Txt'
$Group      = 'Enterprise Admins'
"On:  [$(Get-Date)]  Group [$Group] was changed" |
  Out-File -Force $LogFile -Append -Encoding Ascii
$ADGM = Get-ADGroupMember -Identity $Group
# Display who's in the group
$ADGM | Format-Table Name, DistinguishedName |
  Out-File -Force $LogFile -Append  -Encoding Ascii
$OKUsers = Get-Content -Path C:\Foo\OKUsers.Txt
# Look at who is not authorized
foreach ($User in $ADGM) {
  if ($User.Name -notin $OKUsers) {
    "Unauthorizsed user [$($User.Name)] added to $Group"  |
      Out-File -Force $LogFile -Append  -Encoding Ascii
  }
}
"************************************`n`n" |
Out-File -Force $LogFile -Append -Encoding Ascii
'@
$MONITOR | Out-File -Path C:\Foo\Monitor.ps1
```

These commands create a file, `C:\Foo\Monitor.ps1`, which you want WMI to run each time the event occurs. The script outputs information about the current membership of the Enterprise Admins group. Then it looks in the `C:\Foo\OKUsers.txt` file to ensure that all users in the AD group are valid and outputs a message to the `C:\Foo\Grouplog.txt` file if not. Depending on your needs, you could adjust the `Monitor.ps1` script to remove any users in the Enterprise Admins group that are *not* contained in the `OKUsers.txt` file and take any other actions appropriate for your situation (such as sending an email message to a help desk or to a security group).

Creating an Event Consumer

The event consumer tells WMI what to do if and when an event occurs. For permanent event handlers, this means defining the specific event handler you want WMI to invoke when the event occurs—in this case the Command Line event consumer. You also provide the name of the program you want to run (which is PowerShell 7) and the parameters for that program, namely, the script file you want to run. To create the event consumer, you add a further object to the CIM database, with this snippet:

```
# 6. Create an Event Consumer
#    The consumer runs PowerShell 7 to execute C:\Foo\Monitor.ps1
$CLT = 'Pwsh.exe -File C:\Foo\Monitor.ps1'
$Param =[ordered] @{
  Name                = 'EventConsumer1'
  CommandLineTemplate = $CLT
}
$ECHT = @{
  Namespace = 'root/subscription'
  ClassName = "CommandLineEventConsumer"
  Property  = $Param
}
$InstanceConsumer = New-CimInstance @ECHT
```

These commands add a new WMI object to the `CommandLineEventConsumer` class in the `root/subscription` WMI namespace. As with the event filter, you save the results of `New-CimInstance` in a variable for later use.

Binding Event Filter and Event Consumer

Now that you have the event filter and event consumer, you create a third WMI object that binds these two objects together. In effect, you instruct WMI to listen for a specific event; when that event occurs, WMI is to invoke the event consumer. You achieve this binding by adding a further CIM instance to the `__FilterToConsumerBinding` class in the `root/subscription` namespace, like this:

```
# 7. Bind the filter and consumer
$Param = @{
  Filter   = [ref]$InstanceFilter
  Consumer = [ref]$InstanceConsumer
}
$IBHT = @{
  Namespace = 'root/subscription'
  ClassName = '__FilterToConsumerBinding'
  Property  = $Param
}
$InstanceBinding = New-CimInstance   @IBHT
```

These commands create a new instance in the __FilterToConsumerBinding object, which tells WMI to start listening for this event and invoke the event consumer when the event happens. Since Windows runs the program (that is, PowerShell 7, running Monitor.ps1) in a separate process, any Write-Host statements in Monitor.ps1 do not appear on your console, unlike temporary WMI event handling.

Displaying Event Filter Details

As you are adding the records, and especially after you have all three added, it's useful to ensure you have the right objects added. You can do that by using the Get-WMIPE function you created in "Defining Helper Functions," like this:

```
# 8. Get the event filter details
Get-WMIPE
```

You can see in Figure 9.33 the three related WMI objects.

```
PS C:\Foo> # 8. Get the event filter details
PS C:\Foo> Get-WMIPE
***Event Filters Defined:

Name        Query
----        -----
EventFilter1  SELECT * From __InstanceModificationEvent Within 10  …

***Consumer Defined:

Name        Commandlinetemplate
----        -------------------
EventConsumer1 Pwsh.exe –File C:\Foo\Monitor.ps1

-InputObject***Bindings Defined:

Filter                              Consumer
------                              --------
__EventFilter (Name = "EventFilter1") CommandLineEventConsumer (Name = "EventConsumer1")
```

Figure 9.33: Viewing event details

Testing Event Filtering

Once you define the binding, WMI is able to carry out the filtering. To test this, you add a user to the Enterprise Admins group.

```
# 9. Add a user to the Enterprise Admins group
Add-ADGroupMember -Identity 'Enterprise Admins' -Members Sylvester
```

This adds the user Sylvester (created in Chapter 3), to the group. Unlike with temporary event handling, WMI does not display any output to indicate that the event has occurred and has been handled.

Viewing Results

When the event occurs, assuming correct configuration, WMI runs `Monitor` `.ps1`, which outputs the current membership of the group and displays any nonapproved users, as follows:

```
# 10. View Grouplog.txt file
Get-Content -Path C:\Foo\Grouplog.txt
```

You can see the output of this command in Figure 9.34.

```
PS C:\Foo> # 10. View Grouplog.txt file
PS C:\Foo> Get-Content -Path C:\Foo\Grouplog.txt

On:  [04/24/2020 10:03:09]  Group [Enterprise Admins] was changed

Name           DistinguishedName
----           -----------------
Sylvester      CN=Sylvester,OU=IT,DC=Reskit,DC=Org
Administrator  CN=Administrator,CN=Users,DC=Reskit,DC=Org

Unauthorized user [Sylvester] added to Enterprise Admins
***********************************
```

Figure 9.34: Viewing event details

In the figure, you see the current membership of the group. Since Sylvester is not an approved user (that username is not contained in the `OKUSers` `.Txt` file). Depending on your situation, you could extend `Monitor.ps1` to remove the unapproved user from the group.

Removing Event Filter Details from WMI

Once you have defined and tested the filter, you can leave it in place to protect the membership of the group. In that case, you should probably extend `Monitor` `.ps1` to alert you when the event occurs. Alternatively, you can remove the relevant records by running the `Remove-WMIPE` function and removing Sylvester from the Enterprise Admins group.

```
# 11. Tidy up
Remove-WMIPE
$RGMHT = @{
  Identity = 'Enterprise Admins'
  Member   = 'Sylvester'
  Confirm  = $false
}
Remove-ADGroupMember @RGMHT
Get-WMIPE
```

These commands run the Remove-WMIPE function to remove the three objects from the CIM database, remove Sylvester from the Enterprise Admins group, and then rerun Get-WMIPE to verify that the filter details are no longer contained in WMI.

Summary

In this chapter, you have taken a look at WMI in Windows using PowerShell 7. You began by discovering details about the namespaces that exist on a host and the classes contained in those namespaces. You then saw how to retrieve data from the WMI CIM database using the Get-CimInstance command. Next you looked at invoking WMI methods and how you can use a WMI method to add an object to the CIM database. You concluded with looking at both temporary and permanent event handling.

Reporting

Reporting is a process of obtaining information and presenting it to an intended audience. Since audiences vary, the content and layout of a report changes. Senior management, for example, might like to see a dashboard-like report, showing just key status items. The IT group could benefit from performance graphs or System Diagnostics Reports to enable them to spot issues as early as possible. And the team supporting a new virtualization project might want high-level views of both stability and resource utilization.

PowerShell along with Windows applications provides IT pros with a variety of reporting options. You can use many of the PowerShell commands to retrieve information and report on it. You can use the AD cmdlets, for example, to retrieve information about who is in a high- security group to ensure that group membership is appropriate. The Windows Performance Logs and Alerts (PLA) feature logs various performance counters, enabling you to review the performance of the system or some application.

Some applications or Windows features, such as File System Resource Manager (FSRM), provide reports you can request using PowerShell.

In this chapter you look at the following:

- In "Reporting on AD Users and Computers," you learn to create reports with details of AD users as well as summary reports of computer or user accounts that have not been used recently. You use the cmdlets in the Active Directory module to retrieve and summarize AD usage.

- In "Managing Filesystem Reporting," you learn about the FSRM. You investigated FSRM in Chapter 5, "Managing Storage" (sections "Managing Filestore Quotas" and "Managing File Screening"). FSRM can create reports that can help you to manage file storage. You can use PowerShell to produce up-to-the-minute reports in a predefined layout or get the underlying information from FSRM and build your own reports.

- In "Collecting Performance Information Using PLA" and "Reporting on PLA Performance Data," you learn to use the PLA feature. PLA provides the ability to capture detailed performance information that can form the basis for capacity planning and other uses.

- In "Creating a Performance Monitoring Graph," you learn how to create graphs to show performance over time.

- In "Creating a System Diagnostics Report," you learn to produce diagnostic reports that provide details about your system, typically used for troubleshooting purposes.

- In "Reporting on Printer Usage," you use the printing features you reviewed in Chapter 7, "Managing Printing." Specifically, you can develop a report showing printer usage, which might be useful for usage chargeback.

- In "Creating a Hyper-V Status Report," you use PowerShell 7 to produce a basic status report for VMs running on a Hyper-V host. This is another summary-level report that could be useful.

- In "Reviewing Event Logs," you learn all about Windows event logs, which contain a huge amount of information about events that occurred on a Windows system. You can use PowerShell 7 to summarize the mountain of information contained in Windows event logs.

This chapter shows you several approaches you can take when creating reports; all of the reports shown in this chapter demonstrate ways you can use PowerShell to create rich and useful reports.

Systems Used in This Chapter

In this chapter, you use PowerShell 7 to report on the activities of many servers. The scripts in this chapter make use of the following servers:

DC1.Reskit.Org: This is a DC in the Reskit.Org domain. You have used this DC throughout this book.

SRV1.Reskit.Org: You implemented FSRM on this host in "Managing Filestore Quotas" in Chapter 5.

PSRV.Reskit.Org: You deployed and managed a print server on this system in Chapter 7.

HV1.Reskit.Org: This is one of two Hyper-V hosts you used in Chapter 8, "Managing Hyper-V."

You can see a diagram of these hosts in Figure 10.1.

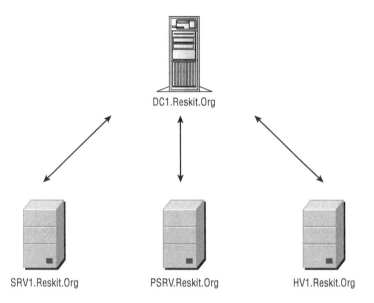

DC1.Reskit.Org

SRV1.Reskit.Org   PSRV.Reskit.Org   HV1.Reskit.Org

Figure 10.1: Systems used in this chapter

Reporting on AD Users and Computers

All organizations need to secure user and computer accounts. If user accounts are compromised, an attacker could use the account credentials to enter and damage the organization. Likewise, AD computers need to be secured. As a basic security feature, a computer that has not been used in more than 30 days loses its machine AD password, leaving the computer (and any user attempting to use it) unable to log on to the domain.

In this section's example, you create a report of potential security issues related to user accounts. Specifically, you report the following:

- Each user's basic information, including a count of bad password attempts
- Members of key high-security AD groups (Enterprise Admins, for example)
- Computers that have not been used in a long time and may be lost or stolen

To create the AD user and computer report, you use PowerShell's powerful string-handling capability. You begin by defining an empty report body. Then you build the report, section by section, and add the output to the report body. Finally, you output the report to the console, save it to a file, or send the report in email.

Before You Start

You run the code in this section on DC1.Reskit.Org, the main domain controller in the Reskit.Org forest. You have used this host throughout this book, and it should have a number of user and computer accounts created. However, in the various code snippets you have run, many of the AD objects were created but not used; as a result, values such as bad password count or last logon date might not be as well-populated as in a real-life AD domain. You may want to generate some activity on some of the user accounts. For example, log in to one of the hosts in the Reskit.Org VM farm using one of the user accounts.

Defining a Function to Retrieve User Accounts

As a first step to creating an AD user and computer report, you define a function, Get-ReskitUser, to retrieve all user accounts in the AD. To simplify the report, this function creates custom PowerShell objects for each AD user account. Each object contains only the properties needed for the report.

```
# 1. Define a function Get-ReskitUser
#    The function returns objects related to users in reskit.org
Function Get-ReskitUser {
    # Get PDC Emulator DC
    $PrimaryDC = Get-ADDomainController -Discover -Service PrimaryDC
    # Get Users
    $P       = "DisplayName","Office","LastLogonDate","BadPWDCount"
    $ADUsers = Get-ADUser -Filter * -Properties $P -Server $PrimaryDC
    # Iterate through them and create $Userinfo hash table:
    Foreach ($ADUser in $ADUsers) {
        # Create a userinfo HT
        $UserInfo = [Ordered] @{}
        $UserInfo.SamAccountName = $ADUser.SamAccountName
        $Userinfo.DisplayName    = $ADUser.DisplayName
        $Userinfo.Office         = $ADUser.Office
        $Userinfo.Enabled        = $ADUser.Enabled
        $Userinfo.LastLogonDate  = $ADUser.LastLogonDate
        $UserInfo.BadPWDCount    = $ADUser.BadPwdCount
        New-Object -TypeName PSObject -Property $UserInfo
    }
} # end of function
```

This function is an example of one you might define for your environment. You could store this function in a custom PowerShell module for use in reporting. You can extend this simple function to obtain other information that might be relevant when you generate reports. You might be able to get information from other systems and applications that you can add to the output of this function.

Getting Reskit Users

Having defined the `Get-ReskitUser` function, you use it to retrieve summary information about AD users.

```
# 2. Get the users
$RKUsers = Get-ReskitUser
```

Depending on the size of your AD, you might want to create reports grouped by organizational unit (OU). For example, you might create an IT Team Users report that just reported on the users in the IT Team OU. In that case, you could extend the function to take an OU name as a parameter and have the function return users in that OU only.

Building the Report Header

You begin to build the report by creating the report header.

```
# 3. Build the report header
$RKReport = '' # Define initial report variable
$RKReport += "*** Reskit.Org AD Report`n"
$RKReport += "*** Generated [$(Get-Date)]`n"
$RKReport += "********************************`n`n"
```

These commands create a variable named `$RKReport` that you use to hold the report. You add to that variable as you build the report.

Reporting on Disabled Users

An AD account that is disabled is one that a user cannot use to log in or to access resources. There are a variety of reasons you might disable an AD user account, such as when a user has left the company or is on long-term leave, or an account could have been accidentally disabled. You can filter the disabled accounts via `Where-Object` and add that information to the report.

```
# 4. Report on Disabled users
$RKReport += "*** Disabled Users`n"
$RKReport += $RKUsers |
    Where-Object {$_.Enabled -ne $true} |
        Format-Table -Property SamAccountName, DisplayName |
            Out-String
```

Reporting on Unused Accounts

In most cases, a disabled account is probably not much of a security risk, although it does potentially consume resources. User accounts that have not been recently used represent more of a risk. You can use the `LastLogonDate` property in the `AD User` object to determine the last logon date.

```
# 5. Report users who have not recently logged on
$OneWeekAgo = (Get-Date).AddDays(-7)
$RKReport += "`n*** Users Not logged in since $OneWeekAgo`n"
$RKReport += $RKUsers |
    Where-Object {$_.Enabled -and $_.LastLogonDate -le $OneWeekAgo} |
        Sort-Object -Property LastLogonDate |
            Format-Table -Property SamAccountName,LastLogonDate |
                Out-String
```

One issue with this section of code is that Active Directory does not replicate the last logon date property between domain controllers. Thus, the last logon date for users from DC1 is not accurate for users authenticated from other hosts. If you have a large number of DCs, this part of your report would be improved by calculating the last logon date across all servers. You could extend the Get-ReskitUser function to contact each DC in the domain to retrieve the accurate last logon date.

Reporting on Invalid Password Attempts

When you log on to Windows, you need to provide credentials; if those fail, Windows does not log you. An AD user account contains a count of bad password attempts, which you can use to report on users who show a high number of failed attempts.

```
# 6. Users with high invalid password attempts
#
$RKReport += "`n*** High Number of Bad Password Attempts`n"
$RKReport += $RKUsers | Where-Object BadPWDCount -ge 5 |
   Format-Table -Property SamAccountName, BadPWDCount |
     Out-String
```

If an account has a high number of bad password attempts, it could indicate an attacker attempting to guess a user's password. Of course, there may be other causes, which you can address with user training.

Determining Privileged Users

Several AD groups have high privileges. In particular, adding a user to the Enterprise Admins group gives them significant power throughout your domain. So it is useful to ensure that these high-privilege groups contain only those users who need the permissions. Three specific AD groups you should monitor are Enterprise Admins, Domain Admins, and Schema Admins. In the report, you create a section containing details of group membership for these groups as follows:

```
# 7. Query the Enterprise Admins/Domain Admins/Schema Admins
#    groups for members and add to the $PUsers array
# Get Enterprise Admins group members
$RKReport += "`n*** Privileged  User Report`n"
$PUsers = @()
$Members =
  Get-ADGroupMember -Identity 'Enterprise Admins' -Recursive |
    Sort-Object -Property Name
$PUsers += foreach ($Member in $Members) {
  Get-ADUser -Identity $Member.SID -Properties * |
    Select-Object -Property Name,
                  @{Name='Group';Expression={'Enterprise Admins'}},
                  WhenCreated,LastLogonDate
}
# Get Domain Admins group members
$Members =
  Get-ADGroupMember -Identity 'Domain Admins' -Recursive |
    Sort-Object -Property Name
$PUsers += Foreach ($Member in $Members) {
  Get-ADUser -Identity $Member.SID -Properties * |
    Select-Object -Property Name,
                  @{Name='Group';Expression={'Domain Admins'}},
                  WhenCreated, LastLogondate
}
# Get Schema Admins members
$Members =
  Get-ADGroupMember -Identity 'Schema Admins' -Recursive |
    Sort-Object -Property Name
$PUsers += Foreach ($Member in $Members) {
  Get-ADUser -Identity $Member.SID -Properties * |
    Select-Object -Property Name,
                  @{Name='Group';Expression={'Schema Admins'}},
                  WhenCreated, LastLogonDate
}
```

Depending on your organization, you may have other high-privilege groups you can report on. You can use the code here as a template.

Adding Privileged Users to the Report

Once you have identified the set of highly privileged accounts, you add them to the report.

```
# 8. Add the special users to the report
$RKReport += $PUsers | Out-String
```

This completes the report.

You built this report using the simple technique of compiling it as a set of concatenated strings. For simple reports you might create in your environment, adapt the approaches shown here. Depending on how much reporting you need to carry out, you can always refactor the code snippets in this section to create functions to each report section and use these functions in other reports.

Displaying the Report

You can view the report like this:

```
# 9. Display the report
$RKReport
```

You can see the report in Figure 10.2.

Figure 10.2: AD user and computer report

The details you see in the report you generate may differ from this figure. Depending on what you have done—for example, logging on as different users (successfully and unsuccessfully)—you may see different output.

Managing Filesystem Reporting

File Server Resource Manager is a Windows feature that provides tools to help you manage a file server. You examined the installation and use of FSRM in Chapter 5.

FSRM includes the ability to generate a variety of reports related to files stored on a file server. It can create incident reports (as a result of a quota threshold, for example), scheduled reports (run at some specific time), or on-demand reports (interactive reports).

In Windows Server 2019, FSRM supports 10 report types.

Duplicate Files: Identifies files that appear to be duplicates based on size and last modification time

Files by File Group: Lists files belonging to specified FSRM file groups, such as backup files or image files

Files by Owner: Lists files by owner, where you can specify all or selected owners

Files by Property: Lists files based on the value of specified FSRM classification properties

Large Files: Lists files over a specified size, such as 10MB

Least Recently Accessed: Lists files that have not been accessed in some specified time, such as 90 days

Most Recently Accessed: Lists files accessed in a recent specified time period, such as the past week

Quota Usage: Lists any FSRM quotas whose usage exceeds a specified value

File Screen Audit Files: Lists any file screening audit events that occurred during a specified time period

Folders by Property: Lists folders based on the value of specified FSRM classification properties

FSRM provides reports in several different output formats. FSRM can produce report output in DHTML (saved with the .html extension), HTML (.htm), text (.txt), and XML (.xml). The DHTML, HTML, and text files have predefined formats, which you cannot change. The XML output type returns the same information shown in the other reports, but as XML. As an alternative to the predefined report layouts, you can use the XML to build reports better suited for your specific needs.

The documentation for FSRM reporting is sparse. There are some high-level overview web pages and cmdlet documentation, although those pages are light on detail. They lack examples and contain no end-to-end advice and guidance. Additionally, there is not much up-to-date information on the Internet—much Internet content is old (although still useful!). But with that said, the workings are straightforward and pretty easy to get working.

Before You Start

This section uses SRV1, on which you installed and used FSRM in Chapter 5's "Managing Filestore Quotas," and "Managing Files Screening" sections.

Creating a Storage Report

To create a new interactive storage report, you use the New-FSRMStorageReport command.

```
# 1. Create a new Storage report for large files on C:\ on SRV1
$REPORT1HT = @{
  Name              = 'Large Files on SRV1'
  NameSpace         = 'C:\'
  ReportType        = 'Large'
  ReportFormat      = ('DHTML','XML')
  LargeFileMinimum  = 10MB
  Interactive       = $true
  MailTo            = 'DoctorDNS@Gmail.Com'
}
New-FsrmStorageReport @REPORT1HT
```

This command creates a new Large Files report and produces the output you see in Figure 10.3.

This report shows all large files on the c:\ volume that are bigger than 10MB. The report also generates both a DHTML file and an XML output file and mails a copy of them to the specified email address.

New-FSRMStorageReport is a complex command with parameters for all the options for all report types. Typically, you do not need many for any given report.

When you create an interactive storage report, FSRM runs the report (and generates requested output).

```
PS C:\Foo> # 1. Create a new Storage report for large files on C:\ on SRV1
PS C:\Foo> $REPORT1HT = @{
            Name           = 'Large Files on SRV1'
            NameSpace      = 'C:\'
            ReportType     = 'Large'
            ReportFormat   = ('DHTML','XML')
            LargeFileMinimum = 10MB
            Interactive    = $true
            MailTo         = 'DoctorDNS@Gmail.Com'
          }
PS C:\Foo> New-FsrmStorageReport @REPORT1HT

FileGroupIncluded           :
FileOwnerFilePattern        :
FileOwnerUser               :
FileScreenAuditDaysSince    : 0
FileScreenAuditUser         :
FolderPropertyName          :
Interactive                 : True
LargeFileMinimum            : 10485760
LargeFilePattern            :
LastError                   :
LastReportPath              :
LastRun                     :
LeastAccessedFilePattern    :
LeastAccessedMinimum        : 0
MailTo                      : DoctorDNS@Gmail.Com
MostAccessedFilePattern     :
MostAccessedMaximum         : 0
Name                        : Large Files on SRV1
Namespace                   : {C:\}
PropertyFilePattern         :
PropertyName                :
QuotaMinimumUsage           : 0
ReportFormat                : {DHtml, XML}
ReportType                  : LargeFiles
Schedule                    :
Status                      : Queued
PSComputerName              :
```

Figure 10.3: Creating a new FSRM report

Viewing FSRM Reports

You can view the active FSRM reports by using the following commands:

```
# 2. View FSRM Reports
Get-FsrmStorageReport * |
  Format-Table -Property Name, ReportType, ReportFormat, Status
```

You can see the output from these commands in Figure 10.4.

```
PS C:\Foo> # 2. View FSRM Reports
PS C:\Foo> Get-FsrmStorageReport * |
            Format-Table -Property Name, ReportType, ReportFormat, Status

Name                  ReportType ReportFormat  Status
----                  ---------- ------------  ------
Large Files on SRV1 LargeFiles {DHtml, XML} Running
```

Figure 10.4: Viewing the FSRM report

FSRM does not come with much in the way of display XML, so PowerShell by default displays objects such as the storage report objects, with all properties displayed in a list. You may find it easier to display only the properties you actually need.

Once you start the report, it can take some time to finish, especially for larger file servers. You can use Get-FSRMStorageReport, specify the report you want, and watch for the job to move from being queued, to running, then to ready (that is, finished for now and ready to be run again).

Viewing FSRM Report Output Files

Once FSRM has completed creating the report output files, you can view them. FSRM stores the generated report output for interactive reports in the C:\StorageReports\Interactive folder.

```
# 3. Viewing Storage Report Output
$Path = 'C:\StorageReports\Interactive'
Get-ChildItem -Path $Path
```

You can see the output files in Figure 10.5.

```
PS C:\Foo> # 3. Viewing Storage Report Output
PS C:\Foo> $Path = 'C:\StorageReports\Interactive'
PS C:\Foo> Get-ChildItem -Path $Path


    Directory: C:\StorageReports\Interactive


Mode            LastWriteTime     Length  Name
----            -------------     ------  ----
d-----    30/04/2020     10:33            LargeFiles40_2020-04-30_10-33-02_files
-a----    30/04/2020     10:33    206699  LargeFiles40_2020-04-30_10-33-02.html
-a----    30/04/2020     10:33    374064  LargeFiles40_2020-04-30_10-33-02.xml
```

Figure 10.5: Viewing the FSRM report output files

In this figure, you see the two output files: the DHTML file stored with the .html extension and the XML output. The DHTML report contains a few graphics, and FSRM puts these into a subfolder.

Viewing the Large Files Report

Now that FSRM has completed the Large Files Report, you can view the report in your browser with this snippet:

```
# 4. View the DHTML report
$Rep = Get-ChildItem -Path $Path\*.html
Invoke-Item -Path $Rep
```

Figure 10.6 shows the report.

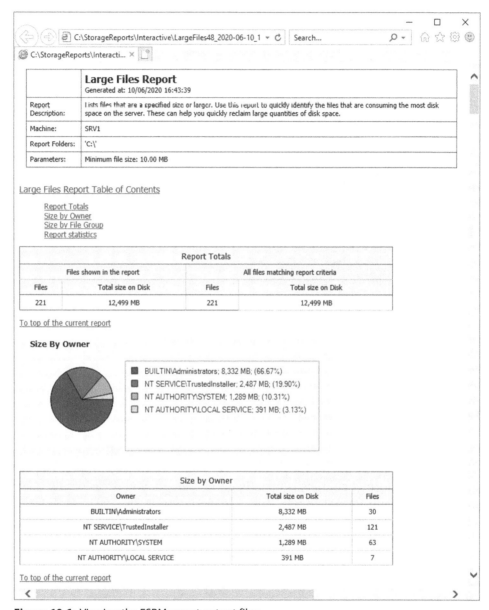

Figure 10.6: Viewing the FSRM report output files

Using FSRM XML Output

FSRM provides the information in the reports in the form of an XML document. You can use PowerShell to find and load the XML and then pull key information from the XML, as follows:

```
# 5. Extract key information from the XML
$XF   = Get-ChildItem -Path $Path\*.xml
```

Continues

continued

```
$XML  = [XML] (Get-Content -Path $XF)
$Files = $XML.StorageReport.ReportData.Item
$Files | Where-Object Path -NotMatch '^Windows|^Program|^Users' |
   Format-Table -Property Name, Path,
                @{ Name ='Size MB'
                   Alignment = 'right'
                   Expression = {(([int]$_.size)/1mb).ToString('N2')}},
                DaysSinceLastAccessed -AutoSize
```

You can view my output from these commands in Figure 10.7; yours may differ as discussed earlier.

```
# 5. Extract key information from the XML
PS C:\Foo> $XF   = Get-ChildItem -Path $Path\*.xml
PS C:\Foo> $XML  = [XML] (Get-Content -Path $XF)
PS C:\Foo> $Files = $XML.StorageReport.ReportData.Item
PS C:\Foo> $Files | Where-Object Path -NotMatch '^Windows|^Program|^Users' |
            Format-Table -Property Name, Path,
                @{ Name ='Size MB'
                   Alignment = 'right'
                   Expression = {(([int]$_.size)/1mb).ToString('N2')}},
                DaysSinceLastAccessed -AutoSize


Name                                                Path                          Size MB DaysSinceLastAccessed
----                                                ----                          ------- ---------------------
23{3808876b-c176-4e48-b7ae-04046e6cc752}  System Volume Information                    0
pagefile.sys                                                                    1,470.64 0
Winre.wim                                           Recovery\WindowsRE             406.28 170
```

Figure 10.7: Using FSRM XML output

These commands retrieve the details of files larger than 10MB from the XML file and then display them nicely. While the default output of properties performed by the format cmdlets is usually good enough, you occasionally need to override default formatting. In this case, you output the size of each large file as a right-aligned value, overriding the default format to produce a report that is easier to use.

Creating a Scheduled FSRM Report Task

FSRM also supports scheduled reports—reports that run at specified times. For example, you could create a monthly report showing each file owner and what files they own. Creating a scheduled report is a two-step process. First, you need to create an FSRM report task that runs at the appropriate time, using the New-FsrmScheduledTask command.

```
# 6. Create a monthly FSRM Task
$Date = Get-Date '04:20'
$NTHT = @{
  Time     = $Date
```

```
      Monthly = 1
   }
   $Task = New-FsrmScheduledTask @NTHT
```

This creates a scheduled task that runs monthly, in this example at 4:20 a.m. on the first day of every month.

Creating the Scheduled Report

The second and final step in creating a new scheduled report is to call New-FSRMStorageReport, passing it the details of the report that FSRM is to generate, along with the schedule created in the previous step.

```
# 7. Create a new FSRM monthly report
$ReportName = 'Monthly-Files By Owner'
$REPORT2HT = @{
   Name            = $ReportName
   Namespace       = 'C:\'
   Schedule        = $Task
   ReportType      = 'FilesByOwner'
   MailTo          = 'DoctorDNS@Gmail.Com'
}
New-FsrmStorageReport @REPORT2HT | Out-Null
```

These commands create a new FSRM storage report, which you can view using the Get-FSRMStorageReport cmdlet.

Viewing the Report Scheduled Task

Creating the FSRM scheduled report also created a Windows schedule task, and you can view the task using Get-ScheduledTask.

```
# 8. Get details of the scheduled task
Get-ScheduledTask |
   Where-Object TaskName -match $ReportName |
     Format-Table -AutoSize
```

You can see the details of the scheduled task in Figure 10.8.

```
PS C:\Foo> # 8. Get details of the scheduled task
PS C:\Foo> Get-ScheduledTask |
           Where-Object TaskName -match $ReportName |
             Format-Table -AutoSize


TaskPath                                          TaskName                              State
--------                                          --------                              -----
\Microsoft\Windows\File Server Resource Manager\ StorageReport-Monthly-Files By Owner Ready
```

Figure 10.8: Viewing a scheduled task

The scheduled task runs PowerShell at the appointed hour and has Power-Shell run the command.

Running the Report Interactively

When you create a new FSRM scheduled report, you may need to wait a while to ensure that the output is what you want and need. It's usually a good idea to run the report immediately and view the output. You can do this by starting, and then viewing, the scheduled task, as shown here:

```
# 9. Run the task interactively
Get-ScheduledTask |
  Where-Object TaskName -match $ReportName |
    Start-ScheduledTask
Get-ScheduledTask -TaskName '*Monthly*'
```

This snippet starts and then views the scheduled task associated with the scheduled report, as you can see in the output in Figure 10.9.

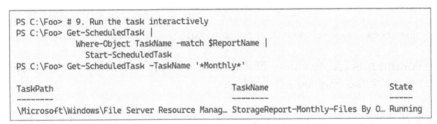

```
PS C:\Foo> # 9. Run the task interactively
PS C:\Foo> Get-ScheduledTask |
             Where-Object TaskName -match $ReportName |
               Start-ScheduledTask
PS C:\Foo> Get-ScheduledTask -TaskName '*Monthly*'


TaskPath                                        TaskName                        State
--------                                        --------                        -----
\Microsoft\Windows\File Server Resource Manag... StorageReport-Monthly-Files By O... Running
```

Figure 10.9: Running the report interactively

Although you are running the report immediately, FSRM sends output details to the C:\StorageReports\Scheduled folder.

Viewing the Report

Once the scheduled task has completed, it can take FSRM a bit of time to make the output available. Once the output has been stored, you can view the HTML file using Invoke-Item.

```
# 10. View the report
$Path = 'C:\StorageReports\Scheduled'
$Rep = Get-ChildItem -Path $path\*.html
Invoke-Item -Path $Rep
```

You can see the report in Figure 10.10.

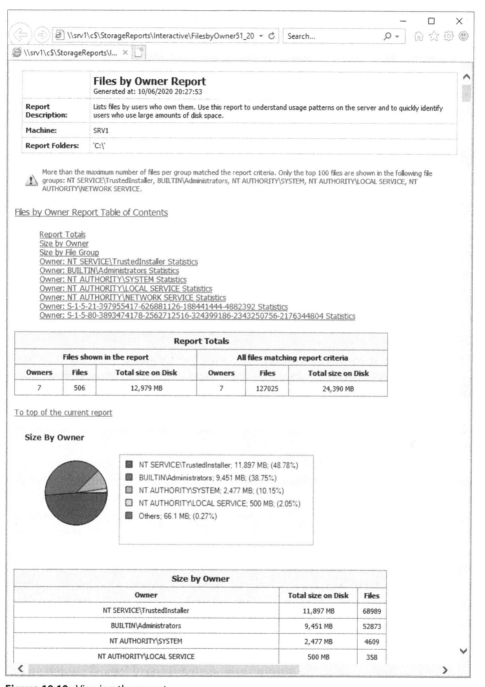

Figure 10.10: Viewing the report

Removing the Reports and Scheduled Task

To remove the FSRM reports and the FSRM schedule reporting task, you can do the following:

```
# 11. Remove the objects
#   Remove the scheduled task
Get-ScheduledTask |
  Where-Object TaskName -match $ReportName |
    Unregister-ScheduledTask -Confirm:$False
Remove-FsrmStorageReport $ReportName -Confirm:$False
Get-Childitem C:\StorageReports\Interactive,
             C:\StorageReports\Scheduled |
  Remove-Item -Force -Recurse
```

These commands first remove (unregister) the scheduled task, then remove the FSRM scheduled task and the storage report, and also remove any FSRM report output files in the two storage report output folders.

Collecting Performance Information Using PLA

There are several ways you can report on the performance of your Windows systems. You can use the Get-Counter command to get individual performance counters. You can also retrieve performance information using WMI (Get-CimInstance). There are around 400 WMI performance classes in Windows Server 2019 that you can retrieve and use in your reports. A final way is to use the PLA subsystem built into Windows.

Using Get-Counter or WMI to retrieve counter information is slow, and using those tools does not scale well. While using these cmdlets is great for retrieving a few performance counters to give you an up-to-the minute look at some aspect of a Windows host, these mechanisms are not well suited for long-term performance data collection. PLA is an excellent method for continuous performance reporting.

PLA enables you to create a *data collector set*, which defines the specific performance counters whose details you want to retrieve. You can then set a schedule for starting the data collection (say 6:00 a.m. tomorrow) and for how many days to collect performance information. Finally, you can start the collector set.

Once the collector set is running, Windows retrieves the counter value based on the sample interval you specified and stores the information in a file. You have several options as to the output type, such as binary logs, CSV, and so on.

You can analyze performance data using a number of different tools and performance file types. Setting up a data counter set to log to a binary log file allows you to use perfmon.exe to view the counter data. You can create a counter set that outputs to a CSV file, which enables you to use other tools to analyze and report on the performance information.

There are no PowerShell cmdlets for setting up and using PLA to collect performance data. Instead, you use COM and script the related COM objects.

In this section, you set up and start two PLA data collector sets. The first you set up to deliver the information in a binary log file, and the second you use to deliver the data using a CSV file. Setting up the two collectors is similar—you just specify a different log file output and a different collector set name.

Before You Start

You run the PowerShell code for this section on SRV1.

Creating a Data Collector

You create a data collector by using the New-Object command and then populate key attributes of the collector, as shown here:

```
# 1. Create and populate a new collector
$Name = 'SRV1 Collector Set'
$SRV1CS1 = New-Object -COM Pla.DataCollectorSet
$SRV1CS1.DisplayName               = $Name
$SRV1CS1.Duration                  = 12*3600
$SRV1CS1.SubdirectoryFormat        = 1
$SRV1CS1.SubdirectoryFormatPattern = 'yyyy\-MM'
$JPHT = @{
  Path      = "$Env:SystemDrive"
  ChildPath = "\PerfLogs\Admin\$Name"
}
$SRV1CS1.RootPath = Join-Path @JPHT
$SRV1Collector1 = $SRV1CS1.DataCollectors.CreateDataCollector(0)
$SRV1Collector1.FileName             = "$Name_"
$SRV1Collector1.FileNameFormat       = 1
$SRV1Collector1.FileNameFormatPattern = "\-MM\-dd"
$SRV1Collector1.SampleInterval       = 15
$SRV1Collector1.LogFileFormat        = 3 # BLG separated
$SRV1Collector1.LogAppend            = $True
```

These commands create a new PLA data collector set that collects data for a total of 12 hours and stores data in binary log (BLG) format.

Defining Counters

Now that you have created the data collector set, you define the specific performance counters you want to capture, as follows:

```
# 2. Define counters of interest
$Counters1 = @(
    '\Memory\Pages/sec',
```

Continues

continued

```
    '\Memory\Available MBytes',
    '\Processor(_Total)\% Processor Time',
    '\PhysicalDisk(_Total)\% Disk Time',
    '\PhysicalDisk(_Total)\Disk Transfers/sec',
    '\PhysicalDisk(_Total)\Avg. Disk Queue Length'
)
```

Adding the Performance Counters to the Collector Set

You can update the data collector set with the specific counters you want to capture.

```
# 3. Add the counters to the collector
$SRV1Collector1.PerformanceCounters = $Counters1
```

Creating a Schedule

You can run a data collector set—that is, capture performance information—based on a schedule you set up and add to the set.

```
# 4. Create a schedule — start tomorrow morning at 06:00
$StartDate = Get-Date -Day $((Get-Date).Day+1) -Hour 6 -Minute 0 -Second 0
$Schedule = $SRV1CS1.Schedules.CreateSchedule()
$Schedule.Days = 7
$Schedule.StartDate = $StartDate
$Schedule.StartTime = $StartDate
```

Creating and Starting the Data Collector Set

You can add the schedule to the data collector set and then start it, as follows:

```
# 5. Create, add and start the collector set
try
{
    $SRV1CS1.Schedules.Add($Schedule)
    $SRV1CS1.DataCollectors.Add($SRV1Collector1)
    $SRV1CS1.Commit("$Name", $null, 0x0003) | Out-Null
    $SRV1CS1.Start($false)
}
catch
{
    Write-Host "Exception Caught: " $_.Exception -ForegroundColor Red
    return
}
```

These commands add the schedule to the collector set and then add this collector set to the system (and commit the change). You then start the collector set.

Once you start the data collector set, you need to wait a few days to see the data being logged.

Creating a Second Data Collector Set

You can create a second data collector set that logs data to a CSV file rather than a BLG file. CSV files allow you to parse and report on performance data, as you see later in this chapter.

This second data collector set is similar to the first one, except that the output type is CSV.

```
# 6. Create a second collector that collects to a CSV file
$Name = 'SRV1 Collector Set2 (CSV)'
$SRV1CS2 = New-Object -COM Pla.DataCollectorSet
$SRV1CS2.DisplayName              = $Name
$SRV1CS2.Duration                 = 12*3600
$SRV1CS2.SubdirectoryFormat       = 1
$SRV1CS2.SubdirectoryFormatPattern = 'yyyy\-MM'
$JPHT = @{
  Path       = "$Env:SystemDrive"
  ChildPath = "\PerfLogs\Admin\$Name"
}
$SRV1CS2.RootPath = Join-Path @JPHT
$SRV1Collector2 = $SRV1CS2.DataCollectors.CreateDataCollector(0)
$SRV1Collector2.FileName             = "$Name_"
$SRV1Collector2.FileNameFormat       = 1
$SRV1Collector2.FileNameFormatPattern = "\-MM\-dd"
$SRV1Collector2.SampleInterval       = 15
$SRV1Collector2.LogFileFormat        = 0 # CSV format
$SRV1Collector2.LogAppend            = $True
# Define counters of interest
$Counters2 = @(
    '\Memory\Pages/sec',
    '\Memory\Available MBytes',
    '\Processor(_Total)\% Processor Time',
    '\PhysicalDisk(_Total)\% Disk Time',
    '\PhysicalDisk(_Total)\Disk Transfers/sec',
    '\PhysicalDisk(_Total)\Avg. Disk Queue Length'
)
#  Add the counters to the collector
$SRV1Collector2.PerformanceCounters = $Counters2
# Create a schedule — start tomorrow morning at 06:00
$StartDate = Get-Date -Day $((Get-Date).Day+1) -Hour 6 -Minute 0
-Second 0
$Schedule2 = $SRV1CS2.Schedules.CreateSchedule()
```

Continues

continued

```
$Schedule2.Days = 7
$Schedule2.StartDate = $StartDate
$Schedule2.StartTime = $StartDate
# Create, add and start the collector set
try
{
    $SRV1CS2.Schedules.Add($Schedule2)
    $SRV1CS2.DataCollectors.Add($SRV1Collector2)
    $SRV1CS2.Commit("$Name", $null, 0x0003) | Out-Null
    $SRV1CS2.Start($false)
}
catch
{
    Write-Host "Exception Caught: " $_.Exception -ForegroundColor Red
    return
}
```

These commands build and start a second data collector set.

Viewing the Collector Sets

An easy way to view the data collector sets is to use the Windows Performance Monitor (`perfmon.exe`). You can run `perfmon.exe` either from PowerShell or by clicking the Windows Start button and typing **perfmon**.

When you open `perfmon.exe`, you can expand the Data Collector Sets node in the left pane and then expand the User Defined node to see the two data collector sets, as shown in Figure 10.11.

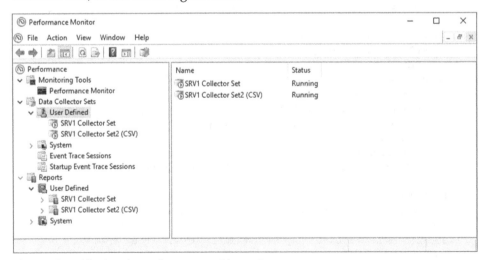

Figure 10.11: Viewing data collector sets with `perfmon.exe`

As you can see in the figure, both collector sets are running. Each collector set is logging values of the requested performance counters to the folders you specified when creating the data collector sets.

Reporting on PLA Performance Data

As noted in "Collecting Performance Information Using PLA," Windows can write performance counter data to files in a different format. You then use different techniques to leverage the different file formats. In this section you use the data collected earlier to report on performance data from SRV1.

Before You Start

You use SRV1 for this section. You need to have created and run the data collector sets on this host, as in "Collecting Performance Information Using PLA."

Importing the Performance Counters

In "Collecting Performance Information Using PLA" you set up a data collector that writes performance counter information to a CSV file. The files are stored in C:\PerfLogs\Admin. You can discover the specific files with this code:

```
# 1. Import the CSV file of counters
$Folder = 'C:\PerfLogs\Admin'
$File = Get-ChildItem -Path $Folder\*.csv -Recurse
```

This finds the CSV file of performance counters. Depending on your monitoring, you may have more than one CSV file of performance measurements; thus, you might need to be more specific as to the CSV file of performance counter data.

Importing Performance Counter Data

You can retrieve the performance counter information by using the Import-CSV command.

```
# 2. Import the performance counters.
$Counters = Import-Csv $File.FullName
"$($Counters.Count) measurements in $($File.FullName)"
```

You can see the output from this command in Figure 10.12.

```
PS C:\Foo> # 2. Import the performance counters.
PS C:\Foo> $Counters = Import-Csv $File.FullName
PS C:\Foo> "$($Counters.Count) measurements in $($File.FullName)"
2603 measurements in C:\PerfLogs\Admin\SRV1 Collector Set2 (CSV)\2020-05\DataCollector01-05-01.csv
```

Figure 10.12: Counting available performance counters

Fixing the Data Collection Problem

A long-standing bug with PLA data collection is that the first counter measurement is incorrect and does not contain a complete measurement. To resolve that, you just overwrite the first measurement with the second, as shown here:

```
# 3. Fix issue with 1st row in the counters
$Counters[0] = $Counters[1]
```

Obtaining CPU Statistics

You can pull out basic CPU statistics using this syntax:

```
# 4. Obtain basic CPU stats
$CN = '\\SRV1\Processor(_Total)\% Processor Time'
$HT = @{
 Name = 'CPU'
 Expression = {[System.Double] $_.$CN}
}
$Stats = $Counters |
   Select-Object -Property $HT |
     Measure-Object -Property CPU -Average -Minimum -Maximum
```

These statements measure the collection of performance statistics to find the maximum, minimum, and average CPU measurement.

Determining the 95th Percentile

In reviewing the basic performance statistics generated, it's likely that over the measurement period you might see high CPU measurements. To put such measurements into overall context, it's useful to calculate a 95th percentile measurement, as follows:

```
# 5. Add 95th percent value of CPU
$CN = '\\SRV1\Processor(_Total)\% Processor Time'
$Row = [int]($Counters.Count * .95 )
$CPU = ($Counters.$CN | Sort-Object)
$CPU95 = [double] $CPU[$Row]
$AMHT = @{
  InputObject = $Stats
  Name        = 'CPU95'
  MemberType  = 'NoteProperty'
  Value       = $CPU95
}
Add-Member @AMHT
```

These commands sort the CPU performance measurements and then find the row equating to 95%. That is the measurement number that is at the 95th percentile, the value that 95% of the CPU measurements are below (and 5% above). While you may have a single high CPU usage of, say, 99%, if 95% of all measurements are below, say, 10%, then the server probably has adequate CPU power.

Combining CPU Measurements

You next combine the various CPU measurements into a single variable.

```
# 6. Combine the results into a single variable
$Stats.CPU95    = $Stats.CPU95.ToString('n2')
$Stats.Average = $Stats.Average.ToString('n2')
$Stats.Maximum = $Stats.Maximum.ToString('n2')
$Stats.Minimum = $Stats.Minimum.ToString('n2')
```

These statements format the minimum, maximum, average, and 95th percentile CPU measurements into a single variable.

Displaying CPU Statistics

You can display the results of the calculations by piping the results to Format-Table.

```
# 7. Display statistics
$Stats | Format-Table
```

You can see the output from this command in Figure 10.13.

```
PS C:\Foo> # 7. Display statistics
PS C:\Foo> $Stats | Format-Table

CPU95 Count Average Sum Maximum Minimum StandardDeviation Property
----- ----- ------- --- ------- ------- ----------------- --------
5.14  2603  1.54        99.98   0                         CPU
```

Figure 10.13: Viewing CPU Information

In the output, you can see that there were 2,603 measurements used in this calculation. Also, CPU usage averages 1.54%, with its 95th percentile at 5.14%. For most uses, these measurements show a fairly low CPU usage for this server over the measurement time period. The 95th percentile value, 5.14%, indicates that CPU usage was low almost all the time during the measurement period. For any general Windows server, this suggests that CPU is not a performance bottleneck.

The commands in this section pull together the CPU status for one day for one system. If you are managing multiple servers, you could implement performance counters on each one (as shown in "Collecting Performance Information Using PLA"). You could add counters to the counter set, for example, to record network traffic for your hosts.

Creating a Performance Monitoring Graph

The performance summary you saw in "Reporting on PLA Performance Data" can give you a high-level view of performance information. You can also use the performance details captured by PLA and create graphs to show performance over time. There are two ways to create a graph of performance data. You can use perfmon.exe to view the performance information captured (using BLG format), as you saw in the previous section, or you can use .NET to create more customized graphs. This section looks at creating a customized graph of CPU usage over time for SRV1.

Before You Start

For this section, you use SRV1 and make use of the performance measurement data you collected in "Collecting Performance Information Using PLA." You use the data visualization features of .NET Core. These classes also exist in the full .NET Framework, which means you could use the code here with Windows PowerShell.

Loading the Forms Assembly

You create a graph using .NET; however, by default, PowerShell does not load the assembly containing the necessary objects. You do that with this code:

```
# 1. Load the Forms assembly
Add-Type -AssemblyName System.Windows.Forms.DataVisualization
```

Importing Performance Data

You use the same technique you used in "Reporting on PLA Performance Data" to import the data and fix row 0.

```
# 2. Import the CSV data from earlier, and fix row 0
$CSVFile     = Get-ChildItem -Path C:\PerfLogs\Admin\*.csv -Recurse
$Counters    = Import-Csv $CSVFile
$Counters[0] = $Counters[1] # fix row 0 issues
```

Creating a Chart Object

Next you create a chart object.

```
# 3. Create a chart object
$TYPE     = 'System.Windows.Forms.DataVisualization.Charting.Chart'
$CPUChart = New-Object -Typename $TYPE
```

Defining Chart Dimensions

You define a width and height for the chart with this snippet:

```
# 4. Define the chart dimensions
$CPUChart.Width  = 1000
$CPUChart.Height = 600
$CPUChart.Titles.Add("SRV1 CPU Utilisation") | Out-Null
```

You can adjust the dimensions (and the chart title) as you need.

Defining the Chart Area

You can also create an area in the chart where .NET will place the performance graph.

```
# 5. Create and define the chart area
$TYPE2 = 'System.Windows.Forms.DataVisualization.Charting.ChartArea'
$ChartArea = New-Object -TypeName $TYPE2
$ChartArea.Name        = "SRV1 CPU Usage"
$ChartArea.AxisY.Title = "% CPU Usage"
$CPUChart.ChartAreas.Add($ChartArea)
```

These statements first create a new chart area, provide a name and y-axis titles, and then add the chart area to the chart.

Identifying the Date/Time Column

You use the following statement to work out which column in the performance counter information holds the date/time for each measurement:

```
# 6. Identify the date/time column
$Name = ($Counters[0] | Get-Member |
        Where-Object MemberType -EQ "NoteProperty")[0].Name
```

The first note property in each counter measurement holds the date and time of the counter measurement.

Adding Performance Data to the Chart

You can use the following statements to add the performance counter information to the chart:

```
# 7. Add the data points to the chart.
$CPUChart.Series.Add("CPUPerc")  | Out-Null
$CPUChart.Series["CPUPerc"].ChartType = "Line"
$CPUCounter = '\\SRV1\Processor(_Total)\% Processor Time'
$Counters |
  ForEach-Object {
    $CPUChart.Series["CPUPerc"].Points.AddXY($_.$Name,$_.$CPUCounter) |
      Out-Null
  }
```

Saving a Chart Image

With the previous statements, .NET has built the chart. You can now save the chart as a graphic file in a folder (after making sure the folder exists).

```
# 8. Ensure folder exists, then save the chart image as
#    a png file in the folder
$NIHT = @{
  Path        = 'C:\Perflogs\Reports'
  ItemType    = 'Directory'
  ErrorAction = 'SilentlyContinue'
}
New-Item @NIHT
$CPUChart.SaveImage("C:\PerfLogs\Reports\SRV1CPU.Png", 'PNG')
```

Viewing the Chart Image

The final step in this section is to view the generated chart.

```
# 9. View the chart image
& C:\PerfLogs\Reports\Srv1CPU.Png
```

You can see the output from these steps in Figure 10.14.

The information in the chart you see may differ from the figure because your SRV1 may be performing differently in your environment.

This section shows how you can use .NET's data visualization capabilities to build a performance graph. In production you would probably want to add to this graph to add in, for example, memory utilization, I/O, and network traffic.

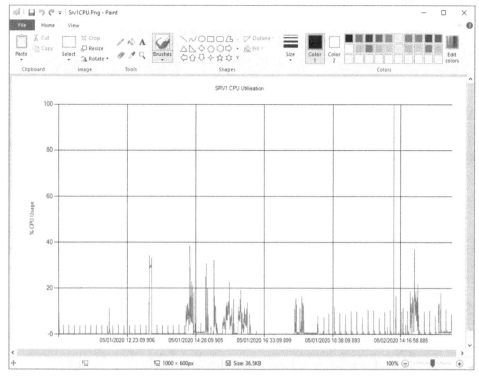

Figure 10.14: Viewing the CPU usage chart

Creating a System Diagnostics Report

In "Collecting Performance Information with PLA," you saw how you can use PLA to create customized data collection. Windows, since Windows Vista and Server 2008, has also contained a number of system-defined data collectors. One of those is the System Diagnostics Report.

Before You Start

You run the commands in this section on SRV1. You can run these commands on any server (or all servers).

Starting the Built-in Data Collector

You use PLA to start the built-in Systems Diagnostic Report.

```
# 1. Start the built-in data collector on the local system
$PerfReportName = "System\System Diagnostics"
```

Continues

continued

```
$DataSet = New-Object -ComObject Pla.DataCollectorSet
$DataSet.Query($PerfReportName,$null)
$DataSet.Start($true)
```

Waiting for Data Collector to Finish

The data collection process takes some time to complete the System Diagnostics Report. You build in a wait period, as follows:

```
# 2. Wait for the data collector to finish
Start-Sleep -Seconds $Dataset.Duration
```

In Windows Server 2019, by default the System Diagnostics Report has a built-in duration of 600 seconds. This is probably generous, as the collection takes only 60 seconds.

Saving the Report as HTML

At the end of the wait period, you save the report as HTML.

```
# 3. Get the report and store it as HTML
$Dataset.Query($PerfReportName,$null)
$PerfReport = $Dataset.LatestOutputLocation + "\Report.html"
```

Viewing the System Diagnostics Report

You view the report with this command:

```
# 4. View the report
& $PerfReport
```

You can see the output—that is, the System Diagnostics Report—in Figure 10.15.

This report is large and contains a lot of details about the server, some of which may be important if you need to perform troubleshooting on it. You could package up the commands in this section and run them via a scheduled task on each production server. Each time you run the diagnostics report, you could save it, say on a file server, for review if and when you need it. PLA and the Windows Task Scheduler make it pretty straightforward to collect and store your diagnostics reports.

The Windows Task Scheduler enables you to run PowerShell scripts at predetermined times. For more information about this tool, see `docs.microsoft.com/windows/win32/taskschd/about-the-task-scheduler`.

Figure 10.15: Viewing the System Diagnostics Report

Reporting on Printer Usage

In many organizations, printers are a shared resource for which management wants to charge back usage to specific departments. You might also want to know which users are using the printers heavily. You can configure Windows Server–based print servers to report details of each print job to an event log for later analysis and/or chargeback.

Before You Start

You run this set of commands on the print server, PSRV, which you set up and used in Chapter 7.

To report on printer usage, you need to have generated some print job on which to report. You can use the built-in Windows PDF printer for this purpose. If you are in an environment where you have real print devices and Windows printers, you can use that printer to generate better output for your organization.

Turning on Print Job Logging

By default, the Windows Printer Server does not log details of print jobs to the Windows Event logs. But you can use `wevtutil` to turn on logging of printer job details as follows:

```
# 1. Run WevtUtil to turn on printer monitoring.
wevtutil.exe sl "Microsoft-Windows-PrintService/Operational" /
enabled:true
```

PowerShell 7 does not (currently) include commands to enable or disable event logs.

Defining a Get-PrinterUsage Function

Event logging can create a lot of data to wade through, much of it not particularly useful in most cases. An approach to reporting is to create a function to extract the details that are of use and return them as objects. You can then use the objects to create reports of printer usage.

```
# 2. Define Get-PrintUsage function Get-PrinterUsage {
# 2.1 Get events from the print server event log
$LogName = 'Microsoft-Windows-PrintService/Operational'
$Dps = Get-WinEvent -LogName $LogName |
        Where-Object ID -eq 307
Foreach ($Dp in $Dps) {
# 2.2 Create a hash table with an event log record
  $Document          = [ordered] @{}
# 2.3 Populate the hash table with properties from the
# Event log entry
  $Document.DateTime = $Dp.TimeCreated
  $Document.Id       = $Dp.Properties[0].value
  $Document.Type     = $Dp.Properties[1].value
  $Document.User     = $Dp.Properties[2].value
  $Document.Computer = $Dp.Properties[3].value
  $Document.Printer  = $Dp.Properties[4].value
  $Document.Port     = $Dp.Properties[5].value
```

```
$Document.Bytes      = $Dp.Properties[6].value
$Document.Pages      = $Dp.Properties[7].value
# 2.4 Create an object for this printer usage entry
$UEntry = New-Object -TypeName PSObject -Property $Document
# 2.5 And give it a more relevant type name
$UEntry.pstypenames.clear()
$UEntry.pstypenames.add("Wiley.PrintUsage")
# 2.6 Output the entry
$UEntry
} # End of foreach
} # End of function
```

This function begins by getting all the printer log entries relating to completed print jobs (with the ID 307). It then pulls out key details from the event log entries and creates an object containing the details chosen.

At the end of the function, you adjust the object type name by changing it to `"Wiley.PrintUsage"`. This allows you to create XML that you can add to your system to format the output nicely. For more details on creating `format.ps1xml` files, see docs.microsoft.com/en-us/powershell/module/microsoft.powershell. core/about/about _ format.ps1xml?view=powershell-7.

Creating Print Output

To view printer event log entries, you need to produce some actual print output. To demonstrate print reporting, you can use the Microsoft Print to PDF printer that is built into Windows.

```
# 3. Create three print jobs
$PrinterName = "Microsoft Print to PDF"
'aaaa' | Out-Printer -Name $PrinterName
'bbbb' | Out-Printer -Name $PrinterName
'cccc' | Out-Printer -Name $PrinterName
```

Each time you send text to `Out-Printer`, Windows opens up a dialog box allowing you to save the PDF file to a named location. Save each of the output files separately. By default, this printer sends PDF output to your Documents folder in your user profile, which is adequate for the purposes of this demonstration.

Viewing PDF Output Files

You can use `Get-ChildItem` to view the PDF files created by the previous step.

```
# 4. View PDF output
Get-ChildItem $Env:USERPROFILE\Documents\*.pdf
```

You can see the output from this command in Figure 10.16.

```
PS C:\Foo> # 4. View PDF output
PS C:\Foo> Get-ChildItem $Env:USERPROFILE\Documents\*.pdf


    Directory: C:\Users\administrator.RESKIT\Documents

Mode                 LastWriteTime         Length Name
----                 -------------         ------ ----
-a---          03/05/2020     14:29         45841 a.pdf
-a---          03/05/2020     14:29         45739 b.pdf
-a---          03/05/2020     14:29         46049 c.pdf
```

Figure 10.16: Viewing PDF output files

Viewing Printer Usage

With those three print files created using the Microsoft Print to PDF printer, you can run the Get-PrinterUsage function to output details of the print jobs on PSRV.

```
# 5. Get printer usage
Get-PrinterUsage |
  Sort-Object -Property  DateTime |
    Format-Table
```

You can see the output from this command in Figure 10.17.

```
PS C:\Foo> # 5. Get printer usage
PS C:\Foo> Get-PrinterUsage |
          Sort-Object –Property  DateTime |
          Format-Table

DateTime             Id Type              User         Computer Printer               Port                                                       Bytes Pages
--------             -- ----              ----         -------- -------               ----                                                       ----- -----
03/05/2020 14:29:25 4  Print Document administrator \\PSRV    Microsoft Print to PDF C:\Users\administrator.RESKIT\Documents\a.pdf 49415 1
03/05/2020 14:29:33 5  Print Document administrator \\PSRV    Microsoft Print to PDF C:\Users\administrator.RESKIT\Documents\b.pdf 49318 1
03/05/2020 14:29:43 6  Print Document administrator \\PSRV    Microsoft Print to PDF C:\Users\administrator.RESKIT\Documents\c.pdf 49599 1
```

Figure 10.17: Viewing printer usage

The output shows the three print jobs that you created earlier in this section. For production printers in use in your organization, you might expect significantly more event log records.

In Figure 10.17, you see the output generated at the PowerShell console. As an alternative, you could package up these steps into a script you can run regularly via the Windows Task Scheduler to produce regular printer usage reports. You can update the steps to add any information that you might find useful in your environment.

Creating a Hyper-V Status Report

In Chapter 8, you set up and managed Hyper-V. In this section, you create a Hyper-V status report to show basic information about your Hyper-V servers and the VMs running on those servers.

To build the report, you create a few hash tables that contain the key information you add to the report. Then you format those hash tables and add the formatted information to the overall report. The report itself contains two sets of information: details about the Hyper-V host and details of each VM. Depending on your needs, you can extend either of these to provide the details you need.

Before You Start

You run this section on the HV1 (or HV2, wherever HVDirect is) server, which you created in Chapter 8. Run this after you have created the HVDirect VM on HV1. If you moved the HVDirect VM to HV2 as described later in that chapter, ensure that HVDirect is moved back to HV1.

You should also note that the HV1 host, however, runs only one VM (HVDirect), so the output may not be representative of a busy Hyper-V server.

Creating a Basic Report Object Hash Table

You begin by creating an ordered PowerShell hash table. You use this hash table to hold details of the Hyper-V server.

```
# 1. Create a basic report object hash table
$ReportHT = [Ordered] @{}
```

Adding Host Details to the Report

Next you obtain basic VM Host details from WMI and add them to the report hash table.

```
# 2. Get the host details and add them to the report hash table
$HostDetails = Get-CimInstance -ClassName Win32_ComputerSystem
$ReportHT.HostName = $HostDetails.Name
$ReportHT.Maker = $HostDetails.Manufacturer
$ReportHT.Model = $HostDetails.Model
```

These statements add the host name, make, and model of your Hyper-V server to the report.

Adding PowerShell and OS Version

You obtain the PowerShell version from the $PSVersiontable built-in object and retrieve details of the OS from WMI. You then add them to the report hash table.

```
# 3. Add the PowerShell and OS version information
# Add PowerShell Version
```

Continues

continued

```
$ReportHT.PSVersion = $PSVersionTable.PSVersion.ToString()
# Add OS information
$OS = Get-CimInstance -Class Win32_OperatingSystem
$ReportHT.OSEdition    = $OS.Caption
$ReportHT.OSArch       = $OS.OSArchitecture
$ReportHT.OSLang       = $OS.OSLanguage
$ReportHT.LastBootTime = $OS.LastBootUpTime
$Now = Get-Date
$UTD = [float] ("{0:n3}" -f (($Now -$OS.LastBootUpTime).Totaldays))
$ReportHT.UpTimeDays = $UTD
```

This section adds the PowerShell version you are using to run this script along with details about the OS.

Depending on which version of Windows Server you used to create the HVDirect VM, you may observe a different OS version in the final report output.

Adding Processor Count

You retrieve a count of the CPUs and add it to the report.

```
# 4. Add a count of processors in the host
$PHT = @{
    ClassName  = 'MSvm_Processor'
    Namespace  = 'root/virtualization/v2'
}
$Proc = Get-CimInstance @PHT
$ReportHT.CPUCount = ($Proc |
    Where-Object elementname -match 'Logical Processor').count
```

If your host has hyper-threading enabled, WMI views each hyperthreaded core separately. Thus, for a host with two physical processors, each of which has 6 cores, WMI would return 12 CPUs (without hyper-threading) or 24 (with hyper-threading enabled). To learn more about the allocation of CPU cores to VMs, see docs.microsoft.com/en-us/windows-server/virtualization/hyper-v/manage/manage-hyper-v-scheduler-types.

Adding Current CPU Usage

You can use the Get-Counter command to retrieve the current CPU usage and add that information to the report hash table.

```
# 5. Add the current host CPU usage
$Cname = '\processor(_total)\% processor time'
$CPU = Get-Counter -Counter $Cname
$ReportHT.HostCPUUsage = $CPU.CounterSamples.CookedValue
```

Adding Total Hyper-V Host Physical Memory

Next, you retrieve the total memory you have given the HV1 host and add it to the report.

```
# 6. Add the total host physical memory
$Memory = Get-CimInstance -Class Win32_ComputerSystem
$HostMemory = [float] ( "{0:n2}" -f ($Memory.TotalPhysicalMemory/1GB))
$ReportHT.HostMemoryGB = $HostMemory
```

Adding Memory Assigned to VMs

You can determine how much memory has been assigned to all the VMs on the server.

```
# 7. Add the memory allocated to VMs
$Sum = 0
Get-VM | Foreach-Object {$Sum += $_.MemoryAssigned}
$Sum = [float] ( "{0:N2}" -f ($Sum/1gb) )
$ReportHT.AllocatedMemoryGB = $Sum
```

Creating the Host Report Object

You have created a hash table containing details of your Hyper-V server. You next create a new report object.

```
# 8. Create the host report object
$Reportobj = New-Object -TypeName PSObject -Property $ReportHT
```

Creating the Report Header

Next, you create the header for the Hyper-V report and add it to the report object.

```
# 9. Create report header
$Report =  "Hyper-V Report for: $(hostname) `n"
$Report += "At: [$(Get-Date)]"
```

Adding the Report Object to the Report

You add the report object, containing the details of your Hyper-V host, to the report.

```
# 10. Add report object to report
$Report += $Reportobj | Out-String
```

Creating an Array for the VM Details

In the steps so far, you have created a report that contains details about the Hyper-V host, to which you add details about the VMs.

```
# 11. Create VM details array
#     VM related objects
$VMs = Get-VM -Name *
$VMHT = @()
```

Getting VM Details

You populate the VM details array with information from each VM. For each VM on the host, you use details returned from Get-VM and add each VM's details to the array.

```
# 12. Get VM details
Foreach ($VM in $VMs) {
  # Create VM Report hash table
  $VMReport = [ordered] @{}
  # Add VM's Name
  $VMReport.VMName = $VM.VMName
  # Add Status
  $VMReport.Status = $VM.Status
  # Add Uptime
  $VMReport.Uptime = $VM.Uptime
  # Add VM CPU
  $VMReport.VMCPU = $VM.
  # Replication Mode/Status
  $VMReport.ReplMode = $VM.ReplicationMode
  $VMReport.ReplState = $VM.ReplicationState
  # Create object from Hash table, add to array
  $VMR = New-Object -TypeName PSObject -Property $VMReport
  $VMHT += $VMR
}
```

Completing the Report

You complete building the report by adding the details of each VM, contained in the $VMHT to the report.

```
# 13. Finish creating the report
$Report += $VMHT | Format-Table | Out-String
```

Viewing the Report

You now have the report, held in the `$Report` variable, which you can view as follows:

```
# 14. Display the report
$Report
```

You can view the report output in Figure 10.18.

```
PS C:\Foo> # 14. Display the report:
PS C:\Foo> $Report

Hyper-V Report for: HV1
At: [05/04/2020 10:54:34]
HostName          : HV1
Maker             : Microsoft Corporation
Model             : Virtual Machine
PSVersion         : 7.0.0
OSEdition         : Microsoft Windows Server 2019 Datacenter
OSArch            : 64-bit
OSLang            : 1033
LastBootTime      : 03/05/2020 18:04:00
UpTimeDays        : 0.702
CPUCount          : 4
HostCPUUsage      : 2.35353417587558
HostMemoryGB      : 8
AllocatedMemoryGB : 1.02


VMName    Status             Uptime           VMCPU ReplMode ReplState
------    ------             ------           ----- -------- ---------
HVDirect  Operating normally 00:17:22.4770000     1     None  Disabled
```

Figure 10.18: Viewing the VM report

In this case, you are viewing the report in the PowerShell Console or in VS Code. If you want to run this report regularly, you could use the Windows Task Scheduler to run it as needed and modify the script to send the report via email.

This report is somewhat small in that there is only one VM. In production you typically have more than one VM running on a given host. If you run this report against a busier Hyper-V host, you can see more information, as shown in Figure 10.19.

Reviewing Event Logs

With the introduction of Windows NT 3.1 (on which both Windows 10 and Windows Server are based), Microsoft introduced the Windows event logs. Today, those key event logs, Application, System, and Security, contain a large number of event entries. Each entry alerts you to some fact that various developers thought you should know about.

```
Hyper-V Report for: COOKHAM24
At: [05/04/2020 10:46:39]
HostName          : COOKHAM24
Maker             : Dell Inc.
Model             : Precision WorkStation T7500
PSVersion         : 7.0.0
OSEdition         : Microsoft Windows 10 Enterprise Insider Preview
OSArch            : 64-bit
OSLang            : 2057
LastBootTime      : 01/05/2020 21:05:26
UpTimeDays        : 2.57
CPUCount          : 24
HostCPUUsage      : 13.0474057885482
HostMemoryGB      : 96
AllocatedMemoryGB : 40.1


VMName         Status              Uptime           VMCPU ReplMode ReplState
------         ------              ------           ----- -------- ---------
Hyper-V Server Operating normally 00:00:00                None     Disabled
FS1            Operating normally 02:18:14.0450000         None     Disabled
***Cookham1    Operating normally 2.14:25:05.3000000       None     Disabled
HV2            Operating normally 17:34:41.5380000         None     Disabled
FS2            Operating normally 1:11:14.4820000          None     Disabled
DC1            Operating normally 1.21:34:23.6550000       None     Disabled
HV1            Operating normally 17:34:41.9420000         None     Disabled
SRV2           Operating normally 11:12:04.7130000         None     Disabled
PSRV           Operating normally 11:12:08.0680000         None     Disabled
SRV1           Operating normally 11:12:12.9820000         None     Disabled
DC2            Operating normally 1.21:34:29.9110000       None     Disabled
```

Figure 10.19: Viewing the VM report on another Hyper-V host

These logs were extended with Windows Vista to include Application and Services logs—event logs for individual applications and services. In a Windows Server 2019 host, such as DC1, there are more than 400 separate logs. Among those, only about 100 have more than 750,000 log entries. Each entry is yet another fact that a developer felt you should know about.

The vast majority of event log entries are not interesting to most IT professionals, at least most of the time. However, troubleshooting issues such as setting up WMI filters or management information like printer usage can make use of these additional logs.

You can retrieve the Windows event log entries by using the Get-WinEvent command. You can use that command to retrieve a list of event logs (using the -ListLog parameter) or entries from a given log. You can also filter events using XPath queries, structured XML queries, and hash table queries. You can find some examples of XML and hash table queries at docs.microsoft.com /powershell/ module/microsoft.powershell.diagnostics/get-winevent?view=powershell-7.

You can use the Get-WinEvent command to retrieve logon events from the system's Security event log. You can then report on the users who logged on to a given system, including date and time. In Windows, there are a number of different kinds of logon events such as logging on to a physical host, logging on to a VM or remote host using the Hyper-V `vmconnect.exe` program, or using the Remote Desktop client. Services and drivers can also generate logon events.

Before You Start

You run this section on `DC1`, a domain controller in the Reskit.Org domain.

Counting Event Logs

You can use the `Get-WinEvent` cmdlet to get a listing of all the event logs on a given system.

```
# 1. Count logs and logs with records
$EventLogs  = Get-WinEvent -ListLog *
$Logs       = $EventLogs.Count
$ActiveLogs = ($Eventlogs | Where-Object RecordCount -gt 0).count
"On $(hostname) there are $Logs logs available"
"$ActiveLogs have records"
```

You can see in Figure 10.20 that on DC1, there are a total of 409 separate event logs, of which 115 have records.

```
PS C:\Foo> # 1. Count logs and logs with records
PS C:\Foo> $EventLogs  = Get-WinEvent -ListLog *
PS C:\Foo> $Logs       = $EventLogs.Count
PS C:\Foo> $ActiveLogs = ($Eventlogs | Where-Object RecordCount -gt 0).count
PS C:\Foo> "On $(hostname) there are $logs logs available"
PS C:\Foo> "$ActiveLogs have records"

On DC1 there are 409 logs available
115 have records
```

Figure 10.20: Viewing a count of event logs

The number of event logs on a given system can vary as you add more features to the system.

Getting the Total Number of Event Records

You can also look at each event log and calculate the total number of event log entries across all the logs.

```
# 2. Get total event records available
$EntryCount = ($EventLogs | Measure-Object -Property RecordCount
-Sum).Sum
"Total Event logs entries: [{0:N0}]" -f $EntryCount
```

You can see in Figure 10.21 that on my system there are a total of 783,122 log events across all logs. The number of entries you see when you run this code is likely to be different depending on how long your system has been up, whether event logs have been cleared, and so on.

```
PS C:\Foo> # 2. Get total event records available
PS C:\Foo> $EntryCount = ($EventLogs | Measure-Object -Property RecordCount -Sum).Sum
PS C:\Foo> "Total Event logs entries: [{0:N0}]" -f $entrycount

Total Event logs entries: [783,122]
```

Figure 10.21: Viewing the total number of event logs

Getting Event Counts in Key Logs

You can also see the number of event log entries in the System, Application, and Security logs.

```
# 3. Get count of events in System, Application and Security logs
$Syslog = Get-WinEvent -ListLog System
$Applog = Get-WinEvent -ListLog Application
$SecLog = Get-WinEvent -ListLog Security
"System Event log entries:       [{0,10:N0}]" -f $Syslog.RecordCount
"Application Event log entries: [{0,10:N0}]" -f $Applog.RecordCount
"Security Event log entries:    [{0,10:N0}]" -f $Seclog.RecordCount
```

You can see the output from these commands in Figure 10.22.

```
PS C:\Foo> # 3. Get count of events in System, Application and Security logs
PS C:\Foo> $Syslog = Get-WinEvent -ListLog System
PS C:\Foo> $Applog = Get-WinEvent -ListLog Application
PS C:\Foo> $SecLog = Get-WinEvent -ListLog Security
PS C:\Foo> "System Event log entries:       [{0,10:N0}]" -f $Syslog.RecordCount
PS C:\Foo> "Application Event log entries: [{0,10:N0}]" -f $Applog.RecordCount
PS C:\Foo> "Security Event log entries:    [{0,10:N0}]" -f $Seclog.RecordCount

System Event log entries:      [    12,768]
Application Event log entries: [       253]
Security Event log entries:    [   198,479]
```

Figure 10.22: Viewing the total numbers of System, Application, and Security event logs

This snippet uses PowerShell's -f (format) operator and .NET's composite formatting features. You can find more details about composite formatting at docs.microsoft.com/ dotnet/standard/base-types/composite-formatting. This technique allows you to create good-looking output. In this case, you format the number of log entries into a number with thousand separators and right-justify it within a 10-character space. That way, the numbers line up vertically within the output, which makes reading the information much easier. Using composite formatting is a common practice in reporting scripts.

Getting All Windows Security Log Events

You can use Get-WinEvent to get all the log entries in the Security log and display a count of how many records you found with this syntax:

```
# 4. Get all Windows Security Log events
$SecEvents = Get-WinEvent -LogName Security
"Found $($SecEvents.count) security events"
```

You can see the output from these commands in Figure 10.23.

```
PS C:\Foo> # 4. Get all Windows Security Log events
PS C:\Foo> $SecEvents = Get-WinEvent -LogName Security
PS C:\Foo> "Found $($SecEvents.count) security events"

Found 198099 security events
```

Figure 10.23: Viewing the Security log events

As you saw earlier, on a busy server there can be a large number of events in the Security log. This means getting all the events and performing any detailed processing of the Security log will be slow. Retrieving all the events in the security log is going to take a while, possibly half an hour, so please be patient. Because retrieving the security events takes so long, in most cases event log processing is best done as a background task run by the Windows Task Scheduler.

Getting Logon Events

You can pick out individual logon events.

```
# 5. Get Logon Events
$Logons = $SecEvents | Where-Object ID -eq 4624    # logon event
"Found $($Logons.count) logon events"
```

You can view the different types of logons recorded on DC1 in Figure 10.24.

```
PS C:\Foo> # 5. Get Logon Events
PS C:\Foo> $Logons = $SecEvents | Where-Object ID -eq 4624    # logon event
PS C:\Foo> "Found $($Logons.count) logon events"

Found 60484 logon events
```

Figure 10.24: Getting logon events

Creating a Logon Type Summary

In Windows, there are several different logon types, as described in detail at docs.microsoft.com/previous-versions/windows/it-pro/windows-server-2003/cc787567(v=ws.10). A logon type of 2 indicates a local console logon (that is, logging on to a physical host), while a logon type of 10 indicates logon over RDP. Other logon types include service logon (type 5), Batch or scheduled task (type 4), and console unlock (type 7). You can review the logon events and summarize the different logon types with this code:

```
# 6. Create summary array of logon events
$MSGS = @()
Foreach ($Logon in $Logons) {
    $XMLMSG = [xml] $Logon.ToXml()
    $t = '#text'
    $HostName    = $XMLMSG.Event.EventData.data.$t[1]
    $HostDomain  = $XMLMSG.Event.EventData.data.$t[2]
    $Account     = $XMLMSG.Event.EventData.data.$t[5]
    $AcctDomain  = $XMLMSG.Event.EventData.data.$t[6]
    $LogonType   = $XMLMSG.Event.EventData.data.$t[8]
    $MSG = New-Object -Type PSCustomObject -Property @{
        Account   = "$AcctDomain\$Account"
        Host      = "$HostDomain\$Hostname"
        LogonType = $LogonType
        Time      = $Logon.TimeCreated
    }
    $MSGS += $MSG
}
```

Each event log entry contains event details in XML stored as a text attribute of the event log entry. You can use PowerShell's built-in XML support to get the account that logged on, the host, and at what time. The code creates an array of objects that summarize the details.

The approach of parsing the event entry's XML to pull out relevant details of the event is one you can use to report from any log. Finding the specific details of what properties are contained at what position in the XML may require you to use the Event Viewer (eventvwr.exe) to work out where to find the information you need within the entry or the entry's XML.

There are several different types of audit log entries that Windows writes as appropriate, such as a logon that failed because the account is disabled or expired. You may want to extend the set logon event codes to look for other possibly suspicious activity.

Displaying Logon Events by Logon Type

You can view the logon summary as follows:

```
# 7. Display results
$MSGS |
  Group-Object -Property LogonType |
    Format-Table Name, Count
```

You can view the different types of logons in Figure 10.25.

```
PS C:\Foo> # 7. Display Results
PS C:\Foo> $MSGS |
            Group-Object -Property LogonType |
              Format-Table Name, Count

Name Count
---- -----
0        3
10       4
2       34
3    59021
5     1422
```

Figure 10.25: Getting logon event types

As you can see in the output, there are a large number of logons across most logon types. Since DC1 is a virtual machine, you would not expect any interactive logons but would expect logon type 10 events, logging on via RDP.

Examining RDP Logons

To drill down further, you can view the individual RDP logons as follows:

```
# 8. Examine RDP logons
$MSGS | Where-Object LogonType -eq '10'
```

You can see the type 10 logon events recorded on DC1 in Figure 10.26.

```
PS C:\Foo> # 8. Examine RDP logons
PS C:\Foo> $MSGS | Where-Object LogonType -eq '10'

LogonType Time                 Account               Host
--------- ----                 -------               ----
10        03/05/2020 20:47:37 RESKIT\administrator RESKIT\DC1$
10        30/04/2020 16:04:43 RESKIT\administrator RESKIT\DC1$
10        26/04/2020 15:49:43 RESKIT\administrator RESKIT\DC1$
10        22/04/2020 20:51:07 RESKIT\administrator RESKIT\DC1$
```

Figure 10.26: Getting RDP logons

Summary

In this chapter you have used a variety of tools, orchestrated by PowerShell 7, that create reports to help you manage your organizations. You saw how you can retrieve information from AD about logon failures and view users someone may have added to a high privilege security group. You used the FSRM reporting features to generate reports on the use of a file server. You can get preformatted reports or use the XML returned from FSRM to create your own report. PLA enables you to collect performance information, and you can use that information to create basic reports. You can also take that information and use .NET's visualization tools to create performance graphs. You also used PLA to run the System Diagnostics Report. You saw how to enable the Windows printing subsystem to log details of printer usage. Once you enable the logging, you can then retrieve usage details. You saw how you retrieve details of VMs and create Hyper-V status reports. Finally, you looked at one way to comb through the event log and create reports on the contents.

Index